Breeding Ornamental Plants

Breeding Ornamental Plants

Edited by
Dorothy J. Callaway
and M. Brett Callaway

TIMBER PRESS
Portland • London

Published in 2000 by
TIMBER PRESS, Inc.
The Haseltine Building
133 S.W. Second Avenue, Suite 450
Portland, Oregon 97204-3527
www.timberpress.com

2 The Quadrant
135 Salusbury Road
London NW6 6RJ
www.timberpress.co.uk

Library of Congress Cataloging-in-Publication Data

Breeding ornamental plants / Dorothy J. Callaway and M. Brett Callaway, editors.
    p.   cm.
    Includes bibliographical references.
    ISBN-13: 978-1-60469-094-1
    1. Plants, Ornamental—Breeding. I. Callaway, Dorothy J. (Dorothy Johnson)
II. Callaway, M. Brett (Mitchell Brett), 1960–

SB406.8 .B74 2000
635.9′152—dc21

                                                                99-087325

To our parents

Bill Callaway (1930–1997)
who expressed such joy at our accomplishments

Barbara Callaway
for her support and kind words

and

Sydney and Nedra Johnson
for their continued encouragement in our endeavors

Contents

8   Contents

10   Contents

Color plates follow pages 48 and 240

Preface

Plant improvement is at least as old as agriculture, the growing and tending of crops and raising of livestock. Long ago, humans began plant selection by choosing a specific plant or group of plants to care for. With selections began the earliest form of plant improvement, a conscious choice to care for some plants and discard or ignore others. Before agriculture, humans were hunter-gatherers whose activities (hunting and migration patterns, for example) undoubtedly influenced the flora around them and thus shifted the genetic makeup of plant communities. Some of these activities, such as burning, were carried out with the *intention* of changing the plant community to better suit the needs of the human community. This is the fundamental activity of plant improvement: intentionally changing the characteristics of a plant to better suit the needs of the selector. As humans began to practice agriculture, they gradually became more sophisticated in their selection of plants. A vast literature is available on the selection, maintenance, and in some cases, development of crop varieties by prehistoric peoples. (See Baker 1965; Harlan 1976; Kaplan 1971; Manglesdorf 1974; Marcus 1982; Mathewson 1984; Popenoe 1920; and Wilson 1987 for interesting examples.)

Genetic variation among individual plants is the raw material upon which selection pressure, whether natural or human-induced, exerts its influence, causing evolutionary changes. Over the centuries, agricultural practices acted upon this genetic variation, resulting in plants that were better suited for agriculture. In grains, for example, wild plants rely on their ability to "shatter" and scatter the seed when ripe, thus ensuring regeneration. Domesticated grains, under human selection, do not shatter, making it easier to harvest grains without losing seeds. Similarly, human selection would favor fruits with fewer seeds, whereas natural selection would likely favor fruits with more seeds (and therefore more offspring); non-prickly food plants (thornless blackberries, for example) would be selected and maintained by humans as food sources, whereas wild plants may be better off retaining their spines to ward off wildlife.

Since food is a necessity, food plants were naturally of greatest interest to early humans. Food plants were cultivated and selected much more intensively and extensively throughout history compared to ornamental plants. Ornamentals were used by humans only later and in much smaller quantities. If cultivated at all, they were originally used in very small plantings, allowing precious space for the more essential food plants. As a result, selection of ornamental plants has a much shorter history. Of the approximately 250,000 known species of higher plants, only about 3000 have been used by humans, and of these, only about 150 have been extensively cultivated (Briggs and Knowles 1967). These include, of course, primarily food plants.

Plant breeding is the application of scientific principles to plant improvement and, unlike plant selection, is a relatively recent activity in human history. The origins of plant breeding are generally dated to the 1900s with the rediscovery of Gregor Mendel's work on inheritance (see Chapter 1). The rediscovery of the principles of genetics catalyzed a century of unprecedented advancements in plant improvement, such as the development of hybrid corn (Wallace and Brown 1988; Jenkins 1978; Steele 1978); improved varieties of rice and wheat, upon which "The Green Revolution"* was based (Jennings 1976); and the use of biotechnology to develop insect-resistant varieties of corn and other crops using genes from organisms entirely outside the plant kingdom. The most urgent application of plant improvement has been to better feed the world's population, and public and private institutions have successfully devoted vast amounts of resources to this end. As a result, few opportunities remain today for amateur plant breeders to make significant improvements in the area of food crops.

The world of ornamental plant breeding, on the other hand, remains wide open. Hobbyist plant breeders—whether medical doctors, teachers, lawyers, or businesspeople—with little or no professional training in botany, horticulture, or plant genetics, are still able to make significant contributions to the improvement of ornamentals because of the vast array of plants and the seemingly endless combinations among them. All that is

---

*The "Green Revolution" refers to the period of the 1960s and 1970s which saw dramatic increases in the productivity of cereal agriculture in underdeveloped countries. These increases resulted from the transfer of technology (including use of improved cereal varieties and greater use of fertilizer) from temperate regions to primarily tropical regions.

required are some basic background of genetics (Chapter 1) and plant breeding (Chapter 2), an understanding of the specific plants one chooses to work with (Chapters 3–17), and a desire to create interesting and beautiful new plants.

It is our belief that the genetic improvement of ornamental plants must rely largely on the work of plant enthusiasts. There are simply too many groups of ornamental plants and too few professional ornamental-plant breeders. Woody ornamentals, especially, have great potential for improvement, as most of the focus thus far has been on annuals and herbaceous perennials. By providing gardeners with the basic knowledge necessary to successfully select and improve desired traits of ornamental plants, we hope to encourage them to venture into plant breeding. The specific plant groups highlighted in this book, from daffodils to African violets and lilacs to oaks, are presented in an effort to provide general guidelines and to illustrate the broad range of possibilities. The dedicated efforts of thousands of backyard plant breeders would surely result in many new and exciting ornamentals to enrich the landscape. A Chinese proverb says: "Give a man a fish and you feed him for a day. Teach a man to fish and you feed him for a lifetime." We hope this book will provide information leading to a lifetime of nourishment for the senses of ornamental plant enthusiasts.

References and Additional Reading

Baker, H. G. 1965. *Plants and Civilization*. 2nd ed. Belmont, Calif.: Wadsworth Publishing.

Briggs, F. N., and P. F. Knowles. 1967. *Introduction to Plant Breeding*. New York: Reinhold Publishing.

Harlan, J. R. 1976. The plants and animals that nourish man. In *Food and Agriculture: A Scientific American Book*. San Francisco: W. H. Freeman and Co. 57–68.

Jenkins, M. T. 1978. Maize breeding during the development and early years of hybrid maize. In *Maize Breeding and Genetics*. Ed. D. B. Walden. New York: John Wiley and Sons. 13–28.

Jennings, P. R. 1976. The amplification of agricultural production. In *Food and Agriculture: A Scientific American Book*. San Francisco: W. H. Freeman and Co. 125–136.

Kaplan, L. 1971. Archeology and domestication in American *Phaseolus* (Beans). In *Prehistoric Agriculture*. Ed. S. Struever. Garden City, N.Y.: The Natural History Press.

Manglesdorf, P. C. 1974. *Corn: Its Origin, Evolution, and Improvement*. Cambridge, Mass.: Harvard University Press.

Marcus, J. 1982. The plant world of the sixteenth- and seventeenth-century lowland Maya. In *Maya Subsistence*. Ed. K. V. Flanner. New York: Academic Press.

Mathewson, K. 1984. *Irrigation Horticulture in Highland Guatemala.* Boulder, Colo.: Westview Press.

Popenoe, W. 1920. *Manual of Tropical and Subtropical Fruits.* New York: Macmillan.

Steele, L. 1978. The hybrid corn industry in the United States. In *Maize Breeding and Genetics.* Ed. D. B. Walden. New York: John Wiley and Sons. 29–40.

Wallace, H. A., and W. L. Brown. 1988. *Corn and Its Early Fathers.* 2nd ed. Ames: Iowa State University Press.

Wilson, G. L. 1987. *Buffalo Bird Woman's Garden.* St. Paul: Minnesota Historical Society Press.

Acknowledgments

In the few years it has taken to put this book together, we have become indebted to many people who have provided help and encouragement. The most important of these, of course, are the contributors themselves, all of whom were willing to work with us to produce a book we thought would be useful to gardeners interested in plant breeding. Like so many plant breeders, some of our contributors breed plants as a hobby rather than a profession, and therefore gave willingly of their free time to prepare their portion of this book. Those who breed plants professionally had plenty of things to do without taking on this project, but they willingly agreed to help just the same. We are grateful to all of them, for surely this book would not have come about without them.

Similarly, we are indebted to Josh Leventhal at Timber Press, who helped shape and refine the book in an effort to provide information useful to would-be plant breeders, and to present it in an interesting and easily understandable format.

1 Genetics and Its Applications

M. Brett Callaway and Dorothy J. Callaway

Just the word *genetics* is often enough to conjure up ideas of complicated combinations of science and math in the minds of those not accustomed to using genetics in their work. If that describes your thoughts, don't let those ideas overwhelm you or stop you from reading further. The basic concepts can be made clear without requiring that the reader have advanced degrees. Those wishing to improve plants through the crossing and selection techniques described later in this book will need only the basic foundation presented in this chapter. Out of necessity, the discussions will be brief. For those who become fascinated with genetics (and it is a fascinating subject) and want to learn more, the references listed at the end of the chapter provide such an opportunity.

Plant improvement results from the selection of desired traits whose expression is *repeatable*. Selection of a desirable form does no good, for example, if the trait is the result of physical damage to the plant by a virus, pesticides, cold damage, or other isolated environmental forces, because the form will not be expressed in clones or progeny of the selected plant—in other words, the trait has no genetic basis. In this discussion, we will only concern ourselves with traits that have a genetic basis, traits that are controlled by *genes*. A review of some basic biological processes will help to clarify the structure and function of genes.

The Basics: Cells, Chromosomes, and Genes

Heredity, the process through which characteristics of the parents are transmitted to their offspring, is one aspect of the larger process of reproduction. In flowering plants, characteristics of the male and female parents are contributed to the offspring through pollen and egg cells, respectively, via sexual reproduction. This first section of the chapter describes at the cellular level how these characteristics are transmitted. In the following sections we will discuss the genetics of how these characteristics are transmitted.

Cells are the building blocks of all plants and are made up of five main components (Figure 1-1): 1) a *cell wall*, which keeps the contents of the cell intact; 2) *chromosomes*, which are strands of genetic material; 3) a *nucleus*, which contains the chromosomes; 4) a *nuclear membrane*, which keeps the chromosomes inside the nucleus; and 5) *protoplasm*, which comprises various other materials found between the nuclear membrane and the cell wall, including the *cytoplasm*. For our purposes, cells can be grouped into two basic types: sex cells, or *gametes*, which make up reproductive tissue, as in pollen and egg cells; and *somatic cells*, which make up nonreproductive, or vegetative, tissue. These two types of cells are generated by two types of cell division: *meiosis*, which produces gametes, and *mitosis*, which produces somatic cells.

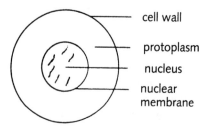

Figure 1-1. The main components of a cell.

Every species of plant has a characteristic number of chromosomes; for example, *Magnolia macrophylla* has 38. The parental, or somatic, chromosome number consists of n pairs of identical, or *homologous*, chromosomes, where n is the characteristic chromosome number of the gametes. So, the parental chromosome number is twice n, or $2n$. With our example of *M. macrophylla*, the parental chromosome count is expressed in shorthand as $2n$ = 38; the gametic chromosome number is n = 19. Each of the n pairs differs from other pairs in size, shape, and genetic information but is consistent for all individuals in a species. For example, chromosome 3 for a particular species may contain the gene for flower color, and that chromosome will determine the flower color in each individual. When one plant is crossed with another of the same species in sexual reproduction, the offspring will also exhibit the characteristic number of chromosomes—but how is the chromosome count maintained at the typical number, instead of doubling? Meiosis, known more descriptively as *reduction division*, is the cellular process that allows this characteristic chromosome number to be maintained by halving the parental chromosomes into gametes. These gametes are then united through sexual fertilization, reconstituting the full chromosome number and simultaneously combining characteristics from both parents into the offspring.

MEIOSIS

Details of the process of meiosis can be best described by breaking it down into a series of defined steps. Meiosis has two main phases (Figure 1-2). In the first phase, the parental chromosome number is halved and the parent cell is divided into two daughter cells. The daughter cells are multiplied in the second phase. The following simplified description is adapted from L. R. House's excellent presentation (House 1985).

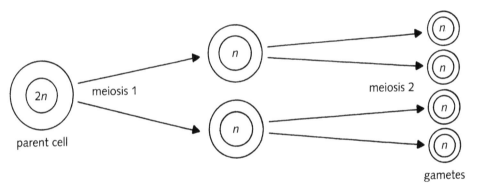

Figure 1-2. The two phases of meiosis.

Phase 1. During the first step of meiosis, prophase 1, each chromosome of each homologous pair divides lengthwise, forming two *chromatids* (Figure 1-3a). In the next two steps, known as metaphase 1 and anaphase 1, the nuclear membrane dissolves and chromosomes of each homologous pair, comprising two chromatids, move to opposite poles within the cell (Figure 1-3b). A nuclear membrane then forms around each of the two sets of chromosomes, and the cell divides (telophase 1) (Figure 1-3c).

Phase 2. A short "resting phase," called *interphase*, sometimes takes place before the second main phase of meiosis begins. In the first stages of Phase 2 (prophase 2, metaphase 2, and anaphase 2), the nuclear membrane again disappears, and the chromatids separate and move to opposite poles in each of the two cells (Figure 1-3d). In the final step, telophase 2, the four groups of chromosomes are each enclosed in a nuclear membrane and cell division

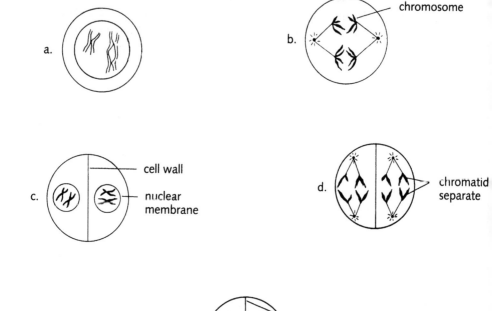

Figure 1-3. The stages of meiosis. a) prophase 1: the homologous chromosomes separate into two chromatids. b) anaphase 1: the nuclear membrane dissolves and the chromosomes, each comprising two chromatids, move to opposite poles of the cell. c) telophase 1: a nuclear membrane forms around each of the two sets of chromosomes, a cell wall forms between the two poles of the cell, and the cell divides. Phase 2 of meiosis begins and the nuclear membrane again dissolves. d) anaphase 2: the chromosomes (chromatids) separate and move to opposite poles. e) telophase 2: nuclear membranes form around each of the four nuclei and cell walls form to produce four daughter cells, each with n chromosomes.

takes place, forming four cells each with n chromosomes (Figure 1-3e). These cells are the gametes.

MITOSIS

An increase in cell number is fundamental to plant growth, and mitosis and cytokinesis are the two processes that together accomplish this. House

(1985) defines mitosis as "the division of the nucleus to form two nuclei, each having the same number of chromosomes as, and identical genotype to, the parent cell." *Cytokinesis* is the division of the rest of the cell. As in meiosis, mitosis takes place in four defined steps. In the first three steps (prophase, metaphase, and anaphase), the nuclear membrane disappears and the chromosomes double and migrate to opposite poles of the cell. In the final step (telophase), nuclear membranes form around each set of chromosomes and a cell wall forms, dividing the cytoplasm into two equal parts. The end result is two daughter cells, each identical to the original mother cell.

FERLITIZATION

Fertilization is the process by which traits from each parent are brought together in the offspring. It also completes our discussion of how the $2n$ chromosome number is maintained from parents to offspring. In fertilization, pollen of the male parent lands on the stigma of the female parent, germinates, and grows down the style and into the ovary where it releases two nuclei. One nucleus unites with the egg cell and forms a $2n$ cell known as a *zygote*, which through mitotic division grows into the embryo. The second nucleus unites with two other nuclei, known as *polar nuclei*, to form a $3n$ cell, which through mitotic division develops into the endosperm. The process by which these two unions—the forming of a $2n$ zygote and a $3n$ cell—take place is referred to as *double fertilization*. Double fertilization brings together traits contributed from each parent to the seed. When that seed germinates, the resulting plant has genetic material from both of its parents.

Genetic material is carried in the form of deoxyribonucleic acid, or DNA. Within the DNA are the four bases adenine (A), thymine (T), guanine (G), and cytosine (C). These bases form specific pairs—A links with T and G with C. Genetic information is coded by the order in which these bases occur and by the location of these base sequences along a chromosome. Therefore, genes are sequences of base pairs that affect the expression of a particular trait. The genes' location on a chromosome is called the *locus* (plural, *loci*).

Exactly how the information coded in a gene is consistently and reliably turned into a product is a fascinating process, but it is beyond the scope of this book. Those interested in understanding more about how this process works are referred to Lewin (1987) and Stryer (1981). Suffice it to say, each trait—such as growth rate, flower color, flower size, fall color—is the result of a series of biochemical reactions, each of which is triggered by an enzyme, which is controlled by a gene. If you were selecting for red flower color and four compounds were necessary in the production of red pigment, then four genes would be involved. The final product may be affected by changes in any of the four genes.

CHROMOSOME NUMBERS

As mentioned earlier, every plant species has a characteristic number of chromosomes. *Magnolia macrophylla* has a chromosome number of 38 ($2n = 38$), meaning that it has 38 chromosomes consisting of two strands each. This chromosome number is called the *diploid* number (*di* means "two," referring to the $2n$ state). When meiosis occurs and reproductive cells are formed, each chromosome strand separates from its partner. Each reproductive cell will have one strand from each chromosome. In the case of *M. macrophylla*, the reproductive cells— pollen and ovules—each have a total of 19 chromosome strands. The number of chromosomes in a reproductive cell is known as the *haploid* number and is written as $n = 19$. During fertilization, one set of chromosomes is contributed by the pollen parent, and one set by the ovule parent. With *M. macrophylla*, each parent contributes 19 chromosomes, which combine in the offspring to produce a diploid ($2n = 38$) *M. macrophylla*, thus completing the cycle.

Until now we have discussed organisms in which the gametes contain only one of each kind of chromosome characteristic of that species. When gametes unite to form somatic cells, the result is a diploid organism containing two strands of each type of chromosome. Each strand will only pair with the other strand of the same chromosome type—for example, a strand of chromosome 8 will pair only with another strand of chromosome 8, and never with a chromosome 2 strand—because the sequence of genes on one strand is identical to the gene sequence on the corresponding strand of the chromosome type. These strands are said to be *homologues* of each other, and chromosomes constituted from homologous strands are called *homologous chromosomes*.

Not all organisms conform to the diploid situation just described. Exceptions can be considered in two groups. The first group consists of organisms in which chromosome sets have duplications or deletions for one or a few chromosome types. These organisms are known as *aneuploids*. For example, a somatic cell in an aneuploid may have four sets of chromosome 8, rather than the two sets typical of a diploid. (Within the aneuploid group, other terms are used to specify the number of duplications or deletions; see Allard 1999.) The second group consists of organisms in which somatic cells contain some multiple of the complete set of chromosome types. These organisms are known as *euploids*. Certain types of euploids are commonly found in the plant world: triploids, containing three complete chromosome sets, tetraploids with four sets, hexaploids with six sets, octoploids with eight sets. Euploids can be further categorized into *autopolyploids*, which have homologous chromosome sets (from the same genome) and thus the chromosomes are able to pair along their entire length, or *allopolyploids*, which have *homoeologous* chromosomes that are from different genomes but share common segments, as in different species. These terms are used with reference to the number of chromosome sets—for example, a tetraploid with homologous chromosomes is called an autotetraploid.

EXTENT AND UTILITY OF POLYPLOIDS

It is estimated that more than one-third of all flowering plants are polyploids. From the standpoint of plant improvement, the utility of polyploidy varies greatly depending on the type of polyploidy (euploid vs. aneuploid, allopolyploid vs. autopolyploid), the trait(s) of interest, and how the plant is to be propagated (from seed or vegetatively).

Aneuploids are more useful for academic studies of genetics than for direct use in commercial production because they are typically sterile and lacking in vigor. Autopolyploidy, on the other hand, often increases the vigor and size of vegetative parts of plants. Allopolyploidy generally results in a blending of the physical characteristics of the species from which the genome is derived. Autopolyploids and allopolyploids that contain odd numbers of chromosome sets (such as triploids and pentaploids) are usually sterile, whereas those with even numbers (tetraploids, hexaploids) are often fertile. For ornamental plants that can be propagated vegetatively, reduced fertility is not a serious flaw, while larger flower and fruit size may be highly desirable. Therefore, euploidy may be useful to ornamental plant breeders.

Different species within a genus can have different chromosome numbers. This is important in breeding because it can affect the ease with which species cross or the direction in which the cross can be made, the fertility of the resulting hybrid, or the inheritance of certain traits. Obtaining hybrids from parents with the same chromosome number is easier than hybridizing plants with different chromosome numbers.

Increasing the chromosome number, or ploidy, of breeding materials can be beneficial for making crosses that might not otherwise be possible because the plants have different chromosome numbers. For example, doubling the chromosomes of a diploid ($2n$), making it tetraploid ($4n$), might allow it to be more easily crossed with another tetraploid, producing a tetraploid hybrid. The hybrid in this case is also more likely to be fertile than a triploid ($3n$) hybrid produced by a diploid × tetraploid cross.

CAUSE AND INDUCTION OF POLYPLOIDY

Chromosome doubling is caused by irregularities in the process of mitosis. It occurs naturally at low frequencies in all plants. Chromosome doubling is most commonly induced artificially by treatment with colchicine, an alkaloid derived from the autumn crocus, *Colchicum autumnale.* Colchicine disrupts mitosis and causes some cells to accumulate duplicate chromosomes, resulting in a polyploid. Typically, it is most effective on seed embryos or small seedlings. Colchicine, in a 0.05–0.9% solution, is utilized by soaking seed, immersing roots, or application to the meristem (growing point). The proper treatment methods and concentration varies with the plant group; more information on application for particular ornamentals can be found in such articles as Kehr (1996) and Austin (1998), and in some of the chapters of this book as well. Colchicine is a potentially harmful chemical that should be handled with caution.

Mendelian or Qualitative Inheritance

As explained previously, genes are specific sequences of base pairs located at specific positions (loci) along strands of DNA, and genes control particular functions, which in turn lead to the expression of traits. Genes may occur in alternate forms known as *alleles.* As an example, in flower color, one allele, which we can call *R,* causes plants to have red flowers. Since there are two chromosome strands, one contributed from each parent, plant breeders would designate the red-flowered plant in this example as *RR* to indicate that each parent contributed the allele for red flower color. An allele for white flower color may also exist, which we can call *R'* to differentiate from *R.* So, plants carrying the *R'* allele from each parent (*R'R'*) would have white flowers. What if a red *RR* parent were crossed with a white *R'R'* parent? Since each parent would only contribute one chromosome strand, the offspring would be *RR'* and, in this case, would have a flower color intermediate between that of the parents—that is, pink. In such a situation where one gene (or very few) is responsible for controlling the expression of a trait, the pattern of inheritance is known as *qualitative genetics* or, more commonly, Mendelian genetics to honor the monk Gregor Mendel, who is credited with discovering this type of inheritance.

At this point, introducing some key terms will simplify future discussions of plant breeding. First, the observable expression of a trait (red, white, or pink flower color) is the *phenotype,* or physical appearance, for that trait. The actual genetic constitution (*RR, R'R',* or *RR'*) is known as the *genotype.* In our example, the expression of *R* and *R'* was neither red nor white in *RR'* offspring. Instead, those individuals had a phenotype (pink flowers) in which neither parental phenotype (red or white flowers) was dominant. In plant breeding terminology this is called *codominance.* If the *RR'* individuals had all been red, however, we would say that *R* was *dominant* to *R'* and *R'* was *recessive* to *R.* In other words, if the *R* allele were dominant, any plant having *R* in its genotype would produce red flowers. Plants in which both alleles at a locus are the same (as in $R'R'$ or RR) are said to be *homozygous* for that locus, and plants with different alleles at a locus (as in $R'R$ or RR') are *heterozygous* for that locus. Plants that exhibit the same physical appearance, or phenotype, are called *homogeneous*.

You can immediately put some of this information to use if you want to make a cross between two plants and you know what alleles each one has and whether the alleles interact in a dominant, recessive, or codominant fashion. But what if you don't know how the alleles interact? Or what if you don't know what alleles exist for a given trait? The inheritance of genes follows the rules of probability, and so we can use probability to determine how alleles are interacting and how many genes are affecting a trait. First, let's review some of the basics.

What a plant breeder can expect to see in the field, and consequently the decisions to be made, will vary with the degree of homozygosity and homogeneity of the plant material, referring to the genotype and phenotype, respectively. Using the previous example of the alleles R and R' for determining flower color, where R (red) is dominant with respect to R' (white), if all of a breeder's material has the genotype RR, all the offspring will be homozygous (both alleles being R) and homogeneous (all will have the same appearance, red flowers). If an RR is crossed to an $R'R'$, all the offspring material will be heterozygous (RR' or $R'R$) and homogeneous (exhibiting the red-flower trait of the dominant R). This example is illustrated in Table 1-1, with the alleles of the red (RR) parent included across the top of the table and those of the white ($R'R'$) along the left-hand side. The boxes in which R and R' intersect display the possible genotypes of the offspring.

Since the degree of homozygosity is determined by the degree of inbreeding (selfing and crossing of relatives), plant breeders categorize their breeding material according to the generation of breeding. The first generation from a cross between two parents is the F_1, or first filial, generation. The F_2 generation is obtained by self-pollinating or making crosses

Table 1-1. First-generation (F_1) offspring of a cross between red (RR) and white ($R'R'$) parents. All offspring are heterozygous (having one R and one R') and would have red flowers, since the dominant R is present in all four possible offspring genotypes.

	R	R
R'	RR'	$R'R$
R'	RR'	$R'R$

among individuals from the F_1 generation (Table 1-2). Subsequent generations are determined in a similar fashion.

Table 1-2. Second-generation (F_2) offspring of a cross between red (RR)
and white (R'R') parents. In this case, some offspring (R'R') would be white
flowered.

	R'	R
R'	R'R'	R'R
R	RR'	RR

Returning to the original example of two homozygous diploid parents,
to simplify our discussion we have added subscripted numbers to the alleles:
the red parent has the alleles R_1 and R_2 and the white parent has the alleles
R'_1 and R'_2. (We'll say that $R'_1R'_2$ is recessive in this example.) Again, in
Table 1-3, the alleles of the red parent are included across the top of the
table and those of the white parent along the left-hand side, with the possible genotypes of the offspring indicated in the boxes where the alleles intersect. Because each allele has an equal chance of being passed on to the offspring, R_1 has a 50% chance of appearing in the offspring and R_2 has a 50%
chance of appearing in the offspring; the same is true for R'_1 and R'_2. Applying the rules of probability, we can multiply the chances of each allele being
passed on to the offspring to determine the frequency of each genotype in
the offspring. For example, to determine the likelihood of R'_1R_2 offspring,
we multiply the probability of R'_1 (50%) by that of R_2 (50%). So, on average,
R'_1R_2 will appear in 25% (50% × 50% = 25% or 0.5 × 0.5 = 0.25) of the offspring. Using the same formula, Table 1-3 shows the frequencies of all the
possible genotypes.

Table 1-3. First-generation (F_1) offspring genotypic frequencies, genotypes,
and phenotypes of a cross between red (RR) and white (R'R') parents.

	R_1	R_2
R'_1	25% $R_1R'_1$ (red)	25% R'_1R_2 (red)
R'_2	25% $R_1R'_2$ (red)	25% R'_2R_2 (red)

We have already established that R' is recessive to R, so any plant that
has a genotype that includes R will have a red phenotype. Since all the geno-

types in Table 1-3 have an *R*, all offspring have red phenotypes. Now, if we cross two (or self one) of the offspring from Table 1-3, we find white phenotypes (*R'R'*) in 25% of the F_2 offspring, as shown in Table 1-4 (subscripts have been dropped).

Table 1-4. Second-generation (F_2) offspring genotypic frequencies, genotypes, and phenotypes of a cross between red (*RR*) and white (*R'R'*) parents.

	R	*R'*
R	25% *RR* (red)	25% *R'R* (red)
R'	25% *RR'* (red)	25% *R'R'* (white)

   Table 1-4 demonstrates two important frequency distributions used by plant breeders: the genotypic and phenotypic distributions for traits controlled by a single, dominant gene. The genotypic distribution is 1*RR*: 2*RR'*: 1*R'R'*, or simply 1:2:1. The phenotypic distribution is 3 red: 1 white, since all genotypes with the dominant *R* will be red and only *R'R'* will be white. Thus, 75% of the offspring should be red and 25% should be white.
   Once understood, this general rule can be used without going through the process of multiplying and creating the diagrams. If we are interested in, for example, a yellow flower, and we know that flower color is controlled by a single dominant gene where yellow is recessive, we know that two generations of breeding are necessary: the F_1 hybrids will all be heterozygous and the yellow flower color will be masked by the dominant, typical flower color. But the F_2 hybrids created by crossing two of the F_1 hybrids will contain about 25% yellow-flowered plants.

More Than One Gene

Expanding the previous discussion to include two traits controlled by a single gene each, or single traits that are controlled by two or more genes, is straightforward. For example, we may be interested in both flower color and plant height, and we want a white plant with a dwarf stature. Say the allele for dwarfing (*D'*) is recessive to that for normal height (*D*). If we cross two plants that are heterozygous for both traits (as in *RR'DD'* × *RR'DD'*), what frequency of offspring will have the desirable phenotype? As shown in Table 1-5, each parent will pass along one allele for each trait, and so each gene combination (*RD*, *R'D*, *RD'*, *R'D'*) has a 25% chance of being passed along to the offspring. Each genotype would therefore occur in the offspring 25% × 25%, or 6.25% of the time. The phenotypic distribution would be 9 red-normal: 3 red-dwarfs: 3 white-normals: 1 white-dwarf, and so there is a 1 in 16 (6.25%) chance that the offspring exhibits both white flower color and dwarf stature.

Table 1-5. Genotypes and phenotypes for F₂ plants from parents heterozygous for two traits.

	RD	R'D	RD'	R'D'
RD	RRDD (red normal)	R'RDD (red normal)	RRD'D (red normal)	R'RD'D (red normal)
R'D	RR'DD (red normal)	R'R'DD (white normal)	RR'D'D (red normal)	R'R'DD' (white normal)
RD'	RRDD' (red normal)	R'RDD' (red normal)	RRD'D' (red dwarf)	R'RD'D' (red dwarf)
R'D'	RR'DD' (red normal)	R'R'DD' (white normal)	RR'D'D' (red dwarf)	R'R'D'D' (white dwarf)

The approach just described can be used to predict genotypic and phenotypic frequencies for any number of traits. However, the size of the table quickly expands to an inordinately large size with the addition of traits, thus quickly reducing its utility. So, how does one deal with traits controlled by many genes? Quantitative genetics provides such an approach.

Many Genes—Quantitative Genetics

Let us first consider what the phenotype of a trait controlled by a single gene would look like if it were a measurable trait, such as height, and we graphed the percentages for each height found in the F₂ offspring. Graph 1-1 shows the phenotypic distribution of such a trait where dominance is not present. Three discrete groups are found within the offspring population: those that express the parent 1 genotype (call it *AA*), making up 25% of the population and having a height of 50 inches (125 cm); the parent 2 genotype (*aa*), making up 25% of the population and having a height of 62 inches (155 cm); and the heterozygous genotype (*Aa*), making up 50% of the population and having a height of 56 inches (140 cm). Remember, in this example we are assuming no dominance, so the offspring are intermediate between the parents in their height.

We will assume that there are 12 inches (30 cm) of height difference

One Gene No Dominance

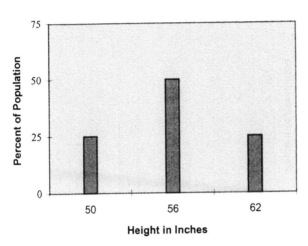

Graph 1-1. Phenotypic distribution for a trait controlled by one gene with no dominance. (Adapted from Allard 1960)

between the parents. (To keep things simple, we are making several other assumptions as well. Readers wishing greater detail on the subject should read Allard 1999.) If two equally contributing genes are responsible for a phenotypic difference of 12 inches, the distribution would appear as in Graph 1-2. Graphs 1-1 through 1-4 demonstrate that as the number of genes involved in determining the expression of a trait increases, the number of inches separating the groups of offspring becomes smaller and smaller until one's ability to measure a difference between groups becomes impractical, if not impossible.

In this example, the addition or subtraction of one gene would not have a dramatic, or *qualitative*, effect, as in the examples of the single gene for flower color. Instead, these genes act incrementally, or *quantitatively*. The process is known as *quantitative genetics*. This distinction is the essence of how plant breeders work differently with traits that are controlled by one or a very few genes (Mendelian or qualitative genetics) as compared to those traits controlled by many genes.

Quantitative Traits and the Effect of the Environment

Quantitative genetics can be a daunting subject to those who are not fond of statistics. Our purpose here is to provide enough of an introduction to allow someone with no other training in quantitative genetics to under-

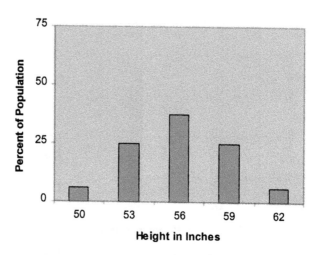

Two Genes No Dominance

Graph 1-2. Phenotypic distribution for a trait controlled by two genes with no dominance. (Adapted from Allard 1960)

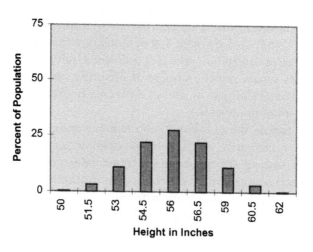

Four Genes No Dominance

Graph 1-3. Phenotypic distribution for a trait controlled by four genes with no dominance. (Adapted from Allard 1960)

Eight Genes No Dominance

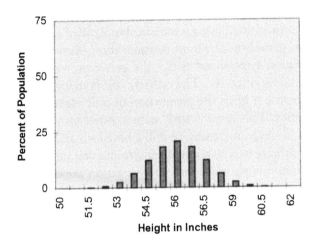

Graph 1-4. Phenotypic distribution for a trait controlled by eight genes with no dominance. (Adapted from Allard 1960)

stand the basic tools for manipulating quantitative traits and how they may be used in the simplest manner possible. Several good texts are available for those wishing detailed information (Allard 1999; Briggs and Knowles 1967; Falconer 1981; Fehr 1987; Moore and Janick 1983; Poehlman 1979; Simmonds 1979; Stoskopf et al. 1993).

A plant breeder concerned with improving a quantitative trait attempts to increase the frequency of favorable alleles for that trait. The essence of this approach is to separate the phenotypic expression into what is attributable to environment and what is attributable to genetics. Plants with the largest values attributable to genetics are selected. An obvious question is, how does one separate phenotypic expression into genetic and nongenetic components? For example, in a plant with larger-than-typical flowers, how much of this expression is due to genetics, and how much to some environmental factor like fertilization, soil type, or water availability?

So far, we have been assuming that the phenotypic expression of a trait is the result of one factor—the genotype. There is, of course, another factor that influences the phenotypic expression of traits—the environment. If, for example, a corn plant (*Zea mays*) with a genotype for high yield (as measured by kernel number) is not provided with sufficient water, nutrients, and sunlight, it will produce a low yield. The genotype and environment interact to influence the phenotypic expression of a trait. As the environment influences the phenotypic expression of genotypes, the values become more variable, until the lines between the phenotypes become blurred, finally becoming a continuum. The variation on either side of the "true" genotypic values is quantified using a statistical tool called a *variance*. For quantitative traits, plant breeders must consider three primary variances: a phenotypic variance, symbolized as σ_p^2; the genotypic variance, σ_g^2; and the environmental variance, σ_e^2. The ratio σ_g^2/σ_p^2 is an important one in plant breeding because it gives the proportion of trait variation that is actually due to genetics. This ratio is aptly named *heritability* and is customarily abbreviated h^2. As h^2 increases, so will a breeder's ability to make genetic progress; h^2 is increased by reducing environmental variation. Useful techniques for minimizing environmental variation are outlined in the next chapter.

Inheritance in Polyploids

As mentioned earlier in the chapter, euploids are of most interest to plant breeders, and here we will focus mainly on that type of polyploid organism. Allopolyploids, being composed of at least two more or less distinct genomes, have segregation ratios similar to those of diploids, which we have just discussed. (Segregation ratios for autopolyploids can be complex due to the larger number of possible alleles for each locus.) For diploid individuals, two different alleles are possible at a single locus. For autopolyploids, the number of different alleles possible at a single locus is equal to the ploidy level. For example, an autotetraploid would have four possible alleles (call them *a*, *b*, *c*, *d*) at a single locus. Five genotypes may be derived from these four alleles (Table 1-6). Table 1-7 shows the possible gametes, or the *gametic array*, produced by an autotetrapolid for each genotype. The genotypic ratios resulting from selfing any of the five genotypes can be determined by squaring the gametic array (Table 1-8).

Phenotypic ratios can be understood with a slightly different description of the genotypes using only two alleles, where *A* is dominant and *a* is recessive (Table 1-9). The gametic array is given in Table 1-10. Self-fertilization of *AAaa* (or crossing two *AAaa* individuals) would give F_2 genotypes in the proportion shown in Table 1-11. If *A* is completely dominant over *a*, the phenotypic ratio would be 35:1 (since only 1 out of 36 possible genotypes is all *a*). Other phenotypic ratios can be determined in a similar manner for crosses between various autotetraploid genotypes (Table 1-12). These ratios are only some of those possible for autotetraploids, however— remember that in order to keep our discussion simple, the ratios were based on only two alleles. Autotetraploids may have four alleles. In addition, gamete formation during meiosis is not as straightforward in polyploids as in

Table 1-6. Descriptions, terms, and examples of autotetraploid genotypes. (Adapted from Fehr 1987)

Genotype Description	Term	Examples
Only one allele present	Nulliplex	*aaaa, bbbb*
One allele present in three copies, another allele present in only one copy	Simplex	*aaab, abbb*
Two alleles, each present in two copies	Duplex	*aabb, bbcc*
One allele present in two copies, two different alleles present in one copy	Trigenic	*aabc, bbcd*
Four different alleles present	Tetragenic	*abcd*

Table 1-7. The gametic array for each possible genotype of an autotetraploid.

Genotype	Gametic Array
Nulliplex, *aaaa*	*aa*
Simplex, *aaab*	*aa + ab*
Duplex, *aabb*	*aa + 4ab + bb*
Trigenic, *aabc*	*aa + 2ab + 2ac + bc*
Tetragenic, *abcd*	*ab + ac + ad + bc + bd + cd*

Table 1-8. Autotetraploid genotypic ratios obtained by squaring the gametic array.

Selfed Plant	Genotypic Array of Progeny
$aaaa \rightarrow (aa)^2 =$	all nulliplex
$aaab \rightarrow (aa + ab)^2 =$	1/4 duplex + 1/2 simplex + 1/4 nulliplex
$aabb \rightarrow (aa + 4ab + bb)^2 =$	1/2 duplex + 4/9 simplex + 1/18 nulliplex
$aabc \rightarrow (aa + 2ab + 2ac + bc)^2 =$	1/2 trigenic + 1/4 duplex + 2/9 simplex + 1/36 nulliplex
$abcd \rightarrow (ab + ac + ad + bc + bd + cd)^2 =$	1/6 tetragenic + 2/3 trigenic + 1/6 duplex

Table 1-9. Phenotypes of an autotetraploid with only two alleles, one dominant (A) and one recessive (a).

Term	Genotype
Nulliplex	aaaa
Simplex	Aaaa
Duplex	AAaa
Triplex	AAAa
Quadriplex	AAAA

Table 1-10. The gametic array and frequency resulting from autotetraploids, considering two alleles at a single locus.

Genotype	Gametic Array and Frequency
Nulliplex, aaaa	1 aa
Simplex, Aaaa	1/2 aa + 1/2 Aa
Duplex, AAaa	1/6 aa + 4/6 Aa + 1/6 AA
Triplex, AAAa	1/2 aa + 1/2 Aa
Quadriplex, AAAA	1 AA

Table 1-11. Genotypic proportions resulting from selfing AAaa individuals.

Genotype	Proportion
AAAA	1/36
AAAa	8/36
AAaa	18/36
Aaaa	8/36
aaaa	1/36

diploids. For example, under certain conditions a triplex, AAAa, can give rise to aa gametes, through a process called *double reduction*. A discussion of double reduction, how it works, and its probability of occurrence is beyond the scope of this book; several texts are available for readers wishing to explore this subject (Allard 1999; Sanford 1983; Stoskopf et al. 1993).

Table 1-12. Phenotypic ratios for an autotetraploid with one dominant allele *(A)* and one recessive allele *(a)* with no double reduction.

Parents	Progeny (dominant:recessive)
AAAA × *AAAA*	1:0
AAAa × *AAAa*	1:0
AAaa × *AAaa*	35:1
AAaa × *Aaaa*	11:1
AAaa × *aaaa*	5:1
Aaaa × *Aaaa*	3:1
Aaaa × *aaaa*	1:1
aaaa × *aaaa*	0:1

An obvious consequence of these phenotypic and genotypic ratios is that homozygosity will be approached more slowly by selfing polyploids compared to diploids. More undesirable recessive alleles are carried along in a breeding program with polyploids because these recessives are not expressed as quickly and therefore cannot be selected against as quickly. An additional consequence of the slower approach to homozygosity is that more variation is retained in the genomes of polyploid individuals, waiting to be uncovered and exploited by plant breeders.

Our intent in this chapter has been to present some basic principles so that the specific plant chapters are more meaningful. It is hoped that this chapter has provided the background necessary for amateurs to feel confident in their understanding of the genetic basis for plant breeding.

References and Additional Reading

Allard, R. W. 1999. *Principles of Plant Breeding.* 2nd ed. New York: John Wiley and Sons.

Austin, B. 1998. Engineering superior daylilies. *American Nurseryman* 187 (1): 24–29.

Briggs, F. N., and P. F. Knowles. 1967. *Introduction to Plant Breeding.* New York: Reinhold Publishing.

Emsweller, S. L. 1974. Fundamentals in plant breeding. In *Breeding Plants for Home and Garden.* Brooklyn Botanic Garden Record 30 (1): 7–11.

Falconer, D. S. 1981. *Introduction to Quantitative Genetics.* 2nd ed. London: Longman Group.

Fehr, W. R. 1987. *Principles of Cultivar Development.* Vol. 1. New York: Macmillan Publishing.

House, L. R. 1985. *A Guide to Sorghum Breeding.* 2nd ed. International Crops Research Institute for the Semi-Arid Tropics.

Kehr, A. E. 1996. Woody plant polyploidy. *American Nurseryman* 183 (3): 38–47.

Lasley, J. F. 1987. *Genetics of Livestock Improvement.* 4th ed. Englewood Cliffs, N.J.: Prentice-Hall.

Lewin, B. 1987. *Genes III.* New York: John Wiley and Sons.

Moore, J. N., and J. Janick, eds. 1983. *Methods in Fruit Breeding.* West Lafayette, Ind.: Purdue University Press.

Poehlman, J. M. 1979. *Breeding Field Crops.* 2nd ed. Westport, Conn.: AVI Publishing.

Sanford, J. C. 1983. Ploidy manipulations. In *Methods in Fruit Breeding.* Eds. J. N. Moore and J. Janick. West Lafayette, Ind.: Purdue University Press.

Simmonds, N. W. 1979. *Principles of Crop Improvement.* London: Longman Group.

Stoskopf, N. C., D. T. Tomes, and B. R. Christie. 1993. *Plant Breeding Theory and Practice.* Boulder, Colo.: Westview Press.

Stryer, L. 1981. *Biochemistry.* 2nd ed. San Francisco: W. H. Freeman.

van Harten, A. M. 1998. *Mutation Breeding: Theory and Practical Applications.* Cambridge, England: Cambridge University Press.

Zobel, B., and J. Talbert. 1988. *Técnicas de Mejoramiento Genético de Árboles Forestales.* Mexico: Editorial Limusa.

2 Plant Breeding— Practical Matters

M. Brett Callaway and Dorothy J. Callaway

Program Objectives

Progress in any breeding project is typically due to incremental advances. Even sudden large advances are almost always the result of several less dramatic, but necessary, steps. A breeder must have a clear understanding of the breeding goal and what is required to achieve it; otherwise the incremental advances will not be recognized as advances but as failure to achieve a desired result. Without clear objectives and an organized plan to achieve those objectives, chances of success are very low and the would-be breeder will likely become frustrated and give up. Every successful breeder has specific objectives and plans for reaching those objectives.

Any plant breeder must first ask, "What specifically do I want to end up with?" The objective might be a plant that will be cold hardy in the northern United States, or a plant that produces 20% more flowers than typical, or a plant that has white flower color rather than the typical red. Being specific about one's goals helps to clarify and focus. "I want to make a nicer plant" is not specific enough to be helpful. Setting measurable objectives is essential to gauging progress.

Once specific objectives have been established, the next question should be, "What are the necessary steps to achieve these objectives?" For example, will it be necessary to cross an ornamental but cold-sensitive plant to a cold-hardy yet less attractive distant relative to obtain cold hardiness, or can cold hardiness be obtained by crossing among more desirable, more closely related cultivars? How will the selection pressure be applied to identify differences? In the case of cold hardiness, the breeding program would most likely need to be located in the targeted hardiness zone so that winter temperatures would provide appropriate selection. How will differences in plants be measured? Or in our example, how will we determine which plants to keep? Perhaps those that survive a selected temperature without damage, or with a previously determined amount of damage, would be kept for further evaluation. These issues must be thought out in advance, and the chapters that follow give guidance on such questions as they pertain to the various plant groups.

Improving Efficiency

Plant breeding has often been called a numbers game. Intelligent choice of parents for crossing, and good methods for applying selection pressure, can greatly reduce the numbers necessary to make progress. But a plant breeder's success will continue to be largely dependent on the efficiency with which large numbers of plants can be evaluated. Organization and focus are critically important to operating efficiently, and the two must work together. A breeder can be very organized yet inefficient by focusing on issues that have little or no impact on furthering program objectives. Some common constraints to evaluation efficiency are time, space, and cost.

Time constraints can involve the time required to reach the stage at which evaluation can occur or the time required to make evaluations. Speeding growth or maturity is a good way to reduce the time delay before beginning evaluations, thereby increasing the number of plants that can be evaluated in a given time period—providing ideal growing conditions through the use of fertilizers and irrigation is the most obvious method for speeding up growth and maturity. Maturity and growth are closely associated, but there are important reasons for considering them separately. Maturity, as in reproductive maturity (flowering and seed production), can be delayed by ideal growing conditions. Knowing how to manipulate the growth and maturity of the plants you are working with is essential. Growth and maturity can be influenced in many ways, including controlling the intensity of light, adjusting the length of time spent in light or in darkness, spraying with growth regulating chemicals, pruning, and girdling, among others. The methods you choose will depend on the plant you are breeding, the goals of your program, and the value you place on saving time to evaluation.

Nonprofessional breeders often plant the intended parent plants for their breeding program using spacing similar to what they would use in the landscape. This is particularly wasteful when dealing with trees and shrubs, due to their large mature sizes. If cold hardiness is the breeding objective, for example, selection may be possible at a young age. If that age happens to be one year, then the plants should be spaced only as far apart as one year's growth requires.

Ruthlessness is another important tool for the plant breeder, especially as pertains to space. The quickest way to bog down a breeding program is to keep too many plants in the evaluation stage. Discarding the various "interesting things" that result from the crosses you make is often a difficult prospect, but progress depends on staying focused on your objectives. You will soon be overwhelmed with material, and will run out of space, if you do not mercilessly discard those plants not meeting your objectives for that step of the breeding program.

Sampling

The number of individual plants that need to be evaluated in order to have a high (for example, 95%) probability of obtaining the desired phenotype depends on the frequency of the allele(s) in the population being evaluated, the number of alleles controlling the expression of the trait, and the amount of environmental variation in the selection environment. Determining precise estimates for the number of plants to evaluate can be a complex exercise; Narain (1990) provides further information for those interested in pursuing this topic. However, some general practices will improve your probability of identifying the phenotype you are after without having to resort to complex calculations. First, begin your search in a population with as high a frequency as possible of the alleles you are looking for. In other words, if you are looking for cold tolerance, do not look for it in a population from the tropics, if at all possible. Second, increase the number of plants you evaluate as the number of alleles controlling the trait increases. For example, a trait controlled by a single gene may only require tens of plants for evaluation, whereas a quantitative trait may require that thousands of plants be evaluated. Finally, make your selection environment as uniform as possible. In the previous chapter, we discussed the effect of environment on the phenotypic expression of traits. Creating a uniform environment in which to make selections helps ensure that the differences you find in your evaluation plots are a result of genetics rather than environmental factors.

Several techniques are key to minimizing environmental variation. 1) Keep growing conditions as uniform as possible. Use the same soil mix, water and fertilizer regime, planting dates, and so forth, for all plants from which selections will be made. If plants are field-grown, make sure the field is uniform in soil type, drainage, fertility, and other conditions. 2) Replicate. If selections are being made on clonal plants or families at or above the F_3 generation, grow multiples of each clone or family and average out the results. The ideal number to use depends on many factors—among them the amount of variation in the testing environment, the degree of precision desired, the ability to measure with precision, the amount of resources available—but four replications is sufficient for most circumstances. This way your decision will be based on how the four plants of that clone performed as a whole, rather than how any single individual performed, thus minimizing any localized environmental effects. 3) Randomize the placement of replicated clones or families. The principle behind this is that plants grown together may be subjected to undetected and unintended similarities in their growing environment. Do not plant your four replicates of a particular clone side-by-side, but scatter them throughout the planting so that you are less likely to have all four subjected to a quirk in the growing environment (such as a spot that is not well-drained or receives less sunlight) that might affect the expression of the trait in which you are interested. By randomly placing plants in the greenhouse or field, the chance of unintentionally favoring or discriminating against a clone or family is reduced.

Putting It All Together

One possible example of how a breeding program might take shape is outlined here. Other examples are given in the chapters on specific plants.

Let's start with a few assumptions. Our program involves ornamental trees and our objective is to develop a red-flowered, cold-hardy hybrid by obtaining cold hardiness from one parent and red flowers from the other. We have set specific, measurable levels of redness (as red as the red parent) and cold hardiness (withstands −10°F [−23°C] when fully dormant). The area where these plants will be evaluated consistently reaches winter temperatures of −10°F (−23°C). We have selected a plot of land uniform in its soil type, drainage, and fertility in which to do our selection, and we will provide good growing conditions. We know that the alleles for cold hardiness are rather infrequent even in the cold-hardy parent, but this parent was the best source of cold hardiness available in the species, and we did not want to expand the search for cold-hardiness alleles to related species because they are far inferior in other important traits. We also know that several alleles influence the expression and intensity of the red flower color, even though the red parent is always red. So, most likely at least a few thousand plants must be evaluated to obtain the phenotype we are after. Furthermore, it is known that the trees begin flowering at about 5 feet (1.5 m) tall and the flowers are representative of those that would appear on mature trees. We could grow these trees in containers, but we have done our homework and know that we can obtain a similar amount of growth at far lower cost by planting them in the ground. We have determined that we can reliably get at least 5 feet (1.5 m) of growth in 4 years and still get a few flowers (we do not need many to make our selection) using a spacing of 3 feet (1 m) within the row and 6 feet (2 m) between rows. We only have 1 acre (0.4 ha) available to us. We can plant ¼ acre every year so that after the first 4 years of establishment, we will always be planting ¼ acre and selecting and clearing ¼ acre. After making selections, we can transplant out of the field those meeting our criteria (a very small number of plants). Everything else should be destroyed to free up space for the next planting cycle. Destroying these plants will not be an easy task because we like these plants (or else we would be pursuing another hobby) and have 4 years of time invested in them. But, destroy them we must because over time we can evaluate more promising crosses by sticking to a disciplined cycling of materials. Every cycle we are able to plant 605 new trees in our ¼ acre.

Labeling and Record Keeping

Once a breeding program has been initiated, it is imperative that attention be given to organization and record keeping. These are very important components of any breeding program, and the authors of the following chapters will reiterate this. A good, consistent system of labeling helps prevent a breeding program from becoming hopelessly confusing and unproductive. Of course, parent plants must be correctly labeled with a permanent label so that there is no question about the parentage of the hybrids. Once crosses are made and seedlings are grown out, each seedling needs to be labeled, recorded, and tracked until evaluation. Each program will have somewhat different goals and priorities, but information of importance to most programs includes location (a code for where the plant was collected, or where its originating cross was made), date (when a cross was made or when seeds were collected or planted), cross or seedpod number, and seedling number. For example, GA9601007 would describe the seventh seedling (digits 007) resulting from the first cross (01) obtained from a breeding program in Georgia (GA) in the year 1996 (96). With this code permanently attached to a seedling in the evaluation plot, the breeder can refer back to more detailed notes in his or her record book. Notes might indicate that the breeding program in Georgia was, for example, at the University of Georgia, the cross was made on 15 March 1996 between *Magnolia liliiflora* seedling PA8503025 and *M. sprengeri* 'Diva', and the hybrid seedling bearing this label was the fastest growing and earliest flowering of the 10 seedlings resulting from the cross. Used in this manner, labeling will greatly aid the breeder's organization and ability to make informed selection decisions. Never rely on memory alone. Many a plant breeder has discovered that what is obvious and foremost in our mind today may very well get pushed to the back and blurred over time. Labeling and detailed notes are the only way to keep important information close at hand.

Pedigrees

Many systems for writing pedigrees have been developed over the years, and some breeders prefer to create their own system. Attempts to standardize the writing of pedigrees have found only modest success. A system advanced by the United States Department of Agriculture (USDA) is frequently used and will be described here. For more information on this and other systems, see Jennings et al. (1979).

In the USDA system, the female parent is always on the left in the pedigree. A slash (/) separates the female parent and the male parent in a single cross (A/B). If a single cross is crossed to another parent, C, two slashes (//) separate the single cross from parent C (A/B//C). When a third cross is added using a parent, which we'll call D, three slashes (///) are used to separate D from the rest of the pedigree (A/B//C///D). For additional crosses, the number of the cross is enclosed between slashes (for example, /5/ for the fifth cross). A four-way cross, sometimes called a double-cross, is a cross between two single-crosses. Therefore, the two single-crosses are separated by two slashes (//). A backcross is when offspring of a cross between two parents are repeatedly crossed back to one of the parents. The parent that is repeatedly used in this manner is referred to as the recurrent parent and an asterisk is always placed next to it. The dosage, or number of times that the plant has served as a parent, is placed next to the slash that separates the parents.

To illustrate, let's say A is crossed to B, then the offspring are crossed again to A, with A being the female in each case; the pedigree would be written A*2/B. If A is crossed to B, and the offspring are then crossed to A and their offspring are also crossed to A, with A being the male in each case, the pedigree should be written B/3*A. If the cross B/3*A is then used as a female in a cross with parent C, the resulting pedigree is B/3*A//C. Additional examples of pedigrees for various crosses, using the U.S. Department of Agriculture pedigree system, are given in the following table.

Single cross	A/B
Backcross	A*2/B
Three-way cross	A/B//C
Four-way cross	A/B//C/D
Compound cross	A/B//C///D/4/E/5/F

If the USDA system seems too complicated or overwhelming, do not give up on writing pedigrees. The important thing is to keep the necessary records. Conforming to a particular pedigree system is not necessary as long as the information is presented in such a way that makes clear what has taken place. A simple notation of parents, and which was the male or female parent, may suffice. But again, keeping the records, regardless of the system or manner in which they are kept, is critical.

Propagation of Selections

Once a breeder has evaluated the hybrids and determined that a particular selection is worthy of being named and introduced, several steps must then be taken. The first matter that should be addressed is propagation. Whether the breeder will be sending the plant out to nurseries for introduction into the trade or to other growers for further testing, the plant must be successfully propagated before it can go any further. With very few exceptions, the plant will have to be propagated vegetatively through division, layering, rooted cuttings, or grafting. The appropriate means of vegetative propagation will vary depending on the type of plant. A plant that is stubborn and difficult to propagate will be a disadvantage. If propagation seems impossible, or if there is no intention of propagating or distributing the plant, then the breeder should be discouraged from naming and registering the plant.

Naming Selections

After propagation, many breeders choose to send their plants out to other growers for testing before determining whether or not to introduce the plant. Sometimes the plants are sent out for testing with just the hybrid number (such as GA9601007), and some are given names before they are sent out for testing. Either approach is acceptable, and the plant must be accurately labeled with a name or number that corresponds to the plant breeder's detailed notes.

When it comes time to give a selection a cultivar name, careful consideration is necessary. Just as scientific names are governed by the *International Code for Botanical Nomenclature*, cultivar names are governed by the *International Code of Nomenclature for Cultivated Plants*, or the Cultivated Code. Article 17 of the code outlines rules and recommendations for assigning names to cultivars. Some of these rules are as follows:

1. The name must be in a modern language; Latin cultivar names such as 'Alba' or 'Variegatum' are no longer acceptable, although such names previously assigned to plants when it was acceptable are still valid.
2. The name should consist of no more than 10 syllables or 30 letters; this simply keeps names reasonably short.
3. The name should not consist solely of adjectives, such as 'Large Red', but may do so if one of the adjectives can be considered substantive (as in 'Gold and Silver', 'Velvet Cream') or if the adjectives describe a well-known color (as in 'Royal Blue').

4. The name should not include any common or vernacular names of plants unless it is only part of the cultivar name and is not the final word. For example 'Rose Queen' is acceptable since *rose* is only part of the cultivar name and is not the last word; 'Sweet Petunia', however, would not be acceptable since *petunia* is the last word.

5. Words exaggerating the merit of a cultivar should not be used; for example, 'Best Yellow' would be unacceptable since future introductions may prove to be even "better" yellows!

6. As common sense would dictate, a new cultivar name should be sufficiently different from existing names so as to avoid confusion; thus 'Geneva' would not be acceptable as a name for a new African violet since there is already a cultivar called 'Lady Geneva' with which it could be confused. (Note that it is acceptable to have, say, a magnolia named 'Little Gem' and a lilac named 'Little Gem', but obviously not two magnolias or two lilacs.)

These guidelines are among the more important rules for naming new cultivars; the code gives other rules and recommendations. The best way to ensure that your selected cultivar name is within the rules is to contact the registration authority for that particular group of plants. The International Registration Authority (also known as an IRA or registrar) is knowledgeable about the code and the rules involved in naming. Some larger ornamental plant genera have their own registrar, while others are lumped together under such groups as "other woody plants," "conifers," or "bulbous plants." Registrars maintain a list of all registered cultivars and can guide you in selecting your plant name, especially when it comes to number 6 in the preceding list—that is, not giving a name that can be confused with existing names. As unlikely as it may seem, there have been occasions when two different people have written to a registrar proposing exactly the same cultivar name (for different selections), each unaware of the existence of the other. The registrar can catch this *before* the plants go into circulation, thus eliminating a lot of confusion that would have come about by having two entirely different plants in the trade under the same name.

Though registration of cultivar names is strongly advised, it is not required and is done on a purely voluntary basis. Registration usually involves filling out a form, perhaps including a picture, and in rare cases a small fee. Many plant societies then publish the registrar's list so that those interested can see what plants have been recently named.

One last piece of advice regarding plant names: remember that the name you give your plant cannot be changed and so should be something of which you are proud. You might want to think about the marketability of the name, and you should not give a misleading name. 'Golden Glow' creates a nice image in the mind of the potential buyer, but if there is no golden glow, don't name it that. Nor do you want to name your plant something that evokes potentially unpleasant images, such as 'Green Swamp'. Even if the plant was selected from Green Swamp, and even if you like green swamps, you might want to come up with a more marketable name. Many breeders give their plants "stable names," intended only for use in identifying which plant was which in the field, only to have the names stick with the plant forever. *Magnolia* 'Two Stones' came about in just such a way: the breeder located the plant in his field by using two stones nearby as a landmark. Once a name is mentioned in a society journal, a nursery catalog, or other similar situation, it is considered to be the name of the plant, "validly published" as the code says. If you intend to write an article on your breeding program, consider referring to plants by their label number or giving them permanent names.

Plant Protection and Trademarks

Plant protection is becoming more popular with plant breeders around the world, and in the United States this protection comes in the form of a plant patent. A plant patent allows the breeder or originator of an exceptional plant form or new cultivar to obtain protection and monetary rewards for his work. Plants discovered in the wild are generally excluded from patenting, but a selection from a cultivated field of plants can be patented, as can the result of a breeding program. Plant patents are granted through a legal process similar to that of patenting inventions and are not governed by either of the nomenclatural codes. Consultation with an attorney knowledgeable about patents is usually required to begin the process. In the United States, plant patents require an abstract outlining the history of the plant and its description and unique characteristics. This is usually accompanied by supporting photographs. A patent application is then sent to the U.S. Patent and Trademark Office, where reviewers investigate the plant and similar forms to determine whether or not it is truly distinct. If a patent is granted, the patent holder alone has the authority to propagate and sell the patented cultivar, or to assign rights to others to do so. New plant patents are effective for a period of 20 years from the date of first filing the patent. (This term was recently extended from 17 years. Plant patents granted before 8 June 1995 may be in effect for 20 years, or 17 years from the date of filing, whichever is longer.)

Plant names can also be trademarked, in which case the selection is given not only a cultivar name but also a trademark name. The owner of the trademark cannot restrict the use, propagation, or distribution of the plant, but controls use of the trademark name only. Trademarking is becoming more popular in recent years as a marketing strategy for nurseries. The actual cultivar name given to the plant (and not controlled by trademark law) is often something unattractive or nonsensical that would not create much attention for the plant (for example, 'Swefm'), and the more attractive and marketable name is patented (such as, Pink Swirl™). In this instance, anyone can grow the plant under the name 'Swefm', but only the nursery holding the trademark name Pink Swirl can sell it under that name. Those seeking more information on plant patents and trademarks will find a good discussion in Moore and Janick (1983).

References and Additional Reading

Allard, R. W. 1999. *Principles of Plant Breeding.* 2nd ed. New York: John Wiley and Sons.

Briggs, F. N., and P. F. Knowles. 1967. *Introduction to Plant Breeding.* New York: Reinhold Publishing.

Fehr, W. R. 1987. *Principles of Cultivar Development.* Vol. 1. New York: Macmillan Publishing.

Jennings, P. R., W. R. Coffman, and H. E. Kauffman. 1979. *Rice Improvement.* Los Banos, Philippines: International Rice Research Institute.

Moore, J. N., and J. Janick, eds. 1983. *Methods in Fruit Breeding.* West Lafayette, Ind.: Purdue University Press.

Narain, P. 1990. *Statistical Genetics.* New York: John Wiley and Sons.

Simmonds, N. W., ed. 1976. *Evolution of Crop Plants.* London: Longman Group.

Stoskopf, N. C., D. T. Tomes, and B. R. Christie. 1993. *Plant Breeding Theory and Practice.* Boulder, Colo.: Westview Press.

Trehane, P., C. D. Brickell, B. R. Baum, W. L. A. Hettersheid, A. C. Leslie, J. McNeill, S. A. Spongberg, and F. Vrugtman, eds. 1995. *International Code of Nomenclature for Cultivated Plants—1995.* Wimborne, England: Quarterjack Publishing.

Plate 3-1. *Hemerocallis* 'Banquet at Versailles' (Photo by Ted Petit)

Plate 3-2. *Hemerocallis* 'Ferengi Gold' (Photo by Ted Petit)

Plate 3-3. *Hemerocallis* 'Forbidden Desires' (Photo by Ted Petit)

Plate 3-4. *Hemerocallis* 'Gladys Campbell' (Photo by Ted Petit)

Plate 3-5. *Hemerocallis* 'Mardis Gras Ball'
(Photo by Ted Petit)

Plate 3-6. *Hemerocallis* 'Romeo is Bleeding'
(Photo by Ted Petit)

Plate 3-7. *Hemerocallis* 'Winter in Eden'
(Photo by Ted Petit)

Plate 4-1. Division 1, trumpet daffodil:
Narcissus 'Gold Velvet' ('Aurum' × 'Arctic
Gold'), 1Y-Y

4-2. Division 2, large-cupped daffodil:
issus 'Concertina' (['Precedent' ×
*nt'] × 'Spaceship' sibling), 2W-P

Plate 4-3. Division 3, small-cupped daffodil:
Narcissus 'Engagement Ring' ('Silken Sails' ×
'Merlin'), 3W-WWY

4-4. Division 4, double daffodil: *Narcis-*
Spun Honey' ('Gay Time' × 'Daydream'),

Plate 4-5. Division 5, triandrus daffodil:
Narcissus 'Ringing Bells' (sibling to *Narcissus*
'Petrel'), 5W-W

Plate 4-6. Division 6, cyclamineus daffodil: *Narcissus* 'Jetfire', 6Y-O

Plate 4-7. Division 7, jonquilla daffodil: *Narcis.* 'Pink Step' (*Narcissus* 'Quick Step' open pollinated), 7W-P

Plate 4-8. Division 8, tazetta daffodil: *Narcissus* 'Falconet', 8Y-R

Plate 4-9. Division 9, poeticus daffod *Narcissus* 'Angel Eyes', 9W-GYO

Plate 4-10. Division 11, split-corona daffodil: *Narcissus* 'Mission Impossible' (['Wild Rose' × Hillbilly'] × ['Pink Frost' × 'Accent']), 11aW-P

Plate 5-1. *Iris* 'Butter and Sugar', the first nonfading yellow amoena diploid. (Photo by Chandler Fulton)

Plate 5-2. *Iris* 'Nagareboshi', a diploid with six falls. (Photo by Robert Hollingworth)

Plate 5-3. *Iris* 'Pink Haze', introduced in 1969 and still the standard of comparison for newer pinks. (Photo by Elsie McGarvey)

Plate 5-4. *Iris* 'Strawberry Fair', an extremely ruffled tetraploid with crimped edges and signals of unusual size. (Photo by Robert Hollingworth)

Plate 5-5. *Iris* 'White Swirl', Fred Cassebeer's milestone in the development of the modern Siberian iris. (Photo by Currier McEwen)

Plate 5-6. *Iris* 'White Triangles', a pure white diploid of triangular form. (Photo by Edward White)

Plate 6-1. Hostas come in a variety of attractive forms and foliage types useful for the garden. (Photo by James W. Wilkins Jr.)

Plate 6-2. Sports of *Hosta sieboldiana* 'Elegans' and *Hosta* 'Dorothy Benedict'. From left to right, top row: 'Color Glory' PPAF, 'Golden Sunburst', 'Dorothy Benedict', and 'Northern Lights'; bottom row: 'Frances Williams', 'Elegans', and 'Northern Halo'. 'Dorothy Benedict' is included to illustrate what a streaked *sieboldiana* type of hosta looks like, showing the effect of chlorophyll dilution on mature leaf size. (Photo by James W. Wilkins Jr.)

Plate 7-1. Diversity in foliage and flower color among aroids (clockwise from upper left): *Aglaonema*, *Spathiphyllum*, *Aglaonema*, *Anthurium*, and *Dieffenbachia* hybrids. (Photo by R. J. Henny)

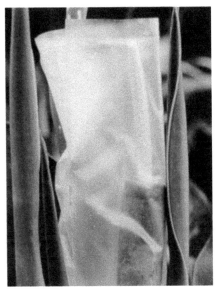

Plate 7-2. Inflorescence of *Aglaonema modestum* with the spathe unfurled and exposing the male and female flowers. (Photo by R. J. Henny)

Plate 7-3. Inflorescence of *Dieffenbachia* that has just been pollinated and wrapped in a paper towel and plastic bag to provide the high relative humidity necessary for pollen germination and eventual seed set. (Photo by R. J. Henny)

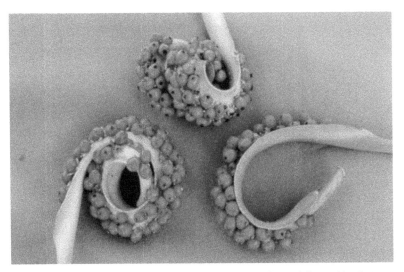

Plate 7-4. *Dieffenbachia* seed heads with mature seeds. Each berry-like fruit contains one seed. The red flesh should be removed before planting seeds, which will begin to germinate immediately once planted. (Photo by R. J. Henny)

Plate 8-1. A view of commercial plants, showing some of the genetic diversity in African violets. (Photo by Jeffrey L. Smith)

Plate 8-2. This commercial seedling is an example of the truest red available in African violets. The color is especially intense when the plants are grown under gro-lux lights. (Photo by Jeffrey L. Smith)

ate 8-3. *Saintpaulia* 'Golden Threads', ne of the best yellow-flowered African olets. (Photo by Jeffrey L. Smith)

Plate 8-4. *Saintpaulia* 'The Alps' is a chimera or pinwheel African violet with white edge strips and a lavender center strip. (Photo by Jeffrey L. Smith)

ate 8-5. African violet seedling with a relatively new muta-on known as 'Raspberry Edge'. The trait is genetic dominant nd is always expressed in pink or red petal edges. (Photo by effrey L. Smith)

Plate 9-1. *Chirita sinensis* 'Hisako' (Photo by Jeanne Katzenstein)

Plate 9-2. *Columnea* 'Hot Spot' (Photo by Michael Riley)

Plate 9-3. *Episcia* 'Silver Skies' (Photo by Jeanne Katzenstein)

Plate 9-4. *Gesneria* 'Lemon Drop' (Photo by John Evans)

Plate 9-5. *Kohleria* 'Strawberry Fields' (Photo by John Evans)

Plate 9-6. *Nematanthus* 'Leytron' (Photo by John Evans)

Plate 9-7. *Sinningia speciosa,* wild type (Photo by Peter Shalit)

Plate 9-8. *Smithiantha* 'Sunset' (Photo by John Evans)

3 Breeding Daylilies (*Hemerocallis*)

Ted L. Petit and Dorothy J. Callaway

Daylilies are among the most popular perennials grown today. They are easy to grow and propagate and are available in a wide range of colors, shapes, and sizes. Bloom time varies with the different cultivars so that a long season of color can be achieved with proper selection of cultivars, and most modern hybrids have combined extensive branching and bud count with frequent recurring scapes to provide nonstop flowers throughout the summer months.

The genus *Hemerocallis* consists of about 20 species native to the Orient. Although the common name would lead one to believe that daylilies belong to the lily family (Liliaceae), they have recently been transferred to their own family, the Hemerocallidaceae. The name *Hemerocallis*, proposed by Linnaeus in 1753, is composed from the Greek words *hemera*, meaning "day," and *kallos*, "beauty." Of course, this name refers to the fact that most daylily species have flowers that are open only for a single day, but each is quite beautiful during its burst of glory. Daylilies have been cultivated in Asia for millennia, dating back at least as far as 2600 B.C.; they were introduced into Europe by the early 1500s and to America by 1890.

Hemerocallis species bear red, orange, or yellow flowers, and it is difficult to believe that the pink, red, lavender, purple, white, and almost black flowers in gardens today arose from such a limited spectrum. The incredible array of *Hemerocallis* hybrids exists primarily because of the efforts of literally hundreds of breeders over many years. The daylily is ubiquitous in gardens and becomes tantalizing to the would-be plant breeder: it is easy to make the crosses (floral structures are large and easily accessible) and the possible combinations seem almost endless.

Key Groups for Breeding

A. B. Stout published his classification of *Hemerocallis* in 1934, and this classification is the foundation for the taxonomy used today. Stout separated the species with branched scapes (flower stalks) from those without branches. Erhardt (1992) outlined five main groups of species: the Fulva, Citrina, Middendorffii, Nana, and Multiflora groups. Plants from the species formed an important first step in the early days of hybridizing daylilies. The daylilies found in gardens today, however, are many generations past the species, and indeed, it has become extremely difficult to find plants of the original daylily species. Therefore, the actual members of the daylily species themselves have become primarily of academic interest. Most of these original daylilies were found growing wild in the Far East, mainly in China and Japan. For the most part, the petals were narrow, the scapes held few flower buds, and the colors were generally restricted to yellows, oranges, and rusty reds.

Now that we are so far beyond the original species, there are a number of key groups that should be considered in hybridizing. The first critical question is ploidy: Are the plants you want to cross diploids or tetraploids? This question is critical since diploids will only cross with diploids, and tetraploids will only set seed with tetraploids. You cannot successfully cross a diploid with a tetraploid; no matter how hard you try to make seed, you are doomed to failure. Although some people suggest that there may be a few plants, containing unreduced gametes (that is, gametes containing the full diploid number of chromosomes), that allow crossing of diploids and tetraploids, if such plants exist they are extremely rare. How do you know whether your plants are diploid or tetraploid? The answer can be found most easily by looking up the plant in the garden catalog that you purchased it from, since most catalogs list the plants' ploidy. If you got the plant from a friend or some other source, you can look it up in a catalog from any major garden or plant source (several are listed at the end of this chapter). The problem is that each nursery catalog only carries a limited number of daylilies, so the plant you are looking for may not be found in any catalog. The ultimate source is the American Hemerocallis Society's *Checklist*, a series of books listing all registered daylilies as well as their characteristics. Most of this information is now readily available on CD-ROM (see "Resources"). An additional source is the *Eureka Daylily Reference Guide*, which is a paperback book published each year (see "Resources"). It lists most daylilies that are in commerce, where you can buy them, and a price comparison between the different sources. The more time-consuming but least expensive way to check for ploidy is to try to set seed with a plant that you know is a diploid or tetraploid. Though opposite-ploidy plants will initially set seed pods, within a week or two the pods will dry up and abort since there are no viable seeds inside.

Once you have established whether your plant is diploid or tetraploid, you can cross it with any other daylily of the same ploidy. You then must decide what direction you want to take the plant. Any two flowers can be crossed, but most crosses are made for the purpose of improving the different key groups. Daylilies are generally divided into categories based on flower size (large, small, or miniature) or flower shape, whether single or double, polytepal, or spider. Double daylilies have more than the typical three petals, with the additional petals found at the center of the flower, making it resemble a carnation or rose. Polytepal daylilies are a new hybridizing direction; therefore, relatively few of them exist. They too have more than the typical three petals, but here the extra petals are added to the original circle of petals rather than to the center of the flower. This results in, for example, a four-petaled daylily, which resembles a dogwood bloom. Daylilies in the spider group have extremely long (sometimes 12 to 14 inches [30–35 cm]), very narrow petals, giving them a unique look, like a daddy longlegs. (See Figure 3-2 for illustrations of these flower shapes.)

Beyond these primary groups, daylilies are also generally characterized according to the color(s) of the petal. For purposes of color classification, the petal is broken into the throat area, the eyezone area, the petal self, and the petal edge. The very center of the daylily, where the petals form a narrow funnel leading back toward the base of the flower, is known as the *throat*. Typically, the throat area is a different color from the rest of the flower. In creating the modern cultivars, most hybridizers try to achieve a green-colored throat since many people find this a cool contrast to the rest of the petal color.

Daylilies are further categorized as either being self colored or having an eye or watermark. Self-colored daylilies are so named because the entire petal (except, perhaps, the throat) is the same color, or "the color of itself." Thus, the flowers appear as a solid color. *Eyed* daylilies have a darker area in the center of the flower surrounding the throat area. This effect can create a dramatic color contrast in, for example, a pink flower with a darker red or purple center. These eyes can be small, forming a dark ring in the center of the flower, or large, taking up most of the area of the petal. If this center circle of the flower is lighter, not darker, than the petal self color, it is referred to as a *watermark*. Many of the hybrids of R. W. Munson were lavender to purple with a large cream watermark. Like the darker eyes, the lighter watermarks can add interesting contrast to the flowers. In addition, the edges of the petals can be darker or lighter than the petal self. Darker petal edges are referred to as *picotee*, as in other flowers. Daylilies can also have lighter edges. These dark or lighter edges can be very narrow, forming a pencil-width line, to very wide, taking up to one-third or, in the case of some picotee forms, even one-half the petal width. Some modern tetraploid hybrids even have dramatic gold edges, with the edges glittering like golden sequences or pearls. Of course, like all other flowers, daylilies are also broken down into overall color, such as red, white, pink, and so forth.

In order to officially fit into the categories listed above, flowers have to meet the American Hemerocallis Society's (A.H.S.) designated criteria for that category (such as the petal length-to-width ratios for spiders). In the real world, however, the flowers often fall between the "official" groups, and yet still may be good candidates for breeding. For example, a flower may be spidery looking (have long, narrow petals), and therefore useful for breeding, but not actually meet the criterion for a spider as set forth by the A.H.S. Also, it is important to realize that just because a flower falls within one group does not mean that it should not be crossed with flowers within another group, especially if you are trying to achieve a particular goal. In fact, such breeding across flower groups is common. For example, the prominent and showy gold edge found on the newer tetraploid hybrids originally appeared only on large-flowered, wide-petaled, single daylilies. Therefore, hybridizers interested in getting this petal edge on miniatures, spiders, or doubles had to breed the gold-edged types into these lines. Naturally, this meant taking a step backward, losing much of the characteristic size, narrowness, or doubling in their first generation in order to achieve the ultimate goal of the gold edge. So, while these categories are listed here since most breeding goes on within specific categories (breeding doubles to doubles and spiders to spiders), enthusiasts should not be afraid to cross flowers of different groups if they have a specific goal in mind.

Brief History of Daylily Hybridizing

To date, more than 40,000 daylily cultivars have been registered and more than 15,000 of them are available commercially. Most of these selections have been made by people who were not professional plant breeders but whose interest in growing the plants led to hybridization of daylilies and selection of improved cultivars. A brief account of the history of daylily breeding might help to put the current hybridization efforts into perspective. The following overview is based on Munson (1989), who offers a more detailed history for the interested reader.

In the United States, daylily breeding began with A. B. Stout during his tenure as director of the New York Botanical Garden. His first selection, 'Mikado', was produced in 1929. As mentioned previously, Stout also produced the first taxonomic treatment of *Hemerocallis*, and his work remains the standard. Stout's breeding work focused on red flower color (such as

'Copper Red' and 'Dominion'), late-blooming selections (most notably 'Autumn Prince'), and *Hemerocallis altissima*, which he hoped would allow him to create tall daylily hybrids.

In the 1940s and '50s breeders such as Ralph Wheeler, Ophelia Taylor, and Betty Nesmith were creating daylilies of new color, form, and beauty. Wheeler's technique of mixing pollen and dusting it on various daylilies yielded many beautiful forms of unknown parentage; the most famous of these cultivars are 'Show Girl', 'Playboy', and 'Naranja'. Taylor produced a hybrid called 'Prima Donna', an evergreen selection with pastel tones that were passed along to offspring when it was used as a parent. Taylor's work opened up new avenues for breeding such pastels. Nesmith experimented with red, pink, and purple flower color. Her pink selections, such as 'Pink Prelude' and 'Sweetbriar', have since been surpassed, but at the time they were breakthroughs in pink coloring. Her 'Royal Ruby' possessed a clear red color that had not previously been accomplished, and it too led the way for future selections. The 1940s also heralded the beginning of hybridization for purple-flowered selections. Betty Nesmith's 'Potentate', Ralph Wheeler's 'Amherst', and A. B. Stout's 'Theron' were the basis for purples to come.

The period from 1950 to 1975 saw many promising advances in the hybridization and introduction of new daylilies. According to Munson (1989), during this period more than 15,000 new cultivars were registered, and more than 450 people were breeding *Hemerocallis*. Most of these breeders were amateurs like David Hall, an attorney who also bred *Iris* as a hobby. Hall worked to create two breeding lines, one pink and one red, and he is credited with bringing these colors into the daylily grower's garden. Another amateur breeder to have great impact during this time was Elmer A. Claar, a businessman and real-estate manager whose hybridizing hobby led to broad-flowered ruffled yellows and, perhaps most notably, rich reds. A professional breeder and botany professor, Ezra Kraus, developed a complex breeding program during this time that was used as a tool to help understand the variability and potential for mutations in the seedlings resulting from his crosses. He created hundreds of cultivars of various colors and forms.

W. B. MacMillan based his breeding program on five cultivars: 'President Giles' (one of his earlier hybrids), 'Chetco', 'Dorcas', 'Dream Mist', and 'Satin Glass'. These five were intercrossed in various combinations in the hopes of producing evergreen hybrids with short scapes and boasting broad, round, flat, ruffled flowers. MacMillan succeeded in producing such hybrids in yellow, pink, and pastels. The round, ruffled form he created was later to be called the "MacMillan" form.

Edna Spalding specialized in crossing pinks and purples, beginning with many of Betty Nesmith's selections. 'Dorcas' is a salmon-coral pink form bred by Spalding, and it was one of the five cultivars selected by Mac-Millan for his breeding work. Frank and Peggy Childs maintained a small breeding program and are credited with creating 'Pink Dream', the first truly clear pastel pink daylily, and 'Catherine Woodbery', a clear pinkish lavender with a whitish green throat.

The 1960s saw an increased interest in breeding tetraploid daylilies. Three of the earliest such workers were Hamilton Traub, Quinn Buck, and Robert Schreiner. Traub developed the Beltsville series of tetraploids, including 'Tetra Apricot', 'Tetra Peach', 'Tetra Starzynski', and many others. However, these tetraploids were inferior to the diploid daylilies of that time. Breeding of tetraploids did not hit its stride until the late 1960s. Today, more than 5000 tetraploid cultivars have been registered, and many more are sure to follow, as the possibilities seem endless!

Virginia Peck worked in the late 1960s to convert diploids into tetraploids, thereby creating a greater variety of tetraploids with which to continue hybridization work. She made remarkable advances in breeding full forms and ruffling in a variety of colors. Her selection 'Dance Ballerina Dance' was widely used in hybridizing because of its excellent ruffling. James Marsh, another amateur breeder, began his work with diploid forms in the 1950s, selecting a series of reds, pinks, and lavenders, each one given the prefix "Prairie" ('Prairie Blue Eyes', 'Prairie Hills', 'Prairie Warrior'). Later, he became interested in tetraploids, and these colors remained the focus of his program. Although other flower colors are included in his tetraploid Chicago series, it is the lavenders for which he is most known.

In the 1950s Orville Fay and Robert Griesbach created the tetraploid Crestwood series ('Crestwood Ann', 'Crestwood Evening', and 'Crestwood Gold', among others). These highly prized plants were the result of Fay and Griesbach's new technique for producing tetraploids, which involved soaking newly germinated seeds in a colchicine solution before planting. In addition to the Crestwood selections, Fay introduced 'Superfine' (large, rose-pink) and 'Satin Glass' (large, cream-melon pastel), two selections that were lauded for their flower size and overall quality.

Brother Charles Reckamp at Mission Gardens was known for his tetraploid pastel flowers with ruffled petals and gold edges. Both he and Steve Moldovan began working with diploids and then later became interested in tetraploids. Both carried out complex breeding programs and kept good records of their work. Moldovan began in the early 1960s to convert diploids to tetraploids by treating young seedlings with colchicine. He also bred winter-dormant northern cultivars with evergreen southern cultivars in an effort to produce hybrids that were more widely adaptable. Other prominent hybridizers of the more recent period include individuals such as

Van Sellers, E. R. Joiner, Clarence Crochet, Jack Carpenter, and Oscie Whatley. Pauline Henry has been a very accomplished breeder with an extensive hybridizing career, producing a large number of prize-winning hybrids in great variety, from miniatures to large flowers to doubles in a variety of colors, including her Siloam series.

R. W. Munson Jr., whose daylily breeding efforts span 50 years, also worked with diploids early in his career, later moving to tetraploids as his interest was captured by them. Munson's early attempts focused on clarifying the color in the early daylilies, producing a line of clear pastels. In 1960 (27 years after beginning his diploid breeding program) Munson became one of the first hybridizers to attempt to create a full line of tetraploid daylilies. The early converted daylilies were almost sterile, so a season of hard work that would have produced tens of thousands of new diploid daylilies produced only a handful of tetraploid seedlings. After many years of arduous work, he succeeded in creating several lines of new tetraploids. He worked with his mother, Ida, and together they produced daylilies in every available color. Their plants 'Betty Warren Woods' and 'Ida's Magic' were the standards for refinement and have been two of the most important and widely used hybrids in recent years. Despite Munson's many extraordinary accomplishments, his passion was always his purples and pastels. Where many hybridizers focused merely on improving the flower, Munson's primary focus was on improving the overall plant habit. He was ever mindful of the problems of short-sighted hybridizing and painfully aware of the problems that hybridizers had ignored in the breeding of other flowers. He was determined to keep the daylily out of the pitfalls that hybridizers of other flowers had ignored—such as the susceptibility to black spot fungus that had come to plague the modern hybrid tea rose, or the rot that had been bred into the newer irises. His goal was to make the daylily a carefree, everblooming perennial that would grow across a broad climatic range with no dependence on chemicals or special treatment.

No one since A. B. Stout has done more to change the face of the modern daylily than Bill Munson. He and Virginia Peck, against a background of great pessimism and what initially seemed insurmountable odds, pioneered the tetraploid daylily and brought it to the forefront, where it remains today. Human spirits such as they are, people were divided into two hostile camps: diploid supporters and tetraploid supporters. The vast majority of the members of the American Hemerocallis Society refused to accept the new tetraploids. As a result, Virginia Peck died without ever receiving the Stout Silver Medal (the highest honor bestowed on a cultivar), and Bill Munson never received it either.

Today the tides have turned, and most of the leading hybridizers are either breeding with tetraploid daylilies or are in the process of converting their programs from diploid to tetraploid; few top hybridizers are working exclusively with diploid lines. The more recent prominent hybridizers include Pat and Grace Stamile, who have worked on a variety of different flower types; Jeff and Elizabeth Salter, who are known for their full-formed flowers and complex eyes; and David Kirchhoff and Mort Morss, who have made significant advances in a variety of areas including doubles and eyed or edged daylilies. In addition, a newer group of hybridizers has begun making major changes in the face of the daylily. This group includes Dan Trimmer, who has focused on bringing converted diploids into the tetraploid lines; Ted Petit, who has created large, ornate single and double flowers; and Matthew Kaskel, who has concentrated on husky single and double flowers. The hybridizers of today are working to broaden the climatic conditions in which daylilies thrive and are putting their own vision of a new look on the daylily.

Important Traits and Breeding Objectives

Not surprisingly, much of the breeding work that is being done with *Hemerocallis* is focused on improvement of the flowers. Flower color and patterning are perhaps the most noticeable traits of a blooming daylily, but the plants have many other attributes that may interest breeders and gardeners.

FLOWER COLOR

In nature, daylilies offer flowers of yellow or orange, sometimes with tones of red or brown. Today, many hybrids are available that go far beyond those basic daylily colors. Almost every color is available, with the possible exceptions of solid blue or green, brown, and true black. Although white color has been achieved in some newer cultivars, breeders are constantly looking for the flower that is an even purer white. These elusive colors are highly sought after and are the focus of several breeding programs.

In order to understand how to successfully breed for a particular flower color, a bit of background on the chemical basis of flower color is useful. Flavonoids are pigments that have little color by themselves (and are sometimes referred to as co-pigments for this reason). Alone they would produce a white or pale creamy color, but when combined with other pigments, either anthocyanins (reds, purples, and blues) or carotenoids (yellows, oranges, orange-reds), flavonoids act to intensify the color produced by the other pigment. Flavonoids and anthocyanins have crystal structures, and when there is an excess of flavonoid pigment, the excess will crystallize and create what is known as "diamond dust," or a glistening or sparkling seen on the petals of the daylily flower (Erhardt 1992). This glittering effect can be considered in breeding programs, and one can breed for or against this characteristic.

The quest for a white-flowered daylily has revealed that the ability of daylilies to retain the carotenoid pigments in the flowers is dominant. This means that the flowers will contain at least a small amount of yellow, orange, or red pigment. If one could eliminate or negate the carotenoids, leaving only the pale flavonoids, a white or creamy-colored flower would result. It is thought that some daylilies carry a substance that neutralizes the carotenoids present. Diploid cultivars such as 'Joan Senior' and 'Gentle Shephard' and the tetraploid 'Wedding Band', 'White Crinoline', and 'Winter in Eden' (Plate 3-7) are good potential parents for a white-flowered hybrid.

Blue flower color has only recently begun to appear, primarily in the eyezone, and breeding efforts have focused on this eyezone area. The closest to a pure blue eye was developed by Elizabeth Salter in her miniature diploids, such as 'In the Navy'. Such eyes are almost nonexistent in the tetraploids, with the closest being 'Douglas Lycett', 'Hiding the Blues', and 'Rhapsody in Time'. The situation is changing rapidly, however, as hybridizers are converting the blue-eyed diploids to tetraploids and breeding them to large flowers.

When breeding for flowers of other colors, the list of available cultivars is almost endless. Although we can give a brief overview here, each flower has its own persona, and it is always recommended that you breed with those that have particular appeal to you. There are many reds to choose from, both diploid and tetraploid, that span the price range. Some popular red diploids are 'Big Apple' and 'Christmas Is', while the tetraploid reds that have received the greatest acclaim are such older, less expensive cultivars as 'Red Volunteer', 'Scarlet Orbit', and 'Seductor' as well as the newer, more expensive 'Dragon King', 'Richard Taylor', and 'Romeo is Bleeding' (Plate 3-6). The diploid 'Barbara Mitchell' almost always comes out at the top of any popularity poll for pinks, along with 'Fairy Tale Pink' and 'Jolyene Nichole'. Bill Munson's 'Shishedo' is considered one of the finest tetraploid pinks, along with 'Ed Brown', 'Effay Veronica', 'Elizabeth Salter', and 'Seminole Wind'.

Among the darker colors, popular purples and lavenders include cultivars from Moldovan, Petit, and Munson, such as the tetraploids 'Court Magician', 'Forbidden Desires' (Plate 3-3), 'Malaysian Monarch', and 'Strutters Ball' or the diploid 'Super Purple'. Although there are few cultivars to choose from in the black color range, 'Edge of Eden', 'Midnight Magic', and 'Quote the Raven' are popular near-black tetraploids.

Yellow, cream, and gold daylilies always make a bright spot in the garden. The most often discussed cultivars in this color range include the tetraploids 'Betty Warren Woods', 'Bill Norris', 'Ever So Ruffled', and

'Ferengi Gold' (Plate 3-2), plus the diploids 'Brocaded Gown', 'Ruffled Masterpiece', and 'Ruffled Perfection'.

COLOR DISTRIBUTION

Color distribution is another variable that can be selected for in daylily breeding. The flower of a daylily hybrid may show one of many color patterns and distributions (Figure 3-1). *Self color* means that the sepals and petals are the same in both color and shading. A *blended* flower has two different colors evenly distributed on both the petals and sepals (for example, yellow and red together on both the sepals and the petals, not red sepals and yellow petals or red petals and yellow sepals). *Polychrome* flowers have more than two colors spread evenly over the petals and sepals—that is, the same as blended but with more than two colors. *Bitone* flowers have petals and sepals of the same color, but with differences in shade and intensity of those colors. In bitone flowers, the sepals exhibit the lighter color. *Reverse bitone* refers to bitone flowers in which the sepals have the darker shades. A *bicolor* flower has petals and sepals of two entirely different colors, with the sepals having the lighter color; in *reverse bicolor* flowers the petals show the lighter color.

Along with color distribution, color patterns in daylily flowers (see Figure 3-1) also allow for interesting combinations to entice the breeder and gardener. Flowers are referred to as *simple* when no pattern exists. *Eyed* flowers have a dark contrasting blotch at the base of the petals and sepals. A *watermark* is similar to an eye, but the blotch on the base of the sepals and petals is lighter than the background color. A flower is called *edged* when the edges of the tepals are a different color or shade. If the edging is found only on the tips of the petals, the flower is known as *tipped*. *Wire edging* refers to a narrow line around the edges of the petals and sepals in a contrasting color to the background color.

Popular daylily cultivars that have been bred with attractive eyed flowers include 'Always Afternoon', 'Daring Dilemma', 'Pirate's Patch', and 'Strawberry Candy', which are all tetraploids, and the diploid 'Dragon's Eye', 'Janice Brown', and 'Siloam Virginia Henson'. The eyes of the daylily have also been bred to contain layers or some other pattern within them, producing what are known as complex or patterned eyes. The complex-eyed diploids such as 'Child of Fortune', 'Enchanter's Spell', 'Little Print', and 'Siloam David Kirchhoff' are fine examples. Only a few complex-eyed tetraploids are available, such as 'Chinese Cloisonne', 'Etched Eyes', and 'Paper Butterfly', although this characteristic is currently the center of intense hybridizing efforts.

A new break in the tetraploid daylily is the development of gold edges, which are currently highly sought after. Some renowned gold-edged day-

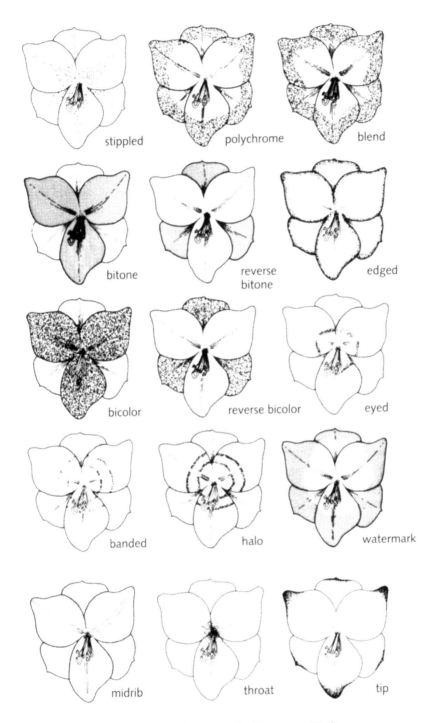

Figure 3-1. Color distribution and patterns in *Hemerocallis* flowers.
(Illustration by Marlene Gemke. Adapted from Erhardt 1992.)

lilies are the lavender 'Ida's Magic', the near-white 'Wedding Band', and 'Admiral's Braid'. The edges are heavier on more recent releases, such as 'Banquet at Versailles' (Plate 3-1), 'Clothed in Glory', 'Ida's Braid', and 'Light Years Away'. Hybridizers have also combined the gold and picotee edges to achieve dramatic double-edged daylilies, such as 'Creative Edge', 'Mardi Gras Ball' (Plate 3-5), and 'Uppermost Edge'. The lighter edged daylilies that are proving to be useful in hybridizing include 'Altered State', 'Avante Garde', and 'Street Urchin', all of which are shades of red with a broad, lighter edge.

Daylily flowers may also have *midrib stripes* along the middle of the petals and sepals, on the petals only, or on the sepals only. Some midrib stripes are raised or "prominent," making them even more noticeable. Midribs can be either lighter or darker than the petal self, providing an interesting contrast. Sometimes a midrib stripe can enhance the overall flower appearance, though in others cases it may detract.

Many flowers have throats of a different color, which provides for further variation in the kinds of flowers that can result from hybridizing. The color of the throat is usually yellow, green, or orange. Similarly, anther color can vary from yellow to orange to deep reddish black. Although neither the throat color nor the anther color is terribly obvious at first glance, it can enhance the overall effect of a particular combination of flower colors and patterns.

FLOWER SHAPE

Hemerocallis flower shapes may be described from the front view, which tells of the geometric shape of the flower, and from the side view or profile (Figure 3-2). The front view may be one of four different shapes. *Circular* flowers have blunt-tipped, short, wide petals that overlap to form a rounded shape. *Triangular* flowers have petals that are relatively narrow (although not narrow enough to be considered a spider), creating a triangular shape. *Spider*-shaped flowers have petals that are even narrower, so much so that they do not overlap. Those flowers that do not reflect any of those three shapes, or that lack uniformity within the flower, are called *informal*.

Profile views of the flowers may be described as *recurved*, with the petal tips curved back toward the throat; *chalice-*, *cup-*, or *trumpet-shaped*, with petals pointed away from the throat, much like a *Narcissus* corolla; and *flat*, in which the petals lay out flat, rather than being chalice-shaped or curved backward.

Flower shape also includes doubles, of which there are two types. *Peony* doubles have extra petals and *petaloids* that stick up, creating a flower that resembles a peony (*Paeonia*). Petaloids are the extra tissues in the center of the flower that look like petals, although careful examination will reveal

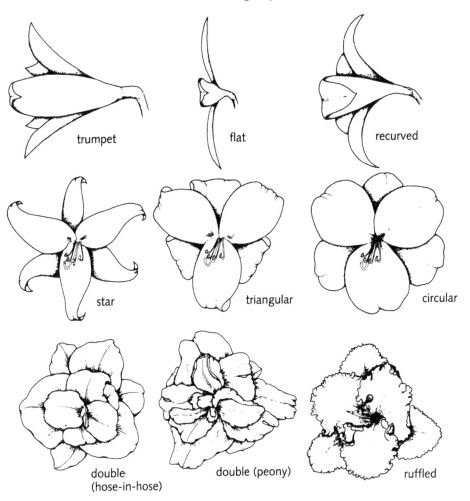

trumpet   flat   recurved

star   triangular   circular

double   double (peony)   ruffled
(hose-in-hose)

Figure 3-2. Flower shapes in *Hemerocallis*. (Illustration by Marlene Gemke. Adapted from Erhardt 1992.)

that they are actually stamens that have been modified to look like petals. (Sometimes the only way to tell the difference is to count the number of stamens present—there should be six, and if there are fewer than six, some have been converted to petaloids.) The *hose-in hose* or *layered* double type has layers of petals or petaloids that lie on top of one another (as in azaleas or camellias). In these flower types, the petaloids, if present, resemble true petals. A few doubles have extra true petals, not just petaloids, but they are rare. The shape of a double flower often varies from bloom to bloom; therefore, a single cultivar may vary in its form daily or, more commonly, as the season progresses.

The shape of the individual flower petals and sepals is also variable. They may be *rounded*, or *pinched* (the petals look as if someone has pinched the petal along the midrib), and *twisted* (with lengthwise twists or twirling, which is most obvious in the long sepals and petals of the spider forms). Many beautiful daylily selections have unusual edging to the tepals, primarily *ruffled* or *crimped*, but edges can also be *tailored* (lacking any real ruffling). Tepal texture is also variable, from smooth to a corrugated or ribbed texture.

Hybridizing for daylily shapes has resulted in some interesting double and spider forms. The diploid 'Betty Warren Woods', 'Francis Joiner', and 'Siloam Double Classic' are ever-popular doubles. Tetraploid doubles are relatively new, and therefore scarcer, but such cultivars as 'Gladys Campbell' (Plate 3-4), 'Highland Lord', 'John Kennibrew', and 'Layers of Gold' are all highly regarded. The rage for spider breeding is also a fairly recent development. Some of the more popular diploids include 'De Colores' and 'Yabba Dabba Do'. Although it is currently the center of intense hybridizing efforts, very few tetraploid spiders are available to date. Among the few tetraploid spiders are 'Red Suspenders', 'Spider Man', 'Swirling Spider', and 'Twist of Lemon'.

TIME OF DAY OF FLOWERING

Some daylilies bloom primarily at night rather than during the day, thus there exists the possibility of extending the life of a particular flower. Nocturnal blooming is inherited from the Citrina group, in which flowers open early in the evening and wilt by midday the following day. Crossing these nocturnal species with diurnal species can lead to extended blooming, or individual flowers that are open for 16 hours or more. Such crosses may yield plants that are day, night, or intermediate bloomers. Although a few modern hybrids may perform as extended bloomers, beginning to open the afternoon before, no modern daylilies bloom for more than one day. This is an area of hybridizing that is completely open for exploration.

FLOWERING SEASON

Peak daylily bloom varies from May to mid-July, depending on the locale and climate. The divisions used in describing daylily flowering season are based on peak bloom time. Since most modern daylilies have many buds, which causes an extended bloom period, as well as rebloom scapes, which extend the season even more, the categorization of bloom time is generally based on the time at which the daylilies begin blooming. The daylily season varies greatly between geographical areas—being quite extended in Florida and quite compressed in New England, for example—so it is not possible to give exact time frames for the subcategories of bloom season. Extra early (EE) daylilies, such as 'April Elf', begin blooming at the very beginning of the *Hemerocallis* season. Daylilies are categorized into further groups as flowering early (E) or early midseason (EM) if they begin blooming before the main season. Midseason (M) types, including 'Absolutely Fabulous', bloom during the main or peak season. Late midseason (LM), late (L), and very late (VL) bloomers begin their bloom progressively later in the season, after most other daylilies have begun blooming. Among the notable cultivars in these groups are 'Acapulco Gold' (LM), 'African Shadows' (L), and 'Bookwood New Era' (VL).

Some new hybrids have an extended season and therefore may begin blooming very early and continue through the entire bloom season. Similarly, some flowers may bloom during a particular season, then bloom again later for a second bloom season. These are referred to as *reblooming* or *recurrent* (Re). Many breeders strive for an everblooming hybrid, one that blooms throughout most of the season. 'Stella d'Oro' is the most popular long-blooming selection, although its popularity is primarily for commercial plantings (such as highways and malls). Though it has been surpassed as a garden plant by more modern cultivars, 'Stella d'Oro' remains among the longest blooming cultivars, particularly for northern gardens. Long-blooming daylilies require good branching, a high bud count, and the continuous production of recurrent scapes. At this time, many modern daylilies are approaching this goal. Two examples are 'My Darling Clementine' and 'Ferengi Gold'.

FLOWER FRAGRANCE

Most daylilies have a soft, pleasant fragrance. The modern hybrids do not offer the strong fragrance found in other species such as the rose or jasmine. A few hybridizers are trying to breed a stronger fragrance into the daylily flower by crossing the most fragrant cultivars in the hopes of enhancing the smell. Flower fragrance is another area very much open for hybridizers.

FLOWER SIZE

The size of daylily flowers is described by the following terms: *miniature* (less than 3 inches [7.5 cm]), *small* (3 to 4½ inches [7.5–11 cm]), or *large* (greater than 4½ inches [11 cm]). The term *pony* is often used informally to refer to flowers that are small but not miniature. Most hybridizing today goes on within the group of large-flowered cultivars. However, the small-flowered cultivars of the Siloam series are very popular among gardeners and breeders, as are the small and miniature flowers of Elizabeth Salter ('In the Navy', 'Little Print') and Grace Stamile ('Broadway Gal', 'Broadway Imp'). Efforts are also being made to further increase flower size to create giant-sized daylilies. There are few very large, full-formed daylilies, although the spider forms can be extremely large.

SCAPE CHARACTERISTICS

It is generally thought that flower size and scape height should have an appropriate ratio so that the plant does not look out of proportion—that is, small flowers should appear on short scapes and tall scapes should carry large flowers. These proportions allow the daylily to be used throughout the border, with the small-flowered varieties in the front, the large flowers in the middle, and the tallest and largest flowers at the back of the border. However, there are dwarf selections with large flowers and tall-scaped cultivars with a profusion of small blooms. Most people prefer some correspondence between flower size and scape height, but one need not be constrained by convention.

Scape branching is also important because a branched scape can support more flowers than can a single, unbranched scape. Scapes may be *top-branched*, in which there is very little branching limited to the top of the scape; *well-branched*, a more desirable form in which a number of branches occur along the length of the scape; *low-branched*, as in some miniature forms, where the scape is not much taller than the foliage and scape branching begins amidst the leaves; or *multiple-branched*, in which the branches have branches. Branch angle is another consideration to keep in mind, as it determines how close together the flowers appear. Flowers should not be so crowded as to detract from their individual appearance.

DORMANCY

Daylilies are classified as either dormant, evergreen, or semievergreen. *Dormant* daylilies have leaves that turn brown and die back to beneath ground level in the winter—the plant loses its foliage, generally regardless of climate (although it may not go dormant in a tropical setting where there is little change of season). *Semievergreens* are more dependent on climate and may be evergreen in mild climates and go dormant in areas with more harsh winters. In some cases, the upper part of the foliage may be killed by frost while new leaves continue to be produced. *Evergreen* forms remain green during the entire winter in warmer climates, although the foliage will often be killed in colder climates. Dormancy of a hybrid is inherited from its parents.

GARDEN PERFORMANCE AND CULTURAL CONDITIONS

As is the case for any plant group, the criteria for selecting daylilies must include the plants' ability to perform well in the garden. Garden conditions, and therefore selection pressure, may vary depending on the climate, and selections can be made accordingly. Historically, dormant daylilies tended to prefer cooler areas, and the evergreens performed best in the warmer south. Still today, some hard-dormant daylilies will not survive in the south (dwindling each year and eventually dying since they do not get the required chilling), and some tender evergreens will freeze and die in northern winters. Hybridizers have crossed the dormant and evergreen daylilies for so many generations, however, that today most modern evergreen daylilies thrive well into Canada, and most dormant daylilies perform well even into central Florida. It is generally recommended that gardeners in cold climates place some mulch over evergreen daylilies for the first winter so that the plants have a year to become established. Unfortunately, there is little that southern gardeners can do to provide sufficient chilling for those few hard dormants, short of potting them up and putting them in the refrigerator for a few weeks in midwinter, an effort most gardeners are not willing to expend.

Selections that resist fading of flower color are also desirable for many garden situations. The darker colors found in today's cultivars—particularly the reds, purples, and blacks—often melt, slick, or burn up in full sun. These color forms generally have to be planted in partial, or afternoon, shade so that they can be enjoyed, and breeding for sun-resistant cultivars in this color range is an important hybridizing goal.

Breeding Tetraploids

The history of tetraploid daylily breeding was outlined earlier in the chapter, and all the objectives just discussed can be pursued using either tetraploid *or* diploid parents. (Remember, tetraploids and diploids cannot be successfully intercrossed, as both parents used in a cross must have the same number of chromosomes.) Tetraploid forms have 44 chromosomes, rather than the typical 22 found in diploid species of *Hemerocallis*, and along with this increase in chromosome number come some desirable characteristics: bigger flowers with thicker petals, more intense flower colors, hardier and more robust plants, sturdier flower scapes, thicker and more rigid foliage, increased heat tolerance, and resistance to diseases and pests. A diploid daylily can be converted to a tetraploid through the careful use of colchicine. Austin (1998) outlines the procedure for artificially inducing polyploidy, should you wish to do so. However, it is not necessary to convert diploids to tetraploids in order to begin breeding with tetraploids, since so many tetraploids have already been introduced into the trade.

Hybridization Mechanics

The mechanics of hybridizing daylilies is, on the surface, quite simple. There are a number of possible pitfalls, however, as well as tricks that can make the process easier. The process is outlined here, and it is also beautifully demonstrated in a full-length color video now available. (See

"Resources" at the end of this chapter for information on obtaining the video.)

One reason daylily breeding is so popular among backyard breeders is that the flowers are large and the floral parts are easy to recognize and to reach. The showy tepals are made up of three outer sepals (which resemble petals) and three inner petals. At the center, a single (female) pistil is surrounded by six (male) stamens. Hand pollinations can be made in two ways. The simplest method is to break off a single stamen and use it as a brush to dust pollen onto the pistil of the seed parent. A more professional procedure involves collecting the stamens from unopened flowers early in the morning. The stamens themselves will also be closed when collected. They are then placed in shallow containers and allowed to dry. When dry, the stamens release the pollen, which is collected and dabbed onto receptive stigmas with tweezers, cotton swabs, or artist's brushes. Most hybridizers simply place the entire fresh flower in the refrigerator, where it will remain relatively fresh for two or more days, using one or more stamens each day. The flower's pollen should be collected while it is fresh and fluffy yellow, from a newly opened flower. Exposure to heat causes a progressive loss in pollen viability. The pollen of some cultivars (such as 'Exotic Echo') is hard and whitish and is not viable; in such cases the plant can be used only as a pod parent.

Since the pistil is such a distance from the stamens, few hybridizers bother to emasculate (remove the stamens of) the flowers of the plant chosen to be the seed (female) parent before pollinations are made. Early morning is the best time for pollination of tetraploid daylilies; diploids can be successfully pollinated throughout the day. In either group, successful pollination becomes less and less likely as the day progresses beyond midday. Successful seed set is temperature dependent. Particularly hot days are not good for pollination since few pods will set, whereas cool, overcast days generally result in excellent seed set, even on crosses made late in the day. Some breeders cover the pollinated stigmas with small pieces of aluminum foil to ensure that no foreign pollen reaches them. Pollination by foreign pollen is very rare, however, since the stigmas are only receptive for a short period of time, and the flower is only open for a single day.

Labeling the crosses as you make them is crucial. Use weatherproof tags and markers so that your label will be permanent, and include the names of both parents, indicating which was the pollen and which was the seed parent. You may wish to record the information in a notebook as well so that you can include more detailed information about the cross. The flowers can also simply be tagged with numbers that correspond to an entry in the record book, where the parentage and other details are recorded. Methods of labeling, numbering, or otherwise recording crosses vary from person to person, and each breeder must find a system that works best for him or her. How it is done is not critical, but seeing that it is done is very important.

If the potential parents of a particular cross do not bloom at the same time, pollen may be collected from the male when it is in bloom and stored for use when the female blooms. As already mentioned, refrigerated flowers remain usable for several days before degenerating. For longer storage periods, the following procedure may be used: brush the pollen into gelatin capsules, or place the entire anther(s) in a sealed container (inexpensive contact-lens holders work well); label the capsules or containers carefully; and place them in an airtight jar, ideally, but not necessarily, with a desiccant enclosed. Prepared in this manner, pollen will remain viable in the refrigerator for one season, or for a full year or even longer if stored in the freezer. When it is time to use the pollen, simply open the capsule and dip the stigma of the female parent into the capsule or remove the anther with a pair of tweezers (reverse tweezers, which are normally clamped rather than open, are useful here). Alternatively, an artist's brush can be used to transfer the pollen from the capsule to the stigma. If the latter method is used, the brush must be thoroughly cleaned after use in each type of pollen to avoid contamination from one pollen capsule to another.

A few days after pollination, the daylily flower will drop off. If pollination has been successful (if it has led to fertilization), the ovaries at the base of what was once the flower will begin to swell and seed development will begin. Development and maturation of the seeds usually takes about 8 to 10 weeks. If the pollination is not successful, no such seed pods will be formed. But do not despair! Even under ideal conditions, it is estimated that only about half of all attempted crosses will actually set seeds.

Seeds will be ripe in midsummer to early fall depending on the climate, usually 60 to 80 days after pollination. Left on its own, each seed pod will turn brown and split into sections to reveal one or more glossy black seeds. In order to keep the seeds from being scattered in the garden, seed pods should be watched closely, and as soon as they become completely brown and crack open on their own, the seed pods should be collected by removing them from the plants. If frost threatens to come before all the pods in the garden have ripened, they can be ripened indoors. To collect unripened pods, break off the entire flower scape and bring the stems indoors and place them in vases of water. Allow the pods to ripen there, then collect the seeds.

The seeds can be easily collected and stored in envelopes or zip-lock bags, each labeled with the cross that yielded the enclosed seeds. The seeds should be refrigerated for a minimum of 3 weeks if they are being planted directly—that is, if they are not being overwintered outside in a cold climate. Pure evergreen varieties will sprout without any chilling, but daylilies that have some dormancy in their background will require refrigeration in order to sprout. Some research suggests that seeds that are completely dried out do not receive the benefit of refrigeration. Therefore, most hybridizers attempt to keep the seeds in a moist environment during chilling. This can be accomplished by placing a moist paper towel in the zip-lock bag with the seeds. Ideally, the paper towel should not be soggy, as the seeds can rot if they get too wet. Hybridizers may place a mild fungicide in the bags during refrigeration to prevent rot.

Some gardeners prefer to soak seeds overnight in warm water just before planting in order to soften the seed coats and hasten germination, although this is not necessary, particularly if the seeds were kept moist during refrigeration. Daylily seeds may be started in the greenhouse on a heating mat set at 70–80°F (21–27°C). The heat helps improve germination, but this step is optional. If no greenhouse or heating mat is available, the seeds can be started in small flats or boxes on a well-lit windowsill. Seeds can be started outdoors once the danger of frost has passed. They can also be sown outdoors in the fall in cold climates, although you run the risk of losing some tender plants. In warmer climates, the seeds can be started outdoors in late summer to early fall, and they will grow all winter. Indoors or out, germination can be rapid (especially when using heat) but may take as long as 2 months.

When planting seedlings into outdoor beds, you should set them about 4 inches (10 cm) apart in rows 1 to 1½ feet (0.3–0.5 m) apart. If the seedlings have been growing indoors or in the greenhouse, be sure to allow them to harden off before bringing them outside permanently. To harden off, place the seedlings outdoors for a couple of hours for the first day or two, and then increase the time outdoors each day for 1 or 2 weeks before planting them out in beds. Be sure to transfer the label information to the garden with the plants, in order to maintain accurate records.

Once in the beds, these hybrid seedlings will likely grow for 1 or 2 years before flowering. This typically means that it will be 2 to 3 years between pollination and bloom, except for hybrids grown in a greenhouse or in very warm climates. In warm climates or greenhouses, if the seeds are planted out early and the plants are fertilized heavily, they can bloom the following spring, or within about 9 months. It is recommended that you wait until the second or third flowering season before evaluating a hybrid, allowing it to clump up and become established before making the final judgment.

Propagation

Once a new selection of daylily has been made, it must be propagated vegetatively so that all the offspring share the desirable characteristics of the parent. As any gardener who grows them knows, daylilies are easily propagated by division. Daylilies form fans of leaves bearing roots that can easily be separated from the parent plant. A single daylily clump can be divided into as many fans as have developed in that clump, or divisions can include two or three fans each, allowing for larger new plants. Depending on the cultivar and the health of the plant, daylilies can form from one to fifteen fans per year. Large, crowded clumps may produce fewer blooms or blooms of inferior quality. Therefore, daylily clumps should be divided periodically as needed.

Division is typically done in the fall or early spring. Single fans can be separated from a plant that is still in the ground, but this may result in damaged fans and/or damage to the parent plant. A better approach is to dig the entire clump of the daylily to be divided in order to see exactly how the plantlets are situated. Shake any loose soil from the roots; if necessary, use water to completely remove the soil. Large clumps can be dried in a shady place to loosen the soil. Once the soil has been removed, try to remove a single fan from the clump without cutting. A large knife, machete, or even shovel may be used to cut the fans apart, if necessary; place the knife between two divisions and cut straight down. Continue removing the fans until the clump has been divided into as many pieces as you desire. Be sure that, with each division, some roots remain attached to the crown of the new plantlet. After removing a fan, especially those cut from the parent plant with a knife or shovel, clean off any root pieces and other debris not attached to that fan. Root pieces alone (without a crown) will not grow and should be discarded. Some growers recommend dusting the cut portion of the crown with a fungicide powder to prevent rotting.

Once separated, the plantlet will benefit from having its leaves trimmed. This helps prevent loss of moisture through the leaves while the plant generates a good root system. After trimming, the fan should be about one-third its original size. The new, trimmed plant may then be planted in the garden, and the crown covered with about 1 inch (2.5 cm) of soil.

Daylilies often develop proliferations, which are small fans of leaves presented on the flower scapes. Although these small plantlets usually lack roots, roots may occasionally form, particularly in humid weather. A proliferation can be easily removed by breaking it from the scape. The extracted proliferation can then be planted in a small pot with a glass jar over it, thus creating a miniature greenhouse with humid conditions suitable for root production. A proliferation can also be rooted by cutting the scape 1 or 2 inches (2.5–5 cm) above and below the fan, then pushing the base of the fan (and the scape piece) into a mixture of sand and peat. Alternatively, the proliferation can simply be placed in a glass of water in a sunny window until roots form. The plantlet will use food reserves found in the scape piece until its own root system is established.

Daylilies can be propagated by dividing the crown of the plant, or by wounding the crown and treating it with plant hormones. These methods allow breeders to obtain many new plants in a short period of time, but at a cost: they are considerably more complicated and risky than the two methods mentioned above, and therefore are not discussed here. Crown-division techniques, as well as propagation by tissue culture, are discussed by Erhardt (1992).

Resources

COLLECTIONS

Hundreds of display gardens officially recognized by the American Hemerocallis Society are located across North America. A complete current list can be found in the spring issues of *The Daylily Journal* (a publication of A.H.S., discussed under "Plant Societies"). Most of the nurseries listed as "Suppliers" can be visited during bloom season to view the daylilies.

SUPPLIERS

Most daylilies found in large gardening centers are very old hybrids or unnamed varieties. Newer named varieties can be found from the sources listed here. When first introduced, daylilies from the top hybridizers can be quite expensive, often in the $100–$150 price range. The price quickly drops, however, as the plants multiply and become more readily available. Many excellent daylilies are available in the $10 range, as well as every price in between. The following suppliers range from expensive new introductions to inexpensive, tried-and-true daylilies. Many produce catalogs with color pictures.

United States

Bell's Daylily Garden
1305 Griffin Road
Sycamore, GA 31790
phone: 912-567-2633

Brookwood Gardens
303 Fir Street
Michigan City, IN 46360

Browns Ferry Gardens
1315 Browns Ferry Road
Georgetown, SC 29440
phone: 888-329-5459
fax: 803-546-0318

Coburg Planting Fields
573 E. 600 N.
Valparaiso, IN 46383
phone: 219-462-4288

Covered Bridge Gardens
1821 Honey Run Road
Chico, CA 95928-8850
phone: 530-342-6661

Daylily World
P.O. Box 1612
260 N. White Cedar Road
Sanford, FL 32772-1612
phone: 407-322-4034
fax: 407-322-4026

Floyd Cove Nursery
1050 Enterprise-Osteen Road
Enterprise, FL 32725-9355
fax: 407-860-0086

Jeff and Jackie's Daylilies
179 E. Smith Road
Clinton, TN 37716-5005
phone: 423-435-4989

Joiner Gardens
9630 Whitfield Avenue
Savannah, GA 31406

Klehm Nursery
4210 N. Duncan Road
Champaign, IL 61821
phone: 800-553-3715
fax: 217-373-8403
web site: www.klehm.com

Ladybug Daylilies
1852 S.R. 46
Geneva, FL 32732
phone: 407-349-0271

Le Petit Jardin
Ted L. Petit
P.O. Box 55
McIntosh, FL 32664
phone: 352-591-3227
fax: 352-591-1859
web site: www.distinctly.on.ca

Majestic Gardens
2100 N. Preble County Line Road
West Alexandria, OH 45381
phone: 937-833-5100

Marietta Gardens
P.O. Box 70
Marietta, NC 28362
phone: 910-628-9466
fax: 910-628-9993

Oakes Daylilies
8204 Monday Road
Corryton, TN 37721
phone: 423-687-3770 or
    800-532-9545
fax: 423-688-8186
e-mail: paradisegarden@oakes.html
web site: www.oakesdaylilies.com

Pinecliffe Daylily Gardens
6604 Scottsville Road
Floyds Knob, IN 47119-9202
phone: 812-923-8113
fax: 812-923-9618
e-mail: dcs923@aol.com

Roycroft Daylily Nursery
P.O. Box 2553
942 White Hall Avenue
Georgetown, SC 29440
phone: 843-527-1533 or
    800-950-5459
fax: 843-546-2281
e-mail: rdn@sccoast.net
web site: www.roycroftdaylilies.com

Singing Oaks Garden
1019 Abell Road
Blythewood, SC 29016
phone: 803-786-1351

Tranquil Lake Nursery
45 River Street
Rehoboth, MA 02769-1395
phone: 508-252-4002 or
    800-353-4344
fax: 508-252-4740

Canada

Strong's Daylilies
48 Lakeshore Road
Stoney Creek, Ontario L8E 5C7
phone: 905-643-3271
e-mail: mstrong@cgocable.net

We're in the Hayfield Now Daylily
    Gardens
4704 Pollard Road, R.R. 1
Orono, Ontario L0B 1M0
phone: 905-983-5097
fax: 905-983-6271
e-mail: withndg@osha.igs.net

Australia

Mead's Daylily Gardens
203 Watson Road
Acacia Ridge
Brisbane, Queensland 4110

REGISTRATION AUTHORITY

American Hemerocallis Society
Attn: W. C. Monroe
7015 Chandler Drive
Baton Rouge, LA 70808
U.S.A.

PLANT SOCIETIES

The best way to begin enjoying daylilies is to join the American Hemerocallis Society. Membership costs only $18 a year and includes a subscription to *The Daylily Journal*. Published four times a year, *The Daylily Journal* is a thick publication printed on glossy paper with many full-color pictures of daylilies and articles about daylily gardening. To join A.H.S., contact

Pat Mercer
American Hemerocallis Society
P.O. Box 10
Dexter, GA 31019
U.S.A.
phone: 912-875-4110
e-mail: gmercer@nlamerica.com
web site: www.daylilies.org/daylilies.html

ADDITIONAL INFORMATION

Much of the information presented in this chapter concerning the techniques of hybridizing daylilies is contained in a very helpful and informative, beautiful color video. The video, entitled *We're in the Hayfield Now Daylily Gardens Video*, is available from

Henry Lorrain
We're in the Hayfield Now
4704 Pollard Road, R.R. 1
Orono, Ontario L0B 1M0
Canada
phone: 905-983-5097
fax: 905-983-6271
e-mail: withndg@osha.igs.net

A common problem when one first gets involved with daylilies is being overwhelmed with the thousands of named varieties. Color images as well as flower and plant information on thousands of the more popular daylilies is now available on a CD-ROM, entitled *A Pictorial History of the Daylily*. The CD-ROM may be obtained from

John Peat
Distinctly Creative Designs
16 Douville Court
Toronto, Ontario M5A 4E7
Canada
phone: 416-362-1682
e-mail: jpeat@distinctly.on.ca

The *Eureka Daylily Reference Guide*, published annually, is another excellent source of information. It includes price comparisons of thousands of commercially available daylily cultivars (with a few photographs), as well as the addresses of nurseries from which to purchase these cultivars. It is available from

Ken and Kathy Gregory
Eureka Daylily Reference Guide
P.O. Box 946
Granite Falls, NC 28630-9538
U.S.A.
phone: 704-396-4495

References and Additional Reading

Austin, B. 1998. Engineering superior daylilies. *American Nurseryman* 187 (1): 24–29.
Erhardt, W. 1992. *Hemerocallis*. Portland, Ore.: Timber Press.
Munson, R. W. 1989. *Hemerocallis: The Daylily*. Portland, Ore.: Timber Press.
Stout, A. B. 1934. *Daylilies*. New York: Macmillan.

4 Breeding Daffodils

Elise Havens

The daffodil (*Narcissus*) has long been considered the flower of spring, a symbol of new life, a flower with character yet simplicity, elegance yet commonality. Its traditional yellow flower color is only one of many possibilities in a broad range that includes deep orange-red, bright red-pink, golden orange, pastel lemon or pink, and white. The range of plant and flower form is even greater: huge flowers 4½ inches (11 cm) across to miniatures as small as ½ inch (12 mm) in diameter; heights of 3 inches (7.5 cm) to 20 inches (50 cm) or more; long trumpet-shaped flowers to very short cups; flat petals to reflexed to nearly nonexistent; pendant flowers or upright flowers; one flower per stem to 20 per stem. The challenge of breeders is to merge the broad range of color with an almost infinite range of forms, in pleasing combinations. Much has been done and even more is waiting to be done. Colors thought impossible 30 years ago are becoming common today.

Key Groups for Breeding

A few definitions relating to daffodil flowers are key to understanding the categorization of daffodil types. The *perianth* includes the six floral leaves, comprising three sepals and three petals. The *corona* is the cup-, trumpet-, or disc-shaped outgrowth that arises from the inner surface of the perianth at the base of the segments.

Two often-misused terms are *Narcissus*, which is sometimes used to refer to one type of daffodil, and "jonquil," which is sometimes used to refer to daffodils in general. In truth, *Narcissus* is the genus name and comprises all the species of daffodil, which is the English vernacular name for *Narcissus*. A member of the family Amaryllidaceae, *Narcissus* is divided into 13 distinct divisions, one of which is jonquilla daffodils. The divisions are defined as follows (abridged from the Royal Horticultural Society system of classi-fication) and are illustrated in Figure 4-1 and Plates 4-1 through 4-10.

Division 1. Trumpet daffodil cultivars: one flower to a stem; corona ("trumpet") at least as long as the perianth segments. (See Plate 4-1.)

Division 2. Large-cupped daffodil cultivars: one flower to a stem; corona ("cup") more than one-third but less than equal to the length of the peri-anth segments. (See Plate 4-2.)

Division 3. Small-cupped daffodil cultivars: one flower to a stem; corona ("cup") not more than one-third the length of the perianth segments. (See Plate 4-3.)

Division 4. Double daffodil cultivars: one or more flowers to a stem; doubling of the perianth segments or the corona or both. (See Plate 4-4.)

Division 5. Triandrus daffodil cultivars: usually two or more pendant flowers to a stem; perianth segments reflexed. (See Plate 4-5.)

Division 6. Cyclamineus daffodil cultivars: one flower to a stem; perianth seg-ments significantly reflexed, flower at an acute angle to the stem with a very short neck. (See Plate 4-6.)

Division 7. Jonquilla and apodanthus daffodil cultivars: usually one to five flow-ers to a stem; leaves narrow, dark green; perianth segments spreading, or reflexed; flowers usually fragrant. (See Plate 4-7.)

Division 8. Tazetta daffodil cultivars: usually 3 to 20 flowers to a stout stem; perianth segments spreading, not reflexed; flowers usually fragrant. (See Plate 4-8.)

Division 9. Poeticus daffodil cultivars: usually one flower to a stem; perianth segments pure white; corona usually disc-shaped, with a green or yellow center and red rim; flowers usually fragrant. (See Plate 4-9.)

Division 10. Bulbocodium daffodil cultivars: usually one flower to a stem; peri-anth segments insignificant compared to the dominant corona; anthers dorsifixed (attached more or less centrally to the filament); filament and style usually curved.

Division 11. Split-corona daffodil cultivars: corona split rather than lobed and usually for more than half its length.

a) Collar daffodils: split-corona daffodils with the corona segments oppo-site the perianth segments; the corona segments usually in two whorls of three. (See Plate 4-10.)

b) Papillon daffodils: split-corona daffodils with the corona segments alter-nate to the perianth segments; the corona segments usually in a single whorl of six.

Division 12. Miscellaneous: all daffodils not falling into any one of the previous divisions.

Division 13. Daffodils distinguished solely by botanical name: species and hybrids occurring naturally in the wild.

Each daffodil hybrid is assigned a classification, which is composed of the division number (as just described) and a color code. Color abbrevia-

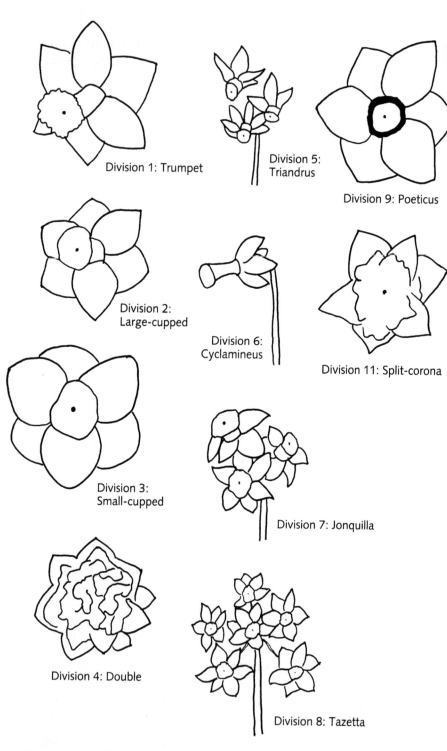

Division 1: Trumpet

Division 5: Triandrus

Division 9: Poeticus

Division 2: Large-cupped

Division 6: Cyclamineus

Division 11: Split-corona

Division 3: Small-cupped

Division 7: Jonquilla

Division 4: Double

Division 8: Tazetta

Figure 4-1. Daffodil divisions.

tions are as follows: W = white or whitish; P = pink; G = green; O = orange; Y = yellow; R = red.

The color code consists of two letters or groups of letters separated by a hyphen. The letter(s) before the hyphen describe the perianth color(s) and those after the hyphen describe the cup color(s). A yellow-colored trumpet daffodil would be labeled 1Y-Y, and a large-cupped daffodil with white perianth and pink corona would be 2W-P. A large-cupped daffodil with a white perianth and a yellow cup with a red rim would be 2W-YYR. Thus, it is easy to have a general idea of the appearance of a daffodil just by knowing its classification. Color codes were designed and computerized by the eminent hybridizer Tom Throckmorton of Des Moines, Iowa, and adopted by the Royal Horticultural Society.

Important Breeding Lines

The history of breeding daffodils is relatively recent, a very high percentage of the breeding work having been done in the last 100 years. Until the 1940s the vast majority of breeding work was done in Divisions 1 through 4, since that is where the show potential of the day was placed, both in Great Britain and in New Zealand and Australia.

During the late 1940s and '50s Grant Mitsch, of Oregon, began rather extensive work in Divisions 5 through 7, and a great deal of interest in these divisions currently exists in the American Daffodil Society. The challenge is to provide top-quality show flowers, with perfection of form and diversity of color, in all divisions, while not neglecting health, vigor, and garden potential.

Over the years, experience has taught us that, even without being particularly adept at genetics, we can identify cultivars that carry on desirable traits. Many hybridizers use line breeding (intercrossing progeny and crossing them back to the parents), and this method has provided many breakthrough traits. Of course, bringing in "new blood" from other outstanding lines is also important. This is an area in which computer technology is extremely useful in giving family trees. In fact, sometimes we find that "new blood" is not necessarily new. A cultivar originating in England may have common ancestry to one originating in New Zealand or the United States, for example.

The following discussion of important breeding lines makes mention of a few cultivars that have been used by a number of breeders, but it is not meant to be an exhaustive list by any means. It is only a sampling of the many cultivars so valuable to hybridizers, both in the past and currently.

Three much-used yellow-flowered *Narcissus* cultivars are 'Arctic Gold', 'Camelot', and 'Galway', all bred by Lionel Richardson of Ireland. The depth of color and smooth texture of 'Arctic Gold' is passed on to many progeny. 'Camelot', a rather short-stemmed, very robust flower possessing exceedingly heavy substance, has been most useful in combination with more delicate reverse bicolors (yellow perianth and white corona), as well as with yellow trumpets. Such crosses have resulted in some top-rate flowers combining smooth texture with heavy substance.

A white perianth combined with a yellow corona is usually called a bicolor. Among the most important bicolors to hybridizing is 'Green Island'. Its excellent form has made it useful in breeding perfection into whites as well as pinks. Reverse bicolors (the opposite combination of yellow perianth and white corona) were originated in the late 1930s by Guy Wilson of Ireland, and they made tremendous strides forward during the 1940s and '50s. 'Daydream', originated by Grant Mitsch in 1960, is among the most successful reverse bicolors. It was used so extensively in hybridizing that nearly all modern reverse bicolors of high quality have 'Daydream' in their background.

In the area of pink cups, 'Accent' and, later, 'Eclat' and 'Spaceship' have probably been used as much as any in the United States to produce bright coloration, and 'Precedent' (bred from 'Green Island') has been used extensively to introduce good form. Two particularly useful pinks from Great Britain are 'Dailmanach' and 'Romance'. In New Zealand and Australia, 'C. E. Radcliff', 'Dear Me', and 'Verran' figure in the parentage of many successful pinks. The diversity of background allows for useful combinations of Southern Hemisphere pinks with American and European originations. Currently, a plethora of pinks is available for hybridizing, in many sizes and shapes. To name a few, 'Berceuse', 'Decoy', 'Fragrant Rose', 'Magician', 'Music', 'Obsession', 'Pink Silk', 'Rainbow', 'Refrain', and 'Vahu' have all proven to be excellent parents.

As for whites, 'Chinese White', 'Easter Moon', 'Empress of Ireland', and 'Panache', all from Guy Wilson of Ireland, are a few that have been used worldwide and are in the parentage of a large percentage of the best of today's whites. Many beautifully formed whites are currently available and are being used extensively in hybridizing programs; these include 'Ashmore', 'Bridal Chorus', 'Chaste', 'Cool Crystal', 'Immaculate', 'Seadream', 'Seafoam', 'Silent Valley', and 'White Star'.

Marvelous advances in orange or red cups with yellow perianths have been made in Great Britain, New Zealand, and Australia. 'Ceylon' and 'Falstaff' have both produced excellent progeny. American-bred 'Paricutin' and 'Resplendent' are still used in hybridizing, as are a number of British cultivars, such as 'Bunclody', 'Loch Hope', and 'Torridon'.

Species daffodils are generally fertile (having both pollen and seed) so that they can propagate in the wild. Most daffodils in Divisions 5 through

7 are crosses between species daffodils and standard hybrids. Unfortunately, they are often sterile or have much reduced fertility due to triploidy. As a result, second-generation hybrids (for example, jonquilla × jonquilla) are not always possible.

Some Division 5 triandrus daffodils set seed readily, but most do not. 'Silver Bells' has produced a few of the current cultivars, among them 'Mission Bells', which strongly resembles its mother but is much healthier and a more rapid increaser.

In Division 6, 'Jetfire', with yellow perianth and red corona, often sets open-pollinated seed and has produced a broad array of fine offspring. Unfortunately, when crossed with other Division 6 cultivars, it sets few if any seed. Other fertile Division 6 daffodils include 'Inca' (a reverse bicolor), 'Cotinga', and 'Foundling' (both pinks). 'Foundling' has been used a great deal in Great Britain.

Jonquilla daffodils of Division 7 are frequently sterile, so it was a surprise when it was found that a white and pale pink jonquilla, *Narcissus* 'Quick Step', was fertile, setting copious amounts of seed. Many interesting intermediate-sized flowers resulted. 'Quick Step' was also crossed with *Narcissus triandrus* var. *triandrus* to create some excellent Division 5 triandrus daffodils, including *Narcissus* 'Petrel', one of the most widely grown of its type. In the early 1980s, the reverse-bicolor jonquilla 'Hillstar' was found to be very similar to 'Quick Step' in its breeding capability. 'Hillstar' and 'Quick Step' have been crossed, beginning a new line of fertile jonquillas. 'Hillstar' was crossed with *N. triandrus* (just as 'Quick Step' had been years previously), and some pleasing and fragrant reverse-bicolor triandrus daffodils have resulted. 'Quick Step' and 'Hillstar' both have some unusual and beautiful progeny, some of which are fertile.

It should be made clear that even though some cultivars appear to be totally sterile, a few seed are occasionally set. Some of the most famous cultivars, including 'Tête-à-Tête', resulted from breeding a supposedly sterile parent. Though discouraging, efforts to breed these would-be parents should be and are being made (see Galyon 1994).

Important Traits and Breeding Objectives

As indicated earlier in this chapter, breeding daffodils has a dual objective: 1) to provide top-rated show flowers, and 2) to provide vigorous garden flowers. Obviously, plant health is of utmost importance in both categories. The ultimate "good flower" should meet both objectives.

For showing, daffodils are rated according to the following qualities (with slightly different weights in various countries): condition, form, substance and texture, color, pose/poise, stem, and size. Most of the seven categories are important for both objectives of show quality and garden capability. Of course, smooth texture and perfection of form is likely considerably more important to a show flower, whereas healthy increase would be of prime importance in the garden.

Isolating dominant and recessive traits is a difficult process, and thus breeding daffodils is not an exact science. Experience has revealed that some cultivars pass on certain desired traits to their progeny. For example, some cultivars are quite predictable in their ability to pass on excellent form; others seem to carry the potential for color. As indicated in the discussion of pink cups, we have found that 'Eclat' and 'Spaceship' transmit brilliant red-pink color and 'Precedent' lends refinement and heavy substance. A number of other examples are given in the previous section on "Important Breeding Lines."

Hybridization Mechanics

The basic process of hybridizing daffodils is very simple. The prime time for crossing is about 1 to 3 days after the flower opens, when the pollen has matured. One of four methods can be employed in hybridizing. (Figure 4-2 illustrates the various flower parts.)

1. Use tweezers to remove the stamen from the pollen (male) parent and spread the pollen thoroughly on the stigma of the intended seed (female) parent.
2. Rub a small brush across the anther to pick up pollen, and use the brush to

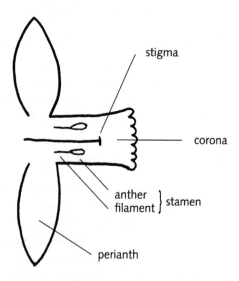

Figure 4-2. Anatomy of a daffodil flower.

spread the pollen on the stigma of the seed parent. The brush should be sterilized after each cross.

3. Use a sharp object, such as a knife, to scrape pollen from the anther and place the pollen on the stigma of the seed parent.

4. For species with very small flower parts, tear the flower apart to expose the anthers and rub them directly on the stigma of the receiving parent.

Ideally, the pollen should be taken directly to the seed parent. If this is not possible (such as if the seed parent is not in bloom yet or is in a remote location), pollen may be stored in an open container or a gelatin capsule in the house for several weeks; freezing the pollen is best for storage. If not needed until the following year (as in crossing a late cultivar on an early one), pollen may be enclosed in gelatin capsules and placed in the freezer in a jar with a desiccant and frozen. All containers should be properly labeled with a waterproof marker—careful labeling cannot be overemphasized.

After pollination, the seed parent should be tagged with the parentage (seed parent × pollen parent); this can be done with small paper tags (1½ × 1¼ inches [3.8 × 3.1 cm]) and a soft lead pencil (#2 or softer) that will be legible after rain. In approximately 6 to 8 weeks the seed is ready to be harvested. The right time to pick the seed is when the dead blossom will fall off easily, and it can be done promptly if the plant is carefully watched. Some breeders prefer to use cotton gauze, or other material with a very open weave, to band over the seed parent so that if the seed shatters, it will not fall to the ground and be lost. Care should be taken to be sure that the material lets water through and dries easily, or else rot or mold may result. If the pod is picked before it has opened, it may be stored in an open container for a few days until the seed is fully ripe and then shelled out.

Propagation

Generally, planting the seed immediately is preferable, but seeds may be stored in packets at room temperature until early September (at the latest) and planted in pots, flats, or beds, about 2 to 3 inches (5–7.5 cm) deep. (Some people prefer to plant seeds about ½ inch [12 mm] deep in protected pots.) The soil should be porous and well drained. Daffodils are light feeders and prefer a pH near 6.5. Some soils may need amending to provide the desired pH and good drainage.

After 2 years the small bulbs should be transplanted so that they have plenty of space to grow to flowering size. (It takes approximately 5 years from seed to flower.) The size of 2- or 3-year-old bulbs varies a great deal, but generally they will be about ½ to 1 inch (12–25 mm) in height and ¼ to ½ inch (6–12 mm) in diameter and should be planted at least 4 to 5 inches (10–12.5 cm) apart to allow for a mature bulb size.

Species daffodils increase best from seed but can to a limited extent also be propagated by bulb division. Traditionally, hybrid daffodils are propagated by natural bulb division, which gives a bit under double the number of plants per year, depending on the variety. More recently, growers are widely using the twin scaling or parting method. In this procedure, the bulb is cut and treated with fungicide and the pieces are grown on. Tissue culture has also been used for daffodils, but it is still very expensive and its use is limited.

Some people might say that developing new daffodils is much too time-consuming. After experiencing breakthrough colors and forms, however, most would agree that it was well worth the wait. Picturing what the average daffodil will look like 50 years from now truly taxes the imagination, if there are as many changes as there were in the last 50 years.

Resources

COLLECTIONS

A number of botanical gardens have daffodil collections. In addition to those listed here, check with the botanical gardens near you. A unique collection and one of the best planted for public viewing is Whetstone Garden in Columbus, Ohio. It is maintained by the Central Ohio Daffodil Society and is monitored for correct labeling and healthy plants by the society's dedicated volunteers. Many bulb suppliers also have extensive collections of cultivars, which may be viewed during flowering season. Generally it is best to verify if they are open to the public and if an appointment is needed.

Chicago Botanic Garden
P.O. Box 400
1000 Lake Cook Road
Glencoe, IL 60022
U.S.A.

Cincinnati Zoo and Botanical
  Garden
3400 Vine Street
Cincinnati, OH 45220
U.S.A.

Kingwood Center
900 Park Avenue W.
Mansfield, OH 44906
U.S.A.

Longwood Gardens
P.O. Box 501
409 Conservatory Road
Kennett Square, PA 19348
U.S.A.

U.S. National Arboretum
3501 New York Avenue, N.E.
Washington, DC 20002
U.S.A.

Royal Horticultural Society's
  Garden, Wisley
Woking, Surrey GU23 6QB
England

SUPPLIERS

The American Daffodil Society can provide a list of sources for those interested in purchasing plants. For information, contact the ADS at the following address:

American Daffodil Society
Naomi Liggett
4126 Winfield Road
Columbus, OH 43220
U.S.A.
web site: www.mc.edu/~adswww/

INTERNATIONAL REGISTRATION AUTHORITY

Royal Horticultural Society
80 Vincent Square
London SW1P 2PE
England

North American Regional
  Representative:
American Daffodil Society
Attn: Mary Lou Gripshover
1686 Grey Fox Trail
Milford, OH 45150
U.S.A.

PLANT SOCIETIES

A number of countries have societies devoted to daffodils. Generally, they provide informative publications that often have articles about hybridizing. They also give useful information on which cultivars are winning in shows. The Royal Horticultural Society in London is mentioned here because it is the worldwide authority for daffodil name registration. The R.H.S. annually publishes a useful book called *Daffodils and Tulips.*

American Daffodil Society
Naomi Liggett
4126 Winfield Road
Columbus, OH 43220
U.S.A.
web site: www.mc.edu/~adswww/

Daffodil Society (U.K.)
Jackie Petherbridge
The Meadows
Puxton, near Weston-super-Mare
North Somerset BS24 6TF
England

Royal Horticultural Society
80 Vincent Square
London SW1P 2PE
England

Northern Ireland Daffodil Group
Richard McCaw
77 Ballygowan Road
Hillsborough, Co. Down
Northern Ireland BT26 6EQ

National Daffodil Association of
  Australia
Jenny Jamieson
11 Bromley Place
Kingsley, Western Australia 6026
Australia

Tasmanian Daffodil Council
Ian Norman
224 East Derwent Highway
Lindisfarne, Tasmania 7015
Australia

National Daffodil Society of New
  Zealand
Wilf Hall, Secretary
105 Wallace Loop Road
Levin R.D.1, 5500
New Zealand

References and Additional Reading

Barnes, D. 1987. *Daffodils for Home, Garden and Show*. London: David and Charles.

Blanchard, J. W. 1990. *Narcissus: A Guide to Wild Daffodils*. Alpine Garden Society.

Galyon, F. 1994. The fertile amphidiploid jonquilla hybrids. *The Daffodil Journal* (American Daffodil Society) 30 (3): 159.

Heath, Brent, and Becky Heath. 1995. *Daffodils for American Gardens*. Elliott and Clark.

Jefferson-Brown, M. 1991. *Narcissus*. Portland, Ore.: Timber Press.

Wells, J. S. 1989. *Modern Miniature Daffodils: Species and Hybrids*. Portland, Ore.: Timber Press.

5 Breeding Siberian Iris

Currier McEwen

Hybridizing is the process of placing the pollen of one species or cultivar on the stigma of another in order to obtain seeds—and eventually plants—containing genes from both parents. The resulting plants are hybrids. At first the term *hybrid* referred strictly to a plant that resulted from a cross of two different species. Over the years, however, its meaning has been broadened to include any seedling in which the genes have been mixed, and thus, by this last definition, even seedlings that result from selfing a flower with its own pollen are hybrids. The ranks of those who make crosses encompass a wide range, from the many who casually cross an occasional flower to the seriously dedicated hybridizer. All serious hybridizers love their gardens, but their chief interest is not the beautiful flowers around them but the still more beautiful ones that do not yet exist.

Planned vs. Natural Crosses

In the late 1800s and early 1900s, when interest in Siberian irises changed from collecting new species to obtaining new, improved cultivars, all the seeds planted came from natural crosses made by insects. New seedlings from such natural crosses are still introduced each year. Some of the most valued cultivars owe their origin to natural crosses, including *Iris* 'White Swirl' (Plate 5-5), which is perhaps the most important Siberian iris ever introduced. For all its significance, however, it came about in a most inefficient way. There was a rather widely accepted idea at the time that it was useless to try to make controlled crosses with Siberian irises because they were believed to cross with their own pollen even before the bud opened.

Adapted from *The Siberian Iris* by Currier McEwen, published in 1996 by Timber Press.

Fred Cassebeer, in whose garden 'White Swirl' originated, believed this erroneous concept and therefore did not make planned crosses with Siberian irises as he did with his tall bearded irises. He told me that he collected a full bushel basket of naturally occurring pods in his large planting of Siberian irises. From the thousands of resulting seedlings came 'White Swirl'.

Neither parent is known in most of Cassebeer's seedlings, which is unusual. More commonly in natural crosses, the pod parent is known, for the iris growers observe pods forming on cultivars they particularly like and plant the resulting seeds. The introducer of such a new seedling may be pleased with it but lacks the satisfaction of having played any very active role in its creation and, of course, knows only the pod parent.

The alternative is the planned, protected cross. Isabella Preston was, in the 1930s, one of the first to make mostly planned crosses and that practice was greatly encouraged by McGarvey (1975). Both parents of the majority of new introductions are now known, a trend that has occurred for two principal reasons. The first is the greater efficiency of the method, and the second is the obvious advantage of being able to record the full genetic background of the plant.

Important Traits and Breeding Objectives

Once the decision has been made to take up hybridizing in a serious way, the beginner had best settle upon goals toward which to work. It is natural simply to start crossing pretty flowers and, indeed, this can provide lovely new seedlings, but very probably, few will be enough better than the parents or other cultivars in commerce to warrant introduction. The end results are still less worthwhile if one starts with inferior parents, as the neophyte all too often does. Clearly, one is not likely to produce the flower of the future by starting with cultivars long since outdated, except when their use is indicated by a particular hybridizing goal. By all means, define goals and then start with the best parents to reach those goals.

A primary decision is whether to work with the 28-chromosome cultivars (those of Subseries *Sibiricae*) or the 40-chromosome cultivars (Subseries *Chrysographes*), or both. Relatively few hybridizers are working with the 40-chromosome group, so it is perhaps a more open field for the beginner. On the other hand, cultivars of that group are less easy to grow in regions that are very cold or dry.

The selection of goals is naturally a matter of personal choice, but here are some possibilities:

- new colors, such as green, orange, and brown;
- new color combinations and patterns;

- improved colors, to obtain spectrum reds and blues and true pinks, un-mixed with lavender;
- improved features, such as ruffling, crimped edges, feathered midribs, and wide, tufted styles;
- improved branching and bud count;
- improved resistance to pests and diseases;
- miniatures with short stalks bearing flowers of proportionately small size;
- early, late, and—especially—repeat bloomers, to extend the season;
- adaptability to unfavorable conditions, to extend the growing range;
- vigorous plants and handsome foliage;
- fragrance.

Discussion of floral forms needs special attention. Hybridizers were so attracted to the lovely round, flaring form and wide falls (the three lower petals, or sepals) of 'White Swirl' that it was chosen again and again as a parent, and most cultivars introduced since 1960 show its influence. There can be no question that this new form is a most valuable advance in Siberian irises. Unfortunately, cultivars with the traditional form of gracefully arched, more narrow falls have tended to be neglected by hybridizers. Renewed efforts with these more traditional forms is yet another important hybridizing goal. Not only are they beautiful in their own right but they also provide lovely contrast for the flowers descended from 'White Swirl'. I am continually impressed by the way in which the more traditional flowers—'Chartreuse Bounty', 'Soft Blue', and 'Shaker's Prayer', for example—when intermixed with the big, round tetraploids, enhance the beauty and interest of our entire display bed.

GENETIC NOTES

The novice iris breeder should be aware of several practical considerations before beginning. The violet-blue color of Siberian irises of the 28-chromosome group is genetically dominant, as would be expected of the predominant color of the species. Both white and the wine-red typical of the "red" Siberian irises are recessive to blue. If one crosses a blue with a white, all the resulting seedlings will be blue, but if one of those seedlings is selfed or crossed with siblings, blue and white progeny will result in the ratio of roughly three to one, blues to whites, in accordance with Mendelian laws. Often, crossing two blue cultivars yields some white seedlings. In the same way, crossing the recessive wine-red color with the dominant blue results in all blues in the first generation and roughly three blues to one red in the next.

Crossing reds and whites also usually results in only blue seedlings in the first generation, with segregation into white, blue, and red in approximately Mendelian ratios in the second. Although only blues are expected in the first generation, the blue often has a reddish tinge and a few light reds can also occur. Crosses of pinks with whites give similar results.

Trials by Tiffney (1971) indicate that results of crossing white Siberian irises with other whites depends on the background of the parents. Albino forms of *Iris sanguinea* are a lovely pure white, whereas the rarer albino forms of *I. sibirica* are a less pure white, with some bluish gray tones at the base of the falls. Crossing the *I. sanguinea* type white with modern white Siberian irises resulted in only white, but crossing 'White Swirl', 'Snow-crest', and 'Snow Queen' with an albino *I. sibirica* resulted in only medium to light blue seedlings. Further crossing of these same first-generation seedlings led to some white and some blue flowers (Tiffney 1971).

These results suggest that *Iris sanguinea* predominates in the background of most modern white Siberian irises. Supporting this view is the lovely color and form of 'Snow Queen', a collected cultivar of *I. sanguinea* that made a major impression when it was brought to the West from Japan in 1900. Surely the popularity of 'Snow Queen' in the early decades of the twentieth century led to its prevailing use as a white parent, just as the outstanding features of 'White Swirl' did 50 years later.

Hybridization Mechanics

APPROACHES

After settling on certain goals, the hybridizer's next question is to consider the various types of breeding approaches that may be used to achieve them. The inefficiency and limitations of harvesting seeds from natural crosses made by insects have been pointed out. A better approach is the planned cross, which is of three general types: selfing, outcrossing, and line breeding.

Selfing is the term used for fertilizing a cultivar with its own pollen. It can be used in the hope of exaggerating some promising genetic feature in that plant but is of limited value in developing new features. Outcrossing and line breeding are the hybridizer's basic tools.

Outcrossing is the practice of selecting unrelated cultivars for a cross. An extreme example of outcrossing is the crossing of different species, such as the interspecies crossing of *Iris sibirica* and *I. sanguinea* in the 1930s and '40s, which led to the modern Siberian iris hybrids. More recently, outcrossing focuses on plants from different genetic breeding lines, crossed in the hope of introducing new features in seedlings. Even more commonly, the hybridizer is unconcerned with the background parentage of the cultivars selected for crossing but instead selects plants that on the basis of their appearance give promise of developing some particular goal.

Once the hybridizer has developed seedlings of real merit, with distinctive, desirable features, the time has come to turn to line breeding, crossing related seedlings to establish a personal breeding line. This can involve crossing a seedling with one of its parents (backcrossing) or with siblings or less closely related relatives. The hybridizer must, however, be alert to the continued usefulness of outcrossing, which approach should be revisited from time to time to introduce some new, desired feature and, perhaps, to maintain hybrid vigor.

BASIC PRINCIPLES

The reproductive organs of the Siberian iris flower—the anthers, stigmas, and ovary—are illustrated in Figure 5-1; all standards, falls, and spathes have been removed the better to reveal the reproductive features. The female reproductive organ, or pistil, consists of the ovary, styles, and stigmas. The ovary is made up of three longitudinal compartments, each one of which extends upward to one of the three styles. Each style ends near its top in a stigma; the function of each stigma is to receive the pollen. The ovary contains the ovules, which in turn contain the egg cells. After fertilization, these develop into the seeds. The male organ is the stamen, consisting of a pollen-bearing anther held at the end of a slender filament.

The falls and standards serve to support and protect the reproductive organs and perhaps, through their colors, to attract nectar-seeking bees. The bees land at the base of the falls at the signal area and then work their large, hairy bodies down between the falls and styles to reach the nectar at their juncture. As seen in Figure 5-1, the anthers are just under the styles and very close to the stigmas. After a flower opens, the anthers mature and open (dehisce), exposing their pollen; the stigmas mature and open shortly thereafter. Hence it is inevitable that as the bee works its way down between style and fall, it will brush against both the stigma and anther, fertilizing the flower with either its own pollen or with pollen from the last visited flower.

The basic principle in making a planned cross is obvious and very simple—yet absolutely essential: the hybridizer must make the cross before the bud has opened spontaneously and must protect all flowers selected to be parents from foraging insects. If the cross is made after the flower has opened, the hybridizer can be sure of only the pod parent of resulting seedlings. The pollen parent may not be the one used by the hybridizer but rather some unknown parent whose pollen was carried by a bee before the cross was made; the bee may have either selfed the flower or brought the pollen from another plant. Some natural protection against selfing is in place: the anther matures some hours earlier than the stigma, and thus the pollen may be largely dispersed by the time the stigma opens.

The biological process of fertilization is remarkable. Almost immedi-

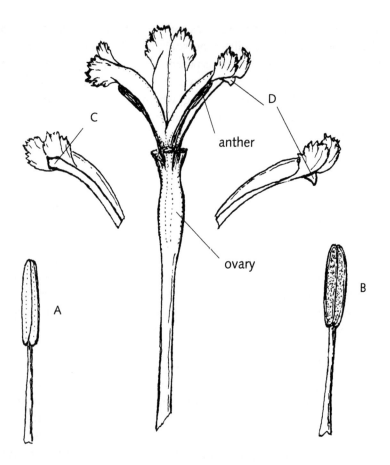

Figure 5-1. The reproductive organs of a Siberian iris flower: A) immature anther, not yet dehisced; B) mature, dehisced anther, dotted with pollen; C) style's underside, with an immature stigma tightly closed against it; and D) mature stigmas, opened and ready for crossing. (Illustration by Jean G. Witt)

ately after the pollen grains are deposited on the stigma, a microscopically narrow tubule starts to grow from each pollen grain down through the style to the ovary, a distance of 1½ inches (about 3.5 cm) or more. This is accomplished in a few hours. In the ovary a nucleus on the tubule fuses with an egg cell in the ovule and fertilization occurs. Within a week one can judge whether the cross has been successful for, if it has, the ovary begins to grow larger and forms a seed pod. By the end of 2½ to 3 months, the capsule is mature and filled with seeds, each one of which came from a single egg cell fertilized by a single pollen grain.

The basic rule of hybridizing Siberian irises is to make the cross before the bud has opened naturally. All the various methods employed by hybridizers thus begin in the same manner: the bud is opened by hand and the anthers removed to prevent self-pollination. A quick check of the stigma for any visible pollen grains will give the breeder additional assurance that the flower has not yet been pollinated. In some cases the cross is made at once with pollen collected for the purpose; in others the flower is protected in such a way that insects cannot gain entrance, and the cross is made later when pollen and stigma are fully mature. A colleague and I carried out a series of trials to determine how mature pollen and stigma must be for a successful cross (McEwen and Warburton 1971). Immature pollen and stigmas were those in buds not expected to open naturally for another 12 hours or more. Mature stigmas and pollen were defined as those in balloon-stage buds expected to open in another hour or two; stigmas and pollen are not fully mature at that time but are approaching maturity. As might be expected, crosses made with either immature stigmas or immature pollen—or both—were not often successful (14–23% successful), whereas much greater success was achieved when both stigmas and pollen were approaching maturity (72–79% successful).

In the 1950s, the importance of making planned crosses and also the need to protect the flower from foraging bees first became appreciated. The buds of plants selected to be parents were gently opened by hand, anthers were removed, the cross was made, and the flower was then protected by "bagging" it, that is, by tying a paper bag or piece of cheesecloth or other light cloth over it. McGarvey later modified this by omitting the bagging and instead lifted the falls up after the cross had been made and tied them at the top. His purpose, in addition to protecting the flower, was to keep the pollen and stigmas cool and fresh while they finished maturing. In the aforementioned study, McGarvey's new method of tying up the falls proved better than the traditional method of bagging the flowers, resulting in distinctly more successful crosses (McEwen and Warburton 1971). One other trial in the study is worth mention. In it, 20 buds opened at balloon stage had the standards, falls, and anthers removed and were left unprotected. Even with the stigmas left open to the bees, not one set a pod.

Hybridizers use various methods to achieve a cross; my three preferences are as follows. With method one, balloon-stage buds of the two selected parents are gently opened by hand, and standards and stamens are carefully removed with forceps or tweezers. The stamens are placed—anther end down—in the cuplike space formed by the styles, where they are conveniently stored until needed. The falls are then raised and tied with a piece of the plant's leaf or a twist tie. Next day the flowers are again opened, the reciprocal crosses are made, and the falls are again tied up. This method has proven very successful and is quite satisfactory if one has only a few crosses to make, but if one has many flowers prepared for crossing, widely distributed in a large hybridizing garden, remembering and finding those flowers the next day, or even later the same day, can be time-consuming and frustrating.

Method two is the same as method one except that the crosses are made at once. Even though the blossom will open naturally in another hour, the anthers will at best be only partly dehisced, and the stigmas will still be closed against the styles. Using a wooden toothpick along the anther's line of opening will expose the pollen. The toothpick can then be gently used to lift open the stigma of the other parent flower and to spread pollen on it. The falls are then brought up and tied.

Method three works on the assumption that flowers with standards, falls, and anthers removed—and only the styles left—can be expected to remain unfertilized even though the stigmas are not protected. Such a flower is crossed with the aid of a toothpick as in method two, and that is all there is to it. Schafer (1989) reports a success rate of 85%, which is at least as high as mine using methods one and two. I had assumed that the flowers with only the styles left in place remained unfertilized because the bees were not attracted to them and perhaps did not recognize them as flowers, but this is not the case. In recent years I have used this method almost exclusively and have been surprised at the frequency with which the bees go to these dismembered flowers. Indeed, they seem to prefer them, perhaps because some attractant is made more apparent to them. Certainly it is easier for the bees to have the nectar laid open for them than to have to work their way down between fall and style to reach it. I have watched many bees come to these flowers, but in no instance did their bodies touch a stigma as there was nothing to prevent them from flying directly to the nectary at the juncture of fall and style.

To test the reliability of method three, a simple experiment was carried out. Approximately 100 buds of Japanese irises were allowed to open in the normal fashion. A similar group of buds was opened by hand, and falls, standards, and anthers were removed. Pods were set on 46% of the normal flowers but on only 2% of those with falls, standards, and anthers removed. I conclude from these results that although method three is not 100% safe, it is very nearly so, and I believe similar results can be expected within Siberian irises. Indeed, our small-scale experiment (McEwen and Warburton 1971) and the larger trials by Schafer (1989) bear this out.

Whatever method is used, the tag identifying the cross must be fastened on as soon as the cross is made. Many hybridizers attach small cardboard tags with string. This is satisfactory in some gardens, but in areas subject to rain accompanied by high winds, plastic tags fastened with light wire are much safer and are very easy to use. Fasten the tag below the ovary, where it will identify the pod as it develops.

Crosses are much more likely to be successful when it is cool and moist than when it is hot and dry. They are rarely successful on very hot days. Since the entire process from pollination to fertilization takes only a few hours, a subsequent rain should not spoil the cross. If rain threatens soon, protect the cross with a "raincoat." Place a plastic sandwich bag over the flower and tie it around the stem. Be sure to tear off the fold of a fold-lock sandwich bag; otherwise it fills with water and can become heavy enough to break off the flower.

All hybridizers have their own system of record keeping. At a minimum, the serial number of the cross should be written on the tag corresponding with the number of the cross entered in the record book, commonly referred to as the stud book. One should also record the date and the names or seedling numbers of the two parents, writing the pod parent first.

Whether they are the result of planned or of natural crosses, pods wanted for their seeds must be watched and harvested before they can open and spill their precious cargo. If the hybridizer must be away at this critical time, a loose netting can be tied around the pod in advance to catch seeds as they fall, or the pod can be harvested if reasonably close to maturity. The subject of seed harvest is taken up in more detail in McEwen 1996.

POLLEN STORAGE

In the three methods of making crosses just described, the pollen involved has been freshly obtained at the time of the cross. Often, however, the hybridizer wishes to use as the pollen parent a plant that will have finished blooming before the desired pod parent starts, or one from a friend's garden, a great distance away. One can then choose the best storage method from a variety of options, depending on the length of time the pollen is to be kept.

If it is to be stored only a day or two, the pollen can be scraped off the anther into a folded square of waxed paper and placed in a screw-top jar. Refrigerate the jar at temperatures above freezing and make sure that no moisture can get into it. If storage is to be for several weeks, add 1 teaspoon (5 ml) or more of a drying agent, such as silica gel or anhydrous calcium chloride, to the jar along with the pollen. The small paper or capsule-like packets that pharmaceutical companies place in medicine containers before shipping make very convenient drying agents; the pharmacist discards these and will provide them without charge. As a rule of thumb, the packets should fill approximately one-quarter of the jar's volume.

Pollen placed in a tightly sealed screw-top jar and stored in the freezing compartment of the refrigerator remains effective for several months. Still longer storage, as from one season to the next, requires more elaborate laboratory equipment than the average gardener has. If frozen and dried at high vacuum in hermetically sealed glass vials, pollen can remain effective for years.

Developments for the Future

The extraordinary achievements made possible by the new techniques of genetic engineering, including gene transfer, are widely appreciated (Smith 1993; Zimmermann 1994). In their application to plants, these high-tech scientific methods are very different from those of traditional hybridizing, but the two have in common the purpose of changing and, one hopes, improving upon what has occurred in nature. The hybridizer hopes to reach certain goals—such as the development of a spectrum red Siberian iris— by combining and recombining genes of promising parent plants by crossing them. Unless some lucky break occurs, as happened with the color yellow (McEwen 1987), this process takes many generations, if indeed it can be accomplished at all. In genetic engineering, the gene or genes that will produce the true red color can, at least theoretically, be obtained from a donor plant that could not be used in a traditional cross and inserted into the host plant in a single generation.

Naturally, first efforts have been directed toward food plants; the techniques of gene transfer are bringing about desirable changes in cereals, vegetables, and other food plants that would have taken hundreds of years using ordinary hybridizing methods. But some experiments have already been carried out with ornamentals (Meyer et al. 1987). The possibilities are many—true colors and new colors; repeat bloom and rebloom; fragrance; built-in resistance to diseases and pests; ability to withstand drought, cold, or adverse conditions of various kinds—but the methods are extremely complex. First the particular gene or genes that control the desired trait must be identified. Next one must find those complete genes among the thousands of genes in the donor plant. That gene must then be "cut" from the DNA molecule of the donor plant in such a way that it can permanently attach itself into the new recipient DNA molecule. This gene is then cloned into a plasmid or virus, which allows the gene to replicate and, if the carrier is suitable, permits the gene to be transferred from donor to recipient. The carrier of the gene into the new cell is called the vector. A common vector is the Ti plasmid of the bacterium *Agromycetum tumificiens*, which causes crown gall in certain plants. This plasmid is capable of carrying the desired donor DNA into some host plants but is ineffective with monocot plants and thus cannot be expected to succeed with irises. Just developing a suitable vector for Siberian irises could be a major challenge. One method involves coating minute tungsten or gold pellets with the desired gene or genes and "shooting" them into the cells of the recipient plant by means of a "gun" powered with high-pressure gas.

The procedures that result in the identification, isolation, and cloning of genes and their introduction into new plants are very expensive and time-consuming, requiring complex laboratory technology. Although it is conceptually possible, for example, to introduce petunia red into a Siberian iris using genetic engineering, it is not yet economically feasible. As the technology is simplified, it is likely that such experiments can and will be done. These dramatic new developments will require years to be achieved in irises, but that they can eventually be achieved appears to be certain.

Resources

COLLECTIONS

Display gardens of Siberian irises are located throughout the world. In addition to the public gardens listed here, many of the gardens and nurseries listed under "Suppliers" also have extensive collections open for viewing. Since some gardens are open by appointment only, it is generally best to call first. The dates indicate approximate bloom time.

Denver Botanic Gardens
909 York Street
Denver, CO 80206
phone: 303-331-4000
20 May to 10 June

Iowa Arboretum
Lois Girton
2025 Ashmore Drive
Ames, IA 50014-7804
phone: 515-795-3216
25 May to 10 June

U.S. National Arboretum
Lynn R. Batdorf
3501 New York Avenue, N.E.
Washington, DC 20002
phone: 202-245-5965
mid-May to early June

Royal Botanical Gardens
P.O. Box 399
Hamilton, Ontario L8N 3H8
phone: 905-527-1158
early June to late June

SUPPLIERS

Many of the suppliers in the following list also have display gardens open for viewing, which is indicated by the inclusion of bloom-time dates.

United States

Abbey Gardens
32009 S. Ona Way
Molalla, OR 97038
phone: 503-829-2928
15 May to 15 June

Aitken's Salmon Creek Garden
608 N.W. 119th Street
Vancouver, WA 98685
phone: 360-573-4472
10 May to 10 June, by appt.

Amberway Gardens
5803 Amberway Drive
St. Louis, MO 63128
phone: 314-842-6103

Louise Bellagamba
11431 Old Saint Charles Road
Bridgeton, MO 63044-3075
phone: 314-739-5413
15 May to 25 May, by appt.

Borbeleta Gardens
15980 Canby Avenue
Faribault, MN 55021
phone: 507-334-2807
1 June to 30 June

Borglum Irises
2202 Austin Road
Geneva, NY 14456
phone: 716-526-6729
early June to late June

Bush Gardens
1739 Memory Lane Extd.
York, PA 17402
phone: 717-755-0557
mid-May to early June

Busse Gardens
5873 Oliver Avenue S.W.
Cokato, MN 55321
phone: 320-286-2654
1 June to 30 June, by appt.

Caprice Farm Nursery
15425 S.W. Pleasant Hill Road
Sherwood, OR 97140
phone: 503-625-7241
late May to mid-June

Chehalem Gardens
P.O. Box 693
Newberg, OR 97132
phone: 503-538-8920
late May to mid-June

Draycott Gardens
16815 Falls Road
Upperco, MD 21155
phone: 410-374-4788
15 May to 5 June, by appt.

Eartheart Gardens
R.R. 1, Box 847
South Harpswell, ME 04079
phone: 207-833-6327
7 June to 1 July, by appt.

James L. Ennenga
1621 N. 85th Street
Omaha, NE 68114
phone: 402-391-6337
late May to late June

Ensata Gardens
9823 E. Michigan Avenue
Galesburg, MI 49053
phone: 616-665-7500
1 June to 15 June, by appt.

Fieldstone Gardens
620 Quaker Lane
Vassalboro, ME 04985-9713
phone: 207-923-3836
mid-June to 1 July

Dale Hamblin
152 N. Idlewild
Mundelein, IL 60060
phone: 708-949-6822
15 May to 27 June, by appt.

Larry L. Harder
208 First Street
Ponca, NE 68770
phone: 402-755-2615
20 May to 15 June, by appt.

Heschke Gardens
11503 77th Street S.
Hastings, MN 55033
phone: 612-459-8381
late May to late June, by appt.

Illini Iris
Route 3, Box 5
Monticello, IL 61856
phone: 217-762-3446
7 May to 10 June, by appt.

Sterling Innerst
2700-A Oakland Road
Dover, PA 17315
phone: 717-764-0281
20 May to 20 June

The Iris Pond
7311 Churchill Road
McLean, VA 22101
15 May to 15 June

Joe Pye Weed's Garden
337 Acton Street
Carlisle, MA 01741
phone: 508-371-0173
1 June to 20 June

Klehm Nursery
4210 N. Duncan Road
Champaign, IL 61821
phone: 800-553-3715
15 May to 1 June

Laurie's Garden
41886 McKenzie Highway
Springfield, OR 97478
phone: 503-896-3756
May to late June

Mid-America Garden
3409 N. Geraldine
Oklahoma City, OK 73112-2806

Miller's Manor Gardens
3167 Route 224
Ossian, IN 46777

Mountain View Garden
2435 Middle Road
Columbia Falls, MT 59912
phone: 406-982-5020
10 June to 1 August, by appt.

Nicholls Gardens
4724 Angus Drive
Gainesville, VA 20155
phone: 703-754-9623
mid-May to late June

Old Brook Gardens
4 Larkdale Drive
Littleton, CO 80123
phone: 303-795-9718
30 May to 20 June

Old Douglas Perennials
6065 N. 16th Street
Kalamazoo, MI 49007
phone: 616-349-5934
26 May to 20 June, by appt.

Phoenix Gardens
8404 Cherry
Kansas City, MO 64131
phone: 816-523-4849
15 April to 15 June, by appt.

Pine Ridge Gardens
832 Sycamore Road
London, AR 72847
phone: 501-293-4359

Pleasure Iris Gardens
425 E. Luna
Chaparral, NM 88021
phone: 505-824-4299

Pope's Perennials
39 Highland Avenue
Gorham, ME 04038-1701
phone: 207-839-3054
10 June to 25 June, by appt.

Quail Hill Gardens
2460 Compton Bridge Road
Inman, SC 29349-8489
phone: 803-472-3339
1 May to 15 May

Redbud Lane Iris Garden
Route 1, Box 141
Kansas, IL 61933
phone: 217-948-5478
15 May to 15 June

Harold L. Stahly
8343 Manchester Drive
Grand Blanc, MI 48439
phone: 810-694-7139
5 May to 15 May

Stephens Lane Gardens
Route 1, Box 136-H
Bells, TN 38006

Terra Nova Gardening (formerly
    Coopers Garden)
P.O. Box 19149, Diamond Lake
    Station
Minneapolis, MN 55419
phone: 612-825-7770
10 June to 25 June, by appt.

Thistle Ridge Gardens
R.R. 1, Box 625
Spencer, IN 47460

Tranquil Lake Nursery
45 River Street
Rehoboth, MA 02769
phone: 508-252-4002
1 June to late June

Valente Gardens
123 Dillingham Road
North Berwick, ME 03906
phone: 207-457-2076
mid-June to 1 July, by appt.

Walnut Hill Gardens
999 310th Street
Atalissa, IA 52720
phone: 319-946-3471
20 May to 10 June, by appt.

White Flower Farm
Route 63
Litchfield, CT 06759
phone: 203-496-9600
late May to late June

Windwood Gardens
124 Sherwood Road E.
Williamston, MI 48895
phone: 517-349-8121
1 June to 15 June

John W. Wood
2654 Prospect Church Road
Mooresboro, NC 28114
phone: 704-657-5149
15 April to 15 May

York Hill Farm
18 Warren Street
Georgetown, MA 01833
phone: 508-352-6560
1 June to 4 July

Australia

Rainbow Ridge Nursery
Taylor Road
Dural, New South Wales 2158
phone: (61) 2-6512857
late October to late November

Tempo Two
P.O. Box 60A
Pearcedale, Victoria
phone: (61) 59-786980
1 November to mid-December

Belgium

Koen Engelen
Kawana
Wijnegembaan
2520 Ranst
phone: (32) 3-35402
25 May to 31 June

Alphonse Van Mulders
Rue du Plangelois 17
5210 Javiers
phone: (32) 81-812271
mid-May to late June

Canada

Les Jardins Osiris
818 Rue Monique
St. Thomas de Joliette, Quebec
    J0K 3L0
phone: 514-759-8621
early June to late June

McMillen's Iris Garden
Route 1
Norwich, Ontario N0J 1P0
phone: 519-468-6508
early June to late June

France

Bourdillon Nursery
Gaec de Champagne
41230 Soings-en-Sologne
mid-May to mid-June

Cayeux Nursery
Poilly-lez-Gien
45500 Gien
mid-May to mid-June

Germany

Friesland Staudengarten
Uwe Knöpnadel
Husumer Weg 16
26441 Jever-Rahdum
May to June

Eberhard Schuster
Post Gaedebehn
19089 Augustenhof
early June to late June

Schöppinger Irisgarten
Bürgerweg 8
48624 Schoppingen
early June to late June

Tomas Tamberg
Zimmerstrasse 8
12207 Berlin
phone: (49) 30-712-4235
1 June to 15 June, by appt.

New Zealand

Bay Bloom Nursery
Box 502
Tauranga
7 November to early December

Ranch North Iris Gardens
RD 3
Whangarei
7 November to early December

Mossburn Iris Gardens
Box 96, Private Bag
Mossburn, Southland
late November to mid-December

United Kingdom

Beth Chatto Gardens
Elmstead Market
Colchester, Essex CO7 7DB
phone: (44) 1206-822007
late May to late June

Croftway Nursery
Yapton Road
Barnham, near Bognor Regis
West Sussex PO22 0BH
phone: (44) 1243-552121
15 May to late June

David Austin Roses
Bowling Green Lane
Albrighton
Wolverhampton, West Midlands
   WV7 3HB
phone: (44) 1902-376300
early June to late June

Four Seasons
Forncett St. Mary
Norwich, Norfolk NR16 1JT
phone: (44) 1508-488344
early June to late June

Jennifer Hewitt
Haygarth, Cleeton St. Mary
Kidderminster, Hereford and
   Worcester DY14 0QU
phone: (44) 1584-890526
1 June to 30 June, by appt.

Holden Clough Nursery
Holden
Bolton-by-Bowland
Clitheroe, Lancashire BB7 4PF
phone: (44) 1200-447618
early June to late June

V. H. Humphrey
Westlees Farm
Logmore Lane
Westcott
Dorking, Surrey RH4 3JN
phone: (44) 1306-889827
mid-May to 30 June

Lingen Nursery and Garden
Lingen, near Bucknell
Shropshire SY7 0DY
phone: (44) 1544-267720
early June to late June

Perryhill Nurseries
Hartfield, East Sussex TN7 4JP
phone: (44) 1892-770377
mid-May to late June

Rowden Gardens
Brentor, near Tavistock
Devon PL19 0NG
phone: (44) 1822-810275
1 June to 30 June, by appt.

Water Garden Nursery
Highcroft
Moorend, Wembworthy
Chulmeigh, Devon EX18 7SG
phone: (44) 1837-83566
mid-May to mid-June

INTERNATIONAL REGISTRATION AUTHORITY
American Iris Society
Attn: K. Keppel
P.O. Box 18145
Salem, OR 97305
U.S.A.

Regional representative in the United Kingdom:
British Iris Society
Attn: Jennifer Hewitt
Haygarth, Cleeton St. Mary
Kidderminster, Hereford and Worcester DY14 0QU

PLANT SOCIETIES

American Iris Society
Marilyn Harlow, Membership Secretary
P.O. Box 8455
San Jose, CA 95155-8455
U.S.A.
phone: 408-971-0444
fax: 408-971-6072

Society for Siberian Irises (A Section of the American Iris Society)
Howard L. Brookins
N75 W14257 North Point Drive
Menomonee Falls, WI 53051-4325
U.S.A.
phone: 414-251-5292
fax: 414-251-8298

British Iris Society
C. E. C. Bartlett
The Old Mill House, Shurton
Strogursy, Somerset TA5 1QG
England

References and Additional Reading

McEwen, C. 1976. Historical note on hybridizing of Siberian irises. *The Siberian Iris* 4 (3): 8–14.

———. 1987. 'Butter and Sugar': Its background. *The Siberian Iris* 6 (5): 5–6.

———. 1996. *The Siberian Iris*. Portland, Ore.: Timber Press.

McEwen, C., and B. Warburton. 1971. Report of a research project to test various methods of making crosses of Siberian irises. *The Siberian Iris* 3 (4): 19–22.

McGarvey, W. G. 1975. The culture and hybridizing of Siberian irises: A short history and report of current work. *Bulletin of the American Iris Society* no. 219: 20–27.

Meyer, P., J. Heidmann, G. Forkmann, and H. Saedler. 1987. A new petunia flower color generated by transformation of a mutant with a maize gene. *Nature* 330: 677–678.

Randolph, L. G., ed. *Garden Irises*. St. Louis, Mo.: American Iris Society.

Schafer, M. 1989. New thoughts on pollination. *The Siberian Iris* 6 (9): 5–6.

Smith, R. G. 1993. Transgenic modifications of irises. *Bulletin of the American Iris Society* no. 289: 54–58.

Tiffney, S. 1971. Notes on hybridizing Siberians. *The Siberian Iris* 3 (4): 6–12.

Warburton, B., and M. Hamblen, eds. 1978. *The World of Irises.* Wichita, Kans.: American Iris Society.

Zimmermann, E. 1994. A slice of life: A gardener's guide to genetic engineering. *Minnesota Horticulturist* (February): 20–22.

6 Breeding Hostas

James W. Wilkins Jr.

Hostas are hardy herbaceous perennial plants. Their primary use is as land-scape plants grown for the ornamental effect of their foliage (Plate 6-1). They are easily grown in temperate zones, and many varieties are shade tolerant. Hostas are monocotyledons that occur in the wild in Japan, Korea, and China, growing in many niches, including alpine, meadows, open woods, bogs, and river banks. Numerous hostas were introduced to Europe by Phillip Von Siebold beginning in 1829 (Schmid 1986). In the past 30 years, they have increased in popularity due to many exciting new varieties and a growing appreciation for the value of foliage in the landscape. Hostas are now among the most popular perennial plants in North America. They are diverse and extremely versatile.

In this chapter the term *variety* is used to include *Hosta* cultivars, species, and specioids. (*Specioid* is a term coined by Hensen [1985] and used by Schmid [1992] to define a taxon that is validly published but is only known in cultivation and is so different from species described from the wild as to be considered a separate taxon of the same rank as a species. This concept is extremely useful in *Hosta* nomenclature, but is unfortunately not sanctioned by the *International Code of Botanical Nomenclature*.) There are more than 3000 recognized hosta varieties (Schmid 1990), coming in many sizes, shapes, and colors. There are varieties of hostas the clump of which could be covered with a teacup, and other varieties with clumps that mature to 3 feet (0.9 m) in height and over 5 feet (1.5 m) in width. Some clumps are very upright, some arching, and others decidedly mounded. Leaf size varies from the size of a thumbnail to that of a large dinner plate. Hosta leaves may be strap-shaped, heart-shaped, or nearly round. Some leaves are cupped, some have down-turned edges, some twist along the long axis, and others have undulating to pie-crusted margins. Hosta foliage can be shiny, seersuckered, or coated with a waxy surface (resulting in the so-called blue hostas or the white-backed hostas). Hosta leaves may be solid colors (green, gold, or blue); they may have marginal variegation (solid colors in the center with a lighter color such as gold or white at the margin of the leaf), reversed variegation (a light-colored gold or white leaf center and a dark-colored margin), or streaked, splashed, or speckled variegation over the entire leaf, the margin, or only the center. Leaf color of several hostas changes from spring to summer.

Hostas do have flowers, and though the bloom is usually not of primary interest, it is often beautiful and may be very fragrant. The season of bloom varies, some varieties blooming in early summer, some midsummer, and some not until autumn (Benedict and Wilkins 1991). Multiple flowers occur along a bloom scape; most often there is one scape per division. Several flowers open each day, usually lasting one day. Flower shape can range from tubular with a flare of the petals, to bell shaped. Flower color varies from white to lavender to intense purple. Some varieties have double flowers (petaloid stamens), and some have flowers that do not open (closed bloom). The bloom scapes may be very tall compared to the clump. Some scapes are straight, and some hang down below the plant (an adaptation to growth on cliffs). Both the petioles of the leaves and the stalks of the bloom scapes may be colored or variegated similar to the plant's leaves and may, in addition, have a red or purple stippling or waxy coat (Wilkins 1994a).

Important Traits and Breeding Objectives

A significant difference in hybridizing *Hosta* compared to most other genera is that the major interest is in the leaf color and adornments, with interest in bloom often secondary. Natural selection has favored the more vigorous all-green hostas in the wild (Schmid 1994; Wilkins 1994c). While a gold- or white-margined hosta may be very lovely and desirable as a landscape plant, it possesses less chlorophyll than its all-green form and, consequently, would compete less well in the wild. What we do as hybridizers and introducers of new plants is breed and select for traits that, in the wild, would often be selected against; many of the plants we grow in the garden would rapidly disappear in the wild.

Variation in hosta leaf color can arise in several ways. Most changes in hostas are not mutations, or genetic changes, but rather chimeral rearrangements (Falstad 1993). Chimeras are formed when two or more different tissue types exist next to each other in the leaf. These rearrangements can occur in the wild, in the garden, or in the test tube during propagation by tissue culture. This phenomenon of chimeral rearrangement is also called sporting, and it has been responsible for many new and wonderful hostas.

An example of a hosta arising as a sport in the wild is *Hosta montana* 'Aureo-marginata'. Examples of hostas arising as sports in cultivation include *Hosta* 'Frances Williams' and *H. ventricosa* 'Aureomarginata'. Examples of hostas arising as sports in tissue culture include *Hosta* 'Northern Lights' and 'Platinum Tiara'. Tissue culture has provided hostaphiles with an entire series of sports from a single progenitor (Plate 6-2). *Hosta sieboldiana* 'Elegans' (all-blue leaf) in cultivation sported 'Frances Williams' (gold margin), which in turn sported 'Golden Sunburst' (all gold) and a medial variegated cultivar 'Color Glory' [plant patent applied for] (gold center). In tissue culture *H. sieboldiana* 'Elegans' sported 'Northern Halo' (white margin) and 'Northern Lights' (white center). A similar series of plants, the so-called Tiara series, has been introduced with tissue culture sports of *Hosta* 'Golden Tiara' (Pollock 1986). An excellent discussion of sporting clones (Hawes 1996) proposes the term *clan* for plants related to each other through sporting. I believe the term is a useful one and will likely be adopted.

It was once thought that a given type of leaf chimeral rearrangement, for example a white margin, would all be the same, but this has not proven to be the case, as some white-margined sports have broad margination and some narrow. The growth rate of narrow margins is often less than the center of the leaf. The result is a distorted, often unpleasant cupping, referred to as the "drawstring effect" (Pollock 1988, 1995). This effect is hardly noticeable in the undersized plants when in tissue culture, but it becomes more obvious in cultivation as the leaves approach mature size. The variability of sports, particularly in tissue culture, initially added confusion to nomenclature, and frustrated hosta buyers. Happily, now that tissue culture laboratories are aware of this problem, propagators attempt to cull defective hostas before they reach the gardening public (Falstad 1995). It is highly likely that mutations and chimeral rearrangements affect traits other than leaf color; however, such changes are apt to be less dramatic and would likely be overlooked.

New hosta varieties can also arise from seeds. In contrast to those arising from sports, new hostas begun as seedlings may vary not only in leaf color but also in shape and size of the leaf or clump, blooming attributes, and virtually any other hosta characteristic. For many hosta enthusiasts, breeding of hostas is an important part of the hobby and has resulted in dramatic new hostas introduced in both North America and abroad.

Hostas as a rule are very fertile when crossed or self-pollinated. There is apparently no barrier to reproduction between species and fertile hybrids. As a result, in cultivation, most hostas do not come true from seed. Some hostas are sterile or of extremely low fertility as pod (female) parents, although some hostas reported to be sterile occasionally produce viable seeds when grown in full sun. Hostas may have reduced fertility for several reasons. *Hosta plantaginea*, for example, originated in southern China and requires a warm climate to flower. It is a night-blooming hosta with a very long style. What was once thought to be infertility may actually be a lack of a nocturnal pollinator, or pollen that produces a pollen tube too short to reach the ova.

The normal diploid chromosome number for *Hosta* is $2n$ = 60. Polyploidy rarely occurs in hostas, although *Hosta clausa* is reported to be triploid ($2n$ = 90) and *H. ventricosa* is reported to have tetraploid forms ($2n$ = 120) (Aden 1988; Schmid 1991). Interestingly, *H. clausa* has closed flowers and rarely sets seeds; seed pod formation has been reported, with pollination likely from an insect burrowing into the flower (Owens 1995). *Hosta ventricosa* exhibits apomixis, which is to say that it produces seed without actual fertilization. Apomixis is frequently seen with polyploidy, the effect being that the progeny are nearly always identical to one another and to the parent.

Very little hard data is available on the genetics of hostas. Most breeders select hostas with desirable traits and make crosses often with each hosta serving as the pod and pollen parent. The genetics of leaf color, particularly variegation, is reasonably well understood. Vaughn (1982) proposes that yellow-leaved hostas that demonstrate a green phase—*Hosta* 'August Moon', for example—have a dominant yellow gene, with the homozygous dominant (*YY*) being lethal, the homozygous recessive (*yy*) being green, and the heterozygous (*Yy*) being either viridescent (sprouting yellow and turning green) or lutescent (emerging pale green and later turning yellow). Vaughn also studied the genetic basis of flower color in hostas, suggesting that white flower color is recessive to lavender, with at least two genes controlling anthocyanin pigment in the *Hosta* blossom, and that red petioles and fragrance are dominant. Aden (1988) found that streaked variegation and possibly vigor may be influenced by mitochondrial DNA.

In a beautifully done series of studies, Vaughn (1980, 1981) has clarified the inheritance of variegation in hosta foliage. Hostas can demonstrate either stable or unstable variegation. In stable variegation the color pattern of the leaves is the same on all leaves in a division and on all divisions in a clump. Both marginal and medial variegation are stable, and Vaughn's research demonstrates that neither one is genetically transferred. Only non-variegated progeny are produced when either parent has stable marginal or medial variegation. This process may be better understood by reviewing the growth and development of the undifferentiated cells of the meristem. Histologically, the meristem has three layers. The first layer (L1) is the epidermal layer, which differentiates into the epidermal and marginal portion of the leaf. The third layer of cells (L3) does not contribute to the leaf but to other tissues such as rhizome and root tissue. Vaughn's data show that in *Hosta*, as has been reported in some other monocots, the subepidermal layer of cells in the meristem (L2) is the source of the tissue for the central portion of the leaf. Ovules and pollen are also formed by cells of L2 origin. Thus, from a genetic standpoint, only the nuclear DNA of the central portion of the leaf is present in the gametes and transferred to the progeny. It is my expectation that the offspring of a truly white-centered hosta would not survive.

Streaky or splashed variegation in hostas is unstable. It differs from leaf to leaf in a division and from division to division in a clump. Streaking in hostas results from a uniparental type of inheritance called non-Mendelian inheritance. A streaked variegated hosta will produce variably streaked progeny only if it is the pod parent. None of the progeny are streaked if streaking is only found in the pollen parent. Streaked variegation is due to mosaicism of the chloroplast (two or more different genetic constitutions). This unstable mutation is in the DNA of the chloroplast and is cytoplasmic rather than nuclear in origin. The paternal (pollen parent) chloroplast is apparently converted to starch granules, perhaps for energy storage—hence, only the DNA of the maternal (pod parent) chloroplasts are expressed (Vaughn 1981).

Streaked variegated hostas represent a mosaic clone in which segments of mutant tissue (devoid of green color) are randomly interspersed between patches of normal tissue (the color of which is determined by nuclear genetics). For this reason, there is no predictable pattern from leaf to leaf. There will also be no predictable pattern to the plastid types in the gametes. Thus, a streaked hosta as a pod parent will contribute a diversity of plastid types to its progeny. As a result, the seedlings may have variable patterns of streaked variegation regardless of the paternal parent. Why anyone would want to raise and breed with unstable (streaked) hostas will be better understood after exploring the phenomenon called *stabilizing*, or sorting out.

Though the variegation in streaked hostas is unstable, with time a streaky hosta will stabilize. That is to say, it will form a division in which all the leaves have a stable pattern of variegation. Through migration (displacement and replacement), the mutant cells become the entire population of either the central portion or marginal portion of the leaf. The result is stable medial or marginal variegation. If a stable division is formed, it may be separated from the clump. These stable divisions then behave genetically like any other stable variegated hosta. If the stable cultivar is worthy of introduction, it can be named but must be given a different name from the streaked hosta from which it stabilized. Lastly, the streaked mutant tissue may be completely replaced by normal cells, resulting in a stable, solid color. Figure 6-1 shows examples of stabilization.

This phenomenon of sorting and stabilizing was delineated by Ralph H. (Herb) Benedict (1986), and it is often referred to as the "Benedict Cross."

Figure 6-1. Stabilization in a streaked hosta. The three leaves in the top row show the variability of leaves in *Hosta* 'Maize and Blue'. The two leaves on the right show (left to right) stabilization into an unnamed stable reversed form. The three leaves on the left show (right to left) stabilization into an unnamed stable marginated form. Horizontally, across the bottom, is an unnamed all-green form. (Photo by James W. Wilkins Jr.)

Benedict has further observed that if the streaking goes to the margin, a marginal variegation will usually develop; if the streaking does not extend to the margin, a medial variegation will usually sort out (Benedict 1989). There is seemingly a directionality to this process, with one portion of the clump sorting out toward marginal variegation and another portion toward medial variegation (Wilkins 1991a). I have observed that it is possible to direct the process to move in one direction or another by stimulating the dormant buds in the crown of the plant. To stimulate the dormant buds, make small vertical incisions in the crown on either side of the leaf that is showing early signs of a stable pattern. This technique was described by Ross (1982) and modified by Zumbar (1991, 1995). The stable variegated patterns that develop from streaked hostas can eventually take over the clump, and it is necessary to remove such divisions, or you risk losing the streaked plant altogether. This has caused some gardeners to become frustrated with streaked hostas (Hyslop 1989) and has limited their appeal in the trade (Schmid 1987). Most breeders fastidiously maintain their breeding stock of streaked hostas by regularly removing divisions showing stable variegation (Benedict 1986). It is possible to recover streaked hostas from old, inactive but viable crowns that were previously streaked. This is done by vertically cutting and replanting these inactive crowns and inducing dormant buds to break (Wilkins 1994b). Some medially variegated divisions, particularly those with white centers (no chlorophyll) are lovely as they develop from a streaked hosta. Once separated from the clump, however, they may die. They were, in a sense, being nursed by the more vigorous divisions in the clump.

Hybridizing, sorting out, and stabilizing streaked hostas is a special type of sporting for creating new variegated hostas (Wilkins 1989b). It is also likely to be a more productive method than sporting alone, because in hybridizing the potential exists to change more than just the leaf color and pattern (Zilis 1984; Wilkins 1990). As previously mentioned, *Hosta sieboldiana* 'Elegans' (all-blue leaf) sported 'Frances Williams' (gold margin). 'Frances Williams' is a beautiful hosta and has repeatedly been highly rated in the American Hosta Society's "Popularity Poll." However, it retains from 'Elegans' the tendency to have flowers very closely spaced on the bloom scape, and bloom scapes that are short, often flowering under the leaves of the clump. How could this be improved? By breeding for longer flower scapes. Pollen from a hosta with tall scapes and well-spaced flowers, such as *H. montana*, *H. fluctuans*, or *H. nigrescens* species or cultivars, could be used on *Hosta* 'Dorothy Benedict', a streaked hosta of *sieboldiana* type. Some of the progeny would be streaked and have tall bloom scapes. These progeny could sort out to form a *sieboldiana* type of hosta with a gold margin and tall scapes. In addition, I have not seen the drawstring effect in marginal variegated hostas that arise from the sorting out process.

In the past, many hostas have been introduced from chance seedlings or sports found in the wild or in cultivation. More recently, the abundance of desirable new hostas has resulted from planned crosses by hybridizers. Insects are much more efficient than most hybridizers at making crosses, but there is no assurance that the progeny will be special. With planned crosses, one controls which two parents are involved and dramatically increases the odds of developing a valuable new plant. More importantly, in subsequent years the progeny can be self-pollinated or crossed back to their parents to bring out recessive traits.

In selecting the parents, the hybridizer is wise to attempt to establish a goal or goals for his or her breeding. Some hybridizers are working on red petioles, hoping to bring red into the leaf blade. Hostas useful for this would include *Hosta tardiflora*, *H. kikutii* var. *tosanna* 'Regal Rhubarb', *Hosta* 'Garnet Prince', and *H. longipes* var. *hypoglauca*. For purple bloom scapes one might use *Hosta* 'Sparkling Burgundy', 'Purple Passion', or 'Cherry Berry'.

Plants to use for breeding white backs might include *H. longipes* var. *latifolia*, *H. rupifraga*, or *Hosta* 'Grand Slam'. For streaked variegated hostas to serve as a pod parent I would recommend 'Breeder's Choice', 'Dorothy Benedict', 'Dorset Clown', 'Galaxy', 'Little Jim', 'Marbled Cream', 'Super Streak', 'William Lachman', and 'Yellow Splash'. In breeding to streaked hostas, especially if the clump is large and has multiple bloom scapes, I have found it most productive to select flowers on those scapes that are themselves variegated, or have streaked scape leaves (sterile bracts) or streaked fertile bracts. Similarly, streaked seed pods, when they form on streaked hostas, are most likely to produce streaked progeny. In breeding for fragrance, consider using *H. plantaginea* (a fragrant, night-blooming species), *Hosta* 'Fragrant Bouquet', and *Hosta* 'Invincible'; for wavy edges, 'Donahue Piecrust', 'Grand Slam', and 'Spritzer'; for dwarfing, *H. venusta*, *H. pulchella*, *Hosta* 'Blue Ice', and *Hosta* 'Popo'; for substance (thick leaves), *H. yingeri*, *H. longipes* 'Maruba', and the specioids of *Hosta tokudama* group. A potentially exciting species for breeding is *H. laevigata*. This hosta has wavy, lance-shaped leaves with good substance and vigor, and it may have multiple bloom scapes without a corresponding leaf crown, which arise in succession from the base of the plant. If this trait is transferable to seedlings, it could be used to hybridize more floriferous hostas with a longer bloom period. The above list is not intended to be all-inclusive but to offer some useful starting plants. What is most fun and productive is to make crosses and initiate one's own breeding line.

Hybridization Mechanics

The mechanics of making a cross are simple. Merely dab ripe pollen on a receptive stigma, cross your fingers, and let nature take over! In general, individual hosta flowers open for one day before declining. It is during this single day that a flower can be crossed and its pollen will ripen. Different techniques and methods can increase the likelihood of success and the integrity of the cross. The first step is to verify that the hosta is fertile. In working with a new hosta, following the suggestion of Benedict (personal communication), I purposely let the bees pollinate several flowers. Try as I might, my success rate with hand pollination varies from 20 to 80%, but the bees are successful almost 100% of the time, unless the temperature is above 90°F (32°C) or heavy rains have fallen during the time that the plant is receptive.

After verifying fertility, the next consideration is to eliminate or greatly reduce the chances of open pollination of the flowers to which you plan to pollinate. This can be accomplished in several ways. First, you can mechanically exclude bees and other flying insects with netting, nylon stockings, or wire-screen cages placed over the bloom scapes. I have not seen seed set on flowers that are isolated from insects and are not hand pollinated, which suggests that self-pollination from pollen shed is rare in hostas. Second, the plant can be potted and isolated in the greenhouse, a screenhouse, or moved to a hosta-free remote site. The third and most common method of preventing open pollination is to emasculate the bloom. The basis of this technique is that bees are attracted to the flower by the petals: remove the petals, and the bees go to other flowers. The petals can be removed with scissors, but I remove them manually as follows. I secure the flower to be emasculated by holding it between my left thumb and forefinger. I gently thrust my right thumb or index finger into the throat of the flower. I grasp the petals between my right thumb and index finger and merely peel off the petals. This leaves behind the pistil and the six stamens. Next, I gently deflect the pistil away from the stamens by placing my thumb under the distal end of the style and grasp the stamens, often all six at once, between the thumb and index finger, pulling them off of the base of the ovary. The stamens are discarded, unless their pollen is going to be used for breeding. Great care must be taken not to bend or injure the style or stigma while preparing the flower for the cross, while making the cross, and when tagging the cross. Some hybridizers use mechanical and isolation techniques along with emasculation to provide additional protection from bee or insect pollination. I have repeatedly and purposely left emasculated flowers without pollinating them and with no barriers to insects; open pollination very rarely occurs on emasculated *Hosta* flowers. In planned crosses, it is also essential to prevent open pollination by keeping the bees away from the flower before you have isolated or emasculated it. The most effective way to do this is to be out at first light and prepare the flower, even if it is several hours ahead of the time to make the cross. The preparation can also be made the night before, but it is sometimes difficult to know which flowers will be opening the next day. One exception is flowers that open at night and are night pollinated, such as *Hosta plantaginea*—here earlier preparation or isolation is mandatory.

The stamens can be collected from the paternal plants in a manner similar to emasculating the flower. I use a Styrofoam egg carton and number the six sections in one row. I place the stamens, anther ends down, into the numbered sections of the cartons. There are sometimes 30 or more stamens in a section. I record which stamens are in which section on a self-stick removable note pad affixed to the top of the carton. In the remaining row of six cells, I place the color-coded yarn or wire used to specify the pollen source after the cross is made. I use yarn 4 inches (10 cm) in length and often will use only one filament of a four-stranded yarn to tie around the pedicel to mark a cross. I always use black yarn to record a self-pollinated cross. Sometimes I use a 3-inch (7.5-cm) long wire from a 50-pair telephone wire to mark a cross. A 50-pair wire consists of 100 wires, each with a distinctive color code. This code is recorded in my hybridizing log book to identify a specific cross. The wire is folded in the middle like a hairpin, slipped over the pedicel, and slightly twisted. Many telephone repair trucks have short pieces of scrap wire that they will give you for this purpose.

The next step is the application of the pollen to the stigma. Most of the time, the pollen is ripe at the same time that the stigma is receptive. The time of receptivity varies in the same plant. The colder the weather, the later in the day the flower is receptive. If the temperature is very high, over 90°F (32°C), seed set is greatly diminished. It would appear that optimal seed set occurs over the range of 55–90°F (13–32°C). If the pollen is not completely ripe, the stamens can still be removed from an open flower and the pollen allowed to ripen off of the flower. The pollen ripens over a period of a few hours and will turn bright yellow. If the day is warm, I leave the egg carton outside; if it's cold, I bring the collected stamens into the warmer house. When the pollen is ripe, usually a bright yellow color, I head to the garden with the egg carton and my hybridizing log book. The pollen can be applied with a fine brush, but the easiest method is to remove a stamen from the carton by picking up the bare end of the filament. The filament can be used like a handle on a brush, and the anther with its pollen is dabbed onto the stigma of the pistil. A receptive pistil will have a slight flare to the end of the stigma, and the pollen will adhere with ease. Often, if I have time, I will reapply the pollen hourly for two to three applications, hopefully to be sure that the pollen is ripe and the stigma is receptive. The stigma ceases to be receptive after several hours, and later in the day the end appears to be sealed by a clear liquid. This seems to happen whether or not the stigma had pollen applied.

I have had some mornings when the pollen to be used for a cross was not yet fully ripe but would still stick to the stigma and literally ripen while on the stigma. This is not an ideal circumstance, but it has allowed some crosses to be made when I was not available at the ideal time. In other situations where pollination could not be done at the appropriate time, I have placed the egg carton with ripe pollen into a plastic bag, which is sealed and refrigerated. Pollen stored in this way has produced successful crosses on the following day.

A common frustration in plant breeding occurs when you wish to cross plants that have different times of bloom. One simple solution to this problem is to collect and freeze pollen until the desired pod parent comes into bloom. Good anecdotal evidence suggests that this approach can be successful with hostas. The pollen is placed in gelatin capsules and stored in sealed containers in the freezer, properly labeled, until needed for a cross. Another approach is to "fool" the hostas into blooming earlier or later than normal (Avent 1992). Early blooming can be induced in a greenhouse or by artificial lighting. Hosta blooming can be delayed by storing the plants in the dark at 40°F (4°C) and bringing them out of storage several months after they would normally have bloomed. Early blooming hostas may also rebloom later in the season, offering the possibility of crossing early and later blooming hostas. Reblooming is most likely if the first bloom scape is removed and the hosta well cared for. It also is apt to be triggered when early blooming hostas are divided immediately after blooming (Solberg 1990). Eric Smith of England created a series of desirable hostas known as the Tardiana Group, when he crossed *Hosta tardiflora* (late blooming) with *H. sieboldiana*, an early blooming hosta that happened to rebloom (Ruh 1984).

When hybridizing, I record in my log book each cross as it is made. My log has a sheet for each pod parent, on which I record its lineage; a plant description (size, leaf and bloom color); the reason why I am using it as a parent; and the day of first bloom, peak bloom, and last bloom. There is a row for each cross with fields to enter the date, pollen parent and reason selected, weather condition, yarn or wire color, whether a pod was set, whether the seed was viable, and the cross number assigned to the progeny. A second sheet is used to record data on the pollen parent: its lineage; a plant description (size, leaf and bloom color); the reason why I am using it as a parent; and the day of first bloom, peak bloom, and last bloom. The data are ultimately entered into a database on my computer. This allows me to search and group data on current and prior years' crosses.

If the cross is successful, it is usually apparent in 2 to 3 days. The ovary is retained on the pedicel and starts to enlarge. When possible, I like to have the seed ripen on the plant, which is never a problem with early bloom-ing hostas. Late-blooming hostas can present some problems in colder regions. If the hosta seeds freeze in the pod, viability is greatly reduced (Benedict and Wilkins 1991). If a freeze is anticipated before the seeds are ripe, the plant can be potted and brought into a greenhouse or placed in a sunny window to finish off the process. Benedict has also ripened seeds of late-blooming hostas by placing the bloom scapes into vases of water and keeping the pods alive for a few weeks indoors (Benedict and Wilkins 1991).

When the pods are ripe, they often begin to split and the seed is black. I harvest the ripened seed pods and place them into small envelopes, such as coin envelopes, with the cross information recorded on each envelope. These are then brought into the house until the seed pods dry and open. If I am collecting a large amount of open-pollinated seeds, I place the cut bloom scape into a brown paper bag and let the seeds mature on the scape. If I have a great quantity of seeds, I just shake the bag and collect the seeds. If I have only one or two pods of a cross, I am more meticulous in cleaning and separating the seeds. Seeds that are white or have no swelling in the embryo end are discarded. The remaining seeds are placed back into their labeled envelopes and stored. If long storage is anticipated, the envelopes are placed in a sealed container in the refrigerator. Benedict has frozen hosta seeds in a sealed container, and viability was retained for 50 months (Benedict 1991, 1993).

As mentioned previously, I record the information regarding my crosses in a computer database. This database can be used to print labels for the seed envelopes. Also, using the same database, I can print on clear, self-adhesive laser labels, which are $1 \times 2\frac{5}{6}$ inches (2.5×7 cm) in size. These can be affixed to metal labels and used in the garden. The labels have lasted at least 3 years in my garden in Michigan.

Propagation

Most hosta hybridizers start their seeds in the fall or winter, growing them indoors under fluorescent lights (Wilkins 1991b). Using high levels of lighting—four 40-watt cool-white bulbs over an 18×48 inch (45×120 cm) bench, with the lights placed 2 to 4 inches (5–10 cm) above the top leaf surface of the plant—left on for 24 hours, hosta seedling growth can be accelerated (Wilkins 1987). This growth is enhanced if the seedlings are replanted into slightly larger containers several times as they increase. Each potting is accompanied by a burst of new leaves. The effect is to delay the onset of dormancy, and this technique has been described for other species of plants (Young and Hanover 1976). One season of accelerated growth produces seedlings equivalent in size to plants grown for three seasons outdoors, and the seedlings often bloom in the first growing season. Alternatively, seeds can be sown in soil in late autumn, but they should be covered with wire to discourage mice from making a winter feast of them. They can also be sown in early spring either in the greenhouse, under lights, or in the soil.

Culling of undesirable seedlings is often done in several stages. The first culling may be done very early, especially if one does not wish to keep hostas bearing or lacking certain traits, such as specific foliage colors, white backs, or red petioles. The next logical time to cull is after the first or second blooming, if certain flower colors or shapes or bloom scape heights are undesirable. Discard plants any time an undesirable trait appears. Sometimes, particularly with unstable streaked hostas, you must wait several years to cull, until the stable pattern develops and can be evaluated. Many hostas become more lovely with time, and quite often age alone makes a hosta look special.

When selecting a hosta for introduction, you need to be objective and unemotional. Seeking the counsel of other growers or entering leaves into competition to get additional input is often desirable. If possible, the hosta should be grown in different parts of the country or at least in different niches in the garden to evaluate its garden worthiness. I like to leave one clump of an introduction to grow to maturity undisturbed. If a hosta is worthy of introducing, it should be registered with the International Registration Authority for the genus *Hosta* (address listed at the end of this chapter) prior to introduction. Measurements and photographs are required and should be taken from a plant approaching maturity. The listing of new hosta registrations is published annually in *The Hosta Journal*, a publication of the American Hosta Society.

Many hybridizers sell their introductions directly to the consumer or through one of the many hosta specialty nurseries. Hostas are vegetatively propagated and, with the exception of streaked hostas, have been extensively propagated by tissue culture. As a result, many exciting new hostas reach the public quickly and relatively inexpensively. Hostas are also propagated by dividing clumps of two or more crowns. An appealing thing about growing hostas is that they rarely require division, even mature clumps, but they can be divided if additional plants are desired. I strongly recommend that initial attempts at dividing be done with plants that are dug out of the ground and from which the soil has been washed away. This allows clear visualization of the crowns and roots. With experience, you can remove a division or two while the majority of the plant is left in the ground and its roots undisturbed. I prefer to divide hostas as they first emerge from the ground, or else late in the growing season, about 4 to 6 weeks before dormancy is expected. Midseason division is acceptable, but the clump will not look good for the remainder of the year. Important root growth for the next season occurs toward the end of the current season, and hostas, whether recent divisions or established clumps, benefit greatly by care and watering during the cool weather of fall.

Hybridizing is a lot of work and a lot of fun. It brings an exciting new element to the wonderful hobby of ornamental gardening. Hostas are easily grown and lovely to work with. They fool most of us into believing that we are competent gardeners and landscape designers. If you wish to find out more about hostas, consider joining one of the hosta societies listed later in the chapter.

Resources

COLLECTIONS—UNITED STATES

Dubuque Arboretum and Botanical
  Gardens
3800 Arboretum Drive
Dubuque, IA 52001

Hidden Lake Gardens
Michigan Route 50, South of US 12
Tipton, MI 49287

Illinois Central College Arboretum
1 College Drive
East Peoria, IL 61635

Inniswood Metro Gardens
940 S. Hempstead Road
Westerville, OH 43081

Longwood Gardens
P.O. Box 501
409 Conservatory Road
Kennett Square, PA 19348

Minnesota Landscape Arboretum
3675 Arboretum Drive, Box 39
Chanhassen, MN 55317

SUPPLIERS—UNITED STATES

Notable hosta suppliers in the United States are listed here. In addition, *The Hosta Finder* references the offerings of more than 20 hosta nurseries by individual cultivar. It is available for purchase annually after late March from Steven H. Greene, 36 Elaine Road, Sudbury, MA 01776, U.S.A.

Adrian's Flowers of Fashion Nursery
855 Parkway Boulevard
Alliance, OH 44601

Azalea Patch
2010 Mountain Road
Joppa, MD 21085

Banyai Hostas
11 Gates Circle
Hockessin, DE 19707

Busse Gardens
5873 Oliver Avenue S.W.
Cokato, MN 55321

Coastal Gardens and Nursery
4611 Socastee Boulevard
Myrtle Beach, SC 29575

Cooks Nursery
10749 Bennett Road
Dunkirk, NY 14048

Dogwood Farms
R.R. 13, Box 288
Brazil, IN 47934

Green Hill Farm
5715 Hideaway Drive
Chapel Hill, NC 27516

Homestead Division of Sunnybrook
  Farms
9448 Mayfield Road
Chesterland, OH 44026

House of Hosta
2320 Elmwood Road
Green Bay, WI 54313

Klehm Nursery
4210 N. Duncan Road
Champaign, IL 61821

Kuk's Forest Nursery
10174 Barr Road
Brecksville, OH 44141

Lakeside Acres
8119 Roy Lane
Ooltewah, TN 37363

Lee Gardens
25986 Sauder Road
Tremont, IL 61568

Miller's Manor Gardens
11974 E. 191st Street
Noblesville, IN 46060

Naylor Creek Nursery
2610 W. Valley Road
Chimacum, WA 98325

Plant Delights Nursery
9241 Sauls Road
Raleigh, NC 27603

Robyn's Nest Nursery
7802 N.E. 63rd Street
Vancouver, WA 98662

Savory's Gardens
5300 Whiting Avenue
Edina, MN 55439

Schmid Nursery and Garden
847 Westwood Boulevard
Jackson, MI 49203

Sea Made Hostas
703 Mt. Lebanon Road
Wilmington, DE 19803

Soules Gardens
5809 Rahke Road
Indianapolis, IN 46217

Stark Gardens
631 G24 Highway
Norwalk, IA 50211

Tower Perennial Gardens
3412 E. 64th Court
Spokane, WA 99223

Walden-West
5744 Crooked Finger Road
Scotts Mills, OR 97375

White Oak Nursery
6145C Oak Pointe Court
Peoria, IL 61614

INTERNATIONAL REGISTRATION AUTHORITY

International Hosta Registrar
Minnesota Landscape Arboretum
3675 Arboretum Drive, Box 39
Chanhassen, MN 55317
U.S.A.
e-mail: steve021@tc.umn.edu

PLANT SOCIETIES

The American Hosta Society annually publishes two journals and a yearbook, holds a national convention, promotes many local and regional activities, and provides the opportunity to meet a lot of nice gardeners. New members receive a list of hosta sources and are placed on the mailing lists for some interesting plant catalogs. The society has an active garden-visiting program, and a listing of private and public gardens that feature hostas is available for purchase by its members. For an application and current membership information, write

American Hosta Society
Cindy Nance, Membership Secretary
338 E. Forestwood Street
Morton, IL 61550
web site: www.hosta.org

Other national hosta societies include the following:

British Hosta and Hemerocallis Society
Lynda Hinton, Hon. Membership Secretary
Toft Monks, The Hithe
Rodborough
Stroud Common, Gloucestershire GL5 5BN
England

Dutch Hosta Society
c/o Arie Van Vliet
Zuidkade 97
2771 DS Boskoop
The Netherlands

Ontario Hosta Society
Box 731
Erin, Ontario N0B 1T0
Canada

Japan Hosta Society
Seiya Onoda
1-9-9 Higashi-cho, Oiso-town
Kanagawa 255
Japan

References and Additional Reading

Aden, P. 1988. *The Hosta Book.* Portland, Ore.: Timber Press.

Avent, T. 1992. Hosta breeders and other strangers. *The Hosta Journal* 23 (1): 58–59.

Benedict, R. H. 1986. Taming the wild ones. *The Hosta Journal* 17 (2): 28–29.

———. 1989. Hosta hodgepodge. Ed. J. Wilkins. *The Hosta Journal* 20 (2): 17–18.

———. 1991. Freezing hosta seeds. *The Hosta Journal* 22 (1): 47.

———. 1992. Personal communication.

———. 1993. Hosta hodgepodge. Ed. J. Wilkins. *The Hosta Journal* 24 (1): 94.

Benedict, R. H., and J. Wilkins Jr. 1991. Fall bloomers: Hosta's finest hour. *The Hosta Journal* 22 (1): 42–43.

Bond, S. 1992. *Foliage Plants in Design.* New York: Sterling Publishing.

Falstad, C. H., III. 1993. Mutations. *The Hosta Journal* 24 (1): 22–23.

————. 1995. Northern, etc. *The Hosta Journal* 26 (1): 57–58.

Grenfell, D. 1990. *Hosta: The Flowering Foliage Plant.* Portland, Ore.: Timber Press.

Hawes, J. 1996. Clans of sporting clones. *The Hosta Journal* 26 (2): 83–85.

Hensen, K. J. W. 1985. A study of the taxonomy of cultivated hostas. *The Plantsman* 7: 19–21.

Hyslop, J. 1989. Some random thoughts on hybridization. *The Hosta Journal* 20 (1): 19.

Owens, C. 1995. A bug opened the door. *The Hosta Journal* 26 (1): 36.

Pollock, W. I. 1986. What's in a hosta name? *The Hosta Journal* 17 (2): 40–43.

————. 1988. Drawstring effect, melting out, scorching and reverting. *The Hosta Journal* 19 (2): 58–63.

————. 1995. The drawstring effect, a.k.a. Pollock's pucker. *The Hosta Journal* 25 (2): 45–46.

Ross, H. A. 1982. A foolproof method of rapidly propagating hostas. *The Hosta Journal* 13: 51–54.

Ruh, P. 1984. Update on *H.* ×*tardiana*. *The Hosta Journal* 15: 26–27.

Schmid, W. G. 1986. Phillip Von Siebold (1796–1866). *The Hosta Journal* 17 (2): 34–35.

————. 1987. Caveat hostae emptor: Let the hosta buyer beware! *The Hosta Journal* 18 (2): 48–52.

————. 1990. A place in the shade? *The Hosta Journal* 21 (1): 78–80.

————. 1991. *The Genus Hosta.* Portland, Ore.: Timber Press.

————. 1992. Species, specioids and such, Part 1. *The Hosta Journal* 23 (1): 9–12.

————. 1994. Questions and answers. Ed. W. Burto. *The Hosta Journal* 25 (2): 79.

Solberg, R. 1989. Hosta registration: What is your role? *The Hosta Journal* 20 (1): 10–11.

————. 1990. Hosta hodgepodge. Ed. J. Wilkins. *The Hosta Journal* 21 (1): 81.

Stevenson, D. H. 1995. The whos, whys, and hows of hosta registration. *The Hosta Journal* 26 (1): 48–49.

Vaughn, K. C. 1980. Chloroplastic mutants in Hosta. *The Hosta Journal* 11: 36–49.

————. 1981. Using genetics to improve Hosta. *The Hosta Journal* 12: 21–28.

————. 1982. The genetics of Hosta. *The Hosta Journal* 13: 44–49.

Wilkins, J. W., Jr. 1987. Accelerated growth of Hosta. *The Hosta Journal* 18 (1): 55–56.

————. 1989a. In defense of streaking. *The Hosta Journal* 20 (1): 41–42.

————. 1989b. The registration of Hosta. *The Hosta Journal* 20 (1): 10–11.

————. 1990. Why hybridize? *The Hosta Journal* 21 (1): 56–57.

————. 1991a. Leaf show exhibit: Hybridizing for variegation. *The Hosta Journal* 22 (1): 17.

————. 1991b. Unpublished data, American Hosta Society hybridizer's round robin.

————. 1994a. Hostas are more than just pretty leaves. *The Hosta Journal* 25 (1): 73–75.

————. 1994b. New jewels form old crowns. *The Hosta Journal* 25 (1): 51–52.

————. 1994c. Questions and answers. Ed. W. Burto. *The Hosta Journal* 25 (2): 79.

Wilson, Jim. 1990. *Masters of the Victory Garden*. Boston, Mass.: Little, Brown and Company.

Young, E., and J. W. Hanover. Accelerating maturity in *Picea* seedlings. *Acta Horticulturae* 56: 105–114.

Zilis, M. R. 1984. What tissue culture can and cannot do. *The Hosta Journal* 15: 80–81.

Zumbar, W. W. 1991. Beginners' propagations of hostas by Ross-izing, an update. *The Hosta Journal* 22 (1): 19–20.

————. 1995. Class materials on the propagation of hostas. The Great Lakes Region, Hosta College. Piqua, Ohio.

7 Breeding Ornamental Aroids

R. J. Henny

Ornamental aroids, members of the family Araceae, are a major component of the foliage-plant industry in the United States, accounting for
roughly one-third of total foliage-plant sales. *Aglaonema, Dieffenbachia, Epipremnum, Spathiphyllum,* and *Syngonium* are routinely among the top 10
foliage plants in annual sales volume.

The genera discussed in this chapter are grown as potted foliage or
flowering plants and used as interior foliage, cut flowers, or landscape
plants. *Aglaonema, Alocasia, Dieffenbachia, Philodendron,* and *Syngonium* are
valued for their showy foliage and good performance as interior plants.
Caladium is grown both as a potted plant and as a landscape specimen, as are
Philodendron and *Zantedeschia. Epipremnum* and *Syngonium* are vines and are
often grown as hanging baskets or on totem poles. *Anthurium, Spathiphyllum,* and *Zantedeschia* produce beautiful inflorescences. See Plate 7-1 for an
illustration of the variety of features among aroids.

Being tropical in nature, ornamental aroids require special cultural conditions for maintenance of good quality. Members of most genera require
shade. A general rule of thumb is that light intensity should be low enough
that your hand does not cast a shadow. If you have access to a hand-held
light meter, light levels should be within the 1500–2500 foot-candle range.
Winter temperatures should be kept at a minimum of 60°F (16°C) to prevent chilling injury. Soil should be well drained and contain at least 50%
organic matter. Many good articles have been published regarding culture
of ornamental aroids (see Henny 1988; Joiner 1981).

Historically, new ornamental aroid cultivars originated from mutations
of established cultivars or by introduction of new plants collected in the
wild. An early exception was the genus *Caladium,* in which many colorful
hybrids were developed in the early 1900s. This was the first instance where

the commercial value of an aroid genus was enhanced through development and introduction of hybrid cultivars. Beginning in 1951, many important *Philodendron* hybrids were developed from interspecific crosses. Most of those hybrids were patented and are still being grown today.

Since the 1970s, breeding has had an expanding role in the introduction of new aroid cultivars. An increase in knowledge of aroid breeding methods and the development of plant tissue culture as a fast, reliable tool for propagation of new cultivars were key factors. Both developments were fostered in part by high crop value and demand for new cultivars. Using tissue culture methods, a new aroid cultivar can be increased rapidly enough to reach commercial production levels within 1 to 2 years, instead of the 5 to 7 years required with standard cutting or division techniques.

Important Traits and Breeding Objectives

Table 7-1 (pages 124–125) includes a list of the 10 major aroid genera, along with key species, important traits, and a summary of breeding work. Studies of inheritance of many of the important traits have produced information valuable to aroid breeders.

SPATHE COLOR

The earliest report concerning inheritance of spathe color involved *Zantedeschia* (Shibuya 1956). Interspecific crosses of *Zantedeschia rehmanii* (pink spathes), *Z. albomaculata* (white), and *Z. elliottiana* (yellow) indicated that anthocyanin color expression depends on the complementary effect of four pairs of dominant genes. Inheritance of yellow coloration was demonstrated to be independent of anthocyanin. In *Anthurium* it was proposed that separate genes, designated M and O, are responsible for production of the five major spathe colors of *Anthurium andraeanum*. The colors and their respective genotypes are red (*MMOO, MMOo,* or *MmOO*), pink (*MmOo*), orange (*mmOo, mmOO,* or *mmoo*), coral (*mmoo*), and white (*mmoo* or *Mmoo*).

FOLIAR VARIEGATION

Inheritance of foliar variegation has been studied in *Caladium, Aglaonema,* and *Dieffenbachia*. The netted venation pattern of *Caladium* is controlled by a single dominant gene, with the recessive genotypes having no pattern (Wilfret 1986). Red main vein in *Caladium* leaves is dominant to green, and white is dominant to both green and red. The gene for a red main vein was also found to suppress (is epistatic to) the gene for netted venation, in that the homozygous genotype for red vein produces a solid red leaf with a green margin (Wilfret 1986). Red and white leaf spots in *Caladium* are governed by codominant alleles (Wilfret 1986; Zettler and Abo El-Nil 1979).

The presence of foliar variegation in *Dieffenbachia* and *Aglaonema* is dominant to non-variegation. A single dominant allele (*Pv*) determines the presence of a variegation pattern typical for *Aglaonema maculata* 'Perfection' (Henny 1982). The same allele controls a similar pattern in *Dieffenbachia maculata* 'Hoffmannii', with slight differences due to modifying genes. Studies showed that mutation of the *Pv* allele to *Pv¹* produced the variegation pattern present in *D. maculata* 'Camille' (Henny 1986a). The *Pv¹* allele masks expression of the *Pv* allele in plants containing both alleles.

Inheritance of a white foliar midrib in *Dieffenbachia* is controlled by a single dominant gene (Henny 1983a) linked to the gene controlling foliar variegation. The dominant alleles for each trait are carried on opposite homologous chromosomes.

Six different foliar variegation patterns of *Aglaonema* were found to be governed by a single-locus, multiple-allelic system (Henny 1986b). Each distinct pattern is controlled by a separate dominant allele. The alleles are codominant, allowing for expression of two variegation patterns in the same plant. Several other variegation patterns in *Aglaonema* currently being studied appear to be inherited in the same manner.

OTHER FOLIAGE TRAITS

Leaf shape and the number of leaf spots on *Zantedeschia* hybrids is highly variable, indicating multigenic inheritance. In *Caladium* the heart-shaped (fancy) leaf is controlled by a single gene. One homozygous genotype produces the fancy leaf and the other homozygote produces a strap (ribbon) leaf, with the heterozygote a lance-shaped leaf. Modifying genes have been implicated in affecting intensity of foliar variegation in *Dieffenbachia*. The tendency for plants to develop basal shoots, or suckers, is a desirable trait and appears to be multigenic in *Anthurium* and *Dieffenbachia*. Highly suckering plants of both genera tend to transmit the trait to hybrids in varying degrees.

Petiole color in *Aglaonema*, which includes green, pink, white, and russet, is inherited independently of foliar variegation and appears to be due to the interaction of at least two genes.

FLORAL CHARACTERISTICS

Aroids have an inflorescence that consists of a spadix enclosed by a modified bract called a spathe (see Plate 7-2). The spathe encompasses the spadix and serves as protection and, in some cases, as an indicator of anthesis. The spadix is a fleshy spike covered with many small flowers that may be unisexual or bisexual depending on the genus. *Anthurium*, *Epipremnum*, and *Spathiphyllum* have bisexual flowers. In genera with bisexual flowers, the entire spadix is covered with similar-appearing flowers. *Aglaonema*, *Cala-*

Table 7-1. Ten Important Aroid Genera and a Summary of Current Breeding Activity

Genus	Major Species	Important Traits	Current Breeding Activity*	Commercial Value
Aglaonema	commutatum costatum nitidum rotundum	leaf shape leaf variegation petiole color branching chilling resistance	academic commercial hobby	high
Alocasia	×amazonica cuprea guttata	leaf shape leaf color branching dwarf size	commercial hobby	fairly low
Anthurium	andraeanum clarinervium crystallinum hookeri scherzerianum	early flowering flower color and size branching	academic commercial hobby	high
Caladium	bicolor ×hortulanum lindenii	leaf shape and color leaf venation color vigor dwarf size	academic	high
Dieffenbachia	amoena maculata	leaf shape and color petiole color branching dwarf or large sizes	academic commercial hobby	high
Epipremnum	aureum	leaf color branching dwarf size	academic	high
Philodendron	bipennifolium laciniatum scandens selloum squamiferum	leaf color and size branching dwarf sizes	commercial	moderate
Spathiphyllum	cannifolium floribundum phryniifolium	early flowering continual flowering disease resistance	academic commercial hobby	high

Genus	Major Species	Important Traits	Current Breeding Activity*	Commercial Value
Syngonium	auritum podophyllum wendlandii	leaf color and size branching dwarf size	commercial	high
Zantedeschia	aethiopica elliottiana rehmannii	flower color vigor	commercial	high

*academic = research conducted at public institutions such as universities or research stations; commercial = research by commercial nurseries or companies; and, hobby = research conducted by private individuals.

dium, *Dieffenbachia*, *Philodendron*, and *Syngonium* flowers are unisexual. Spadices with unisexual flowers usually contain male flowers on the upper half and female flowers on the lower portion, with a small area between devoid of flowers (Figure 7-1).

Colorful and long-lasting spathes, such as those of *Anthurium* and *Zantedeschia*, are highly valued as cut flowers. The showy white *Spathiphyllum* spathes enhance that genus's popularity as a flowering foliage plant.

FLOWERING

In the genus *Anthurium*, flower production is continuous once plants reach maturity. Differences in the natural flowering cycles of aroid species within the same genus can be frustrating for anyone interested in breeding, and careful planning is required to ensure a sufficient supply of usable flowers for breeding. *Aglaonema*, *Dieffenbachia*, *Philodendron*, and *Spathiphyllum* flower naturally in late winter or spring (flowering times vary depending on environmental conditions and the individual species or cultivars). None of these genera produces large numbers of inflorescences. For example, *Aglaonema*, *Dieffenbachia*, and *Philodendron* produce only three to five inflorescences per stem per year.

Aroid breeding has benefited from recent studies demonstrating that *Aglaonema*, *Dieffenbachia*, *Spathiphyllum*, and *Zantedeschia* can be induced to flower at any time during the year when mature plants are treated with gibberellic acid (GA_3), a synthetic plant hormone. Treatment generally con-

Figure 7-1. Typical aroid inflorescences: (left to right) *Spathiphyllum, Anthurium, Dieffenbachia,* and *Aglaonema. Spathiphyllum* and *Anthurium* have bisexual flowers and *Dieffenbachia* and *Aglaonema* have unisexual flowers, with male (M) flowers on the top half of the spadix and female (F) flowers on the bottom.

sists of a single foliar spray with approximately 250 ppm active ingredient of GA₃. Following treatment, plants flower within 3 to 5 months, depending on the genus. Fortunately, different species and cultivars within a genus generally flower together following treatment with GA₃. One additional benefit of using GA₃ to induce flowering is that treated plants tend to produce more flowers than those flowering naturally. Some inflorescences produced following GA₃ treatment are deformed, but I have observed no detrimental effects on fertility. Although rates and methodology are still being tested, data show that GA₃ treatment may also be used to induce flowering of *Epipremnum* and *Syngonium.*

Hybridization Mechanics

GENERA WITH UNISEXUAL FLOWERS

This discussion will focus on *Aglaonema* and *Dieffenbachia,* but the techniques also apply to *Caladium, Philodendron,* and *Zantedeschia* and other aroids that possess unisexual flowers. In these genera, female flowers on the same spadix mature simultaneously, as do male flowers. However, female flowers (located on the lower half of the spadix) are receptive for pollination before male flowers produce pollen. This phenomenon discourages self-pollination while promoting outcrossing in nature. Therefore it is necessary to obtain pollen from a separate inflorescence and manually transfer it to the inflorescence selected as the seed parent. Pollen can be collected by using a small soft brush and brushing the pollen into a container (such as a stiff piece of paper, a cup, or a jar cap), or the entire inflorescence may be removed and turned so that the spathe is on the bottom and acts as the container to catch any pollen that becomes dislodged from the spadix.

Pollination can be easily accomplished using the same brush that was used to collect the pollen. First make the brush sticky by gently touching it to the stigmatic surfaces of the female flowers, then dip the brush into the pollen supply and deposit the pollen on the stigmatic surfaces of receptive flowers (Figure 7-2).

Receptivity of female flowers coincides with the unfurling of the spathe, which makes the flowers accessible for pollination. In some *Philodendron*

Figure 7-2. Close-up of *Dieffenbachia* female flowers (F) being pollinated using a small brush. The white structures are called staminoids (S) and have no known function in seed production.

species the entire inflorescence becomes warm to the touch as an indicator of receptivity. Spathes normally begin to unfurl at night and pollinations may be made anytime the following day. Receptivity of *Aglaonema* and *Dieffenbachia* flowers lasts at least 24 hours, as evidenced by pollen-germination studies. Seed has been obtained from flowers of both genera that were pollinated one day after spathe unfurling, but the number of seeds is small. Female flowers do not support pollen germination once pollen is produced by the male flowers of the same inflorescence. By this time, flower surfaces will have become discolored and mushy.

Following pollination, *Dieffenbachia* flowers require 100% relative humidity for pollen germination (Henny 1980b). To maintain high humidity, the entire spadix should be wrapped with moistened paper toweling and enclosed in a plastic bag (Plate 7-3). The cover is removed the next day so as not to interfere with pollen production. *Aglaonema* also yields better pollen germination when provided with high humidity after pollination, but it is not quite as particular as *Dieffenbachia*. There are no reports that *Caladium*, *Philodendron*, or *Zantedeschia* require high humidity for seed set.

GENERA WITH BISEXUAL FLOWERS

In aroid genera with bisexual flowers, such as *Anthurium* and *Spathiphyllum*, the spathe unfurls to expose the spadix several days before female flowers become receptive. All flowers on a *Spathiphyllum* spadix mature simultaneously, whereas in *Anthurium* new flowers become receptive each day, beginning at the spadix base and advancing gradually toward the top over a period of approximately 2 weeks. In these genera, female receptivity is indicated by a glistening shine of stigmatic surfaces, a stickiness to the touch, and sometimes accompanying small drops of exudate. Female flowers may stay in this state for more than a day, so timing of pollination is not as critical as with unisexual genera.

When no longer receptive, the stigmatic surfaces dry and become brown. At this stage pollen begins to appear along the spadix, usually at the bottom first and proceeding toward the top. Pollen is available for several days on *Anthurium* flowers because of the uneven maturation of individual female flowers. A *Spathiphyllum* inflorescence also will produce pollen over a 2- to 3-day period. *Anthurium* pollen is not wind blown. It can easily be transferred by collecting it on your fingertips then gently rubbing it on the receptive female flowers. *Spathiphyllum* pollen is lighter and tends to blow in the air, so use a brush and collect it in a container before attempting a pollination.

To achieve maximum seed production, an *Anthurium* spadix may need to be pollinated more than once, whereas it is possible to fertilize an entire *Spathiphyllum* spadix with one pollination. No special environmental manipulation is needed to ensure seed set for *Anthurium* or *Spathiphyllum*.

POLLEN STORAGE AND SEED GERMINATION

Very little information is available regarding storage of aroid pollen. However, if pollen is in short supply, it can be stored in a refrigerator. *Philodendron* and *Spathiphyllum* pollen may be stored for several days or weeks in this manner. *Aglaonema* and *Dieffenbachia* pollen is short-lived, and germination ability declines within 1 to 2 days of storage. It is best to use fresh pollen from those genera if possible.

If successfully pollinated, *Caladium* fruit will mature in 5 to 6 weeks and *Dieffenbachia* fruit within 10 to 12 weeks. *Anthurium* fruit will require up to 6 months to ripen, whereas *Philodendron* fruit vary from 2 to 6 months, depending on the species. *Aglaonema* fruit mature in 4 to 6 months, although some hybrids have taken one year to develop ripe fruit. *Zantedeschia* crosses made in June yield mature seed by November.

Seed maturity in *Dieffenbachia* and *Aglaonema* is indicated by the seed covering turning bright red (Plate 7-4). *Anthurium* and *Spathiphyllum* spadices begin to change color, soften, and appear to be emitting the mature seeds.

To achieve good germination, the seed should be separated from the spadix. Cleaning seeds speeds germination and lessens the chance of disease starting in the decaying fruit. For genera like *Dieffenbachia* and *Aglaonema* that have large seeds, pick off the red berry-like fruit, remove the fleshy seed covering, and plant. Genera with large numbers of small seeds, such as *Spathiphyllum*, are more difficult. It is easiest to harvest the entire spadix when mature (indicated by a change in color from green to yellow and a softening of the tissue), placing it in a plastic bag with a little water. The spadix tissue will decay in a few days, allowing the seeds to be removed by gently washing them on a screen small enough to catch the seeds but letting the rotted spadix tissue fall through.

Once cleaned, seeds should be planted before they dry. Good germination is achieved if the seeds are sown on the top of a moist medium and covered with plastic or some other material to prevent drying. Soil temperature should be kept at a minimum of 70°F (21°C). Aroid seed have no dormancy requirements and begin to grow as soon as sown. They can be removed from the germination chambers and repotted once the first true leaves are produced. Most aroid seedlings require at least 1 to 2 years before they are large enough to be evaluated.

There are many other genera of ornamental aroids that have not been specifically discussed in this chapter, and unfortunately little published information is available regarding culture or breeding of these plants. Hopefully, more aroid enthusiasts will take an active interest in studying their unique breeding systems and eventually unleash this vast amount of untapped genetic potential. An ornamental aroid resource list follows and should provide a good starting place for anyone interested in studying this large family of plants.

Resources

COLLECTIONS

Atlanta Botanical Garden
c/o The Fuqua Conservatory
P.O. Box 77246
Atlanta, GA 30357
U.S.A.

Brooklyn Botanic Garden
1000 Washington Avenue
Brooklyn, NY 11225
U.S.A.

Curador da Colecão de Araceae
Jardim Botânico do Rio de Janeiro
Secão de Botânico do Rio de Janeiro
22460.030 Rio de Janeiro
Brazil

Flecker Botanic Gardens
CCC P.O. Box 359
Cairns, Queensland 4870
Australia
phone: (61) 70-502454
fax: (61) 70-321183

Longwood Gardens
P.O. Box 501
409 Conservatory Road
Kennett Square, PA 19348
U.S.A.

Lyon Arboretum
3860 Manoa Road
Honolulu, HI 96822
U.S.A.
phone: 808-988-3177
fax: 808-988-4231

Marie Selby Botanical Gardens
811 S. Palm Avenue
Sarasota, FL 34236
U.S.A.
phone: 941-366-5730
fax: 941-366-9807

Missouri Botanical Garden
P.O. Box 299
St. Louis, MO 63166
U.S.A.
phone: 314-577-5111
fax: 314-577-9595

Royal Botanic Gardens, Kew
Richmond, Surrey TW9 3AB
England
phone: (44) 181-332-5207
fax: (44) 181-332-5278

SUPPLIERS

The International Aroid Society can help those interested in locating hard-to-find aroids. For those just beginning a collection, the Florida Nurserymen and Growers Association is a good place to start.

Florida Nurserymen and Growers Association
1533 Park Center Drive
Orlando, FL 32835-5705
U.S.A.
phone: 407-295-7994 or 800-375-3642
fax: 407-295-1619

INTERNATIONAL REGISTRATION AUTHORITY
International Aroid Society
Attention: John Banta
Route 2, Box 144
Alva, FL 33920
U.S.A.

PLANT SOCIETIES
Members of the International Aroid Society (I.A.S.) receive the quarterly *Aroideana*, which is an illustrated publication containing information relating to all aspects of aroid botany, collecting, horticulture, taxonomy, and breeding. The I.A.S. 1995 directory listed 447 members worldwide.

International Aroid Society
P.O. Box 43-1853
South Miami, FL 33143-1853
U.S.A.

References and Additional Reading

Conover, C. A., and R. T. Poole. 1984. Light and fertilizer recommendations for production of acclimatized potted foliage plants. AREC-A Research Report RH-84-7.

Garner, L. 1983. Hybridizing alocasia for the landscape. *Aroideana* 6: 74–81.

Hartman, R. D., E. M. Hawkins, J. F. Knauss, and F. W. Zettler. 1972. Seed propagation of *Caladium* and *Dieffenbachia*. *Proceedings of the Florida State Horticultural Society* 85: 404–409.

Henny, R. J. 1980a. Gibberellic acid (GA₃) induces flowering in *Dieffenbachia maculata* 'Perfection'. *HortScience* 15: 613.

―――. 1980b. Relative humidity affects *in vivo* pollen germination and seed production in *Dieffenbachia maculata* 'Perfection'. *Journal of the American Society for Horticultural Science* 105: 546–548.

―――. 1981. Promotion of flowering in *Spathiphyllum* 'Mauna Loa' with gibberellic acid. *HortScience* 16: 554–555.

―――. 1982. Inheritance of foliar variegation in two *Dieffenbachia* cultivars. *Journal of Heredity* 73: 384.

―――. 1983a. Inheritance of the white foliar midrib in *Dieffenbachia* and its linkage with the gene for foliar variegation. *Journal of Heredity* 74: 483–484.

―――. 1983b. Flowering of *Aglaonema commutatum* 'Treubii' following treatment with gibberellic acid. *HortScience* 18: 374.

―――. 1985. *In vivo* pollen germination of *Aglaonema* affected by relative humidity. *HortScience* 20: 142–143.

―――. 1986a. Inheritance of foliar variegation in *Dieffenbachia maculata* 'Camille'. *Journal of Heredity* 77: 285–286.

―――. 1986b. Single locus, multiallelic inheritance of foliar variegation in *Aglaonema*. *Journal of Heredity* 77: 214–215.

————. 1988. Ornamental aroids: Culture and breeding. *Horticultural Reviews.* Vol. X. Ed. J. Janick. Westport, Conn.: AVI Publishing. 1–33.

Joiner, J. N. 1981. *Foliage Plant Production.* Englewood Cliffs, N.J.: Prentice-Hall.

Kamemoto, H., R. Y. Iwata, and M. Marutani. 1984. Genetics of spathe color in *Anthurium andraeanum* Andre. *HortScience* 19: 547 (Abstr.).

Kamemoto, H., H. Y. Nakasone, and M. Aragaki. 1968. Improvement of anthuriums through breeding. *Proceedings of the Tropical Region of the American Society for Horticultural Science* 12: 267–273.

Madison, M. 1979. Protection of developing seeds in neotropical Araceae. *Aroideana* 2: 52–61.

McColley, R. H., and H. N. Miller. 1965. Philodendron improvement through hybridization. *Proceedings of the Florida State Horticultural Society* 78: 409–415.

Shibuya, R. 1956. Intercrossing among pink calla, white-spotted calla and yellow calla. Tokyo: Kasai Publishing and Printing.

Wilfret, G. J. 1986. Inheritance of leaf shape and color patterns in *Caladium* (Araceae). *HortScience* 21: 750.

Wilfret, G. J., and T. J. Sheehan. 1981. Development of new foliage plant cultivars. In *Foliage Plant Production.* Ed. J. N. Joiner. Englewood Cliffs, N.J.: Prentice-Hall.

Zettler, F. W., and M. M. Abo El-Nil. 1979. Mode of inheritance of foliage color in caladium. *Journal of Heredity* 70: 433–435.

8 Breeding African Violets

Jeffrey L. Smith

African violets are highly popular and familiar flowering houseplants. Many people, remembering their mother's and grandmother's plants, assume that all African violets have deep blue flowers and plain green leaves. Though this was true of the original plants brought into cultivation in about 1900, mutations and the work of enthusiastic plant breeders have developed modern African violets with many flower colors, leaf types, and plant growth forms (Plate 8-1). Today's African violets have colors that include white, several shades of blue, purple, red, pink, lavender, coral, coral-red, and even flowers marked with green, ivory, and yellow. The flowers may be bicolor, multicolor, and edged in white, pink, or red. Some flowers, called fantasies, are spotted and streaked with blue, red, or white markings. There are singles, semi-doubles, full doubles, star-shaped blooms, bell-shaped blooms, and flowers with fringes or ruffles. The leaves of African violets may be plain, girl leaf, ruffled, longifolia, or bustled. The leaves may have green, silver, or red backings and can be variegated in white, pink, tan, cream, or yellow-green. The plants range in size from miniatures that measure only 1½ to 2 inches (about 3.5–5 cm) across to large trailing specimens that can reach more than one meter in diameter. The explosion of colors and forms in this plant group, especially in the last 50 years, is truly remarkable and stands as a monument to the work of hybridizers and growers.

African violets belong to the genus *Saintpaulia* and are members of the gesneriad family (Gesneriaceae). The common name African violet acknowledges the origin of the genus on the African continent and the observation that the flowers are somewhat similar in color and shape to the woodland violets (family Violaceae). African violets, however, are *not* related to the woodland violets, and hybridization efforts with members of the Violaceae are futile. The genus is found in the forest understory and mountain ledge areas of the east African countries of Kenya and Tanzania.

The genus *Saintpaulia* consists of 20 recognized species and 3 types that are commonly encountered but are not recognized as individual species.

Saintpaulia brevipilosa B. L. Burtt 1964

Flowers are small, usually four per stalk, and light purple with dark purple centers. The leaves are thin, round, and light green with pale undersides. The plant normally forms a single crown. The petioles are often twisted so the leaves do not lay flat.

Saintpaulia confusa B. L. Burtt 1956

Flowers are medium sized, two per stalk, and blue-violet in color. The leaves are longer than wide, slightly pointed, thin, slightly toothed, and medium to light green in color. The plant frequently forms multiple crowns by suckering but is not a true trailer.

Saintpaulia difficilis B. L. Burtt 1958

Flowers are medium sized, five to seven per stalk, and dark blue. The leaves are thin, hairy, pointed, and light yellow-green with pale undersides. The plant grows upright with a single crown.

Saintpaulia diplotricha B. L. Burtt 1947

Several forms of this species are recognized. The plants have five to seven pale lilac blossoms per stalk. The leaves are dark green, thick, serrated, and often have a pale red backing. The plants usually grow with a single crown.

Saintpaulia goetzeana Engler 1900

The flowers have lilac upper lobes and white lower lobes, but are rarely produced due to the extremes in temperature needed to induce flowering. The leaves are small, round, and dark green with smooth edges. The growth habit is creeping, and the plant typically forms multiple crowns.

Saintpaulia grandifolia B. L. Burtt 1958

Several forms of this species are recognized, which differ in the texture of the leaves. The flowers are dark blue and numerous. The leaves are large, thin, and light green with long pliable petioles. The growth form is a single crown and specimens can easily reach 12 to 16 inches (30–40 cm) in diameter.

Saintpaulia grotei Engler 1921

The flowers are medium sized, one to two per stalk, and blue-violet with dark centers. The leaves are thin, large, round, and deeply toothed. The plants are large growing trailers and are an important genetic source of the trailing habit. A tetraploid version and a chimera sport that has flowers with white stripes are known.

Saintpaulia inconspicua B. L. Burtt 1958
This plant is reported to have small, blue-spotted white blossoms and a trailer growth habit. The leaves are small and nearly hairless, except on the leaf margins. Currently believed to be extinct.

Saintpaulia intermedia B. L. Burtt 1958
The flowers are medium blue and clustered five or six to a stalk. The leaves are almost round, toothed, and covered with dense short hair. The leaves are dark green on top and red on the bottom with prominent green veins. The plants are intermediate between rosette and trailing, becoming more trailing with maturity.

Saintpaulia ionantha H. Wendland 1893
The flowers are medium blue and grow four to five per stalk. The leaves are serrated and are dark green with red backing. The leaf blades may cup upwards and the entire leaf may droop slightly when grown in high temperatures. The plants are usually grown as a single crown, but they do show some tendency to sucker. Several forms of this species are known, including a tetraploid and one with white flowers.

Saintpaulia magungensis E. P. Roberts 1950
There are three varieties recognized for this species.
  Saintpaulia magungensis var. *magungensis*—This variety is the original plant described by Roberts. It has flowers that are blue-violet with dark centers and are usually two flowers per stalk. The leaves are round, small, and often cupped downwards. The plant has a trailer growth form.
  Saintpaulia magungensis var. *minima* (B. L. Burtt 1964)—This variety has very tiny light purple flowers. The leaves are smaller than those of the type species and are lightly serrated. The plant has a trailer growth form and was an important source of genetic material for developing miniature trailers.
  Saintpaulia magungensis var. *occidentalis* (B. L. Burtt 1964)—This variety is a reluctant bloomer, but has violet-blue flowers with two to five blooms per stalk. The leaves are ovate, medium green, shiny, and may have red backing. It tends to form multiple crowns and is a more upright trailer than the type species.

Saintpaulia nitida B. L. Burtt 1958
The flowers are small, dark purple, and five to seven per stalk. The leaves are small, round, shiny, and smooth. They are medium green on top, reddish underneath, and often spoon-shaped. The plants can be grown as single crowns or as multiple crown trailers.

Saintpaulia orbicularis B. L. Burtt 1947
There are two varieties recognized for this species.
   Saintpaulia orbicularis var. *orbicularis*—The flowers are small, five to eight per stalk, and are pale blue to lilac with darker centers. The leaves are thin, shiny, round, and medium green with pale undersides. The leaf blade is often at a sharp angle to the petiole. The plant may grow as a single- or multiple-crown specimen.
   Saintpaulia orbicularis var. *purpurea* (B. L. Burtt 1964)—This variety is very similar to the parent species except that the flowers are dark purple in color.

Saintpaulia pendula B. L. Burtt 1958
There are two varieties recognized for this species.
   Saintpaulia pendula var. *pendula*—The original plant described by Burtt has flowers that are pale blue and found only one per stalk. The leaves are thick, hairy, yellowish green, and toothed. This plant has a modest trailer growth habit.
   Saintpaulia pendula var. *kizarae* (B. L. Burtt 1964)—The flowers of this variety are medium blue-violet and grow two to four per stalk. The leaves are thinner than those of the type species, hairy, medium green, and toothed. The growth habit is trailing, but the plants stay relatively upright and compact.

Saintpaulia pusilla Engler 1900
This plant is described as having tiny mauve top petals and white lower petals above tiny purple-backed triangular leaves. The plant grows as a single crown and is unknown in cultivation. It was thought to be extinct but was recently rediscovered in the wild.

Saintpaulia rupicola B. L. Burtt 1964
The flowers are medium sized and light blue-violet. They are usually four per stalk. The leaves are shiny and medium green. They have light green undersides and brownish petioles. The plants have a single crown that is slanted rather than upright. This species frequently produce suckers, often resulting in multiple-crown specimens.

Saintpaulia shumensis B. L. Burtt 1955
The flowers are small and pale blue to almost white with a dark center. They are usually found one to three per stalk. The leaves are small, round, and bright green, with a "strawberry pebbling" on the surface. Plants are compact with a single crown, but often produce suckers. This species was an important source of genetic material for producing miniatures.

Saintpaulia teitensis B. L. Burtt 1958
The flowers are medium sized, medium blue in color, and produced two to six per stalk. The plants require cold nights to trigger blooming. The leaves are thick, brittle, shiny, and pointed. They are dark green with red undersides. The outer leaves are typically spoon-shaped. The plants are upright growers with a single crown.

Saintpaulia tongwensis B. L. Burtt 1947
The flowers are medium sized and light blue and are produced in large quantities. The leaves are very heavy, hairy, longer than wide, and pointed. The leaves usually have a red reverse and may have a paler green midrib. The plants grow as a single crown and rarely sucker.

Saintpaulia velutina B. L. Burtt 1958
The flowers are small, medium violet, and grow many per stalk. In some instances, the flowers may develop white edges. The leaves are heart-shaped, scalloped, and have a velvety texture due to the long hairs that protrude from the surface. The leaves are dark green on top and dark red underneath. The plant grows as a single crown.

Two additional forms are known for this species. The first form is a tetraploid, which is larger than the diploid version and has dark violet flowers. The second form is a mutation and is sometimes called *Saintpaulia velutina* Light. This plant is a miniature version of the species and has very pale lilac flowers. The leaves are less scalloped and more rounded than those of the type species.

'House of Amani'—This plant is not currently recognized as a separate species but is listed on the African Violet Society of America's "Master Variety List." It has blue-violet flowers that are produced three to five per stalk. The leaves are dark green, toothed, and have a red backing. The plants grow as a single crown. This plant is most likely a form of *Saintpaulia ionantha*.

Saintpaulia 'Robertson'—This plant is the most recent "species" to become available, although it has not yet been recognized as a separate species and may be only a form of *Saintpaulia rupicola*. The flowers are medium blue, large, slightly cupped, and four to six per stalk. The leaves are thick, longer than wide, and pointed. They are medium green and paler underneath. The petioles of mature leaves often curve, bending the leaf blades downward. The plant grows as a single crown.

Saintpaulia 'Sigi Falls'—Though not currently recognized as a separate species, this plant is also listed on the AVSA "Master Variety List." It has medium blue flowers that are produced two to four per stalk. The leaves are large, thick, hairy, elongated, and pointed. They are red underneath and often have a yellow-green midrib area. The plants grow as weak trailers, often forming multiple crowns.

While almost all members of the genus are interfertile, there are no confirmed hybrids between genus *Saintpaulia* and other plant genera. Sources of new genetic material in African violets, therefore, is limited to the members of the genus and the processes of mutation and selected breeding. The development of today's miniatures and trailer cultivars, for example, can be traced to the inclusion of the species *Saintpaulia shumensis* and *S. grotei* in plant hybridization programs. The yellow-flowered African violets, in comparison, had to wait for selective breeding of the proper mutation, as the yellow color could not be introduced into the genus by hybridization with other genera.

Important Breeding Materials

African violets were discovered by European colonists more than 100 years ago. In 1891, Baron Walter von Saint Paul-Illaire, the German Governor of East Africa, sent seeds to his father Ulrich in Hanover, Germany. Ulrich gave some seeds to the well-known botanist Herman Wendland, who was the director and taxonomist of the Royal Botanical Gardens. Wendland declared the plants to be a species of a new genus and named the plant *Saintpaulia ionantha*. *Saintpaulia* honors the family of the Baron, while *ion* is Greek for "violet-like" or "violet-colored" and *antha* refers to "flower."

In 1893 these new plants were shown by Wendland at the International Horticultural Exhibit in Germany, where they caused great excitement. These small plants, with their production of flowers at all times of the year, showed great potential as a commercial hothouse species. Seeds and plants were quickly dispersed. Some flowering plants were reported in the Royal Botanic Gardens of Kew, England, later that same year. In 1894, the first plants were taken to the United States by a New York florist, George Stumph. Unfortunately, a lack of knowledge of the proper growing conditions for the species curtailed its commercial value for many years. African violets gained a reputation for being difficult and demanding to raise.

Records of the time suggest that African violets were originally propagated mostly by seed, which was important to the eventual genetic development of the plants as offspring were quickly found that differed from the parents. A "plum-red" African violet was reported in 1894. By the turn of the century, the seedhouse of Ernst Benary in Germany announced the production of deep blue African violets and white African violets. The Sutton seedhouse in England also developed several types, many differing in the shade of blue. Some authorities suspect that Wendland's original seed stock contained two species, *Saintpaulia ionantha* and *S. confusa*, which gave even more genetic diversity to the early cultivars.

In 1926 the Armacost and Royston greenhouse of Los Angeles decided to take a chance on African violets. They imported seed from both the Benary and Sutton seedhouses and bred them. From more than 1000 seedlings, they selected only 10 with commercial potential. All were in the blue-violet-purple color range and were named as follows: 'Admiral', 'Amethyst', 'Blue Boy', 'Commodore', 'Mermaid', 'Neptune', 'Norseman', 'Number 32', 'Sailor Boy', and 'Viking'. These 10 cultivars were propagated vegetatively in large numbers and offered for sale in 1935. Because of the ease with which African violets grow in the California climate and an increasing knowledge of their cultural needs, these "original 10" cultivars were the first large-scale commercial success for the genus. They served as important genetic source material for later hybridization work and are still grown by hobbyists today.

The success of the "original 10" attracted the attention of larger nurseries, which soon realized the potential of the compact, free-flowering plants for indoor growing. Most of these nurseries also carried out programs of hybridization, and new cultivars and colors were soon created. African violets also have a striking tendency to mutate or sport, which created important sources of new genetic material. A few of these mutations are listed in Table 8-1.

During the 1950s, patented lines and cultivars were developed in Germany especially for commercial sales. These plants were selected to have full clusters of blooms held above the center of the plant on strong stems and to hold up well to the demands of commercial propagation and sale. Widely available today, the most popular lines are Rhapsodie, Ballet, and Optimara. Many cultivars, including a variety of flower colors, are found within each line. The genetic traits that have made these lines so successful are still in demand by breeders, and they are frequently included in hybridization programs.

Two types of African violets that have received a great deal of hybridi-

Table 8-1. Important Mutations in African Violets *(Saintpaulia)*

Mutation	Date	Comment
Double flowers	1939	Mutant of 'Blue Boy'.
Pink flowers	1940	Mutant of 'Blue Boy', introduced under the name 'Pink Beauty'.
Girl foliage	1941	Mutant of 'Blue Boy', introduced under the name 'Blue Girl'. The foliage has a predominant splotch of white at the base of the blade.
Fantasy flowers	1949	Mutant with lavender flowers splashed with spots and streaks of dark purple. The first cultivar was 'Fantasy'
Geneva edges	1950	Mutant that produces a white edge on the flower. The first cultivar was 'Lady Geneva'.
Star-shaped flowers	1952	These blossoms consist of five equally spaced petals, giving the appearance of a star. The first cultivar was 'Purple Star'.
Fringed flowers	1953	The petals are fringed, giving the blossoms a ruffled appearance.
Bustled foliage	1957	Mutant of 'Purple Prince' with small leaf blades attached to the side or on the back of the main blade. First cultivar was 'Bustles'.
Tommie Lou variegation	1959	A type of variegated foliage found as a sport of 'White Pride' by Tommie Louise Oden. The variegation is on the leaf edges.
Lilian Jarrett or mosaic variegation	1961	A type of variegated foliage found in a sport of 'Lilian Jarrett'. Variegation appears in the center areas of the leaf blade.
Coral pigments	1963	A new color mutation that gave rise to coral and coral-red flowers. The first cultivar was 'Coral Satin'.
Yellow flowers	1989	The newest color mutation. The first cultivars were 'His Promise' and 'Majesty'.

zation attention in the last 30 years are the miniatures and the trailers. Miniatures are characterized by having a diameter of 6 inches (15 cm) or less when mature. Because they take so little space to grow, the miniatures have become increasingly popular for both hobbyist and commercial growers. Although miniatures appeared sporadically in the early hybridization programs, the inclusion of the miniature species, such as *Saintpaulia shumensis*, as a source of genetic material led to the development of an extremely large number of miniature cultivars. Today's miniatures come in a full range of colors, flower styles, and leaf types and are the focus of the work of a number of commercial and hobbyist hybridizers.

Trailing African violets have elongated stems rather than the rosette growth form found in *Saintpaulia ionantha*. This growth pattern is evident in several of the species, including *S. grotei*, which was used in some of the first crosses. The first trailers were released in 1954 by Frank and Anne Tinari, but they were not well received by the public. The early trailers were large, coarse plants that were not very floriferous. Later work, using *S. magungensis* var. *minima* as the genetic source for trailing, produced miniature and semi-miniature trailers. Possibly because of their size, these smaller versions of the trailing African violet have become more popular. Today's trailers are available in a more limited number of colors and leaf types compared to the miniatures, but breeding efforts are continuing to bring the entire color spectrum to these violets as well.

Hybridization work with the other African violet species appears to be limited. Although the species are likely fertile with any other African violet cultivar, their genetic tendency to produce single-petaled blue flowers that drop from the flower stalk is undesirable and is a detriment to most hybridization programs. Other characteristics, such as different foliage types or blooming in colder temperatures, are available in the genetic material of the species, but these traits have been little utilized in breeding programs.

The current trends in breeding African violets are focused on developing continuous flowering, new colors such as true crimson and canary yellow, improved resistance to disease and pests, new blooming patterns, improved symmetry, and new combinations of currently available traits within the same plant. New mutations are also constantly being sought for inclusion into hybridization programs. Improved knowledge of African violet genetics is permitting the development of new combinations, such as plants with double coral-red flowers on mosaic variegation. Growers are not looking to produce duplicates of existing cultivars, but to develop different and exciting new combinations. With several thousand cultivars already available to choose from, only those plants with exceptional characteristics will stand the test of time and find favor with an increasingly fickle public.

Important Traits and Breeding Objectives

The goals in the breeding of African violets have become polarized since the commercial success of the "original 10" cultivars. There are now two distinct markets for new cultivars, and these markets have different criteria and objectives for what makes a successful plant. Hybridizers working with the goals of one group will usually not produce plants that meet the demands of the other. These two groups are the commercial market (or "supermarket violets") and the hobbyist market.

The production of African violets for commercial sales is a big business. Estimates by Holtkamp Greenhouses, producers of the Optimara series, show production figures of more than 35 million plants in 1992. In order to be profitable, the commercial producers must raise as many plants to flowering size in as short a time as possible. The plants must produce a large number of flowers in eye-attracting colors. They must also hold up well to the changing environmental conditions that may occur en route so that the plants arrive in the best possible condition for sale. Relatively few cultivars meet all these demands, and therefore a commercial grower will often raise many plants of only a selected few (20 to 30) cultivars.

Because of these demands, breeding programs for commercial cultivars often selected plants for the following traits: moderate plant size; rapid growth; flowers in bright colors that are held in a nosegay arrangement above the foliage; soft leaves that do not break when the plants are sleeved for shipping; flowers that do not drop from the bloom stalks; and flower longevity. Traits that are selected against include: full double flowers (they take longer to mature and open than singles or semi-doubles), variegated foliage (they grow slower than solid-foliage types), large plants (not as many can be grown in the same amount of space), and colors such as coral or coral-red (they do not have the same flower longevity or eye appeal as other colors).

Recently, commercial growers have been increasing the number of multicolor-bloom cultivars in their stock. These plants have white or colored edges, or they may have white flowers with colored eyes. The plants are very popular with the buying public, but these traits are sometimes genetically unstable and are often changed in expression by the growing temperatures. Fantasy flowers—those with spots or splashes of a contrasting color—are also popular, but they often do not reproduce true by leaf cuttings. Commercial growers can hardly afford the space for fantasies when more than half of the vegetatively produced offspring may not show the fantasy flower pattern.

Miniature African violets have become an increasingly important crop for commercial growers. These plants require less space and mature more quickly than the standard-sized plants. Miniatures that use a wick system for watering and are sold with small crystal-like water reservoirs have been very popular. They are easy to maintain in the salesroom, they do not require a great deal of display space, and the small size is appealing to many buyers. Miniatures will likely continue to hold a significant percentage of the commercial market in the future.

The hobbyist market provides plants for the persons who grow African violets for pleasure and for show. The plant traits that are attractive to the hobbyist are often very different from those of the commercial growers. The hobbyist is usually willing to keep cultivars that grow slowly, are very large in size, and show unusual colors or traits. In fact, many hobbyists select cultivars based on their unusual traits; the more unusual the better. Some examples of traits selected by the hobbyist grower include: variegated foliage, full double blooms, blooms edged in green or other colors, the coral group of flower colors, yellow flowers (actually white with yellow markings), bell-shaped blooms, fantasy flowers, and extremely large or small plant size.

Miniatures are very popular with the hobbyist grower, and trailers, which have almost no commercial sales, are also becoming more popular. Because of the emphasis on the different and the unusual, suppliers for the hobbyist market often grow as many different cultivars as possible (up to 300 or 400 types), but raise only a relatively small number of plants of each cultivar for sale.

The African Violet Society of America (AVSA), the largest organization for African violet growers, has established guidelines for the judging of plants competing in African violet shows. The AVSA scale of points for judging standard (plants larger than 8 inches or 20 cm in diameter) and miniature African violets is as follows:

Symmetry (leaf pattern)	25 points
Condition (cultural perfection)	25 points
Quantity of bloom	25 points
Size and type of blossom	15 points
Color of blossom	10 points

Since half of the points in the competition are based on the growth of a plant's leaves, successful show cultivars must have large leaves that grow in a perfect rosette or radiate from the center like spokes on a wagon wheel (Figure 8-1). The foliage must grow straight, without twisting or turning, from the center of the plant to the leaf edges. Each row of leaves must overlap the row below without gaps or spaces. Hybridizers that breed cultivars for show must select plants that have these leaf characteristics. Although the flower characteristics are also important, a cultivar that does not have the proper foliage will not win awards and will not become a good selling cultivar on the hobbyist market. Cultivars that are popular on the hobbyist market are not always good show plants, but the ones that remain popular for several years often have a good track record in shows.

Figure 8-1. Hobbyist plant demonstrating the wagon-wheel growth form and Tommie Lou leaf variegation. Note how the leaves all radiate from the center of the plant. (Photo by Jeffrey L. Smith)

The genetic control of traits in African violets has been studied for many years. In many cases, however, hybridizers have relied on a philosophy of "breed the best with the best and hope for the best." Though this method has produced many outstanding cultivars, it does rely on trial-and-error and may prevent the purposeful breeding of plants with specific combinations of traits. A summary of some of the genetic traits in African violets and their inheritance patterns is given in Table 8-2.

Two types of leaf variegation in African violets are maternally inherited. Variegated offspring will only be produced if the seed parent, not the pollen parent, has the variegated foliage. Tommie Lou variegation is characterized by leaves that have white or tan areas on the edges of the leaf blade

Table 8-2. Summary of the Genetic Control of Some African Violet Traits

	Dominant	to	Recessive
Flower Traits	blue flowers		all flower colors
	red flowers		pink flowers
	non-white flowers		white flowers
	non-coral colors		coral colors
	coral red		coral pink
	geneva edges		solid edges
	fringed edges		non-fringed edges
	raspberry edges		solid edges
	dogwood dots		solid flowers
	fantasy flowers		solid flowers
	double flowers		non-double flowers
	semi-double flowers		single flowers
	violet-shaped flowers		star-shaped flowers
	pale colors		dark colors
Leaf Traits	girl foliage		boy foliage
	ruffled foliage		plain foliage
	holly foliage		plain foliage
	plain foliage		spooned foliage
	bustled foliage		plain foliage
	longifolia shape		rounded shape
	red backing		green backing

(see Figure 8-1). The extent of the variegation is variable, with leaves ranging from having only slight markings to being almost completely white. If the genetic factor that gives the lower leaf surface a red pigment is also present, the white areas may be colored pink. Crown variegation, also known as champion variegation, is characterized by the young leaves in the center of the crown showing yellow or pale green color. This variegation is usually lost as the leaves mature. Both Tommie Lou and crown variegation types are unstable and are affected by temperature (cooler temperatures increase the amount of variegation) and fertilizer types (high nitrogen and low phosphorus increase the amount of variegation).

The third type of leaf variegation is known as mosaic or Lilian Jarrett variegation. This foliage type is characterized by splashes of pink or yellow in the center of the leaf blades. Mosaic variegation is inherited as a recessive, but can only be expressed through the maternal line. Using a mosaic variegated plant as the seed parent will not give variegated offspring unless the pollen parent also carries this trait. This genetic complexity has made the mosaic variegation trait difficult to breed for, and relatively few cultivars are available with this trait.

Hybridization Mechanics

The genus *Saintpaulia* is fairly easy to work with for hybridization purposes. The flower parts are relatively large and are easily accessible. The anthers do not dehisce or shed their pollen, so steps such as emasculation or bagging are not usually necessary to prevent unwanted pollinations. There are, however, a few tricks that will make hybridization attempts more successful.

When choosing the pollen parent, select a flower that is newly opened and has large, prominent yellow anthers. Since the double-petal characteristic involves the modification of stamens into petals, using cultivars with single or semi-double flowers will provide the best anthers and pollen. Fully double flowers are frequently male sterile because all the stamens have been converted into petals. These cultivars cannot serve as a pollen source, but they can be used as a seed parent.

The anthers must be split open to release pollen. This can be accomplished by removing the anther from the flower and splitting the anther open with a razor blade or thumbnail. If the insides of the anther are wet-looking or mushy, there will not be any usable pollen for the cross and another anther should be selected. The pollen should appear as a yellow-white powder. It can be spilled onto a small piece of black paper (for easy visibility) or the entire anther can be carried to the selected seed parent flower for pollination.

The pistil of African violet flowers matures several days after the flower opens. When receptive for pollination, the stigma at the tip of the pistil should look slightly wet or shiny. The two stigma lobes may also have spread slightly apart. If the flower has many petals and finding the pistil is difficult, the extra petal material can be carefully trimmed to expose the style and stigma for pollination.

Pollination is accomplished by touching the receptive stigma to the pollen. If the stigma is receptive, the pollen should adhere to it. If the pollen does not stick, then the stigma may not have been mature enough, in which case the cross will usually fail to take.

One method of accomplishing pollination is to split open the anther to expose the pollen, then gently insert the stigma into the opening. This method usually ensures that an adequate supply of pollen covers the stigma and gives a good seed set. The transfer of pollen to the stigma can also be accomplished with an artist's brush, although care must be taken to ensure that enough pollen reaches the stigma, as the pollen will not stick well to the hairs of the brush. The brush must also be thoroughly cleaned with alcohol when different pollen parents are used. After pollination is complete, the flower should be labeled with a small tag indicating the name of the pollen parent and the date of the cross.

Several different crosses can be made on a single plant at the same time, as long as proper labeling clearly identifies the pollen parent for each cross. In fact, the plant is more likely to carry the seed pods to maturity if several flowers on the same flower stalk are pollinated.

Pollen can be stored for later use by placing either anthers or pollen in an air-tight container with a small amount of silica gel desiccant. The jars can be stored in a refrigerator and the pollen will remain viable for at least 2 years.

Key hints for successful pollination are summarized here:

- Use a newly opened flower with prominent anthers as the pollen source.
- Single or semi-double cultivars have larger anthers and make the best pollen sources.
- The pollen should be dry and powdery, not wet and mushy.
- Use as the seed parent a flower that has been open for several days. The stigma should look wet or sticky when receptive.
- Seed set is usually best when the first three to four flowers of the inflorescence or flower stalk are used.
- Setting seed on several flowers on the same inflorescence will help prevent the seed pods from aborting.
- Pollen germination is enhanced by high humidity. Make crosses on rainy days or raise the humidity around the flowers by misting.
- Crosses can be made anytime of the year, but high temperatures may prevent the seeds from maturing. In hot climates, make the pollinations during fall or winter.

If the pollination was successful, the ovary at the base of the pistil should enlarge within 2 weeks. If the petals and pistil appear to shrivel and dry up, then the cross was not successful. Once the seed pods are set, the plant does not require any special watering or fertilization. It may be a good idea to grow the plant a little on the dry side to help prevent the growth of mildew on the seed pods.

The seed pods or fruit of African violets are highly variable in size and shape. Some will be short and round, while others will be long and skinny. The fruit shape is genetically controlled and represents the species ancestry of the cultivar. The seed pods will reach full size quickly and will not change appearance during the several months of their maturation. If necessary, the dead petal material can be carefully removed from the pistil.

The seed pods will take 4 to 6 months or longer to ripen, depending on the size of the seed pod and the number of maturing seeds. Placing the date of pollination on the cross label will help you to determine whether enough time has passed. The seed pod and stalk will dry up at maturity; there is no color change as is seen in the fruit of many other genera. Seed pods that dry before 4 months usually will not contain fertile seed. The seed pod can be left on the plant until fully dry, or it can be removed and placed in a warm dry place. In any event, it is usually a good idea to completely dry the seed pod for 2 to 4 weeks before attempting to sow the seed.

The outer wall of the seed pod is very hard when dry. The easiest way to get at the seed is to cut the seed pod open with a knife or razor blade. Before doing this, place a small sheet of paper under the seed pod to collect the seed. Unless the seed is sown immediately, it should be stored in a small envelope. If the seed is to be kept for any length of time, leave it in the seed pod and store the dry seed pods in a small, air-tight container in a refrigerator. Seed stored this way is still viable after several years.

The seed pods will contain several hundred very tiny seeds. It is amazing that the seeds take so long to mature (4 to 6 months) when they are so small! Viable seed will often be black in color and will have a shiny appearance. Nonviable seed looks brown or gray and will be dull in appearance. It is fairly common to have both types in the same seed pod, and it is not necessary to separate out the viable seed from the nonviable before sowing.

The time from making a cross to seeing the offspring in bloom is approximately one year: 4 to 6 months for the seed pod to mature, 1 month for the seed to dry, 2 to 4 weeks for the seed to germinate, and 4 to 8 months for the seedlings to reach blooming size. The generation time for miniatures can be less than a year, while that for large standards is longer. After a potentially valuable seedling is identified, it may take several years of testing, reproducing by leaf cuttings, growing to show size, and so forth before a new cultivar is ready to be released. Breeding programs that require second or third generations to place the desired combinations of traits within a plant will take even more time before the plants are ready for release. Although African violets do not take as much time to breed as other species, patience is still required in the development of new and improved cultivars.

Propagation

African violet seed is fairly easy to germinate. Because the seed is so tiny, it is best germinated in a closed container. This keeps the moisture high and will prevent the seedling from drying out. Any type of closed container will do, but ones with a shallow soil depth are best, since African violet seedlings do not have deep roots.

The germination medium can be a commercial soil that has been lightened by the addition of fine vermiculite. Another germination medium is a mixture consisting of 1 part soil mix, 1 part peat moss, and 1 part fine vermiculite. Seeds can also be successfully germinated in straight vermiculite. Whatever germination medium is used, make certain that it is broken down into a fine grainy texture and is free of large lumps and clods. The germination medium should be moistened with warm water before sowing the seeds.

To collect the seed for sowing, first fold a piece of paper to make a sharp crease in the middle. Open the seed pod and spill the seeds onto the paper. Sow the seeds over the surface of the germination medium by tapping the paper, scattering the seeds as evenly as possible over the medium. If you are concerned about the seeds being sown unevenly, mix the seeds with a very fine sand, then sow the sand-seed mixture. Do not over-sow! It is better to have the seeds too thin than too thick because separating the seedlings will be a problem. Do not cover the seeds with the germination medium; they must remain on the surface and exposed to the light in order to germinate.

The container should be closed and placed in a warm area where it will receive bright light. Direct sunlight, however, can kill the germinating seeds. Placing the container close to a fluorescent light is ideal. The seed will germinate at the typical growing temperatures for African violets (65–75°F [18–24°C]). Germination can be enhanced by using gentle bottom heating, especially in cooler conditions. Most seed will germinate within 2 to 4 weeks, but not all the seed will germinate at once. In some cases, germination can continue even 3 months after sowing, so do not give up too early.

Seedlings can be removed for individual potting as soon as they are large enough to be handled. Although it is possible to move them before the first true leaves appear, it is better to wait until the seedling has developed at least two or three true leaves. Gently loosen the germination medium around the roots with a toothpick. A notched stick or pickle-fork can then be used to gently lift the seedling out of the germination container. Seedlings of larger size can be moved with your fingers, but be sure to hold the seedling by a leaf rather than the stem. If the plant tissue is accidentally crushed during the transfer, the plant can more easily replace a leaf than it can the stem.

Place the seedling into a small pot (a 2-ounce plastic disposable cup works fine). Add enough new soil to cover the roots, and gently water the plant into place with warm water. A sprayer set for a fine mist is excellent for settling new seedlings in the soil. African violets prefer moist soil but do not tolerate standing in water. The seedling pot should be placed in a tray and covered with a humidity dome. The seedling is grown in the enclosed space for several weeks. Once the roots are firmly established in the new soil, the cover can be gradually removed, exposing the new seedling to the open air. African violet seedlings can be grown under the same conditions as mature plants: moderate light; daytime temperatures of 70–80°F (21–27°C), with about a 10° drop at night; and 40–60% humidity. Use dilute fertilizer solutions (one-eighth strength 20-20-20) until the seedlings are large and growing well, then a regular fertilizer regime can be used.

Variegated seedlings may be mostly white or yellow after germinating. Water these with a weak fertilizer solution that is very high in nitrogen to "green them up." If the seedlings do not develop sufficient chlorophyll quickly, they may die from starvation or fail to thrive when transplanted.

In addition to seeds, African violets can be easily reproduced with leaf cuttings. Select a mature, healthy leaf from the row halfway between the crown of the plant and the outer row of leaves. Remove the leaf from the plant with a gentle sideways jerk. Be sure to remove any remaining petiole from the plant stem. Trim the petiole of the leaf to ¾ to 1 inch (2–3 cm) below the leaf blade. Some authorities recommend cutting the petiole on a slant to increase the surface area for the production of new plantlets. Allow the cut to air dry for about half an hour to help prevent rotting. A piece of masking tape with the name of the cultivar written in permanent marker can be attached to the top of the leaf blade as a label. The cut surface may be dusted with a rooting hormone, but this is not considered essential to root and plantlet production.

A rooting medium that is very light and porous works best for rooting the leaf. One mixture uses equal amounts of vermiculite and perlite. Another option is a 1:1:1 mixture of peat moss, perlite, and vermiculite. Place the leaf petiole into the rooting mixture. Since the new plants will grow at the cut end, insert the petiole into the rooting medium as shallowly as possible. The leaf blade can be supported by leaning it against the sides of the container. The leaf blade can also be supported by inserting a broom straw or toothpick through the blade and into the rooting medium. If the hole created by the broom straw is not in a vein, the leaf can be supported with little damage.

The leaves should be placed in a container with a humidity dome and placed under bright light. If the humidity in the growing area is high, the humidity dome may not be necessary as long as the rooting medium is not allowed to dry out. The leaves should be kept moist, but not soaking wet, which may induce rot.

Within 2 to 3 weeks, the leaf should root. A slight tug on the leaf will confirm that roots have started to grow. After another 3 to 10 weeks, the leaves of the baby plantlets should begin to break through the surface of the rooting medium. Each leaf may produce from 1 to 20 or more plantlets, depending on the cultivar and the vigor of the mother leaf. If the leaf has rooted but has not produced any babies, remove the top third of the leaf blade. This surgery will often stimulate the leaf to produce babies.

When the plantlets have three to four leaves about ½ to ¾ inch (12–19 mm) in size, they can be removed from the parent leaf. Most of the plantlets will separate from the leaf with just a slight tug, but some may need to be separated with a knife. Variegated plantlets should have plenty of green in their leaves before separation from the mother leaf or they may not survive. If necessary, fertilize with a dilute high-nitrogen fertilizer to "green up" the babies before separation. Keep as many of the roots on each plantlet as possible, but a baby that is totally without roots will usually survive and grow. Covering the babies with a humidity dome until their new roots are established will help avoid transplant shock and a slowing of growth. Depending on the cultivar, blooming plants can be obtained within 5 to 8 months after putting down a leaf.

African violets can also be propagated through suckers, crown divisions, bloom stalks, and tissue culture. These methods are usually used for specialized cases, however, such as in reproducing pinwheel or chimera violets (Plate 8-4) that will not reproduce true from leaves. Leaf cuttings are the most popular way of reproducing African violets both commercially and among hobbyists.

Resources

COLLECTIONS

Few botanical gardens keep a large number of African violet species in their collection, although many may have a small grouping of different cultivars. An extensive collection of species plants is found at the Royal Botanic Gardens, Kew, in England. The Uppsala Botanical Gardens in Uppsala, Sweden, also has a number of African violet species. Some members of the African Violet Society of America keep a number of the species in their collections.

SUPPLIERS—NORTH AMERICA

Cape Cod Violetry
28 Minot Street
Falmouth, MA 02540
phone: 508-548-2798
    (after 5:00 P.M.)
A mail-order firm that carries all the available species, the original 10 cultivars, and a large number of old and new cultivars.

Green Circle Growers
15650 State Route No. 511
Oberlin, OH 44074
phone: 216-775-1411
fax: 216-774-1465
Grower of the Ultra-Violet series for commercial sales.

Holtkamp Greenhouses
P.O. Box 78565
Nashville, TN 37207
phone: 615-228-2683
Home of the successful Optimara
and Rhapsodie series, this
international company is the largest
commercial grower of African
violets in the world.

Lyndon Lyon Greenhouses
P.O. Box 249
14 Mutchler Street
Dolgeville, NY 13329
phone: 315-429-8291
A commercial and mail-order firm
that hybridizes its own plants,
including new cultivars with unusual
colors. It also sells a wide selection
of chimera or pinwheel violets and
other gesneriads.

Rob's Mini-o-lets
P.O. Box 9
Naples, NY 14512
phone: 716-374-8592
A mail-order firm that specializes in
miniatures and trailers bred by the
owner, Ralph (Rob) Robinson.

Tinari Greenhouses
Box 190, 2325 Valley Road
Huntingdon Valley, PA 19006
phone: 215-947-0144
One of the first commercial
greenhouses to specialize in African
violets. Carries a number of original
cultivars and growing supplies.

Travis' Violets
P.O. Box 42
Ochlocknee, GA 31773
phone: 912-574-5167
fax: 912-574-5605
A mail-order firm that carries a good
variety of popular show cultivars.

The Violet House
P.O. Box 393
Evinston, FL 32633
phone: 352-591-5373 or
        800-377-8466
A mail-order firm that sells flower
pots, plant labels, potting materials,
fertilizer, and African violet seed.

INTERNATIONAL REGISTRATION AUTHORITY

African Violet Society of America
Attn: Iris Keating
149 Loretto Court
Claremont, CA 91711
U.S.A.

PLANT SOCIETIES

The African Violet Society of America (AVSA) is the official organization that handles all matters dealing with African violets. Founded in 1946, the AVSA is an international society with more than 15,000 members. The purpose of the society is to provide a center through which African violet enthusiasts can obtain and exchange growing information. AVSA is also the International Registration Authority for the genus *Saintpaulia* and offers a "Master Variety List" of all recorded species and cultivars.

The AVSA publishes *African Violet Magazine*, which contains growing information, continuous information on the latest developments in the African violet world, and a number of regular columns (including hybridizing) and feature articles. The magazine is published six times a year and includes color pictures.

African Violet Society of America
2375 North Street
Beaumont, TX 77702
U.S.A.
phone: 409-839-4725 or 800-770-AVSA (2872)

The African Violet Society of Canada (AVSC) publishes a quarterly magazine called *Chatter*, which is dedicated to the growing and showing of African violets and gesneriads.

African Violet Society of Canada
Irene Henry
349 Hyman Drive
Dollard des Ormeau, Quebec H9B 1L5
Canada

AV Association of Australia
For membership and information contact:
Patricia O'Reiley
4 Batavia Place
Baulkham Hills, New South Wales 2153
Australia

Primer Club De Violetas (Mexico)
For membership and information contact:
Alejandrina B. DeGuerrerro, President
P.O. Box 1688
Monterrey NL CP 64000
Mexico

Saintpaulia and Houseplant Society
For membership and information contact:
F. B. F. Dunningham, M.B.E., Treasurer
33 Church Road
Newbury Park
Ilford, Essex 1G2 7ET
England

Taiwan African Violet Club
For membership and information contact:
Fu Chen Tung, President
4 Lane 61 Kuo Shan 3rd Rd.
Kao-Hsiung 840
Taiwan

Transvaal AVS
For membership and information contact:
Lana Marais, President
Box 11141
Centurion 0046
South Africa

ELECTRONIC MAIL GROUPS

An internet mail-list group for growers of gesneriads and African violets allows members to post questions, share information, and learn more about these plants. The address for the group is gesneriphiles@lists.Colorado.Edu. Individuals can join the list by sending the appropriate message to listproc@lists. Colorado.Edu, subscribe gesneriphiles <full name>.

References and Additional Reading

Bartholomew, P. 1995. *Growing to Show*. Oxnard, Calif.: AV Enterprises Press.

Coulson, R. 1993. *Growing African Violets*. 2nd ed. Kenthurst, Australia: Kangaroo Press.

Robey, M. J. 1988. *African Violets: Gifts from Nature*. Cranburyn, N.J.: Cornwall Books.

Van Pelt Wilson, H. 1970. *African-Violet Book*. New York: Hawthorn Books, Elsevier-Dutton.

9 Breeding Gesneriads

Peter Shalit

The gesneriad family (Gesneriaceae) contains 2000 to 3000 species of plants native to all the major tropical regions of the world as well as some temperate areas. None is native to North America, but gesneriads can be found growing there in the homes and gardens of millions of people who love them for their beauty and ease of culture. The gesneriads are considered quite evolutionarily advanced, with flowers that have adapted to attract various pollinators, from insects to birds and bats.

The most famous and popular members of the gesneriad family are the African violet (*Saintpaulia*) and the florist gloxinia (*Sinningia speciosa*), but many, many others have horticultural value. Some are cultivated by hobbyists, and quite a bit of hybridization has been done, but the horticultural and genetic potential of this family is largely untapped. The Gesneriad Hybridizers Association, founded in 1977, continues to stimulate interest in this area. Gesneriads appeal to the amateur horticulturist or hybridizer for a variety of reasons.

- Gesneriads frequently have showy flowers, which have evolved to attract pollinators but are attractive to humans as well. Most have ornamental foliage, which is velvety or sometimes shiny, often with contrasting markings, lending appeal even when the plant is not in bloom. In fact, some types are grown primarily for their foliage.
- As tropical plants, most gesneriads are comfortable in the temperature range of human homes or in greenhouses. Many are adapted to low light levels and are ideal for fluorescent-light culture.
- The wide variety of growth habits, flower colors, shapes, and sizes means that the hobbyist will never be bored with this group. At the same time, the flower structure and principles of hybridizing and culture are fairly similar throughout the family.

- Most gesneriads are easy to propagate from stem cuttings, leaf cuttings, rhizome divisions, or seed, facilitating the dissemination of new hybrids.
- Gesneriad seed ripens and germinates relatively quickly, and plant growth is rapid, allowing breeding programs to produce one generation in a year or less.
- Gesneriad seed is often produced in abundance, and plants can often be grown to blooming stage in a small-sized pot, so large numbers of seedlings can be grown from any given cross, thus facilitating selection. This also facilitates selecting for natural mutations. Several horticulturally valuable gesneriads have arisen as sports in seed-grown lots.
- Gesneriad species that appear quite different may actually be closely related, having evolved to attract different pollinators. Barriers to artificial hybridization, either between species or even between genera, are often weak or lacking. Often such hybrids are fertile, so further generations can be obtained.
- New species are continually being introduced from the wild, adding to the gene pool available to gesneriad hybridizing enthusiasts.

What makes a gesneriad? The typical gesneriad flower is tubular in shape or, at least, has its petals joined at the base. (The closely related families Scrophulariaceae, or snapdragon family, and Bignoniaceae, or trumpet-vine family, also have tubular flowers.) A typical gesneriad flower has two to four stamens, which are attached to the corolla, and a single pistil (Figure 9-1). The flowers are borne in the leaf axils, and sometimes the top of the plant is modified into a terminal floral spike, like that of a foxglove (*Digitalis*). Gesneriad flowers are generally perfect (they have both male and female parts), and most will self-pollinate easily.

Most gesneriads have flowers with bilateral (but not radial) symmetry, with five (or occasionally four) lobes, which are often unequal in size and which can be divided into two upper ones and three lower ones. The upper lobes may be smaller than the lower, as in wild type *Saintpaulia* or *Sinningia speciosa* (see Plate 9-7), or they may be larger and form a hood protruding from a tubular corolla, as in some *Columnea* (see Plate 9-2) and *Sinningia* species. Mutations of horticultural interest include the formation of flowers with five (or more) equal-sized lobes. Such a mutation is called peloric. The most important instance of a peloric mutation is in *Sinningia speciosa*, with upright, bell-shaped flowers; the same mutation has also occurred in *Saintpaulia* hybrids, as well as in *Sinningia cardinalis* (Figure 9-2).

In plant habit, gesneriads range from tiny herbs to hanging vines, shrubs, or small trees. Many are terrestrial in their native habitats, but quite a few are epiphytic (growing on other plants) or lithophytic (growing on rocks). With regard to cultural requirements, the epiphytes and lithophytes prefer a very well-drained medium, and some tolerate drying out. In addition, many herbaceous gesneriads produce underground storage organs,

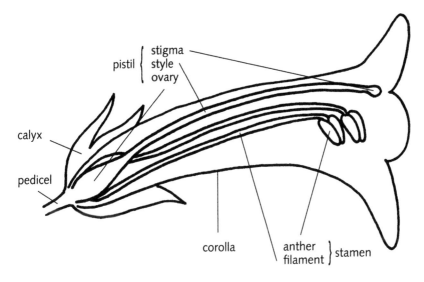

Figure 9-1. Typical gesneriad floral anatomy. (Illustration by John Boggan)

either fleshy tubers or scaly rhizomes, to carry the plant through the dry season in its native habitat. Although dormancy is not a popular feature for houseplants, it does facilitate shipping of these plants, which can be packed and mailed easily as tubers or rhizomes.

Important Breeding Materials

Gesneriads have only been in cultivation to any extent since the early nineteenth century, when species with horticultural potential began to be brought to Europe from the tropics. For horticultural purposes, the gesneriads are best thought of as two groups of plants: those from the New World (*Achimenes, Columnea, Sinningia*, and others) and those from the Old World (including *Streptocarpus, Saintpaulia*, and *Chirita*). Hobbyists tend also to separate gesneriads into those with underground tubers (*Sinningias*, mostly), those with scaly rhizomes (*Achimenes, Kohleria, Smithiantha*, and allied genera), and those with fibrous roots (most other gesneriad genera).

The 1800s saw a frenzy of gesneriad hybridizing, with *Achimenes, Kohleria*, and *Sinningia speciosa* being particular favorites. In all three cases, horticultural forms were developed that were quite far removed from their wild progenitors. Unfortunately, many of these hybrids have been lost. A resurgence of interest in gesneriad cultivation and hybridization began in the mid-twentieth century and has not abated.

Saintpaulia, the African violet, which to many is the perfect flowering

Figure 9-2. *Sinningia cardinalis:* a) wild type; b) peloric form. (Illustration by Peter Shalit, adapted from *The Gloxinian,* 1968)

houseplant, was not discovered and introduced to cultivation until the 1890s, but it quickly became the most popular gesneriad for growers and hybridizers, and it remains so to this day. Because of their popularity, African violets have earned a separate chapter in this book, and so will be discussed only in passing here.

Sinningia is a large New World genus, with upwards of 75 species, mostly tuberous-rooted, which vary greatly in their size and ornamental value. Horticulturally speaking, the genus falls into several distinct groups, which will be discussed separately. *Sinningia* is by far the most popular genus among contemporary amateur gesneriad hybridizers.

Sinningia speciosa—commonly referred to as gloxinia, since it was originally introduced as *Gloxinia speciosa*—is the most popular gesneriad in horticulture, aside from *Saintpaulia*. The original species had lavender-to-purple, nodding (slipper-shaped) flowers (Plate 9-7). By the mid-1800s, plant breeders had developed many color forms, extending the color spectrum of the velvety flowers to white, pink, and red shades, some with elaborate patterning. In addition, a radially symmetric mutant form, with an upright, chalice-shaped flower, arose in 1847. This form is much showier than the original type and has become the standard gloxinia seen in shops today. Forms with double flowers have been developed as well. American hybridizers have worked extensively with this species, creating a vast array of cultivars. These range from the Buell hybrids, which tend to be very large display plants, with flowers several inches across, to quite compact hybrids that can be raised in a 3-inch (7.5-cm) pot and are more suitable for indoor gardening.

The genus *Sinningia* also contains two of the smallest species of flowering houseplant, *Sinningia pusilla* and *S. concinna,* the dimensions of which seldom exceed 1⅛ inches (3 cm) in any direction—a plant could be grown in a thimble, and the whole plant could fit inside a flower of *S. speciosa.*

These species, as well as the white-flowered mutant of *S. pusilla* (*Sinningia* 'White Sprite'), have been bred with each other and with an artificial mutant with fringed flowers to form a number of attractive, "microminiature" *Sinningia* hybrids. All have flowers in shades of purple, lavender, or white, some with speckled flowers or fringed corollas. They are ideal for terrarium growing.

Many of the larger *Sinningia* species, including those formerly placed in the allied genus *Rechsteineria*, can easily be crossed with each other, and a number of attractive hybrids (once called "×Gloxineras") have been created. These hybrids tend to form quite large tubers and can be considered analogous to caudiciform succulents. (The tubers are caudices, and the plants occasionally appear in cacti and succulent shows in the caudiciform succulent class, though the plants are of course not succulent.) In fact, they are beginning to be appreciated by succulent enthusiasts. The species involved include *Sinningia eumorpha* (with white, slipper-shaped flowers), *S. cardinalis* (with red, hooded flowers), *S. leucotricha* (with silvery-hairy leaves and salmon flowers), and many others. A recently introduced species, *S. conspicua*, has flowers that are yellow and fragrant, two unusual and valuable traits to pass along to new hybrids. In addition, several interesting mutations have arisen in *S. cardinalis*, and the mutations can be transferred to these hybrids and may increase their horticultural potential. One such trait, which is recessive, confers an upright, radially symmetric flower. Another, a dominant, transforms the calyx—which is normally small, green, and inconspicuous—into a replica of the corolla, a large, showy structure. The resulting flowers are "double" in the sense that they appear to have two corollas, one inside the other. The end result is either very showy or bizarre, depending on one's taste and the individual plant. These mutations are the focus of this author's breeding program, and other hybridizers are working with them as well.

The aforementioned group of *Sinningias* can be crossed with the microminiatures to create miniature plants that are generally 2½ to 5 inches (6–12.5 cm) in any dimension. Although such hybrids are usually sterile, they can be made fertile by doubling the chromosomes with the chemical colchicine; spontaneous fertile tetraploids have also occurred. When fertile, these hybrids can be intercrossed, and thus a large array of mini-sinningias has been produced. The nodding, slipper-shaped flowers range from white to lavender to red, orange, and purple, often with bold spots, dashes, or stripes. Growing and breeding these plants is increasingly popular, and they are available commercially from several sources. Double-flowered forms have recently been introduced. Popular cultivars include *Sinningia* 'Cherry Chips', 'Cindy-Ella', 'Dollbaby', and 'Super Orange'.

Finally, there is a group of large *Sinningia* species that, though tuberous, have the habit of small shrubs with large numbers of flowers. This group includes *Sinningia tubiflora* (with fragrant white flowers), *S. aggregata* (with pine-scented foliage and orange tubular flowers), and *S. sulcata* (with yellow flowers), among others. These plants can be hybridized with each other, and some of the resulting cultivars (such as *Sinningia* 'Apricot Bouquet') are popular summer patio pot plants among gesneriad enthusiasts.

Although more closely related to the fibrous-rooted genera, *Nautilocalyx* and *Chrysothemis* both produce tubers. Hybrids have recently been created within each genus, and intergeneric hybrids bridge the two genera. These are currently being grown mainly by gesneriad enthusiasts, but there is potential here for hybrids with broader appeal.

Rhizomatous gesneriads—*Achimenes, Gloxinia, Kohleria, Smithiantha*, and others—are excellent breeding subjects, and several genera have been heavily hybridized. In addition, these genera can often be artificially interbred, and at least 20 different intergeneric combinations have been successfully created within this group and with allied fibrous-rooted genera (Table 9-1). In general, such hybrids are sterile but are easily propagated by cuttings or rhizomes.

Table 9-1. Intergeneric Hybrids in the Rhizomatous Group of Gesneriads

×*Achicodonia*	=	*Achimenes* × *Eucodonia*
×*Achimenantha*	=	*Achimenes* × *Smithiantha*
×*Diaskohleria*	=	*Diastema* × *Kohleria*
×*Glocodonia*	=	*Gloxinia* × *Eucodonia*
×*Glokeria*	=	*Gloxinia* × *Koellikeria*
×*Glokohleria*	=	*Gloxinia* × *Kohleria*
×*Gloxinantha*	=	*Gloxinia* × *Smithiantha*
×*Gloxinopyle*	=	*Gloxinia* × *Monopyle*
×*Gloxistema*	=	*Gloxinia* × *Diastema*
×*Heppiantha*	=	*Heppiella* × *Smithiantha*
×*Heppigloxinia*	=	*Heppiella* × *Gloxinia*
×*Heppimenes*	=	*Heppiella* × *Achimenes*
×*Koellikohleria*	=	*Koellikeria* × *Kohleria*
×*Moussogloxinia*	=	*Moussonia* × *Gloxinia*
×*Moussokohleria*	=	*Moussonia* × *Kohleria*
×*Moussoniantha*	=	*Moussonia* × *Smithiantha*
×*Niphimenes*	=	*Niphaea* × *Achimenes*
×*Niphiantha*	=	*Niphaea* × *Smithiantha*
×*Paleria*	=	*Parakohleria* × *Kohleria*
×*Phinastema*	=	*Phinaea* × *Diastema*
×*Smithicodonia*	=	*Smithiantha* × *Eucodonia*

Achimenes, the so-called magic flower, has been in cultivation since the eighteenth century and has been hybridized enthusiastically for the past 200 years or so. This Mexican native is very seasonal, blooming in summer and fall and producing abundant rhizomes that carry it through its dormant period. Many showy hybrids are available, with large flowers in the full color spectrum, and are offered in commercial catalogs as hanging-basket subjects or as summer bedding plants. Double-flowered forms have been introduced and are popular in the trade. Intergeneric hybrids with *Smithiantha* (×*Achimenantha*) and with *Eucodonia* (×*Achicodonia*) have been commercially successful. Further breeding might reduce or eliminate the dormant period, or make these plants less seasonal.

Smithiantha—known in the past as *Naegelia* and in the vernacular as temple bells—is another small genus native to Mexico; recent collections have increased the number of species to seven or so. *Smithiantha* is distinguished by its showy terminal inflorescence of nodding, bell-shaped flowers in colors ranging from white to yellow and orange, and now lavender (Plate 9-8). The plants also have exceptionally nice velvety foliage, in colors from apple green to deep purple. Some older hybrids (the Cornell series) grow quite large, but recent breeding efforts focus on more compact plants. The plants bloom annually, in late summer to fall, and have an obligate dormant period. A *Smithiantha* that blooms repeatedly without a dormant period would be a great advance. *Smithiantha* × *Achimenes* hybrids (formerly called ×*Eucodonopsis*, now ×*Achimenantha*) have been cultivated for over a century. Desirable hybrids have also been created by crossing *Smithiantha* with *Eucodonia* and with *Gloxinia*.

Eucodonia, though containing only two species, is a desirable horticultural subject, with several cultivars and hybrids. Flowers are slipper-shaped and tend to be pale lavender to purple. The attractive leaves are furry and often dark colored. Intergeneric hybrids with *Achimenes*, *Smithiantha*, and *Gloxinia* are available, and some of these are more popular than the eucodonias themselves.

The true *Gloxinia* genus is a diverse genus of rhizomatous plants with tubular, slipper-shaped, or pouched flowers. Some species, such as *Gloxinia sylvatica*, lack the obligate dormant period common to rhizomatous gesneriads, making them valuable for hybridizers. This genus has been heavily hybridized only since the 1960s, and much potential exists. At least two species (*G. lindeniana* and *G. perennis*) have pleasantly scented flowers, a trait that has not yet been exploited by hybridizers. Intergeneric combinations have been created with many other allied genera, the showiest being those hybrids with *Smithiantha*.

Diastema is a small genus of small, generally less distinguished plants. Flowers are also small, in white to lavender shades. The recent introduction of an orange-flowered species, *Diastema comiferum*, broadens the gene pool. Hybrids with *Kohleria* are promising in that they may combine the small size of *Diastema* with the showy flowers of *Kohleria*. A recent cross of *D. racimeriferum* with *Gloxinia racemosa* is an attractive horticultural subject.

Koellikeria is a monotypic genus, the one species being *Koellikeria erinoides*, with several varieties. The compact plants, with silver-flecked leaves and a spike of flowers, are popular among gesneriad enthusiasts. Some people detect a coconut smell in the flowers. Intergeneric combinations with *Kohleria* as well as *Gloxinia* exist, and these have definite potential.

Kohleria (known in the past by many Latin names, including *Isoloma* and *Tydea*) is a genus of larger plants, usually bearing quite showy flowers with interesting markings (Plate 9-5). Although rhizomatous, the genus exhibits a brief or nonexistent dormancy. Several species are available, and hybrids have been worked on for over a century, with much activity in the nineteenth century and again lately. Sterility of hybrids in this genus has been a problem. In addition, natural hybrids occur in the wild, and it appears that many of the "species" material in cultivation is actually of hybrid origin. The plants tend to be tall and/or sprawling, though breeding work has created more compact, well-behaved cultivars. The foliage is velvety and often marked with purple in attractive patterns. The spotted and striped flowers come in unpredictable patterns and colors in hybrids, which adds interest for the hybridizer. Intergeneric combinations with *Koellikeria*, *Parakohleria*, *Moussonia*, and *Diastema* have been achieved. Only the first-mentioned cross has seen any horticultural attention.

Niphaea is a genus of small, spreading plants with white flowers. *Phinaea*, an allied genus, is similar but the plants are smaller in size. As in many other genera, the leaves are at least as showy as the flowers, often dark in color with contrasting markings. Little hybridizing attention has been focused within these genera, but intergeneric hybrids have been created with other rhizomatous genera, and these have potential.

Parakohleria and *Pearcea* have similar, red or orange flowers. They produce rhizomes weakly. Although attractive plants, they have not been bred to any extent. This is a wide-open field for hybridizers, and some very interesting intergeneric hybrids should be possible.

FIBROUS-ROOTED NEW WORLD GESNERIADS

Though in cultivation since the 1800s, the genus *Nematanthus* received no attention from hybridizers until the 1960s. A flurry of hybridizing produced the Saylor hybrids, a group of attractive, easy-to-grow plants that are popular in cultivation. These hybrids were bred from *Nematanthus* as well as an allied genus, *Hypocyrta*, which was subsumed into *Nematanthus* based on this work. Hybridizing efforts in this group have slowed lately, but there is still much potential here. The flowers are in the orange to red to yellow range, some with contrasting stripes, and often with an unusual pouch shape and narrow mouth (Plate 9-6)—hence the popular names guppy plant and candy corn plant. Leaves are tough and shiny (or occasionally velvety), ranging from pale green to dark purple-green, sometimes with a bright red blotch on the reverse. The durable plants ship well and are becoming popular commercially. Some species have unique threadlike pedicels from which the flowers hang. Attractive hybrids with the allied genus *Codonanthe* have been created, and some of these are fertile. Very little hybridizing has been done within the genus *Codonanthe* itself.

The name *Columnea* represents a large group of more than 270 species of shrubby or pendant New World gesneriads, often more interesting when viewed from below than above. Taxonomists differ as to whether the fibrous-rooted plants under the heading of *Columnea* represent one genus or a group of allied genera. *Columnea*, even in the narrow sense, is a large genus that has been actively hybridized for decades, yielding many attractive cultivars that are generally grown as hanging-basket subjects. Flowers in this group, as well as the *Trichantha* and *Pentadenia* group, are tubular, hooded, and showy (Plate 9-2). *Dalbergaria* plants tend to have smaller, less showy flowers, but sometimes have brightly colored calyces and/or berries; in addition, the leaves may be strikingly pebbled or variegated, sometimes with bright red blotches on their undersides. Hybrids within each of these groups are often fertile, whereas hybrids between the groups (including *Columnea*) are always sterile. In the trade one may see these hybrids with intergeneric names, or simply called "Columnea" (Table 9-2).

Table 9-2. Hybrids Within the *Columnea* Alliance

×*Colbergaria*	=	*Columnea* × *Dalbergaria*
×*Coltadenia*	=	*Columnea* × *Pentadenia*
×*Coltrichantha*	=	*Columnea* × *Trichantha*
×*Daltadenia*	=	*Dalbergaria* × *Pentadenia*
×*Daltrichantha*	=	*Dalbergaria* × *Trichantha*
×*Trichadenia*	=	*Trichantha* × *Pentadenia*

Episcia, known as the flame violet or peacock plant, is the gesneriad genus most known for its showy foliage (Plate 9-3). The broad, velvety leaves are often adorned with purple or metallic backgrounds and contrasting ribs. The plants are ground-hugging and spread by forming stolons, which can be used for propagation. *Episcia* thrives in the heat and does not like cool environments. Hobbyists have come up with cultivars with pink or white variegation, either in a set pattern (such as *Episcia* 'Cleopatra') or in random blotches (as in 'Ember Lace'). These cultivars are delicate but very beautiful and desirable. *Episcia* flowers are showy and generally come in shades of red or orange, and occasionally in yellow, pink, white, or lavender. The orange flowers sometimes clash with pink-variegated leaves, but a pink-flowered, pink-leaved type (*Episcia* 'Pink Dreams') has recently been introduced.

Alsobia, a genus of two species, forms stolons like *Episcia* and previously was included in that genus. The leaves are plain, however, and the fringed flower is white, often with purple-brown spots. Hybrids (*Alsobia* 'Cygnet', for example) have been created that are more attractive and easier to grow than either parent.

Gesneria, the genus from which the family is named, consists of herbs and shrubs principally from the West Indies. The tubular yellow, orange, or white flowers are attractive, as are the shiny, holly-like leaves (Plate 9-4). Some of the smaller members of this genus are seen in cultivation, but they are less popular. This may be because of a high-humidity requirement, necessitating terrarium culture in most homes. Some hybridizing has been done (resulting in *Gesneria* 'Lemon Drop', for example), and there is potential for more. An allied genus, *Rhytidophyllum*, which is sometimes combined with *Gesneria*, has little horticultural value.

Other genera of New World gesneriads (*Bellonia*, *Besleria*, *Drymonia*, *Gasteranthus*, *Paradrymonia*, and others), though often treasured by gesneriad fanatics, either are fastidious in their growth requirements, and/or are not attractive enough to be of horticultural potential, and/or have simply been overlooked by horticulturists. However, there is much potential for hybridization here, and new species are frequently introduced from the wild. Given the right plant material, and some talented plant breeders, some of these genera may come into their own in the houseplant world.

OLD WORLD GESNERIADS

The Old World is home to many genera of gesneriads. *Saintpaulia*, popularly known as the African violet, is the best-known Old World gesneriad, and arguably is the most popular flowering houseplant in the world. From the original species, with pale mauve, violet-shaped flowers, have been bred thousands of hybrids, which an East African would never recognize as the same inconspicuous species that grows wild there. Flower colors now include white, pink, red, green, and even yellow, often with spots or stripes of contrasting color. Flowers, as well as leaves, may be plain or ruffled, in a wide array of shapes. Double flowers are common. Tiny miniatures, trailers, as well as huge standard rosette forms exist. Many cultivars have variegated leaves, in several different named patterns. *Saintpaulia* hybridizing is discussed in the previous chapter.

Streptocarpus, the cape primrose, is a large genus of fibrous-rooted African gesneriads. The most popular plants, belonging to subgenus *Streptocarpus*, are native to the southern portion of the continent, and they have been extensively hybridized. These are stemless plants with either a rosette of leaves or a single large leaf. The rosette form tends to dominate in hybrids. Flowers, produced on stalks arising from the leaf base(s), are often showy, with a color spectrum from white to blue, purple, pink, and red. No orange or yellow is found, except occasionally in the throat of the flower.

The Nymph *Streptocarpus* types, which have a flattened face to the flower, are descended from hybrids of *Streptocarpus johannis*. Other types, often thought of as *S. rexii* hybrids but in fact descending from many species, have more open, tubular faces. Most of the red flower color comes from *S. dunnii* ancestry. There are a few fragrant-flowered species (*S. vandeleurii, S. fanniniae*) whose genes have not yet contributed to the hybrid pool, and great potential is to be found here. *Streptocarpus* enjoys cooler temperatures than some other gesneriads. They are increasingly popular worldwide as houseplants and bedding plants. Demand has led to the introduction of more compact cultivars, with some ancestry in the miniature species *S. cyanandrus* and its hybrid with *S. johannis, Streptocarpus* 'Mighty Mouse'. Double, rosebud-form flowers have recently been introduced. Variegated leaf patterns have also occurred.

Streptocarpella is considered a subgenus of *Streptocarpus*, but the plants are very different from the typical cape primroses. They are shrubby or sprawling herbs, with proper stems, relatively small leaves, and a different chromosome number from the *Streptocarpus* subgenus. Flowers range in a narrow color spectrum from white to pale blue to dark purple. Hybrids involving *Streptocarpus saxorum, S. stomandrus, S. kirkii*, and others, are more floriferous and easier to grow than the species. Some of these are carried commercially and promoted as good plants for hanging baskets. The *Streptocarpella* subgenus is seeing little hybridizing activity currently, but the potential is there to broaden the range of flower color and plant habit.

Aeschynanthus (formerly known as *Trichosporum*) is often considered the Asiatic counterpart of *Columnea*. This Southeast Asian genus consists largely of trailing epiphytes, although some species have more upright and/or compact growth. A moderate amount of hybridizing has created some popular hybrids, including *Aeschynanthus* 'Black Pagoda', which shows up in such unlikely places as bank lobbies and dental offices. Flowers are generally in the red-orange-yellow range, though some important species have greenish and/or black-striped flowers. Some species have a showy, tubular calyx, lending the name lipstick plant. *Aeschynanthus marmoratus* has leaves with purple-black marbling and has been a valuable parent. *Aeschynanthus hildebrandii* is compact and floriferous. Although it is difficult to cross, this species has been successfully crossed to produce such attractive hybrids as *Aeschynanthus* 'Hot Flash' and *Aeschynanthus* 'Big Apple'. A recent sport of *A. hildebrandii* has yellow flowers, as opposed to the usual orange ones. *Aeschynanthus* plants tend to have tough, shiny foliage, and they ship well. The commercial and hybridizing possibilities are far from realized. An allied genus, *Agalmyla*, apparently has many species, but only one (*Agalmyla parasitica*) has reached cultivation. There may be significant horticultural potential in this genus.

Chirita is a large and diverse genus of East Asian plants. Some species (*Chirita sinensis*, for example) are rosulate perennials, similar in habit to *Saintpaulia*. Others (such as *C. lavundulacea*) are annual herbs with fleshy stems, reminiscent of *Impatiens* in habit. Still others (including *C. moonii*) are shrubby perennials. *Chirita sinensis* has several stunning forms, with various amounts of silver coloration in the leaves, and a variety of leaf shapes (Plate 9-1). Some allied species have been introduced, and interspecific hybridizing activity has begun on both sides of the Pacific. Some exciting *Chirita* hybrids are appearing in gesneriad shows.

Boea and *Petrocosmea* are two other Asian gesneriads with a flat, rosette habit like that of *Saintpaulia*. Several attractive species are currently in cultivation. No hybrids have as yet been reported, but the potential exists for plants that are similar to the African violet yet different enough to be interesting.

The alpine gesneriads are unique in being frost-hardy and are grown as rock garden plants in temperate climates. The European genera *Ramonda*, *Haberlea*, and *Jancaea* have been in cultivation for hundreds of years. They form ground-hugging rosettes with clusters of star- or bell-shaped flowers produced above the leaves each spring. *Ramonda* in particular has been bred to form a series of hybrids with different flower colors and plant habits. Intergeneric hybrids are reported between these genera and, surprisingly, with their Asian relatives *Briggsia*, *Conandron*, *Didissandra*, and *Opithandra* (Table 9-3). Though attractive, the alpines are fairly fastidious, and attention should be paid to breeding less-demanding cultivars, which could be promoted as "hardy African violets."

Large numbers of Asian gesneriad species have yet to reach cultivation. The largest genus of gesneriads, *Cyrtandra*, is native to the Asian Pacific region. Consisting of large shrubs with inconspicuous flowers, this genus is not horticulturally valuable. Other genera (*Didymocarpus*, *Hemiboea*, *Lysionotus*, *Paraboea*) may have significant potential as more material is brought into cultivation. Taxonomists are working actively on this part of the family, and many species have been moved from one genus to another in recent years. Some promising species have been introduced as a result of this activity.

Table 9-3. Intergeneric Combinations Among the Alpines

×*Jancaemonda*	=	*Jancaea* × *Ramonda*
×*Jancaeberlea*	=	*Jancaea* × *Haberlea*
×*Jancaendron*	=	*Jancaea* × *Conandron*
×*Jancaessandra*	=	*Jancaea* × *Didissandra*
×*Ramberlea*	=	*Ramonda* × *Haberlea*
×*Brigandra*	=	*Briggsia* × *Opithandra*

Important Traits and Breeding Objectives

Many gesneriads make suitable horticultural subjects "straight from the wild." However, breeding has improved their appeal as cultivated plants. Specific traits and objectives for each genus have been mentioned in the preceding discussion. In general, larger flowers, different flower forms (including double flowers), more floriferousness, better plant habit (usually meaning more compact), and fancy leaf forms, all are traits that have been selected by breeders. In many cases the range of flower color has been expanded from the wild type, often by introduction of genes from related species, and sometimes by painstaking selective breeding (as in the case of the new yellow-flowered *Saintpaulia*). Floral fragrance, which occurs in a number of gesneriad species, has thus far been neglected by hybridizers.

Hybridizers have created whole races of gesneriads that have only a remote resemblance to their wild counterparts. This is particularly true in *Saintpaulia*, *Sinningia*, and *Streptocarpus* and to a lesser extent in many other genera. While hybridizers continue to breed exotic new forms for enthusiasts, they must also keep the general public in mind by selecting easy-to-grow, undemanding, compact, yet showy cultivars. The recent *Nematanthus* hybrids, for example, have brought that genus from obscurity into fairly common cultivation as an indoor flowering plant.

The genetics of most gesneriads, other than *Saintpaulia*, have not been well explored. Therefore the inheritance of specific traits is usually poorly understood. Crosses between species, the most common form of hybridizing among the Gesneriaceae, tend to produce offspring that are more or less intermediate between the two parents. The various traits may sort themselves out in the next generation. The inheritance of flower color in *Sinningia speciosa*, as well as in *Streptocarpus*, has been studied scientifically but is too complex to be useful to the amateur hybridizer. A few mutant genes are well understood, however. The *Sinningia cardinalis* albino-flowered mutation, as well as the peloric mutations in this species and in *S. speciosa*, are all recessive. The 'Redcoat' gene of *S. cardinalis*, which converts the calyx into a large, corolla-like structure, is dominant. In addition, the double flower form, as found in *Sinningia speciosa* as well as in *Achimenes, Streptocarpus,* and miniature *Sinningia* hybrids, seems to be inherited as a dominant trait. Floral or foliar fragrance, found in some gesneriad species, tends to be a recessive trait in hybrids.

The gesneriad hybridizer should have sensible goals. A new hybrid should be distinctive; that is, it should be different from whatever is already available. The plant should be showy, with large flowers or many smaller ones, or with attractive foliage. It should be easy and dependable to grow and propagate. For the commercial trade, it should be durable and easy to ship. There are many untapped potential markets. *Streptocarpus,* with its showy, long-stemmed flowers, could be bred for use as cut flowers, especially if the flowers can be made fragrant and long-lasting. The red-flowered forms of *Sinningia, Columnea,* and *Nematanthus* could be bred and promoted for Christmas sale. Many gesneriads are suitable for sale as summer hanging baskets, a market that is currently dominated by fuchsias and some annuals. Similarly, use of gesneriads as bedding plants has barely begun. With the right cultivars and the right promotion, all these uses are possible.

Hybridization Mechanics

All gesneriads have perfect flowers—that is, they have both male parts (stamens) and female (stigma, style, ovary) (see Figure 9-1). In most cases, the pollen matures several days before the stigma is receptive; hence the flower is said to have a male phase and a female phase. The female parent should be emasculated in the bud stage, 1 to 3 days before the flower opens and before the pollen is shed. To do this, slit the bud with a fine scissors or dissecting needle and remove the anthers (Figure 9-3). The flower will continue to develop after emasculation. When the stigma is receptive, the tip tends to open up and become sticky; gesneriad stigmas are either bilobed or capitate (Figure 9-4). Fresh pollen is powdery and is easily brushed from the anthers. A few exceptional genera, *Saintpaulia* for example, have pollen in sacs that need to be opened.

To make a cross, fresh pollen is applied from one flower to another. Some hybridizers use their fingertip, which is fine if only one cross is being made; some use artist's brushes, which must be sterilized between uses; and some simply remove the male flower and dab the anthers onto the stigma. I find it easiest to use a flat toothpick to pack the pollen into the receptive stigma, like spackle. Each toothpick is discarded after one use. Gesneriad pollen remains viable for quite some time. It can be packed in a folded piece of shiny paper and mailed. It can also be frozen for later use. Each paper packet is placed in a glassine envelope, and they are stored in a freezer container. Desiccant granules (silica gel) may be sprinkled in the bottom of the container if the freezer is not a frost-free type. I have made successful crosses with pollen that has been sent in the mail or frozen, or even both. Pollen left at room temperature is generally viable for 1 to 2 weeks. Frozen pollen may remain viable for a year or more.

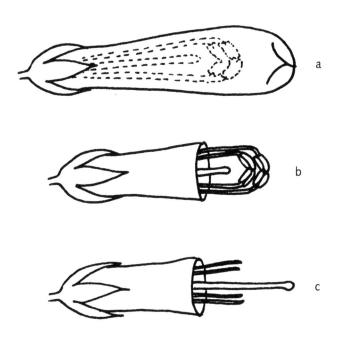

Figure 9-3. Preparing a flower for pollination (flower viewed from top): a) Bud ready for emasculation. The first step is to slit two sides of the corolla. b) Pistil and anthers exposed at early stage. The pollen should now be removed. c) The flower has been emasculated. Apply pollen to the mature stigma. (Illustration by John Boggan)

Figure 9-4. Two different types of stigmas of gesneriads: a) bilobed; b) capitate. (Illustration by Peter Shalit, adapted from *The Gloxinian*, 1995)

Gesneriad flowers may vary greatly in size from one species to the next. In crossing two flowers with disparate sizes, the smaller one should be used as the seed parent so that the pollen does not have too far to grow down the style to get to the ovary. If the larger-flowered species is attempted as the seed parent, the cross will usually fail. One such example is the cross of the diminutive *Sinningia pusilla* with the much larger *S. eumorpha*. This cross only succeeds if *S. pusilla* is used as the seed parent. Flower size tends to be controlled by several genes, so hybrids usually have flowers intermediate in size between those of the parent species. In subsequent generations, a range of flower sizes can be selected.

When a cross is made, the pollinated flower should be labeled immediately with a jeweler's or stationer's tag. The flower will wilt and/or drop off within 24 hours if the pollination "takes," and the ovary at the base of the pistil will swell. Gesneriad seeds take 1 to 6 months to ripen, depending on the genus. New World sorts (*Sinningia*, *Achimenes*) tend toward the shorter end of the range, and Old World sorts (*Saintpaulia*, *Aeschynanthus*) tend toward the longer end.

Propagation

Gesneriad seed may be produced in a dry capsule (*Achimenes*, *Sinningia*, *Streptocarpus*), a fleshy capsule (*Sinningia speciosa*, *Nematanthus*), or a fleshy berry (*Codonanthe*, *Columnea*). When ripe, a capsule will split open, and a berry will simply soften. Capsules should be harvested as soon as they dry and begin to split, or the seeds will be scattered and lost. When soft, a berry should be harvested by crushing it onto a piece of smooth-surfaced paper to dry. If left on the plant for too long after the berry ripens, the seed inside will begin to germinate. Gesneriad seed, stored in a folded piece of paper placed inside a small envelope, can last for years if kept cool and dry, as in a refrigerator.

The tiny seeds are easily grown by distributing them over the moistened surface of fine soil in a container that is kept covered to prevent drying out. They may take several weeks to germinate. Seedlings, depending on the genus and on the mature size of the plant, generally bloom in 6 to 12 months. Some, such as several species of *Sinningia*, go through a juvenile phase and may take a few years to bloom, but these are the rare exception.

Gesneriads are exceedingly easy to propagate vegetatively. *Saintpaulia* is usually propagated by leaf cuttings, a simple trick that no doubt has contributed to this plant's popularity. A leaf is removed and placed in potting media; rooting powder is optional. After several weeks, plantlets grow from the base of the leaf. Each plantlet arises from a single cell, and often new mutations will appear from plants propagated in this way. Many other gesneriad genera can also be propagated by leaves. The tuberous or rhizoma-tous types will often first form a tuber or rhizome from a leaf cutting, rather than forming a plant directly. Propagation by tip or crown cuttings is also quite easy for nearly all gesneriads. Rhizomes can be broken into pieces, or even into individual scales, each of which will form a new plant. Gesneriad tubers can be cut into pieces as well, but this is not recommended because the pieces often rot. Large numbers of gesneriad plants can be obtained by sowing the tiny seeds, but this is not a practical way to propagate hybrids since most do not breed true. Tissue culture has also been used to propagate gesneriads in large quantity, and it is in limited use commercially.

Resources

COLLECTIONS
Most major botanical gardens have some gesneriads; however, there are usually a pitiful few plants and they are often mislabeled. Two excellent collections in the United States are at the Smithsonian Institution, in Washington, D.C., and the Gesneriad Research Foundation, in Sarasota, Florida, although neither is open to the general public. The Royal Botanic Garden in Edinburgh, Scot-land, has a large collection of Old World species. The University of Vienna has a collection of Malaysian gesneriads.

SUPPLIERS—UNITED STATES
Commercial gesneriad growers tend to come and go. The mail-order nurseries listed here carry a large selection. Major seed catalogs also usually list some gesneriads, primarily *Achimenes, Sinningia,* and *Streptocarpus*. A much wider range of gesneriad seed can be obtained from the seed fund of the American Gloxinia and Gesneriad Society.

Belisle's Violet House
4041 N. Metnik Road
Ojibwa, WI 54862

Just Enough Sinningias
P.O. Box 560493
Orlando, FL 32856

Kartuz Greenhouses
1408 Sunset Drive
Vista, CA 92083

Lauray of Salisbury
432 Undermountain Road, Route 41
Salisbury, CT 06068

Weiss' Gesneriads
2293 S. Taylor Road
Cleveland Heights, OH 44118

INTERNATIONAL REGISTRATION AUTHORITY
American Gloxinia and Gesneriad Society
Attn: Judy Becker
432 Undermountain Road, Route 41
Salisbury, CT 06068
U.S.A.

PLANT SOCIETIES

The American Gloxinia and Gesneriad Society (AGGS) is the International Registration Authority for gesneriads, exclusive of *Saintpaulia*. Membership includes the quarterly publication *The Gloxinian*, as well as access to the seed fund, "Round Robins," and opportunities to attend judging schools and an annual convention. AGGS publishes registers of cultivated gesneriads, a valuable resource for hybridizers. Local chapters are found in many parts of North America. AGGS has a site on the World Wide Web (www.aggs.org) that is updated frequently.

American Gloxinia and Gesneriad Society
M. J. and D. B. Tyler, Membership Secretariat
P.O. Box 1598
Port Angeles, WA 98362-0194
U.S.A.

The Gesneriad Hybridizers Association was founded in 1977 to promote the hybridizing of gesneriads. Its journal, *CrossWords*, is published three times a year and is provided to members. In addition, membership includes access to a seed fund of hybrid seed, as well as Round Robin discussion groups. The annual meeting is held at the American Gloxinia and Gesneriad Society convention.

Gesneriad Hybridizers Association
Dan Harris
W-6349 County Road "O"
Appleton, WI 54914
U.S.A.

References and Additional Reading

Unfortunately, no general reference text on gesneriads is in print at this time. The most recent work is *The Miracle Houseplants*, by Virginia F. and George A. Elbert (Crown Publishers, New York, 1984). The Brooklyn Botanic Garden produced a *Handbook on Gesneriads* (Brooklyn Botanic Garden, Brooklyn, N.Y., 1976), which is somewhat more out of date. The best resources are the journals of the aforementioned societies. The Gesneriad Hybridizers Association keeps all back issues of *CrossWords* in print, and they may be purchased in year volumes. In addition, issues of the *Gesneriads Register* may be obtained from AGGS;

these are usually devoted to a single genus or taxonomic group and are invaluable references for the hybridizer. AGGS also publishes a basic hybridizing manual, *Birds and Bees and Gesneriad Seeds*, which is a reprint of an article from *The Gloxinian* and is available from AGGS.

ACKNOWLEDGMENTS

Jeff Smith, John Boggan, and Frances Batcheller all reviewed a draft of this chapter and made valuable suggestions, and John Boggan created the drawings for Figures 9-1 and 9-3. I relied on back issues of *CrossWords* and *The Gloxinian*, as well as volumes of *The Gesneriad Register*, for factual information. Most of all I am grateful to the many gesneriad growers who have created such wonderful hybrids. By and large I have avoided naming individual hybridizers in the text of this chapter, out of fairness to the many that I would not have had the room to name.

10 Breeding Amaryllis

Alan W. Meerow

Hippeastrum, the amaryllis, has yielded popular large-flowered hybrids over a 200-year breeding history. Bulbs are produced for indoor forcing and, to a lesser extent, garden use in mild winter areas (USDA hardiness zones 7B–11). The amaryllis is much appreciated by gardeners for its ease of culture, and amateur plant breeders have found it an easy and rewarding group to hybridize.

Hippeastrum consists of 50 to 60 entirely New World species, though one species, *Hippeastrum reginae*, appears to have been introduced to Africa. The species are concentrated in two main areas of diversity, one in eastern Brazil and the other in the central-southern Andes of Peru, Bolivia, and Argentina, on the eastern slopes and adjacent foothills. A few species extend north to Mexico and the West Indies. The genus is essentially tropical and subtropical, though some species occur far enough south of the equator and at sufficient elevation to be considered temperate plants. Little of this genetic diversity is represented in modern, commercial amaryllis hybrids. Early hybrids were produced from a relatively small number of species, mainly *H. aulicum*, *H. psittacinum*, *H. puniceum*, *H. reginae*, *H. reticulatum*, *H. striatum*, and *H. vittatum* (Bell 1973a; Cage 1978; Shields 1979; Traub 1934a, 1958).

The taxonomic relationships among *Hippeastrum* species have yet to be carefully elucidated. Various botanical groupings have been proposed (Traub and Moldenke 1949) but are of little significance to the plant breeder since virtually all diploid *Hippeastrum* species, regardless of their geographic origins, have been successfully crossed. Species or species groups of special interest are discussed later in this chapter. A number of species sometimes offered as "dwarf amaryllis" in specialists' catalogs (and, in some cases, originally described as species of *Hippeastrum*) are now properly recognized as belonging to the genus *Rhodophiala*. No true *Hippeastrum* has been successfully crossed with a *Rhodophiala* species. Likewise, the Brazilian blue amaryllis, *Worsleya rayneri* (sometimes called *Hippeastrum procerum*), has never been successfully hybridized with *Hippeastrum*. From time to time, there have been reports of wide intergeneric crosses between *Hippeastrum* and other genera of Amaryllidaceae such as *Crinum* or *Eucharis*, though there is no evidence that these hybrids are genuine. To date, the only reported intergeneric hybrids involving *Hippeastrum* that appear to be true are those involving *Sprekelia formosissima* (Aztec lily), though it should be noted that two species of amaryllis, *H. angustifolium* and *H. cybister*, have flowers that resemble those of *Sprekelia*.

History of Amaryllis Breeding

A detailed history of amaryllis breeding and cultivation can be found in Traub (1958) and will only be summarized here. *Hippeastrum* ×*johnsonii* ('Johnsonii'), generally acknowledged as the first amaryllis hybrid, was a hybrid of *H. vittatum* and *H. reginae* made in England in 1799 (Traub 1934a). Many additional hybrids were reported during the first 25 years of the nineteenth century as new species were collected in South America and imported to Europe. The two most significant developments in amaryllis breeding were the development of the Reginae and Leopoldii groups of hybrids.

The Reginae group was developed by Jan de Graaff of Holland and his two sons in the middle of the nineteenth century by breeding *Hippeastrum vittatum* and *H. striatum* with *H. psittacinum* and some of the better hybrids available in Europe. The cultivars *Hippeastrum* 'Graveana' and 'Empress of India' were particularly outstanding and figured importantly in successive breeding efforts.

The introduction of *Hippeastrum leopoldii* and *H. pardinum* from the Andes by the plant explorer Richard Pearce, in the employ of the British firm Veitch and Sons, had lasting impact on amaryllis hybridization. Both species are notable for their large, wide-open, and relatively symmetrical flowers. When bred with the best of the Reginae hybrids, large- and very open-flowered progeny were developed, the best of which carried four to six flowers on the scape. Veitch and Sons dominated the development of the Leopoldii group and thus European amaryllis breeding well into the first quarter of the twentieth century. The best of these Veitch hybrids set the standards that largely have since dominated commercial amaryllis development.

Two additional hybrid groups were developed but either were overshadowed by the Reginae and Leopoldii types or else were never widely distributed. The Vittatum group was produced by crossing *Hippeastrum vittatum* with other species and hybrids. The majority originated in France, but England was a secondary source as well. The late-summer- to fall-blooming hybrids of the Reticulatum group (based on the Brazilian species *H. reticulatum*) were generally smaller in stature than other hybrids, evergreen, and featured a white or yellowish stripe down the midrib of the leaf (transmitted by *H. reticulatum* var. *striatifolium*; see Plate 10-6).

The late nineteenth to early twentieth centuries saw a modicum of amaryllis breeding efforts in the United States, primarily in Texas, California, and Florida. Luther Burbank developed a large-flowered group based on the European Reginae and Leopoldii groups. However, the greatest American contributions to amaryllis hybridization were those of two Florida breeders, Henry Nehrling and Theodore Mead (Bell 1973a; Hayward 1934; Traub 1934b). The Mead hybrids in particular, originating from Nehrling's germplasm, have contributed to modern hybrids when crossed with Ludwig or other Dutch stock (Bell 1973a). Though the Mead hybrids did not match the European groups in flower size and number of scapes produced, they were reliable and vigorous performers under Florida garden conditions (Bell 1973a; Hayward 1934; Traub 1958). As amaryllis production in Florida faded due to disease, competition, and failures in quality control, much of this germplasm was lost.

After the first two decades of the twentieth century, amaryllis breeding and production in Europe declined, largely a result of the two world wars. The exception was the Netherlands, which today is the center of modern amaryllis production and breeding. Large-flowered Ludwig cultivars (for example, *Hippeastrum* 'Apple Blossom', 'Dazzler', 'Dutch Belle', 'White Christmas') have rapidly become dominant among Dutch amaryllis cultivars (Ludwig and Co. 1948). Other important Dutch cultivars include the Gracilis dwarf, multiflora types ('Firefly' and 'Scarlet Baby', for example). The group was originated by H. Boegschoten, by breeding *Hippeastrum striatum* with large-flowered hybrids, and developed commercially by the Van Meeuwan and Sons Company. South Africa has also become an important breeding center and exporter of amaryllis (Barnhoorn 1976, 1991; Buck 1961; Goedert 1961) as well, particularly the Hadeco group (Barnhoorn 1976, 1991).

Before ending this short history, we should acknowledge a legion of amateur and professional breeders of amaryllis in America, Europe, Asia, and Australia. In California, Leonard Doran, C. D. Cothran, and Frederick Meyer have made substantial contributions to the field. The late Mr. and Mrs. Morris Clint and their late daughter, Marcia Wilson, of Texas; William D. Bell of Florida; and the late Ira Nelson at Louisiana State University have also produced some interesting hybrids. Prakash Narian of the National Botanic Research Institute in India and Isamu Miyake in Japan have ongoing breeding programs. Miyake's efforts with small, multiflora types are particularly interesting (Miyake 1991). From time to time, selections from these small-scale breeding programs have been offered commercially or purchased as breeding stock by large commercial endeavors.

Important Traits and Breeding Objectives

The emphasis in commercial breeding efforts in amaryllis, with the exception of the Gracilis group, has traditionally been on large flower size, a trait attributable specifically to genes originating in *Hippeastrum leopoldii* and *H. pardinum* (Bell 1973a; Shields 1979; Traub 1958). Commercial breeding efforts subsequent to the initial flurry of primary hybridization has largely been concentrated on the hybrids themselves, leading to a greater complexity of parentage (much without documentation) and dilution of many unique characteristics of the original component species (Bell 1973a, 1973b; Cage 1978; Shields 1979).

The result of these developments on commercial amaryllis breeding has been a similarity among many of the modern hybrids. The flowers, though large, tend to be of the wide, flat, dinner-plate type with little variety of form and limited variation in color (Doran 1982), despite repeated calls for renewed programs of interspecific hybridization (Bell 1973a, 1977a; Buck 1978; Cage 1978; Doran 1982; Shields 1979).

The pursuit of novelty in amaryllis hybrids has largely been the province of amateur breeders and collectors, most of whom have little inclination to commercially exploit their hobby or have failed in their attempts to do so (Cage 1980; Cothran 1979; Doran 1982; Wilson 1981). Breeding efforts by amateurs have largely been ignored by commercial European breeders, with the possible exception of attempts to develop a large-flowered yellow hybrid (Blossfeld 1973; Cothran 1979, 1980, 1981, 1984, 1985; Goedert 1982). There has also been some commercial interest in double-flowered varieties (Bell 1977b).

Amaryllis hybrids could be improved in a number of ways, including novel attributes of flower form (trumpet or long-tubed perianth, novel pigmentation patterns), reintroduction of fragrance, evergreen foliage, repeat bloom, as well as improvements along more strictly cultural criteria (resistance to hippeastrum mosaic virus and red scorch [*Stagonospora curtisii*]). Bell (1973a, 1977a), Cage (1978), and Shields (1979) discuss potential goals in amaryllis breeding.

BREEDING AND PLOIDY LEVEL

The overwhelming majority of *Hippeastrum* species are diploid, with a somatic chromosome number of $2n = 22$ (Arroyo 1982; Flory and Coulthard 1981; Naranjo and Andrada 1975). Virtually all the complex hybrid materials presently in cultivation are tetraploid (Bell 1973a, 1973b, 1977a; Shields 1979), a result of both selection for tetraploid progeny (often associated with larger plant and flower size in hybrid amaryllis) and incorporation of a few natural tetraploid species in early hybridization efforts (some forms of *Hippeastrum striatum*, for example). A few species of *Hippeastrum* have been reported with higher ploidy levels than $4n$ (Traub 1958), but I am not aware of any breeding efforts with them.

The concentration of recent commercial breeding efforts among the various populations of tetraploids may exist for several reasons: 1) desirable characteristics of flower size, scape number, and plant vigor are already stabilized in the hybrid races; 2) sterile triploid progeny result when diploid species are crossed with tetraploid hybrids (Bell 1973b, 1977a); 3) many of the diploid species are not readily available; and 4) self-incompatibility, which occurs in most diploid species and diploid hybrids, generally breaks down in the tetraploid hybrids (Bell 1973a, 1977a; Cage 1978; Shields 1979; Williams 1980), thereby allowing breeders to obtain a segregating F_2 generation.

BREEDING AT THE DIPLOID LEVEL

The advantages of crossing the diploid species of *Hippeastrum* are several: 1) novel traits can only be found among the species; 2) diploid species are readily interfertile; 3) diploid F_1 hybrids often flower in 18 months or less from seed; and 4) hybrid vigor is frequently expressed in the F_1 generation in the form of higher scape and bud counts. The disadvantages are twofold. Firstly, clonal self-incompatibility, which characterizes most wild species, carries over into the hybrids. I have even found that compatibility barriers between siblings of the same cross are more often the rule than the exception. Secondly, the green throat and/or floral tube of most species, which by and large is considered an objectionable characteristic in the marketplace, appears in the hybrids as well. Diploid hybrids will also have smaller flowers than the commercial cultivars of the Leopoldii group.

BREEDING DIPLOIDS AND TETRAPLOIDS

It is generally believed that diploid and tetraploid amaryllis are difficult to breed. Previous reports have stated that if diploids are used as maternal (seed) parents with tetraploid pollen, only sterile triploid progeny will result, whereas the reciprocal cross (tetraploid as seed parent, diploid as pollen parent) will rarely set any seed at all (Bell 1973b, 1977a). The ovary may begin to swell with developing seeds but then aborts before full term. In the latter situation, progeny can sometimes be obtained through embryo rescue, in which the developing ovule is excised from the ovary several days after pollination and grown on a sterile tissue culture medium, although this is probably beyond the resources of most amateur amaryllis hybridizers. In my experience, however, using tetraploid pollen on diploid seed parents can yield a small number of tetraploid progeny. Interestingly, when I have pollinated some diploid hybrids or species with pollen of certain Dutch hybrids, a full and apparently normal seed capsule will develop. Most of the seeds, however, contain no embryo. Approximately 10% of the seed will germinate, yielding a mix of triploids and tetraploids. Unreduced gametes (that is, egg cells with 22 rather than the usual 11 chromosomes) in the diploid parent are the probable source of the few tetraploid progeny that occur in these crosses.

BREEDING TRIPLOIDS

The triploid progeny that usually result from $2n$ (diploid) $\times 4n$ (tetraploid) crosses of amaryllis are usually sterile both when selfed and crossed (Bell 1973b). Rarely can triploids be crossed with diploid species or hybrids, though techniques of embryo culture can be used to "rescue" progeny of such crosses, as long as fertilization has taken place and the developing seeds are placed in culture before the ovary begins to abort. Greater success has been reported in crossing triploid amaryllis with tetraploids, perhaps due to some degree of random assortment of the third set of chromosomes during gamete formation (Bell 1973b). Triploids may allow introgression of desirable traits into established tetraploid cultivars without rapid dilution of those traits, which occurs with diploid-tetraploid crosses followed by exclusively tetraploid breeding. The success of this strategy is of course dependent on whether the genes for the desired traits are represented on the third set of chromosomes in the triploids.

BREEDING TETRAPLOIDS

The self-incompatibility of most diploid amaryllis almost invariably disappears in tetraploid hybrids and most tetraploid species (Bell 1973a, 1977a; Cage 1978; Shields 1979; Williams 1980). Most tetraploids can be readily self-pollinated and intercrossed with a resulting high percentage of viable seed. This has largely been the source of today's commercial amaryllis cultivars and is the easiest breeding program for the interested amateur hybridizer to undertake, as much due to the wide availability of tetraploid hybrids as to the absence of compatibility barriers.

LESSER KNOWN SPECIES AND SPECIES GROUPS
USEFUL FOR BREEDING PROGRAMS

Hippeastrum papilio. First described in 1970, *Hippeastrum papilio* (Plate 10-4) may be the most significant amaryllis introduction in the twentieth century. It is evergreen, and the foliage is quite handsome relative to most other *Hippeastrum*. The species flowers regularly in late winter or early spring, though some growers have reported fall flowering as well. *Hippeastrum papilio* seems to be resistant (though not immune) to both hippeastrum mosaic virus and red scorch fungus. The flowers, which last for at least a week on the plant, are laterally compressed, with broad lateral tepals that are attractively patterned with red to purple on a background of white and light green. The species is self-compatible (Bell 1977a). It transmits foliage quality and evergreen nature to its F_1 hybrids. To retain the evergreen characteristic, however, subsequent progeny must have at least 50% *papilio* genes. The green background of the flower tends to muddy the colors of F_1 hybrids, but subsequent breeding with pure whites or clean pastel shades will bring out the rich magenta undertones of *H. papilio*. Due to the species's green background, it is probably not desirable to backcross *papilio*-hybrids to the species. F_1 hybrids of *H. papilio* are particularly vigorous and may regularly produce four, even five, scapes from older bulbs each season.

Trumpet-flowered White Species. The group of trumpet-flowered white *Hippeastrum* species has largely been ignored by twentieth-century breeders of commercial amaryllis hybrids. The species are not well understood taxonomically. A number of erstwhile species have been included as variants of *Hippeastrum argentinum* in some taxonomic accounts; for the purposes of this discussion, the original species designations will be followed. The two most useful species are *H. brasilianum* (Plate 10-1) and *H. fragrantissimum*. Both species produce two to four large, fragrant, long-tubed white flowers that resemble Easter lilies (*Lilium longiflorum*). The flowers are longer-lasting than those of other white, trumpet-flowered species. *Hippeastrum brasilianum*, from the state of Espiritu Santo in Brazil, is most useful for breeders in warm climates. *Hippeastrum fragrantissimum*, from Bolivia, requires cool temperatures during its long dormant period, and it will transmit this requirement to its F_1 progeny. If subjected to long, hot, humid summers, the bulbs will decline. Other species include *H. candidum*, which bears six flowers (unfortunately very short-lived) to a scape in late spring, and *H. solandriflorum*, a species broadly distributed throughout Central and South America.

Hippeastrum reticulatum var. *striatifolium*. The *striatifolium* variety of the Brazilian species *Hippeastrum reticulatum* is notable for the distinct white midrib on the leaves (Plate 10-6). The flowers vary in color from pink to almost lavender, and in form from trumpet-shaped and nodding to more widely spreading. Unlike virtually all other species, *H. reticulatum* var. *striatifolium* flowers in late summer to early fall. Some clones maintain their leaves year-round. It is another one of the few amaryllis that can be successfully self-pollinated. The white striping of the leaves segregates in a 3:1

ratio among selfed progeny and carries over into F_1 hybrids with other species (Bell 1977a), suggesting control by a single dominant gene. Mixed populations are frequently observed in the wild in Brazil. Further breeding will, however, dilute the leaf striping unless hybrids are backcrossed to the species or to the F_1's. All clones (striped or not) of *H. reticulatum* are fairly compact plants and can also be useful for breeding smaller-statured hybrids. The species occurs in the understory of tropical forests and requires heavier shade than most other amaryllis species. This lower light requirement seems to be imparted to F_1 hybrids as well.

Breeding for Yellow Amaryllis. Despite the release in recent years of *Hippeastrum* cultivars such as 'Yellow Pioneer', 'Lemon Lime', and 'Germa', a Leopoldii-type clear yellow amaryllis has remained elusive. Three species produce yellow flowers—*Hippeastrum evansiae* (Bolivia), *H. parodii* (Argentina), and *H. algaiae* (Argentina)—and not surprisingly, breeding efforts for yellow have concentrated on these species. Of the three, *H. evansiae* (Plate 10-3) is best adapted for growing in hot, humid climates. These species should be crossed only with green- or white-flowered species and hybrids, as brightly pigmented parents will mask expression of the yellow coloration in the progeny. Cothran (1979, 1980, 1981, 1984) has detailed his efforts (and trials) toward a large, yellow hybrid amaryllis.

Spider- or Orchid-flowered Species. Two species of *Hippeastrum* have unusual, highly asymmetrical flowers with narrow tepals that resemble the flowers of Aztec lily (*Sprekelia formosissima*). The lower tepals form a tube around the staminal filaments and the style. *Hippeastrum cybister*, from Bolivia, has green and maroon flowers (Plate 10-2), and *H. angustifolium*, from Brazil and Argentina, is red flowered. The latter species grows as an emergent aquatic plant along streambanks and in marshes, and it has been observed with as many as nine flowers on a scape. Both species impart some of their unusual spider-flowered character to their hybrids, especially F_1's resulting from crosses with other diploid species. If crossed to tetraploids, this unique characteristic is quickly diluted.

Species with High Flower Number. A number of *Hippeastrum* species regularly produce scapes with six to nine flowers. This character is readily transmitted to their hybrids, sometimes through a second generation of breeding (Bell 1977a). It appears to be a dominant character but is not inherited in simple Mendelian ratios, which indicates that it is controlled by more than one gene. It should also be noted that an increase in flower number sometimes accompanies an increase in ploidy level. Species frequently holding more than four flowers on a scape include *Hippeastrum angustifolium*, *H. breviflorum*, *H. cybister*, *H. fosteri*, and *H. reticulatum*.

Smaller-statured Species. The success of the Gracilis group of amaryllis indicates an interest in amaryllis hybrids with smaller flowers and more compact foliage. The tetraploid *Hippeastrum striatum* has been the primary contributor to the Gracilis group and is still an excellent choice for crossing with Dutch-type tetraploid hybrids with which it is readily compatible due to its own tetraploid genotype. The closely related *H. petiolatum* (Plate 10-5), also tetraploid, will produce Gracilis-like progeny when crossed with large-flowered, tetraploid cultivars. Other dwarf species include *H. reticulatum*, discussed earlier, and *H. espiritense*.

Breeding for Specific Traits

COLOR AND PIGMENTATION PATTERNS

Little is known of the genetics of color inheritance in *Hippeastrum*. Anthocyanin pigments (reds) appear dominant over carotenoid-based pigments such as yellow. Green and white flowers are essentially without pigment expression. In green amaryllis flowers, chloroplasts present in the surface cells of the tepals are responsible for the color expression. These chloroplasts are presumably absent in white-flowered species or cultivars. If the goal is to preserve unique patterns of color in a species or hybrid, further breeding efforts should concentrate on parents with white or light pastel floral shades. Dark reds or pinks will usually overwhelm zonations of color on a white or greenish white background, and the progeny will be mostly or entirely the color of the dark-colored parent (assuming that at least one parent is homozygous for red). If both parents have interesting patterns of pigmentation on a white or greenish white background, the progeny frequently show novel combinations of these patterns. The amount of variation that will appear in an F₁ generation is directly proportional to the degree of heterozygosity and heterogeneity in the parents for genes controlling color formation and expression. By repeatedly intercrossing progeny with the same flower color, generation after generation, it is possible to develop groups of seed-propagated, true-breeding stock for flower color. This is, in fact, what a number of the early European and American breeders and producers did before the advent of large-scale vegetative propagation. Repeated selfing of self-compatible cultivars of pure color will also achieve these results, but it may also result in loss of vigor due to inbreeding depression.

FRAGRANCE

Fragrance in amaryllis appears to be a recessive trait, though no genetic analysis of the characteristic has been performed. Progeny of two fragrant parents are usually fragrant. When a fragrant diploid is crossed to a non-fragrant diploid, the F_1 hybrids will often segregate for this character, suggesting that the nonfragrant parent may be heterozygous for the fragrance gene (if indeed, a single gene is responsible). When nonfragrant diploids are crossed with fragrant tetraploids, the majority of the progeny are fragrant, perhaps due to the presence of two copies of the fragrance gene(s) in the F_1 genome. As is evident from the overwhelming lack of fragrance in many of the modern commercial cultivars, the trait is rapidly diluted and lost unless persistent backcrossing to the fragrant parent or further complex hybridization is performed using other fragrant species or hybrids. Fragrance also appears to be linked with white or pastel-colored flowers in amaryllis.

DOUBLE FLOWERS

Double-flowered amaryllis are an acquired taste, but there has always been some interest in them. The first reported double amaryllis was found in the wild in Cuba, a form of *Hippeastrum puniceum*. Significant breeding for double flowers was first reported by McCann (1937). Additional tepal-like structures apparently result from transformations of both stamens and style (male and female reproductive structures). Observations on the inheritance of double flowers indicate that it is a dominant trait (Latapie and Latapie 1982; McCann 1937, 1950). Recent bulb catalogs have offered some double-flowered cultivars such as 'Double Picotee', 'Lady Jane', and 'Pasadena'. Double-flowered amaryllis may not have any functional reproductive parts or may produce some pollen-containing anthers at the ends of some of the transformed, petal-like stamens. This pollen can used for successive breeding efforts.

RESISTANCE TO DISEASE

Hippeastrum or amaryllis mosaic virus and the fungus *Stagonospora curtisii* (red scorch) are the two most serious diseases encountered by amaryllis growers. Viral mosaic symptoms are rarely if ever encountered on plants in the wild. *Hippeastrum papilio* and *H. reticulatum* do not manifest foliar symptoms as readily as other species and hybrids, but this is no guarantee of actual resistance. However, Williams (1982) has observed that amaryllis species with grayish waxy (glaucous) foliage seem to be resistant to red scorch infection. I have also noticed this resistance among such species in my own germplasm collection. Breeding for disease resistance is an area in which much additional work is needed. When growing progeny trials, breeders of amaryllis should be alert for particular crosses or select clones that seem to show resistance to diseases affecting other progeny.

Hybridization Mechanics

POLLEN COLLECTION AND STORAGE

All *Hippeastrum* flowers are strongly protandrous, which means that the anthers shed their pollen before the surface of the stigma is receptive to pollen. In the wild, this mechanism helps prevent self-pollination. As the flower begins to open, the anthers are noticeably large and no pollen is visible on the surface. Once the flower is completely open, the anther sacs dehisce, the anthers shrink in size, and yellow pollen is clearly visible on the surface of the anthers. In most species, the pollen is bright yellow. Pollen should be collected, for immediate use or storage, as soon as the anthers shrink and the pollen becomes visible. Pollen is most effectively stored in size 00 or 000 gelatin capsules, which can usually be purchased from a pharmacy or pharmaceutical supply house. The anthers with exposed pollen are carefully removed from the filaments with a metal forceps or tweezers and placed into the longer portion of the capsule. The capsule is put back together and then should be stored in one of several ways. I prefer placing single capsules in small plastic vials with hinged snap lids. A small amount of desiccant is placed in the bottom quarter of the vial, and the capsule is inserted over that. I prefer an indicating desiccant (such as calcium silicate) that changes color when it absorbs moisture. Additional desiccant is then poured into the vial until the capsule is covered. The vial should be marked with the name of the plant from which the pollen was taken or by some other system of identification, along with the date that the pollen was collected, using an indelible felt-tip pen. I also prefer to attach a small string label to the vial with the same information. The vial is then maintained at room temperature for 24 hours, at the end of which time the desiccant is replaced if the indicator dye shows absorption of moisture. The vial can then be placed in the refrigerator or the freezer, depending on how long storage will be required. Alternatively, capsules can be stored together in Mason or other tightly lidded jars with desiccant. In this latter case, identification should be written directly on the individual gelatin capsules. Nonfat, powdered milk has also been used effectively as a desiccant for this purpose (Bell 1982).

Pfeiffer (1936) found that amaryllis pollen can be stored for more than 5 months at 50°F (10°C) and less than 50% humidity and will retain germination rates of 50–75%. If the pollen is to be used exclusively during the current flowering season, storage under refrigeration (40–50°F [4–10°C]) should be sufficient. If, however, the pollen will be stored until the following year, the vials should be placed in the freezer. I have repeatedly produced seed with one-year-old pollen that has been frozen since collection.

Anthers can also be collected just before they dehisce, but they must then be dried sufficiently before they can be stored. This is best accomplished by placing the immature anthers on a small piece of white paper and placing the paper in a jar or other chamber over a desiccant such as calcium silicate. Once the anthers shrink and pollen appears, the anthers and pollen can be stored as just described.

DETERMINING STIGMA RECEPTIVITY

Two different types of stigmas occur in *Hippeastrum*. The most common has three distinct lobes of varying length; rarely, the lobes are largely reduced and the stigma appears round or vaguely triangular. When an amaryllis flower first opens, the style is usually shorter than it will be at maturity and is either declined away from the anthers or held horizontally outward from the flower. The stigmatic lobes remain tightly together. As the flower ages, the style elongates and begins to curve upward. When the stigma is fully receptive, the style is fully curved upward, the stigmatic lobes are fully expanded, and the tiny hairs on the stigmatic surface, called papillae, are clearly visible and upright, giving the stigma a furry appearance. If the stigma is not yet receptive, pollen often will not adhere well to the surface. Stigma receptivity is generally reached on the second to third day after the anthers release their pollen, but this varies from species to species. As the flower ages further, a bead of viscous fluid may appear on the stigma. Contrary to some observations, when this sticky exudate appears, the stigma is past peak receptivity to pollen.

EMASCULATION AND BAGGING OF FLOWERS

Emasculation is the removal of the anthers from a flower scheduled for cross-pollination. It is wise to emasculate any amaryllis flower to which foreign pollen will be applied, even if the plant is known to be self-incompatible. The presence of even a small amount of self pollen on the stigma may induce post-pollination physiological reactions that will prevent any further use of that flower. Enclosing the flower in a paper or light fabric pollination bag after emasculation is another precaution against self-pollination or unwanted foreign pollination. However, I have seen no evidence of insect transmission of amaryllis pollen (most species are pollinated in the wild by hummingbirds) and so do not bag the flowers, whether in the field or in the greenhouse.

POLLINATING AMARYLLIS FLOWERS

When the stigma is receptive, pollen should be applied to the entire surface of the lobes. If the desired pollen is in short supply, a small brush can be used to pick up pollen from the storage capsule and dust the stigmatic surface. The brush should be carefully rubbed clean of pollen before making another cross. If large quantities of the desired pollen have been stored, some of the pollen can be poured into the shorter half of the storage capsule or onto a small piece of paper, and the stigma gently dipped into it until the stigma is coated with pollen. If using pollen from another plant in flower at the same time, and if storage of the pollen is not desired, a stamen can be plucked from the flower of the pollen parent and the anther applied directly to the stigma of the seed parent, using the filament as a convenient handle (Figure 10-1). If the plants are located outside and are exposed to rain and wind, enclosing the flower after pollination in a pollination bag will help ensure that the stigma remains coated with pollen. The bag can be removed after two days.

POST-POLLINATION PHENOMENA

Within 1 or 2 days after pollination, the flower will begin to fade. The ovary begins to noticeably swell between 3 days and 1 week after pollination. If the ovary does not abort by the third week after pollination, chances are good

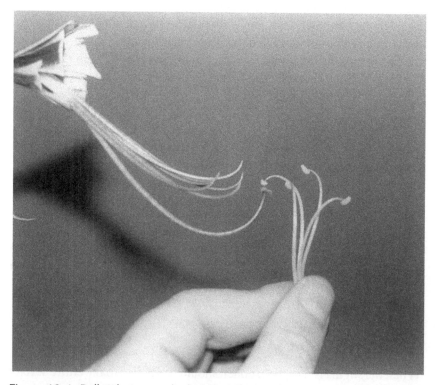

Figure 10-1. Pollen being applied to the stigma of an amaryllis flower using staminal filaments as a handle. Tepals have been removed from the flower for clarity. (Photo by Alan W. Meerow)

that fertilization has been successful and a capsule will mature. Capsule maturation takes 3 to 5 weeks on the average; the time increases as the temperature decreases, and vice-versa. During this time the stalk (pedicel) of the capsule will elongate and the ovary will increase two to three times in size. When the capsule begins to turn yellow, the seeds are fully mature. Shortly thereafter, the capsule will begin to turn brown and split open into three sections (Figures 10-2 and 10-3). When the capsule first noticeably begins to turn yellow, it can be enclosed in a bag or a piece of light fabric tied around its base to allow the capsule to open on the plant. Alternatively, the sealed but mature capsule can be removed and placed upside down in a small paper bag, where it will split open within a few days. Amaryllis seeds are black or dark brown, flat, and winged. If an unbagged capsule is allowed to open on the plant, especially a plant in the garden or the field, the seeds can easily blow away.

Seed Propagation and Growth to Flowering of Hybrids

I prefer to air-dry amaryllis seed for one day after harvest and then plant them immediately. Carpenter and Ostmark (1988a) found that seed of hybrid amaryllis can be stored for a year at 11–52% relative humidity and 40–60°F (4–16°C) without loss of viability. At higher temperatures and

Figure 10-2. Amaryllis seed capsule ready for harvest. (Photo by Alan W. Meerow)

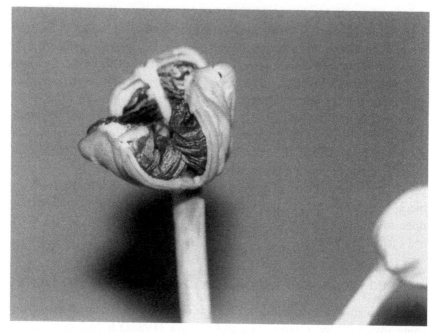

Figure 10-3. Amaryllis seed capsule split open into its three chambers. (Photo by Alan W. Meerow)

humidities, viability loss is rapid. The seed can be sown on any germination medium that drains well but retains moisture, at a temperature between 75 and 85°F (24–30°C) (Carpenter and Ostmark 1988b), and in about 50% shade. The seeds should be spread across the medium in a single layer and covered with no more than ⅛ inch (3 mm) of medium. The medium should not be allowed to dry out.

The first stages of germination (emergence of the cotyledonary petiole) will usually begin within 2 weeks, whereas appearance of the first leaf generally takes 4 to 6 weeks. New seedlings can continue to emerge for several weeks. Seed of some species or hybrids germinates rapidly, others more slowly. The seedlings should be pricked out from the germinating pot or flat when one well-developed leaf is evident. A small bulblet will be visible at that time. Seedlings should be shifted to small pots or cell trays of a sphagnum peat-based mix (ProMix, MetroMix), where they are grown until well-rooted in the cell or pot. In my breeding program, seedlings are next shifted to 4½-inch (11-cm) pots. A sizable number are then transplanted into ground beds in the field from the pots; the balance are transplanted into larger 1-gallon containers, where they are maintained until flowering. After the initial transplanting into cell trays, a coarser container mix is used for the bulbs (for example, 40% pine bark, 30% peat, 20% perlite, 10% coarse sand). The amount of shade that the bulbs require is directly related to the amount of heat they must withstand; in hot tropical or subtropical climates, 50 to 60% shade is essential; in milder zones (montane tropics or more northern latitudes), full sun is possible. Amaryllis are heavy feeders and benefit from regular fertilization.

Diploid amaryllis hybrids, especially primary F_1's between species, can flower in 18 months or less from seed, though 2 years is a more reasonable expectation. Tetraploid hybrids may require 2 to 3 years to reach flowering size.

Evaluating Hybrid Progeny

Hybrid populations should be evaluated on the basis of several criteria, including scapes produced per bulb, flower number, flower size and form, flower pigmentation, and vegetative increase (number of offset bulbs produced), as well as any other characteristic desired by the breeder. Occasionally, a diploid cross will yield one or several tetraploid progeny, probably a result of unreduced gametes in the parents. These may appear larger in all parts than their diploid siblings. It is wise to be liberal when evaluating the first generation of hybrids at their first flowering. At the outset of my own breeding program, I did not dispose of any of my initial F_1 hybrids until they were evaluated through at least 2 years of flowering. As the breeder's goals begin to be realized, larger and larger percentages of successive years' progeny will be consigned to the compost pile. The breeder must be heartless; otherwise, he or she is soon overwhelmed by sheer quantities of germplasm. Only superior selections fulfilling a substantial portion of the breeding program's goals will be used in successive generations of crosses.

BREEDING AFTER THE F_1 GENERATION AT THE
DIPLOID LEVEL

It is always desirable to obtain an F_2 generation if possible. It is in the F_2, obtained either by selfing selected progeny or through sibling crosses, that segregation of parental characters in various combinations occurs. Unfortunately, producing an F_2 is problematic at the diploid level. With repeated effort, the breeder should be able to obtain some sibling crosses among diploid progeny. Successful self-pollination will in most cases be restricted to tetraploid hybrids. The use of complex hybrids between progeny selections from the various F_1 crosses is the most successful strategy for further breeding at the diploid level. If the diploid hybrids share a parent species, desirable characteristics of that species will hopefully predominate in the F_2.

Diploid hybrids of complex parentage—(species A × species B) × (species C × species D)—may show less vigor than the original F_1 parents, as well as lower fertility. These complex second-generation hybrids can then be back-crossed to one or both of their F_1 parents. This tactic will sometimes restore a measure of vigor and fertility. Finally, F_1 primary interspecific hybrids can be crossed to a third species with desired characteristics.

Vegetative Propagation of Selected Clones

Amaryllis have *tunicate* bulbs. This type of bulb consists of tightly overlapping modified leaves called scales and, at the bottom of each bulb, a specialized structure called the basal plate. Amaryllis may be propagated asexually using offsets formed at the base of the parent bulb. Many tetraploid cultivars do not readily form such offsets. Offset production can sometimes be stimulated by cutting small wedge-shaped sections from the base of the bulb, wounding both the basal plate and the base of the bulb scales. The most common type of bulb propagation for amaryllis, however, is bulb scale cuttage or twin-scaling.

PROPAGATING BY THE TWIN-SCALE METHOD

1. Cut off all leaves and the lower portion of the basal plate (from where the roots originate). It is important to leave some of the basal plate intact.
2. Divide the bulb into longitudinal, wedge-shaped sections. One bulb can be divided into 4 to 16 sections, depending on its size.
3. Carefully divide each wedge into sections consisting of two leaf scales and a piece of the basal plate. The scales can be shortened by cutting away some of the top growth.
4. Disinfect the twin-scale cuttings with a 10- to 20-minute soak in any broad-spectrum fungicide.
5. Insert the cuttings on a slant, with the concave side facing down, into flats of moist propagating medium (1:1 by volume perlite and vermiculite or sterile sand) deep enough so that the attached portion of the basal plate is just covered.
6. Place flats under 80% shade, and maintain even moisture in the propagating medium. The medium should be maintained at 75–80°F (24–27°C) if possible. Periodic drenches with fungicide may be beneficial, particularly if temperatures are less than 70°F (21°C) or more than 85°F (30°C).
7. Bulblets should form at the base of the scale cutting 2 to 3 months after the scales are stuck. These may be detached after the first leaf forms and individually potted in small containers. The scales, if not damaged during these operations, can often be used again for additional bulblet production.

The regenerative powers of the basal plate can also be invoked by cutting the plate off just below the bulb scales. The damaged bulb is then stored in sterile medium and kept in shade. A ring of bulblets will usually form around the base in response to the damage.

TISSUE CULTURE (MICROPROPAGATION)

Amaryllis can also be propagated by sterile (aseptic) tissue culture techniques using specialized media (Alderson and Rice 1986; Bose and Jana 1977; Phunsiri et al. 1982; Seabrook and Cumming 1977). These methods are beyond the scope of this book and will not be discussed in detail. Typical materials for micropropagation of amaryllis include twin-scales and developing floral stem tissue. In the latter case, scapes are harvested just as they emerge from the bulb, and a small section of tissue at the base of the individual flower stem (pedicel) is excised under sterile conditions. For reasons unknown, this tissue has the potential to give rise to bulblets but seems more prone to spontaneous mutation than twin-scale explants.

Induction of Polyploidy and Mutations

As mentioned previously, the self-incompatibility system in diploid amaryllis usually breaks down in tetraploids. Attempts to induce tetraploidy in diploid amaryllis with colchicine have only been sparingly successful. Williams (1982) described a protocol for treating amaryllis seedlings with a 0.05% aqueous solution of colchicine mixed with 7 grams per liter of agar. The solution is heated to dissolve the agar and poured off into small containers. Young seedlings (3 to 4 days after germination) are inverted and immersed in the colchicine gel up to the level just above the roots and left for 24 hours. They are thoroughly rinsed, then planted in seedling medium. Of those that survive the treatment (colchicine treatments often prove fatal to amaryllis seedlings), some will be induced tetraploids. Unfortunately, using this method I have found that surviving seedlings are usually unstable tetraploids (cells when prepared for chromosome observation show a mix of ploidy levels) and eventually revert to completely diploid. A far more promising method involves using the herbacide oryzalin as a 0.001% ingredient in sterile medium, upon which twin-scale explants are cultured (Van Tuyl et al. 1992). The method has worked successfully on *Nerine*, another member of the Amaryllidaceae. Irradiation of seed or tissue cultured plantlets is another means of inducing both tetraploidy and mutative morphological changes in amaryllis (Kaicker and Singh 1979), but the necessary equipment is generally unavailable to amateur breeders.

Resources

COLLECTIONS

Germplasm of *Hippeastrum* species is not readily available. Various botanical gardens may have some species in their collections, but these frequently are without collection data and are not correctly identified. Longwood Gardens; the University of California, Irvine Arboretum; and the Royal Botanic Gardens, Kew, all have a number of amaryllis species in their collections. The best collections are in the hands of individuals who will sometimes entertain polite requests for material. Many collectors go to great personal expense to obtain this material, and requests from others often do not take this into consideration.

Longwood Gardens
P.O. Box 501
409 Conservatory Road
Kennett Square, PA 19348
U.S.A.

Irvine Arboretum
University of California-Irvine
Irvine, CA 92717
U.S.A.

Royal Botanic Gardens, Kew
Richmond, Surrey TW9 3AB
England

SUPPLIERS

Commercial dealers of amaryllis species tend to be small "mom and pop" operations that may suddenly disappear from the marketplace. Most of the following listed sources offer tetraploid, Dutch-type cultivars only. If some species are available, this is indicated.

United States

Amaryllis, Inc.
P.O. Box 318
1452 Glenmore Avenue
Baton Rouge, LA 70821
phone: 504-924-5560
Mostly hybrids

The Amaryllis Bulb Company
1409 N.W. 143 Street
Gainesville, FL 32606
phone: 904-332-4672
Hybrids, many with Mead or
Nehrling bloodlines

Dutch Gardens
P.O. Box 200
Adelphia, NJ 07710-0200
phone: 908-780-2713 or
    800-818-3861

Glasshouse Works
Church Street, P.O. Box 97
Stewart, OH 45778-0097
phone: 614-662-2142
Some species

Holland Bulb Farms
P.O. Box 220
Tatamy, PA 18085
phone: 800-283-5082

Park Seed Company
1 Parkton Avenue
Greenwood, SC 29647-0001
phone: 864-223-8555 or
   800-845-3369
Regularly stocks *Hippeastrum papilio*;
occasionally offers other species.
Also available from their subsidiary
Wayside Gardens.

TyTy Plantation Bulb Company
Box 159
TyTy, GA 31795
phone: 912-382-0404

Van Bourgondien Bros.
P.O. Box 1000
245 Route 109
Babylon, NY 11702
phone: 516-669-3500 or
   800-622-9997

United Kingdom

Paul Christian Rare Plants
P.O. Box 468
Wrexham, Clwyd LL13 9XR
Wales
phone: (44) 1978-366399
Species

Harry Hay
Margery Hall Pig Farm
Margery Lane, Lower Kingswood
Tadworth, Surrey KT20 7DG
Seed of some species, small
quantities of bulbs

Australia

Pine Heights Nursery
Pepper Street
Everton Hills, Queensland 4053
phone: (61) 73-3532761
Species

INTERNATIONAL REGISTRATION AUTHORITY

Royal General Bulbgrowers Association (KABV)
Attn: Johan van Scheepen
Postbus 175
NL-2180 Ad Hillegom
The Netherlands

PLANT SOCIETIES

The American Amaryllis Society metamorphosed into the American Plant Life
Society, and finally into the International Bulb Society (IBS). The IBS publishes a semiannual journal, *Herbertia*, and a quarterly newsletter. There is no
finer clearinghouse for information on bulbous plants, especially those of the
amaryllis family. The IBS maintains a seed fund from which members can purchase seed of many rare species for nominal cost. To join the IBS, write

International Bulb Society
P.O. Box 92136
Pasadena, CA 91109-2136
U.S.A.

References and Additional Reading

Alderson, P. G., and R. D. Rice. 1986. Propagation of bulbs from floral stem tissues. In *Plant Tissue Culture and Its Agricultural Applications*. Eds. Lyndsey A. Withers and P. G. Alderson. London: Butterworths. 91–97.

Arroyo, S. 1982. The chromosomes of *Hippeastrum, Amaryllis* and *Phycella* (Amaryllidaceae). *Kew Bulletin* 37: 211–216.

Barnhoorn, F. 1976. Breeding the 'Hadeco' amaryllis hybrids. *Plant Life* 32: 59–63.

———. 1991. Cultivars of *Hippeastrum:* Their evolution from the past and their development for the future. *Herbertia* 47: 76–79.

Bell, W. D. 1973a. New potentials in amaryllis breeding. *Proceedings of the Florida State Horticultural Society* 86: 462–466.

———. 1973b. The role of triploids in *Amaryllis* hybridization. *Plant Life* 29: 59–61.

———. 1974. Stomatal size as an indication of *Amaryllis* polyploidy. *Plant Life* 30: 89–90.

———. 1977a. More potentials in *Amaryllis* breeding. *Plant Life* 33: 65–69.

———. 1977b. Double flowered *Amaryllis. Proceedings of the Florida State Horticultural Society* 90: 121–122.

———. 1982. A simple technique to prolong amaryllid pollen and seed storage. *Amaryllis Bulletin* 2: 42–43.

Blossfeld, H. 1973. Breeding for yellow amaryllis hybrids. *Plant Life* 29: 56–58.

Bose, T. K., and B. K. Jana. 1977. Regeneration of plantlets in *Hippeastrum hybridum* in vitro. *Indian Journal of Horticulture* 34: 446–447.

Buck, Q. Q. 1961. First flowering of newly imported Boshoff-Mostert hybrid amaryllis. *Plant Life* 17: 84–85.

———. 1978. Amaryllis breeding potentials—1977. *Plant Life* 34: 95–98.

Cage, J. M. 1978. The role of *Amaryllis* species in future commercial hybrids. *Plant Life* 34: 98–100.

———. 1980. End of a breeding project. *Plant Life* 36: 79–81.

Carpenter, W. J., and E. R. Ostmark. 1988a. Moisture content, freezing, and storage conditions influence germination of amaryllis seed. *HortScience* 23: 1072–1074.

———. 1988b. Sensitivity of seed germination of amaryllis to light and temperature. *HortScience* 23: 1002–1004.

Cothran, C. D. 1979. Yellow-flowered and other *Amaryllis* hybrids. *Plant Life* 35: 61–65.

———. 1980. The quest for a large yellow-flowering hybrid of amaryllis. *Plant Life* 36: 19–23.

———. 1981. Continuing quest for large yellow flowering amaryllis. *Plant Life* 37: 110–111.

———. 1984. Large yellow amaryllis hybrids. *Plant Life* 40: 105–111.

———. 1985. Quest for large, yellow hippeastrums. *Plant Life* 41: 34–35.

Doran, J. L. 1982. Observations of *Hippeastrum* species hybrids. *Amaryllis Bulletin* 2: 42.

Flory, W. S., and R. F. Coulthard Jr. 1981. New chromosome counts, numbers and types in genus *Amaryllis*. *Plant Life* 37: 43–56.

Goedert, R. D. 1961. Hadeco amaryllis hybrids grown in South Africa. *Plant Life* 17: 85–86.

———. 1982. The continuing pursuit of yellow. *Plant Life* 38: 61–63.

Hayward, W. 1934. The Mead strain of the Nehrling amaryllis. *Yearbook of the American Amaryllis Society* 1: 62–63.

Kaicker, U. S., and H. P. Singh. 1979. Role of mutation breeding in amaryllis. *Plant Life* 35: 66–73.

Latapie, W., and H. Latapie. 1982. Breeding hybrid amaryllis—a rewarding experience. *Plant Life* 38: 15–18.

Ludwig and Co. 1948. The Ludwig hybrid *Amaryllis*. *Herbertia* 15: 69.

McCann, E. J. 1950. McCann double amaryllis. *Plant Life* 6: 107–108.

McCann, J. J. 1937. New double hybrid amaryllis. *Herbertia* 4: 185–186.

Miyake, M. 1991. Observation of an *Hippeastrum* breeding program. *Herbertia* 47: 73–75.

Meerow, A. W. 1988. New trends in amaryllis (*Hippeastrum*) breeding. *Proceedings of the Florida State Horticultural Society* 101: 285–288.

Naranjo, C. A., and A. B. Andrada. 1975. El cariotipo fundamental en el genéro *Hippeastrum* Herb. (Amaryllidaceae). *Darwinia* 19: 566–582.

Pfeiffer, N. E. 1936. Storage of pollen of hybrid amaryllis. *Herbertia* 3: 103–104.

Phunsiri, S., P. Gavinlertvatana, and P. Akavipat. 1982. Propagation of *Amaryllis* through tissue culture. *Kasetsart Journal of Natural Science* 16: 44–51.

Seabrook, J. E. A., and B. G. Cumming. 1977. The in vitro propagation of amaryllis (*Hippeastrum* spp.) hybrids. *In Vitro* 13: 831–836.

Shields, J. E. 1979. The ancestors of the amaryllis. *Amaryllis Bulletin* 1: 2–6.

Traub, H. P. 1934a. A preliminary amaryllis (*Hippeastrum*) checklist. *Yearbook of the American Amaryllis Society* 1: 45–51.

———. 1934b. The Nehrling hybrid amaryllis. *Yearbook of the American Amaryllis Society* 1: 61.

———. 1958. *The Amaryllis Manual*. New York: Macmillan.

Traub, H. P., and H. N. Moldenke. 1949. *Amaryllidaceae: Tribe Amarylleae*. American Plant Life Society.

Van Tuyl, J. M., B. Meijer, and M. P. van Diën. 1992. The use of oryzalin as an alternative for colchicine in in-vitro chromosome doubling of *Lilium* and *Nerine*. *Acta Horticulturae* 325: 625–630.

Williams, M. 1980. Self-sterility in *Hippeastrum* (*Amaryllis*) species. *Amaryllis Bulletin* 1: 20.

———. 1982. A tetraploid *Amaryllis starkii*. *Plant Life* 38: 59–61.

Wilson, M. C. 1981. Amaryllis hybrids of J. L. Doran. *Plant Life* 37: 109–110.

11 Breeding Penstemon

Dale T. Lindgren

Penstemon is not a household name in the community of ornamental plants. However, the broad range of adaptation, wide genetic variability, and great potential for the landscape and other uses make penstemons ideal candidates for the plant breeder interested in developing new and unusual hybrids.

The genus *Penstemon* is taxonomically classified in the family Scrophulariaceae, commonly referred to as the figwort or snapdragon family. There are approximately 270 species of *Penstemon* in the world, with a native range extending from Guatemala and Mexico through the continental United States into Canada and Alaska. Most gardeners use *Penstemon* as landscape or garden plants, but they can also be used for land restoration or reclamation projects, roadside plantings, cut flowers, and potted plants. The majority of *Penstemon* species are considered plants of dry, disturbed areas. However, some species and hybrids tolerate considerable moisture and will, in fact, require additional water to survive. Penstemons are highly variable between and within species. What may hold true for one species may be quite different for another.

Key Groups for Breeding

Penstemon hybrids can originate from natural crosses or from controlled crosses made by plant breeders. Hybrids do occur in the wild but usually only where the natural range of different species overlap. These hybrids are often referred to as hybrid swarms or hybrid colonies. Natural hybrids may also occur when different species or selections are grown in close proximity in gardens. This provides an environment where cross-pollinations between species are more likely to occur.

Numerous interspecific crosses in *Penstemon* have been reported but not all have resulted in named hybrids (Moore 1980; Uhlinger and Viehmeyer 1971). Named hybrids that have resulted from interspecific crosses have been placed into six groups for discussion in this review. These six groups are 1) *Dasanthera* subgenus hybrids, 2) *Penstemon* section hybrids, 3) *Peltanthera* section hybrids, 4) Flathead Lake hybrids, 5) Gloxinoide hybrids, and 6) miscellaneous hybrids.

DASANTHERA SUBGENUS HYBRIDS

Dasanthera hybrids originated between species within the *Dasanthera* subgenus, a group of low-growing, semi-woody plants native to the northwestern United States. Species reported as the most common parents of hybrids in this section include *Penstemon barrettiae, P. cardwellii, P. davidsonii, P. fruticosus,* and *P. rupicola.* The hybrids may have one or more characteristics that make them distinct from their parents. Examples of named hybrids within this section include 'Blue Mink' (*P. rupicola* × *P. fruticosus*), a natural hybrid with rosy purple flowers and leaves edged with a fine red line; 'Breitenbush Blue' (*P. cardwellii* × *P. davidsonii*), natural hybrid; 'Cardinal' (*P. rupicola* × *P. cardwellii*), a smaller version of *P. cardwellii* with red flowers; 'Carol' (*P. rupicola* × *P. fruticosus*), a natural hybrid with a coral-pink corolla; 'Crystal' (*P. barrettiae* × *P. cardwellii* 'Albus'), a hardy, compact bush with translucent white flowers; 'Edithae' (*P. rupicola* × *P. barrettiae*); 'Grape Tart' (*P. cardwellii* 'John Bacher' × *P. davidsonii* var. *menziesii* 'Albus'), with shiny green foliage tinged with orange and a two-tone lavender corolla; 'Keechelus Veronica' (*P. rupicola* × *P. fruticosus*), a close-packed mat with tiny, deeply toothed leaves; 'Martha Raye' (*P. rupicola* × *P. fruticosus*), extra-wide mouth and deep rose; 'Santiam' (*P. rupicola* × *P. davidsonii*), green mat, 2 inches (5 cm) high; 'Sherrard Shell' (*P. cardwellii* × *P. rupicola*), a trailing plant; 'Starkers Blue' (*P. fruticosus* × *P. rupicola*), a low mound of dark green leaves and rosy lilac flowers; and 'Wax Works' (*P. cardwellii* 'John Bacher' × [*P. davidsonii* var. *menziesii* 'Albus' × *P. cardwellii* 'John Bacher']), with wax-thickened, shiny, deep green leaves and bright lavender-purple flowers. Other hybrids in the *Dasanthera* subgenus are *Penstemon* 'Bitterroot' and 'Logan Pass', from crosses of *P. lyallii* × *P. ellipticus.*

Numerous other cultivars in this subgenus are merely forms or variants of a species and not true hybrids. These include *Penstemon barrettiae* 'Gina' (glaucous, silver leaves), *P. cardwellii* 'Floyd McMullen' (low, tight growth with wine red flowers), *P. cardwellii* 'John Bacher' (white form), *P. fruticosus* 'Charming' (pink flowers), *P. fruticosus* var. *serratus* 'Holly' (leaves deeply serrate and dark green), and *P. rupicola* 'Diamond Lake' (pink flowers) (Vesall 1990).

PENSTEMON SECTION HYBRIDS

Several named hybrids have resulted from crosses between species in the section *Penstemon*, a division of the subgenus *Penstemon*. These hybrids include 'Goldie' (*Penstemon confertus* 'Kittitas' × *P. euglaucus*); 'Rose Queen' (*P. calycosus* × *P. digitalis*), which combines the flower shape of *P. digitalis* with the flower color of *P. calycosus;* 'Early Bird' (*P. canescens* × *P. arkansanus*), bearing red-velvet flowers with a white underlip; and 'Dusty' (*P. confertus* × *P. peckii*). 'Husker Red', a selection of *P. digitalis*, was released for its reddish foliage color (Plate 11-2) (Lindgren 1984).

PELTANTHERA SECTION HYBRIDS

Reported hybrids in the *Peltanthera* section include 'Bryantae' (*Penstemon spectabilis* × *P. palmeri*), deep pink flowers on 2- to 3-inch (5–7.5 cm) stalks; 'Dubium' (*P. centranthifolius* × *P. grinnellii*), leaves glaucous, small, and finely serrate; and 'Parishii' (*P. centranthifolius* × *P. spectabilis*). *Penstemon palmeri* has been reported to hybridize with most any species within this section.

FLATHEAD LAKE HYBRIDS

The 'Flathead Lake' hybrid originated as a natural hybrid near Flathead Lake, Montana (American Horticultural Society 1951; Uhlinger and Viehmeyer 1971). It was theorized to be a natural cross between *Penstemon barbatus* and some species in the *Habroanthus* section. This hybrid has deep green lanceolate leaves and flowers with a shark's-head shape that are coral-red to spectrum red in color. Uhlinger and Viehmeyer (1971) determined that this hybrid could accept pollen from many other species and, therefore, could be used as an "intermediate vehicle" or a "bridge" in bringing in germplasm from other species for combining traits. Reported releases involving *Penstemon* 'Flathead Lake' include 'Arroyo', 'Elfin Pink', 'Flamingo', 'Indian Jewels', 'Peacock', 'Prairie Dawn', 'Prairie Dusk', 'Prairie Fire', 'Princess Rose', 'Rainbow Ribbons', and 'Scharf' hybrids. All these have similarly shaped flowers.

GLOXINOIDE HYBRIDS

Gloxinoide hybrids are described as broad-leaved hybrids of *Penstemon hartwegii* with *P. cobaea* or variants of *P. hartwegii*. These plants include many of the European hybrids, such as 'Alice Hindley', 'Blackbird', 'Chester Scarlet', 'King George V', 'Port Wine', 'Stapleford Gem', and 'White Bedder'. This group consisted of some of the earliest hybrids to be used commercially. The flowers of these plants were so large (and similar to gloxinias) that they were popularly referred to as *P. gloxinioides* types. The term "Gloxinoide," however, has no botanical significance in this genus and is an invalid species name (Way and James 1998). There is another group of hybrids that are very popular in the United Kingdom as well, but these have narrow leaves. These selections include 'Firebird', 'Garnet', 'Papal Purple', and 'Threave Pink' (Way 1996).

MISCELLANEOUS HYBRIDS

Numerous reports have been made of other named *Penstemon* hybrids (Lindgren and Davenport 1992). These include *Penstemon murrayanus* crossed with *P. grandiflorus* ('Avalon', 'Fate', 'Fate-Seeba', and 'Seeba'), *P. cobaea* × *P. triflorus* ('Henry' hybrids, 'Prairie Splendor'), *P. hirsutus* × *P. richardsonii* ('Continental'), *P. pseudospectabilis* × *P. eatonii* ('Crideri'), and *P. grinnellii* × *P. speciosus* ('Peirshii'). Bruce Meyers has also released a complex of hybrids known as 'Mexicana' and 'Mexicali'. 'Mexicana' originated from crosses of a mix of species from the *Fasciculus* and *Peltanthera* sections. 'Mexicali' is a result of the 'Mexicana' hybrids crossed with 'Sensation' hybrids. The 'Sensation' hybrids are considered a large-flowered Gloxinoide-type (*P. hartwegii* or *P. hartwegii* × *P. cobaea*) of *Penstemon*. These hybrid complexes are a rich pool of germplasm for plant breeders to work with. Crosswhite (1965) summarized reports of the hybridization of *P. barbatus* with species of the section *Habroanthus*. Many other hybrids between various species are reported but have not been documented, and some are only suspected of being hybrids. Variation in progeny from suspected crosses may only be the result of variation within a selfed species, since self-pollination can result in the expression of recessive genes that are normally not expressed. For a more complete summary of attempted crosses, successful and unsuccessful, refer to the articles by Moore (1980) and Uhlinger and Viehmeyer (1971).

Breeding Objectives

There are numerous traits that plant breeders can work with when hybridizing *Penstemon*. Flowering characteristics are a priority for most hybridizers, specifically flowering time, flowering duration (ever-blooming), flower color, and flower size. Secund flowering (flowering on one side of the inflorescence) is a trait that some breeders want to avoid but others find desirable. Flower fragrance can also be a consideration; *Penstemon haydenii* and *P. palmeri* are considered the two most fragrant species, and both are potential parents when breeding for fragrance.

In the eastern region of the United States and in areas of the world with high precipitation and high humidity, disease resistance is a major concern in selecting and breeding *Penstemon*. Poorly drained soils lead to root rot and similar diseases. The Mexican species are quite tolerant of diseases, especially foliar diseases, and therefore should be considered as parents when breeding for disease resistance. Mexican species that have been used in crosses include *Penstemon kunthii*, *P. campanulatus*, and *P. hartwegii*. Many of the outstanding hybrids grown in England and along the Pacific Coast of the United States are believed to have originated from the Mexican species.

In the colder zones (such as the northern and midwestern United States), winter hardiness and longevity are factors with which to contend. Many of the species found in the southern United States and Mexico will not survive in zones of extreme cold. However, many southern species have attractive flower colors and can be treated as annuals or tender perennials in colder climates. Longevity is important but not a necessity. Annual *Penstemon* selections are available, but most of these are seed-propagated lines best adapted to the milder climates of the United States Pacific Coast area and similar climatic regions of the world. Adaptation to regional soil conditions should also be considered. For example, some species (*Penstemon gormanii*) will show foliar chlorosis (yellowing) when grown on high pH soils in certain regions of the western United States.

Resistance to insects and other pests can also be valuable traits for the plant breeder to incorporate into a breeding scheme. Insects vary greatly from location to location and year to year, so it is difficult, and maybe not practical in some cases, to breed for specific insect resistance. Kelaidis (1989) reported that plants in the *Caespitosi* and *Dasanthera* sections were highly susceptible to attack by the pittosporum pit scale (*Asterolecanium arabidis*), an insect found in California, Colorado, Oregon, and Washington. Other *Penstemon* species exhibit varying degrees of resistance to this scale.

Incorporating attractive and unusual foliage and desirable plant habit into a breeding program should not be overlooked. Height, uprightness, creeping plant habit, and evergreen foliage are traits to consider. The cultivar *Penstemon digitalis* 'Husker Red' (Plate 11-2), for example, was released for its purple-red foliage (Lindgren 1984). Other species with obvious foliar interest include *P. clutei* (wavy, deeply serrated leaves), *P. pinifolius* (pineneedle-like foliage; see Plate 11-3), and *P. hirsutus* (hairy). *Penstemon fruticosus* and its relatives in the *Dasanthera* section have valuable habit characteristics for the rock garden. Other species outside the *Dasanthera* section that are low growing include *P. caespitosus*, *P. linarioides*, and *P. pinifolius*.

The chemical content, mainly iridoid glycosides, of *Penstemon* has been studied both for pharmaceutical purposes and for insect–host plant relationships (Stermitz 1992). There are opportunities for chemists, through breeding and selection, to increase the content of useful chemicals in *Penstemon*. Another trait that might be considered in a breeding program is increasing cut flower longevity. The vase life of *Penstemon* cut flowers varies greatly between species (Lindgren 1986). *Penstemon digitalis* has been reported to work well as a cut flower (Dole 1995; Lindgren et al. 1988). Further studies need to be conducted on handling *Penstemon* as cut flowers. With the interest in backyard wildlife, penstemons can be selected to attract wildlife. Butterflies and hummingbirds are attracted to selective *Penstemon* species. Hummingbirds usually feed on red-flowered species, such as *Penstemon barbatus* or *P. eatonii*. It is difficult for many butterfly species to find a sturdy "landing pad" when collecting nectar from *Penstemon* flowers, and moths are better pollinators of *Penstemon* than butterflies. Breeding *Penstemon* to attract wildlife has received little to no attention.

In a genus as large as *Penstemon*, almost any trait can be found. The problem is combining traits of different species into a single hybrid, a challenge much easier said than done. Natural crossing barriers in *Penstemon* include geographic distance, time of flowering, genetic incompatibility (such as chromosome ploidy level), and other isolation barriers. The basic chromosome number in *Penstemon* is $n = 8$. Diploids are the rule but polyploids are common. Chromosome counts from 16 to 96 have been reported for *Penstemon* species. Species also have specific pollinating agents based on flower size, shape, color, odor, and plant location. For example, some species are pollinated by hummingbirds, others by wasps and bees, and some by moths. If a pollinator only visits plants with a certain size or color of flower, natural cross-pollination between species may be nonexistent even if the plants' natural ranges overlap. Pistil length, rate of pollen tube growth, and other characteristics can also discourage pollination between species.

Remember that the traits you are looking for might be found within the species you are currently working with, as a large amount of genetic variation exists within species. For example, *Penstemon angustifolius* (Plate 11-1) has seven recognized subspecies, exhibiting a wide base of germplasm. It is simpler to combine traits from within a species than from different species because of the greater likelihood of successful pollination. Almost all species contain plants with various flowering traits and plant sizes. Examples of variability within species are listed in Table 11-1. Recent studies comparing DNA and isozyme patterns in *Penstemon* may be useful in determining genetic relationships between species and can lead to valuable information to assist in hybridization (Wolfe and Elisens 1994).

Inheritance of Traits

Very little is known about the inheritance of specific traits in *Penstemon*, as it has not been widely studied. What holds true for one species may not hold true for other species because of the wide variation in ploidy level in *Penstemon* and the large amount of genetic variation within and between species.

Table 11-1. Examples of trait variability within *Penstemon* species that have led to named selections or subspecies.

Species	Typical Trait	Trait Variable
Penstemon barbatus	red/orange flowers	yellow flowers ('Schooley's Yellow')
Penstemon cardwellii	pink flowers	white flowers ('John Bacher')
Penstemon digitalis	green foliage	red foliage ('Husker Red')
Penstemon grandiflorus	pink/lavender flowers	white flowers ('Prairie Snow')
Penstemon hirsutus ('Pygmaeus')	tall habit	short habit
Penstemon pinifolius	orange flowers	yellow flowers ('Mersea Yellow', 'Magdalena Sunshine')

Some generalizations can be made, though, about the inheritance of traits in *Penstemon*. A relationship between foliage or stem color and flower color exists in some species. Viehmeyer (1956) and Lindgren (1990) have both indicated that white-flowered plants of *Penstemon grandiflorus* can be obtained by selecting young seedlings that lack foliage pigment coloration. Meyers (1970) reported that in populations of *P. euglaucus* he was able to find plants that had white flowers by selecting plants with lighter foliage color. This relationship has been observed by others as well. In a study by Mitchell and Shaw (1993), traits including corolla length, corolla width, inflorescence length, nectar production, and total flower production were rated as significantly heritable in *P. centranthifolius*. Scharf (1969) found that secund flowering is dominant to the recessive non-secund flowering and that dwarf-type growth habit is recessive and probably multifactorial. He also speculated that the color of the pink-flowered *P. nitidus* was controlled by a simple recessive gene. Uhlinger and Viehmeyer (1971) reported that in crosses of the red-flowered *P. barbatus* with the blue-flowered *P. strictus*, the progeny were more vigorous than either parent and the flower color of the progeny was purple. When these purple-flowered plants were grown in isolation for seed production, the next generation produced progeny with flower colors in the ratio of 1 red: 2 purple: 1 blue.

In some crosses the progeny will be intermediate between the parents, while in other crosses the progeny will be similar to one or the other parent. Hybrids may be superior to either parent for a particular trait, or they may be at a selective disadvantage (they do not have the adaptive characters of either parent). Some hybrids do, however, have desirable characteristics from both parents. This can only be determined by evaluating the progeny.

Penstemon breeders occasionally bulk pollen of several species and use this bulked pollen as the male source in their pollinations. Although this approach can result in a greater chance of successful pollinations, the exact parentage of the progeny is not known. For heritability studies and in order to repeat specific crosses, bulking pollen is not recommended.

One final important point to consider is the interaction of environmental and genetic factors in plant performance. A trait may be expressed quite differently in different environments. For example, time of flowering will change with location and altitude, and flower colors may be different on the same species depending on light, temperature, and soil type.

Hybridization Mechanics

The main challenges in hand pollinating *Penstemon* involve managing the wind, rain, and insects that may hinder and interfere with breeding techniques. It is much easier to make controlled pollinations indoors or in protected sites where the weather has less impact on pollination conditions. If pollinations are conducted outdoors, plants may need to be staked to keep them upright and flowers bagged with cheesecloth or other materials to keep out insects. Greenhouses work well for pollination if the plants can be induced to flower indoors and insects are excluded. Some species (many of the northern species) require a vernalization period to induce flowering, whereas others (*Penstemon digitalis*) may respond to day length. Plants can be grown outdoors in containers in cold frames and brought indoors to do the pollinations. In the breeding program at the University of Nebraska, *Penstemon* plants are potted up in the spring or summer, placed in a cold frame in the fall, and brought into the greenhouse in January to induce flowering for early spring pollinations.

The *Penstemon* flower is relatively easy to manipulate for emasculation, pollen collection, pollination, and seed collection. The first step in pollinating *Penstemon* is to understand the flowering characteristics of a *Penstemon* plant and to become familiar with the various parts of the flower. *Penstemon* plants begin flowering at the bottom portion of the flower stalk and progress upward. The individual flower consists of a calyx (sepals), corolla (petals), pistil, and stamen (Figure 11-1). It is a perfect flower (contains both male and female parts in the same flower). The pistil, or female sex organ, consists of the stigma, style, and ovary. The stamen, the male sex organ, consists of the anthers and filament. There are five stamens, four fertile (producing pollen) and one sterile (producing no pollen). This sterile stamen is called a staminode. The anthers open (dehisce) in a *Penstemon* flower before the pistil is receptive to pollen, which is an advantage for plant breeders. The two anthers closest to the lips open first, followed by the two back anthers. The petals usually consist of five lobes—two upper and three lower (Figure 11-2).

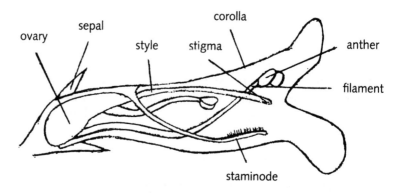

Figure 11-1. Cross-section of *Penstemon* flower. (Illustration by Dale T. Lindgren)

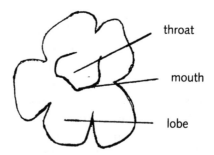

Figure 11-2. End-section of *Penstemon* flower. (Illustration by Dale T. Lindgren)

Numerous techniques can be used for collecting and transferring pollen in *Penstemon*. First, select the female and male parents based on the traits with which you are interested in working. Pollen can be collected and used immediately to make a cross, or it can be stored for later use. Methods for pollen collection include the following:

- Anthers with ripe pollen can be individually collected with a tweezers and then the pollen can be placed immediately on a receptive pistil.
- Pollen can be collected on a pipe-cleaner or small brush and then dabbed on a pistil.
- Pollen can be collected and placed in a small jar or vial, refrigerated, and used when needed.
- Pollen can be collected on a fingernail and then rubbed on a receptive pistil.
- Unopened anthers can be removed and left to lie in a warm location to open-up (dehisce) and release the pollen, which can then be used immediately or refrigerated for later use.

Caution should always be used so as to avoid pollen contamination by other pollen sources. Anthers usually release pollen several days before the pistil of the flower becomes receptive. This time lag will decrease to several hours as temperatures increase. There is considerable variation in anther types, staminodes, corolla types, and time of flowering between species, so modifications in breeding procedures may be necessary.

The following procedure demonstrates one method that works well in pollinating *Penstemon*. Anthers with newly ripe pollen are collected from the male parent either from flowers that are beginning to open or from flowers that have opened recently. Remove the anthers and place them in a small jar or vial and refrigerate. Remove the corolla and stamens of the flower of the female parent by firmly grasping the calyx (sepals) between the thumb and forefinger of one hand and pulling the corolla (petal) with the other hand (Figure 11-3a). This step should be done before the corolla opens. The corolla along with the stamens should pull away, leaving the pistil (Figure 11-3b). This is the emasculation step. The pistil becomes receptive to pollen in a few hours to a few days after the flower normally opens. It remains receptive for several days if not pollinated. When receptive, the pistil tip curves under and forms a small sticky knob at the stigma (Figure 11-3c). (The pistil on flowers of some species may not curve as much as others.) Apply pollen to the receptive stigma. After pollination, the stigma tip will turn brown and the style will dry up (Figure 11-3d). Label the cross to record the parentage and when the cross was made. The label consists of the female parent followed by an "×" and then the name of the male parent. The date of the cross should be included on the label. A jeweler's tag works well as a label.

A "wait and see" period is now required to determine if a successful pollination and subsequent fertilization has occurred. If fertilization occurs, the ovary (seed capsule) will begin to swell and will reach full size in 3 to 4 weeks. It will generally take 6 to 10 weeks after pollination for the seed to mature if crosses are successful. Keep records so you know which crosses

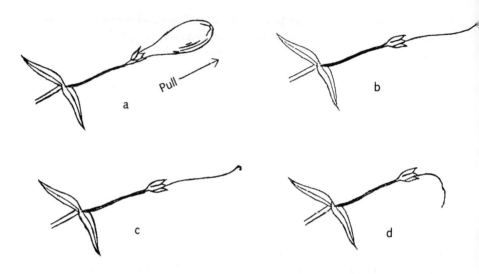

Figure 11-3. Hybridization mechanics: a) removing corolla; b) pistil; c) receptive pistil; d) pistil after pollination. (Illustration by Dale T. Lindgren)

have been successful and which have not. Some selections make good parents that consistently produce good progeny.

Seed Collection and Germination

Seed collection and storage is the final step in the hybridization process. Most *Penstemon* seed capsules, when ripe, will turn a dry brown color. Some sources suggest that the seed can be collected while the pods are still green and seed will germinate without a pregermination treatment, though this has not been documented. Most seed collectors wait to harvest seed until the pods have dried down but before the suture splits to release the seed. Seed capsules, with a small amount of stalk attached, can be harvested when the capsule has almost completely dried but before the capsule has started to dehisce (Figure 11-4). Place the capsules in a dry area in an open container or paper bag so that they will continue to dry. Wait several days until the sutures of the capsules spread apart, then turn the capsules upside down, and shake to encourage the seeds to fall out of the pods. Capsules that do not open can be crushed with a pliers or plied apart with a knife, but the seed and chaff will be mixed together, making seed cleaning more time-consuming. Window screens of various meshes can be used to sort seed from chaff. Store seed in a cool, dry location. Most *Penstemon* seed will be viable for 2 to 3 years and in some cases may be good for even longer.

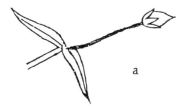 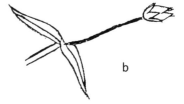

a   b

Figure 11-4. *Penstemon* seed capsule: a) ripe seed capsule; b) dehiscing (opening) seed capsule. (Illustration by Dale T. Lindgren)

Germinating hybrid *Penstemon* seed can be challenging. Several articles on *Penstemon* seed germination have been published and should be consulted (Deno 1991; Kelaidis 1991; Meyer et al. 1995). Pregermination treatments that have been reported to enhance seed germination include cold-stratification, scarification, light, and chemical treatment. Each species or cultivar may require different treatments to encourage germination. In the midwestern United States, one general method that has worked well as a pregermination treatment is to plant the seed in sterilized soil (commercial mixes work well) in containers around 1 January, move to a cool location (preferably 33–40°F [0.5–4.0°C]) for 6 to 8 weeks, then bring indoors and let the seed germinate. Some seed (such as that of *Penstemon barbatus* and its hybrids) will germinate at temperatures of 40–45°F (4–7°C), whereas the optimum germination temperature for other species is 60–70°F (16–21°C). Seedlings can be transplanted outdoors or used as needed. Seed can also be planted directly outdoors in the fall.

Some species and cultivars do not require any pregermination treatment to increase germination rates. In fact, cold-stratification may reduce seed germination in some species (Meyer et al. 1995). Most of the seed selections sold as annuals in the Pacific Coast areas and in Europe, as well as many of the Mexican species, do not require a cold-stratification treatment to induce seed germination.

Damping off, a disease of young seedlings, can be troublesome in *Penstemon*. Damping off can be reduced by 1) using a sterilized growing medium in which to germinate and grow young seedlings, 2) applying registered fungicides for damping off during germination, emergence, and early seedling growth, 3) avoiding overwatering, 4) providing optimum light, and 5) maintaining optimum temperatures for good early growth. Be alert for this disease if you are growing plants from seed of any genus.

Propagation

Plants that have been selected for further evaluation or release as a cultivar will need to be increased or propagated. A *Penstemon* that cannot be easily and reliably propagated is less likely to be accepted in the marketplace. Most *Penstemon* plants can be vegetatively propagated from cuttings, divisions, or layering. Division is a relatively simple method of propagation for plants that normally produce multiple shoots. Plants are pulled or cut apart and each plant is repotted or reset in the garden. Division is best done in early spring, but timing will vary with location, species, and conditions. Some *Penstemon* plants will benefit from division every few years. *Penstemon digitalis* and *P. strictus* (Plate 11-4) propagate very easily from division.

Layering works well to propagate some *Penstemon* selections. Layering consists of mounding soil around the base of the plant and lower stems or by laying stems horizontally on the soil surface and covering them with soil. Penstemons that are receptive to layering will root down where the stem contacts the soil. Layered plants, when rooted, can be separated (divided) from the parent plant and replanted. Division of layered plants can take place in the fall or spring.

Stem cuttings are also used to vegetatively propagate *Penstemon*. There are numerous media and methods that have worked well for rooting *Penstemon* cuttings, depending on the available facilities and resources. One method is to use a product such as perlite for the rooting medium. Cuttings should generally be taken in spring as new shoots are forming. Remove the lower leaves and stick the cutting in moistened perlite. Keep the humidity high around the cuttings by regular misting or by placing them in a container covered to retain the moisture. Roots ¼ to 1 inch (0.5–2.5 cm) long will form in 4 to 8 weeks. The plants can then be placed in a container with growing medium and, when well established, transplanted to the garden. Tissue culture is an additional method of vegetatively propagating plants, but it is usually not feasible for the home gardener (Lindgren and McCown 1992).

The final step in releasing a cultivar is to select a name. *Penstemon* names should be registered with the International Registrar of Names for Penstemon (see "Resources"). Registering reduces the possibility of the same name being used for different *Penstemon* selections and also provides a base description for the registrar file (Lindgren 1993).

Penstemon breeding is in its infancy, but its future is bright. With so much variation within the species, and with so many uses for *Penstemon* selections, many opportunities are out there for those interested in breeding these popular plants.

Resources

COLLECTIONS

Penstemon species can be found naturally throughout the United States, parts of Canada, and Mexico. In many cases, natural areas are the only location where some species can be viewed. National and state parks are often good places to find *Penstemon* in its natural settings. A few sites where *Penstemon* collections are currently on display include the following:

Denver Botanic Gardens
909 York Street
Denver, CO 80206
U.S.A.

University of Nebraska
West Central Research and
    Extension Center
Route 4, Box 46A
North Platte, NE 69101
U.S.A.

Pershore College of Horticulture
Pershore, Hereford and Worcester
    WR10 3JP
England

Royal Botanic Gardens, Kew
Richmond, Surrey TW9 3AB
England

Royal Horticultural Society's
    Garden, Wisley
Woking, Surrey GU23 6QB
England

SUPPLIERS—UNITED STATES

American Penstemon Society Seed
    Exchange
1569 South Holland Court
Lakewood, CO 80232

North American Rock Garden
    Society Seed Exchange
P.O. Box 67
Millwood, NY 10546

Alplains
P.O. Box 489
32315 Pine Crest Court
Kiowa, CO 80117-0489

Agua Fria Nursery
1409 Agua Fria, Dept. MO
Santa Fe, NM 87501-3507

Arrowhead Alpines
P.O. Box 857
1310 N. Gregory Road
Fowlerville, MI 48836

Joy Creek Nursery
20300 N.W. Watson Road
Scappoose, OR 97056
phone: 503-543-7474

Laporte Avenue Nursery
1950 Laporte Avenue
Fort Collins, CO 80521

Plants of the Southwest
Route 6, Box 11A
Santa Fe, NM 87501
phone: 505-438-8888

Rocky Mountain Rare Plants
1706 Deerpath Road
Franktown, CO 80116

Siskiyou Rare Plant Nursery
2825 Cummings Road
Medford, OR 97501

Southwestern Native Seeds
P.O. Box 50503
Tucson, AZ 85703

INTERNATIONAL REGISTRATION AUTHORITY
American Penstemon Society
Attn: Dale T. Lindgren
University of Nebraska—West Central Research and Extension Center
Route 4, Box 46A
North Platte, NE 69101
U.S.A.

PLANT SOCIETIES
American Penstemon Society
1569 S. Holland Court
Lakewood, CO 80232
U.S.A.

North American Rock Garden Society
P.O. Box 67
Millwood, NY 10546
U.S.A.

Alpine Garden Society
AGS Centre
Avon Bank
Pershore, Hereford and Worcester WR10 3JP
England

Hardy Plant Society
Pam Adams, The Administrator
Little Orchard
Great Comberton
Pershore, Hereford and Worcester WR10 3DP
England

NCCPG (National Collection for the Conservation of Plants and Gardens)
The Pines, Wisley Garden
Woking, Surrey GU23 6QB
England

References and Additional Reading

American Horticultural Society. 1951. Special number penstemons. *The National Horticultural Magazine* 30 (1): 1–82.

American Rock Garden Society. 1946. Penstemon number. *Bulletin of the American Rock Garden Society* 4 (4): 53–76.

Crosswhite, F. S. 1965. Hybridization of *Penstemon barbatus* (Scrophulariaceae) of section Elmigera with species of section Habroanthus. *The Southwestern Naturalist* 10 (4): 234–237.

Deno, N. C. 1991. *Penstemon* germination. *Bulletin of the American Penstemon Society* 50 (1): 3–6.

Dole, J. 1995. Mini-culture profile. *The Cut Flower Quarterly* 7 (4): 4.

Kartesz, R. 1994. *A Synonymized Checklist of the Vascular Plants of the United States, Canada, and Greenland.* 2nd ed. Portland, Ore.: Timber Press.

Kelaidis, G. 1989. A *Penstemon* pest: The pittosporum pit scale. *Bulletin of the American Penstemon Society* 48 (2): 49–52.

———. 1991. Germination in penstemons: An interpretation and comments. *Bulletin of the American Penstemon Society* 50 (1): 7–12.

Lindgren, D. 1984. 'Husker Red' *Penstemon. HortScience* 19 (3): 459.

———. 1986. *Penstemon* as cut flowers. *Bulletin of the American Penstemon Society* 45 (2): 19–21.

———. 1990. 'Prairie Snow' *Penstemon. HortScience* 25 (4): 489.

———. 1993. The need to register new cultivar names: *Penstemon,* a case study. *HortScience* 28 (2): 82–83.

Lindgren, D., and B. Davenport. 1992. List and description of named cultivars in the genus *Penstemon.* University of Nebraska Cooperative Extension EC 92-1246-D.

Lindgren, D., and B. McCown. 1992. Multiplication of four *Penstemon* species in vitro. *HortScience* 27 (2): 182.

Lindgren, D., D. Whitney, and J. Fitzgerald. 1988. Response of cut flower spikes of *Penstemon digitalis* 'Husker Red' to floral preservatives and chilling periods. *Bulletin of the American Penstemon Society* 47 (2): 7–8.

Mackaness, F. P. 1959. Experimental hybridization of Columbia River Gorge penstemon. *Northwest Science* 33 (3): 129–134.

Meyer, S. E., S. G. Kitchen, and S. L. Carlson. 1995. Seed germination timing patterns in intermountain *Penstemon* (Scrophulariaceae). *American Journal of Botany* 82 (3): 377–389.

Meyers, B. 1970. Report by Bruce Meyers. *Bulletin of the American Penstemon Society* 29: 53.

Mitchell, R. J., and R. G. Shaw. 1993. Heritability of floral traits for the perennial wildflower *Penstemon centranthifolius* (Scrophulariaceae): Clones and crosses. *Heredity* 71: 185–192.

Moore, G. 1980. Concerning *Penstemon* hybridization. *Bulletin of the American Penstemon Society* 39 (1): 12–16.

Scharf, A. 1969. Report from Canada. *Bulletin of the American Penstemon Society* 28: 52–54.

Scrogin, R., and C. E. Freeman. 1987. Floral anthocyanins of the genus *Penstemon:* Correlations with taxonomy and pollination. *Biochemical Systematics and Ecology* 15: 355–360.

Stermitz, F. R. 1992. Penstemon chemistry. *Bulletin of the American Penstemon Society* 51 (2): 49–50.

Straw, R. M. 1955. Hybridization, homogamy, and sympatric speciation. *Evolution* 9 (4): 441–444.

———. 1956. Floral isolation in *Penstemon. American Midland Naturalist* 90 (850): 47–53.

Uhlinger, R. D., and G. Viehmeyer. 1971. *Penstemon* in your garden. University of Nebraska SC105 (Revised).

Vesall, J. 1990. Dasanthera cultivars and hybrids. *Bulletin of the American Penstemon Society* 49 (1): 3–12.

Viehmeyer, G. 1956. Progress in hybridization and selection at North Platte: Recommendations to society members. *Bulletin of the American Penstemon Society* 15: 11.

Way, D. 1996. *Penstemons*. United Kingdom: The Hardy Plant Society, Shinfield Printers.

Way, D., and P. James. 1998. *The Gardener's Guide to Growing Penstemons*. Portland, Ore.: Timber Press.

Wolfe, A. D., and W. J. Elisens. 1994. Nuclear ribosomal DNA restriction-site variation in *Penstemon* section Peltanthera (Scrophulariaceae): An evaluation of diploid hybrid speciation and evidence for introgression. *American Journal of Botany* 81 (12): 1627–1635.

12 Breeding Rhododendrons and Azaleas

H. Edward Reiley

Growing rhododendrons can be contagious and there is no known cure. Hybridizing can be a further symptom of such contagion and a pursuit that injects a kind of mystique and an element of chance. Goals are set, crosses made, seedlings germinated and planted out, and always with the expectation that something new and outstanding is surely in the genes and about to appear—if not this year, maybe next. Or, one hears about the new superior species just discovered that will of course add enormously to the genetic material available. This kind of excitement motivates and keeps thousands of hybridizers around the world at work. The results are seen as the newly listed cultivar registrations each year, some of which will indeed stand the test of time and improve the variety of first-class rhododendron available. Many other crosses, equally as good, are not registered; some may be introduced, yet most will remain unknown.

New and improved cultivars appear only out of the sustained efforts of hybridizers who grow thousands of seedlings. I will never forget the statement I read years ago that all flowers of all the tomorrows are in the seeds of today. Save for mutants and sports, only seedlings can produce new and exciting plants thanks to the mixing up and rearranging of the genes via the mechanism of sexual reproduction.

A bit of counsel to prospective hybridizers is appropriate here. Only a few hybrids will prove to be superior plants, so there will be many disappointments after thousands of new seedlings have been evaluated. Much patience and a thoroughly disciplined set of judgmental standards are required throughout the long process of evaluation as new crosses are com-

Adapted from *Success with Rhododendrons and Azaleas* by H. Edward Reiley, published in 1995 by Timber Press.

pared to the best available cultivars. Only plants superior to any others in existence at the time should be brought forward for registration and introduction. Complete objectivity is a difficult quality to maintain as one evaluates the seedlings, and advice from others is not only wise but probably necessary. Rhododendron hybridizers are generally friendly, helpful people, ready to assist a new member of the fraternity with hybridizing issues.

The first hybridizers of rhododendrons and azaleas were probably active in Japan over 300 years ago. Evidence of hybrid plants, among the Kurume azaleas in Japanese gardens, dates back at least to the seventeenth century. Beginning in the nineteenth century, extensive hybridizing activity developed in Europe as plant explorers brought back an increasing number of new species.

It was not until the early twentieth century that hybridizing started in earnest in North America with such greats as Joe Gable, Guy Nearing, C. O. Dexter, Tony Shammarello, and James Barto. I urge the interested gardener to read some of the detailed accounts of the contributions of early hybridizers before starting to work. Since that time many more outstanding hybridizers, too numerous to mention, have been at work.

Important Traits and Breeding Objectives

The genus *Rhododendron* is a hybridizer's paradise. The tremendous diversity of flower color and size, plant size, foliage, cold hardiness, heat tolerance, disease resistance, and other attributes presents such a huge reservoir of genetic variability that it seems possible to make any number of useful combinations. However, some combinations of characteristics have defied the best efforts of numerous hybridizers. For example, there are no yellow-flowered, evergreen azaleas; no ironclad, deep yellow rhododendrons; few heat-tolerant, deciduous azalea hybrids; no blue Elepidote or red Lepidote rhododendrons; few disease-resistant plants; and few ironclad, evergreen azaleas. Yet most of these combinations are within the realm of possibility since the genes are there; it is a matter of cleverly arranging them in the proper order. This is a simple statement, yet for the hybridizer it represents a long, problematic undertaking.

The recent discovery of superior forms of some species offers new potential for the production of superior cultivars. The hybridizer is well advised to search out the best form of each species to use in his or her work. Research at the parent selection stage often makes the difference between achieving hybridizing goals or failing to do so. In any circumstance, parent selection can reduce the time required to meet defined goals.

Probably one of the gravest mistakes a hybridizer can make is to start spreading pollen before thoroughly investigating work already done by others. Another weakness can be in failing to define goals. A third failing quite often lies in parent selection. It is essential to identify the parent plants most likely to achieve the goals that are set.

The first step in any hybridizing program is to become thoroughly familiar with previous work. Since much hybridizing work has been done and the results are on record, it makes no sense to repeat crosses already made, especially those which produced poor results. Such research can also identify parents that consistently pass along certain characteristics to their offspring. Obviously those species or cultivars transmitting traits consistent with the goals of the hybridizing program need to be selected for further evaluation and possible use.

Research can, in addition, often eliminate a step in a hybridizing program by starting with first-generation crosses. It is quite possible that two species, identified by the hybridizer as parents, have already been crossed and seedlings selected that carry the genes for the desired characteristic. Since such primary hybrids represent the first step in a successful breeding program, even if the offspring are of mediocre quality, they carry the genetic potential for better things in the next generation where the hybridizers' goal is most likely to be met. I recommend that the beginning hybridizer refer to Leach (1961), West et al. (1978), and Salley and Greer (1992) before starting his or her research program.

The second step is to define goals for the hybridizing program. Since contemporary homes tend to have a low profile, low-growing plants are in increasing demand, while the demand for large-growing plants is declining as vast estates with wooded grounds are decreasing in number. Though many commercial buildings and apartment complexes are of a scale suitable for large-growing plants, there is often little interest in rhododendrons and azaleas in these situations because of their special cultural requirements. The beginning hybridizer might be well advised to aim toward the breeding of low-growing and dwarf forms as one goal. The hybridizer is wise to focus on only one or two goals at a time in order to concentrate the focus and make noticeable progress. Some other goals might include:

1. Increased disease resistance, particularly mildew resistance in deciduous azaleas.
2. Increased insect resistance.
3. Increased cold hardiness in evergreen azaleas and yellow rhododendrons.
4. Increased heat tolerance in all rhododendrons and deciduous azaleas.
5. Larger flowers with cleaner colors on rhododendrons.
6. Fragrance in rhododendrons and azaleas.
7. Development of double flowers.
8. Tightly branched plants.
9. Increased amounts of persistent foliage on evergreen azaleas.

10. Improved fall and winter foliage color on evergreen types.
11. A yellow-flowered, evergreen azalea.
12. Easier-to-root deciduous azaleas.
13. A true blue Elepidote rhododendron.
14. A true red Lepidote rhododendron.
15. Indumentum (hairy covering) on rhododendron leaves.
16. Stronger root systems.

The careful selection of parents possessing the characteristics being sought in the cultivar is the third major step toward a promising hybridizing program. Each generation in the hybridizing program requires from 3 to 7 years. Obviously the hybridizer cannot afford to make many mistakes in the selection of parents. Furthermore, if goals are to be met, the parents must be capable of transmitting the characteristics selected by the hybridizer. A thorough knowledge of characteristics most often transmitted by specific parents becomes of utmost importance. This must be researched before the hybridizer can make selections with any degree of accuracy or expectation of success.

AZALEAS

Azaleas fall into two broad categories, deciduous and evergreen. It is probably sufficient to note that the evergreen species azaleas crossbreed readily, as is also the case among the deciduous species. However, the evergreen species do not readily crossbreed with the deciduous. A handful of hybrids have been produced between an evergreen and a deciduous parent, but they are rare and few of the plants are of much merit. Most azaleas are self-sterile and cannot pollinate themselves yet will readily crossbreed.

Fred Galle's (1987) book on azaleas contains an excellent chapter on hybridizing azaleas written by August Kehr. It presents detailed information on hybridizing and offers some wise advice on selection of parents most likely to transmit specific characteristics to their offspring. The following material on azaleas is taken from Kehr's text.

An informal poll was taken of several azalea breeders and growers to solicit their choices for parents for some specific objectives. As might be expected, replies were varied, but significant points of agreement developed. Listed below are some of the plants suggested to realize particular objectives.

Evergreen Azaleas

Most Cold Hardy: 'Corsage', 'Herbert', *Rhododendron kiusianum*, *R. yedoense* var. *poukhanense*
Best Winter Foliage: 'Glacier', 'Hot Shot', 'Polar Bear'

Reddest Color: 'Girard Scarlet', 'Hino Crimson' (Plate 12-4), 'Mother's Day', 'Ward's Ruby'
Yellowest Color: 'Cream Cup', 'Frostburg', 'Mizu no Yuma Buki'
Fragrance: *Rhododendron mucronatum*, 'Rose Greeley' (Plate 12-5)
Fully Double Flower: 'Anna Kehr', 'Gardenia', 'Elsie Lee' (Plate 12-2), 'Louise Gable', 'Rosebud'
Fall Flowering: 'Dorsett', 'Indian Summer', 'Opal'
Compact Growth: Beltsville dwarfs, 'Dragon', 'Girard Border Gem', *Rhododendron kiusianum*, 'Myogi'
Lasting Quality of Flowers: 'Ambrosia', 'Chojuho', 'Jeanne', 'Rosebud', 'Scott Gartrell', 'Vuyk's Scarlet'
Best All Around Good-Doer: 'Corsage', 'Herbert', *Rhododendron kiusianum*, 'Martha Hitchcock'

Deciduous Azaleas

Easiest to Root: *Rhododendron austrinum, R. atlanticum*, 'Gibraltar', 'Homebush'
Mildew Resistance: 'Coccinea', 'J. Jennings', 'Persil', *Rhododendron speciosum*
Compact Growth: 'J. Jennings', 'Klondyke', *Rhododendron prunifolium*
Red Flower Color: 'Ilam Red Letter'
Yellow Flower Color: 'Klondyke'
Most Floriferous: 'Gibraltar', 'Knap Hill Red'
Double Flowers: 'Homebush', 'Narcissiflora', 'Norma'
Lasting Quality of Flowers: 'Homebush', 'Norma'
Best All Around Good-Doer: 'Gibraltar' (Plate 12-3)

RHODODENDRONS

Rhododendrons also fall into two major groups, the Lepidote or scaly species, which generally also produce small leaves, and the Elepidote or non-scaly, large-leaved species. Lepidotes and elepidotes are cross-sterile. Successful crosses are confined to species or cultivars within each group.

The following plants are suggested as parents with a proven ability to transmit various desirable traits to offspring:

Large Flower Size:
Elepidote—*Rhododendron discolor, R. fortunei*, 'King George'
Cold Hardiness:
Elepidote—'Catalgla', 'Clark's White', *Rhododendron maximum*
Lepidote—*Rhododendron dauricum, R. minus, R. mucronulatum*
Heat/Sun Tolerance:
Elepidote—*Rhododendron catawbiense, R. decorum, R. fortunei, R. hyperythrum, R. maximum, R. metternichii*
Lepidote—*Rhododendron chapmanii, R. compactum, R. minus*
Disease Resistance:
Elepidote—'Caroline', *Rhododendron decorum, R. metternichii, R. pseudochrysanthum, R. yakushimanum*

Lepidote—*Rhododendron aureum* 'Wada', *R. keiskei, R. racemosum*
Compact Size:
   Elepidote—*Rhododendron metternichii, R. williamsianum, R. yakushimanum*
   Lepidote—*Rhododendron keiskei* 'Yaku Fairy'
Late Flowering:
   Elepidote—*Rhododendron haematodes, R. maximum*
Early Flowering:
   Elepidote—*Rhododendron fortunei, R. vernicosum* 18139
   Lepidote—*Rhododendron dauricum, R. mucronulatum*
Fragrance:
   Elepidote—*Rhododendron fortunei*
Red Flower Color:
   Elepidote—'Essex Scarlet', *Rhododendron griersonianum, R. haematodes, R. strigillosum* (Plate 12-6)
Yellow Flower Color:
   Elepidote—*Rhododendron campylocarpum*, 'Gold Mohur', *R. wardii*
   Lepidote—*Rhododendron aureum, R. keiskei*
White Flower Color (usually masked in the first generation and recovered in the second):
   Elepidote—'Clark's White', *Rhododendron yakushimanum*
   Lepidote—*Rhododendron dauricum* var. *album*
Pink Flower Color—nearly all red × white crosses

One way to further demonstrate the process of selecting suitable parents is to present an example. Let us say the goal is to develop a compact, large-leaved rhododendron with large, fragrant flowers. The search begins with research to identify parents with a record of transmitting these characteristics to their offspring. The first observation is that typically the less complex or heterogeneous a plant is genetically, the better the prospect of transmitting the desired traits without passing undesirable traits that would require subsequent crosses to eliminate. In other words, a species or primary hybrid possessing the desired characteristics is a better choice than a complex hybrid. A careful search reveals that *Rhododendron fortunei* (Plate 12-1) has both large flowers and fragrance plus good foliage and resistance to lace bug. Similar research reveals that the species capable of dwarfing or developing compact offspring among the non-scaly rhododendrons include *R. yakushimanum* and *R. williamsianum*. By carrying crosses of these plants through two or more generations and crossing or backcrossing after each generation (depending on those characteristics needing reinforcing or reducing), the hybridizing goal might possibly be met.

A second example: the goal is to develop a compact plant with a dark red flower. *Rhododendron williamsianum* has a dwarfing effect and also has outstanding foliage. *Rhododendron yakushimanum* also has a dwarfing effect but masks red flower color so completely that the chance of producing red offspring is very limited. In this case *R. williamsianum* is the better choice for the parent contributing a dwarfing effect. *Rhododendron* 'Mars' and 'Essex Scarlet' are cultivars that reliably pass red on to their offspring, as does *R. haematodes*; any one of these three is a candidate for obtaining a red flower.

Hybridization Mechanics

After the prospective parents have been researched and carefully selected, it is a good idea to start a record book in which the crosses made, subsequent outcomes, further crosses and outcomes, and other data are meticulously recorded. Any cross should be recorded before it is actually made. The female parent or pod parent is always listed first and the pollen parent second. For example, in the cross 'Mars' × 'America', 'Mars' is the female parent. This record book must be carefully maintained so that all significant events and observations are recorded at the time of their occurrence.

The actual process of cross-pollinating is very simple if both parent plants are growing in the same garden and flower at the same time. The flowers of both rhododendrons and azaleas are fortunately large enough that the male and female flower parts are easy to identify and work with (Figure 12-1).

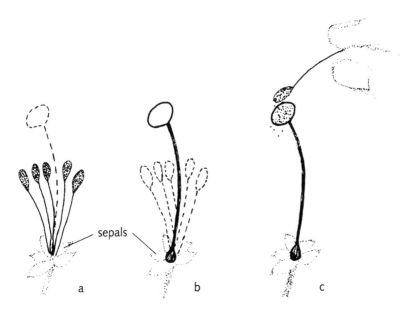

Figure 12-1. Hand pollination, cutaway view of flower parts. a) Male flower parts: stamens with anther (pollen sac). b) Female flower parts: pistil with stigma at top, ovary at base. c) Pollination of stigma: pollen from anther is used to dust stigma of female parent.

Hand pollination requires the following steps:

1. Identify three or four flower buds on two or more stems. More than one bud will be pollinated to insure against loss through physical damage. Flowers should be just ready to open but not yet accessible to insect pollinators. Next, on the plant to be used as a female parent, reduce the attractiveness of the immediate vicinity to pollinating insects by removing any other flowers within one foot (30 cm) of the selected buds.
2. Carefully remove the flower petals (corolla) of the selected flower buds. Pollen from the anthers or male part of the flower must be prevented from reaching the stigma or female part of the flower. To remove the corolla, separate the flower petals with the fingers and pull or cut them free from their base around the ovary.
3. With a tweezers or small scissors remove the anthers of the selected flowers one at a time and discard.
4. When the top surface of the stigma of the prepared flower exudes a sticky substance, it is receptive and can be pollinated immediately. If it is not sticky, cover the stigma with a small paper bag fastened to the stem to prevent accidental pollination. Check the stigma daily to determine when it is sticky and so receptive to pollen. I will note that many hybridizers do not think such stigma protection is necessary as rhododendron pollen is not wind-borne and the emasculated flowers are not attractive to insects.
5. Ideally, when the stigma of the female plant is receptive, remove the corollas to expose anthers on several unopened buds from the male parent plant. Collect the entire flower stem intact and transfer pollen from the anthers to the stigma immediately. If pollen must be held until later, clip the anthers off and place them in a gelatin capsule. Store the capsule containing the male pollen parts in a refrigerator until the female plant is ready. If stored for more than one week, add a desiccant such as silica gel.
6. Apply the pollen from the end of the anther to the sticky surface on the stigma. Since rhododendron pollen is not dusty and does not shake out easily, touch the pollen sac to the surface of the stigma to transfer the pollen. The total surface of the stigma needs to be covered with pollen.
7. Some hybridizers next cover the pollinated flower with a small brown paper bag to protect the fertilized stigma. Others consider such protection unnecessary for the same reasons mentioned for step 4 above.
8. Label the female parent to show the cross, again listing the name of the female parent first.
9. Check the record book to confirm recording and date the cross.

If the selected parents do not flower at the same time, label and store the pollen as discussed for step 5 above. Pollen may be air dried and stored in the open for up to 2 weeks at 50°F (10°C). If the male parent flowers after the female flowers, the pollen may be stored in the freezer at 0°F (−18°C) for a year after it is dried or about a week at 50°F (10°C). If stored for an extended period, enclose the capsule in a sealed jar containing calcium chloride or silica gel as a drying agent. Place the drying agent in the bottom of the jar and cover with a layer of cotton on which the capsules are placed. Be certain the capsule is labeled with the parent name.

Warm frozen pollen to ambient temperatures prior to use by setting the jar with the capsules in warm water. When pollinating with stored pollen, insert the receptive stigma into the capsule to transfer the pollen since the pollen frequently sticks to the sides of the capsule. Unused pollen may be refrozen to use later.

Alternatively, off-season flowering of the female parent can be induced. This is most commonly done by transplanting the female parent into a container the previous fall and placing it in a greenhouse or transplanting into a greenhouse bed. By controlling temperature and day length, the time of flowering can be made to coincide with the flowering time of the pollen parent. If a choice can be made, it is easier to store pollen than to alter flowering dates.

If pollination was successful, the ovaries of the female parent will expand rapidly and produce the seed pod containing the new hybrid seed. Seed usually matures about the end of September, at which time the pod can be removed. There is no need to wait until the seed pod turns brown since the seeds are mature and are capable of germinating a month before changes in pod color. Seed pods must be collected no later than the first killing frost as frost accelerates pod splitting and subsequent seed loss.

Place the pods, collected from one plant, in a separate small envelope or cup that has been labeled to identify the cross. Place the seed container in a warm, dry location to dry the pods so they will release the seeds. Crush pods that have failed to open by drying to remove any seeds. Next, separate the pod and other plant material from the seeds. Since the seeds are very small, it is necessary to take great care not to lose them. Seeds may be sown immediately or stored in a cool, dry place for up to a year.

Seed germination is highest at temperatures of 70–75°F (21–24°C) in an atmosphere of 100% relative humidity. The growing medium needs to hold moisture well, be well drained, and be fine enough that a smooth surface can be prepared. If the tiny seeds fall into small holes on the soil surface, they may become too deeply covered. I would recommend a medium composed of 70% sphagnum peat moss and 30% horticultural perlite, but other organic mixes may be equally satisfactory. Many propagators use 100% milled sphagnum peat moss. The germinating container must be moisture-tight when sealed, must drain well, and must be at least 4 inches (10 cm) deep. The other dimensions depend entirely on the number of seeds to be sown. Containers must be clean, preferably of plastic, metal, or glass. Plastic food storage boxes with clear tops make excellent seedling growing containers. Bottom holes will allow more careful watering once the seedlings are developed. Germination will occur in 2 to 8 weeks after sowing the seed in most cases. Further details on germination and seedling growth is provided in Reiley 1995.

The success or failure of the cross, noted when the seeds are recovered, the disposition of the seed, sowing dates, and other information must all be noted in the record book together with any observations that might prove useful later on. For example, the amount of seed set would indicate the degree of compatibility or success in technique.

The accepted method of ultimately combining in a single cultivar the most desirable characteristics existing separately in the two parent plants is to then cross-pollinate two first-generation seedlings that most closely exhibit the desired characteristics. Intended results are most often obtained in the resulting second generation, the grandchildren of the original parents. It is best to grow as many seedlings of this second generation as possible. This will exploit the maximum number of genetic combinations to turn up the one closest to the desired plant.

If the hybridizing goal is to improve only one or two traits of an otherwise outstanding plant, perhaps tightening the truss or increasing disease resistance, backcrossing is undertaken.

The steps in backcrossing are:

1. Cross the rhododendron needing improvement with a rhododendron having a proven reputation for transmitting the desired trait.
2. Backcross the F_1 (first generation) seedling that best exhibits the trait desired to the pod (female) parent of step 1 needing improvement.
3. If the desired result is not obtained in the resulting F_2 (second) generation, then proceed to cross two sister seedlings of the F_2 generation.

Backcrossing generally requires fewer seedlings to produce the desired results but is also open to the expression of undesirable qualities.

Any physical characteristic is seldom controlled by a single gene. Rather, a number of genes are involved, some of which may work in opposition to others. This fact is one of the reasons that breeding results are difficult to predict.

Furthermore, some characteristics are linked on a single gene. A good example is color and fragrance in rhododendrons. I know of no fragrant red rhododendron, and to my knowledge fragrance only occurs in white or light colored flowers. These two characteristics are probably located on the same gene, in which case a breeding goal of producing a fragrant red rhododendron may be close to impossible to reach.

Sometimes crosses will not produce seeds. This outcome occurs when the two plants selected as parents are too genetically different. For example, an Elepidote × Lepidote rhododendron cross or a deciduous × evergreen azalea cross usually will not produce seed. In addition, polyploids, that is plants bearing two or three times the normal number of 26 chromosomes, are usually incompatible with plants containing 26 chromosomes. In such cases any seed produced is sterile or weak and yields unthrifty or sterile offspring.

Seedling Evaluation

The genetic purity and potential of the parents in terms of their ability to transmit the genetic characteristics being sought determines how many seedlings need to be grown. Fewer seedlings are needed with inbred lines, such as species, while more are needed with hybrid parents. The greater the heterogeneity of the parents, the greater the variety of possible results. Accordingly, a greater number of seedlings must be grown to increase the likelihood of arriving at the desired characteristic.

The following are guidelines as to the optimal number of seedlings to be grown for various crosses. As the list progresses from number 1 to number 3, the parents are increasingly more heterogeneous or variable in genetic makeup, so a greater number of seedlings must be grown.

1. Cross between two different species. As few as 20 seedlings are adequate if resulting seedlings are to be used as primary hybrid parents in a second cross. The expectation is reaching the goal in a second generation.
2. Cross between a species and a hybrid. A minimum of 50 seedlings are needed if the offspring are to be used as intermediate parents to be crossed again as in number 1. If the expectation is to meet the hybridizing goal in the first generation, several hundred seedlings are a minimum.
3. Cross between two hybrids. Since both parents are hybrids and more heterogeneous than species plants, a minimum of 500 seedlings must be grown on for evaluation.
4. Backcrossing. The number of seedlings required depends on the number of characteristics one is attempting to recombine in the progeny. When seeking to recombine two characteristics, 100 seedlings are probably adequate.

These estimates are offered as ballpark figures only. In practice, the greater the number of seedlings grown, the better the chance of reaching the goals set.

Recognize that the first generation of seedlings rarely produces the desired results and usually present a group of mediocre plants. The uncertain blending of parental characteristics indicates that efforts must usually be carried on to at least a second generation. Desired characteristics in selected parents (especially if carried on recessive genes) are often absent in the first generation yet will appear in future generations, hopefully in the combination desired.

All plants not meeting the hybridizer's goals must be eliminated as soon as it is clear that any of them fall short of the goals. All such roguing needs to be recorded in the record book. Any seedlings selected for growing on should also be recorded.

All hybridizers could use assistance in the selection process since it is impossible to be objective about one's own work. Some suggested evaluation practices include

1. Evaluating any new hybrid over a period of at least 10 years.
2. Comparing by planting the seedlings thought to be better in a test garden beside plants widely agreed to be superior.
3. Share the seedlings with other gardeners in different geographic locations for evaluation under different conditions.
4. Introduce and register only plants that prove to be superior to existing cultivars after these practices have been completed.

Far too many new rhododendron and azalea cultivars are registered each year simply because many hybridizers fail to reach an objective assessment of their own work. This assertion is not meant to criticize the registration system. The registrar is after all only doing the job required by the international code—registering the cultivars submitted. The registrar is not expected to judge the garden worthiness of the cultivars submitted. The issue of selection rests with the hybridizer. This can be a difficult position if a hybridizer lacks knowledge of existing cultivars or understands the plant's performance only under limited conditions. It is for these reasons that objective assistance in determining if a new cultivar is worthy of registration and introduction is warranted. Yet there is some advantage in having too many cultivars registered rather than losing a truly great plant when an amateur hybridizer fails to test it adequately before registration.

Superior selections need to be propagated and shared with other growers, first, to make sure they are not lost to cultivation, and second, to test them as widely as possible. Plant sharing is a critical part of the evaluation process, and if the new cultivar is judged to be superior by a widely diverse number of gardeners, registration may be justified. Registration forms require the registrant to provide considerable detail so that the cultivar can be well identified. Precise measurements of leaf and flower, precise flower color, truss size, and shape, and parentage are among the details requested.

Hybridizing is not for everyone. It requires considerable patience, the ability to sustain disappointment, a strong back to transplant thousands of seedlings, and some good, honest gardening friends to help maintain the proper perspective and objectivity for evaluating new hybrids. On the other hand, hybridizing does add an additional level of satisfaction to gardening. Even if the amateur hybridizer never registers or introduces a single plant, the enjoyment of the undertaking can make it all worth the effort.

Resources

COLLECTIONS

So many gardens worldwide have wonderful collections of azaleas and rhododendrons that the reader is referred to the plant societies listed below for information regarding collections in various areas.

SUPPLIERS

As with collections, suppliers abound for rhododendrons and azaleas. Readers may consult the societies listed here for information on suppliers for their region. *Gardening by Mail* by Barbara J. Barton (Sebastopol, Calif.: Tusker Press) also lists many North American nurseries.

INTERNATIONAL REGISTRATION AUTHORITY

Royal Horticultural Society
Attn: Alan C. Leslie
Royal Horticultural Society's
  Garden, Wisley
Woking, Surrey GU23 6QB
England
fax: (44) 1483-211750
e-mail: acl.reg@dial.pipex.com

North American Regional
  Representative:
American Rhododendron Society
Attn: J. W. Murray
21 Squire Terrace
Colts Neck, NJ 07722
U.S.A.
fax: 318-938-5405

PLANT SOCIETIES

American Rhododendron Society
Dee Daneri, Executive Director
11 Pinecrest Drive
Fortuna, CA 95540
U.S.A.
phone: 707-725-3043
fax: 707-725-1217
web site: www.rhodies.org

Azalea Society of America
Membership Chairman
P.O. Box 34536
West Bethesda, MD 20827-0536
U.S.A.

Rhododendron Society of Canada
R. S. Dickhout
5200 Timothy Crescent
Niagara Falls, Ontario L2E 5G3
Canada
phone: 905-357-5981
fax: 905-375-0018

Rhododendron Species Foundation
Vickie O'Keefe
P.O. Box 3798
Federal Way, WA 98063-3798
U.S.A.
phone: 206-838-4646
fax: 206-838-4686

References and Additional Reading

In addition to the publications of the above-mentioned plant societies, the following are suggested reading for those interested in rhododendrons and azaleas.

Davidian, H. H. 1982. *Rhododendron Species.* Vol. I, *Lepidotes.* Portland, Ore.: Timber Press.

———. 1989. *Rhododendron Species.* Vol. II, *Elepidotes* (Arboreum–Lactaeum). Portland, Ore.: Timber Press.

———. 1992. *Rhododendron Species.* Vol. III, *Elepidotes* (Neriiflorum–Thomsonii). Portland, Ore.: Timber Press.

———. 1995. *Rhododendron Species.* Vol. IV, *Azaleas.* Portland, Ore.: Timber Press.

Galle, F. C. 1987. *Azaleas.* Portland, Ore.: Timber Press.

Greer, H. E. 1987. *Greer's Guide to Available Rhododendrons.* Eugene, Ore.: Offshoot Publications.

Leach, D. G. 1961. *Rhododendrons of the World.* New York: Charles Scribner's Sons.

Reiley, H. E. 1995. *Success with Rhododendrons and Azaleas.* Portland, Ore.: Timber Press.

Salley, H. E., and H. E. Greer. 1992. *Rhododendron Hybrids.* Portland, Ore.: Timber Press.

Van Gelderen, D. M., and J. R. P. Van Hoey Smith. 1992. *Rhododendron Portraits.* Portland, Ore.: Timber Press.

Van Veen, T. 1986. *Rhododendrons in America.* Portland, Ore.: Binford and Mort.

West, F. H., et al. 1978. *Rhododendrons and Azaleas for Eastern North America.* Ed. Philip A. Livingston. Newton Square, Penn: Harrowood Books.

13 Breeding *Kalmia*: Mountain Laurel and its Relatives

Richard A. Jaynes

When gardeners hear of the genus *Kalmia*, the beautiful mountain laurel (*Kalmia latifolia*) usually comes to mind. It is the most commonly cultivated of the laurels, and although its showy flowers are perhaps the main attraction, it also serves as a magnificent broadleaf evergreen. But there are seven species in the genus, and each is fairly distinctive, making them easy to differentiate.

Important Breeding Materials

Kalmia microphylla, the western laurel, is an alpine plant and the only species of the genus found west of the Rocky Mountains. The leaves are opposite, leathery, and evergreen. The flowers are rose-purple to pink, arranged in a terminal raceme of few flowers, each ¼ to ¾ inch (6–19 mm) across. Flowers occur in late spring or early summer. This species includes two varieties, var. *microphylla* and var. *occidentalis*. Variety *microphylla*, the alpine laurel or small-leaved kalmia, is distributed throughout mountainous regions of western North America from central California, Nevada, Utah, and Colorado northward through the Rockies to the Yukon and Northwest Territories. Found in alpine meadows and bogs, this variety is quite small, seldom reaching more than 6 inches (15 cm) in height, with leaves usually less than ½ inch (12 mm) long. Variety *occidentalis*, western bog laurel, is found in marshes and bogs at lower elevations in the coastal regions and islands of southern Alaska, British Columbia, Washington, and northwestern Oregon. This variety is larger, growing to 2 feet (0.6 m) in height with leaves ½ to 1½ inches (12–38 mm) long and flowers slightly larger than those of var. *microphylla*. Both varieties may form dense mats in the wet areas where they are native.

Kalmia polifolia, eastern bog laurel, is a small shrub of 3 feet (0.9 m) or less with opposite, leathery, evergreen leaves. The leaf margins are usually revolute (rolled under), and the leaves are distinct in having purple glandular hairs along the midrib. The flowers are borne on a terminal raceme with few flowers per inflorescence. Like those of *K. microphylla*, the flowers are usually rose-purple and ½ to ¾ inch (12–19 mm) across. Flowers appear early in the growing season. *Kalmia polifolia* is also a native of wet areas, generally found along the margins of ponds and lakes. It is the most widely distributed species within the genus and is found from coastal areas to high elevations in the mountains of the northeastern United States and Canada. It ranges from northeastern Alberta, across Canada to the Atlantic Coast, and south to northern Illinois and central New Jersey. This species is similar to *K. microphylla*, but differs in its larger size, revolute leaf margins, and purple hairs on the leaf midrib. A white-flowered variety, *K. polifolia* var. *leucantha*, has been described from a bog in Newfoundland.

Kalmia latifolia, the tall mountain laurel familiar to gardeners, forms dense thickets in rocky and sandy forests throughout most of its range. It is found in the eastern United States from southern Maine west to central Ohio, south to southern Mississippi, and east to the Florida panhandle. It is a spreading shrub reaching about 12 feet (3.6 m), growing taller in some parts of its native range. The leaves are alternate, leathery, and 2 to 5 inches (5–12.5 cm) long. The flowers are borne on a terminal compound corymb, usually produced in late spring or early summer; they are light pink with purple spots around each anther pocket. This is a highly variable species (Plate 13-1), making it well suited for breeding and selection, and five botanical forms are recognized. First reported from Cape May County, New Jersey, forma *angustata* has very narrow, willow-shaped leaves less than ½ inch (12 mm) wide. Forma *myrtifolia* is essentially a smaller form of the species, rarely exceeding 3 feet (0.9 m) in height. The flowers and leaves are also smaller, and the plant is compact and slow growing relative to the species type. Forma *obtusata* is a rare form originating near Pomfret, Connecticut. It has oval leaves, usually 1 to 2½ inches (2.5–6.5 cm) long and up to 1½ inches (3.8 cm) wide, on a compact plant. Forma *fuscata* has flowers with a dark maroon band on the inside of the white to pink flowers at the level of the anther pockets. This form has been reported from many localities in the northeastern United States. Forma *polypetala* boasts flowers with a deeply divided corolla, creating five separate petals. The width of the petals varies from plant to plant, from narrow and threadlike to very broad. The cultivar 'Bettina' has a corolla that is reduced in size and deeply lobed, and a selection that lacks petals altogether, formerly given the name 'Apetala', is also found in forma *polypetala*.

Kalmia angustifolia, sheep laurel, is a multistemmed shrub to 6 feet (1.8 m) tall with reddish brown branchlets. The leaves are leathery, 1 to 1½ inches (2.5–6.5 cm) long, and arranged in whorls of three. Leaves and stems have stalked glandular hairs on their surfaces. Flowers are small, less than ½ inch (12 mm) across, and reddish purple to pink in color. The flowers are borne in small clusters from the axils of the previous year's leaves, and flowering time is a few days before or the same as that of *K. latifolia*. Sheep laurel is common in eastern and northeastern North America, and the species consists of two distinct varieties. The northern sheep laurel, variety *angustifolia*, has glabrous leaves and densely pubescent calyces. This variety occurs in wet places from northern Michigan and eastern Ontario eastward, and southward to the southeastern tip of Virginia. It is highly variable in flower color, leaf size and color, and habit, and several of these variations have been given cultivar names. They are attractive garden plants, though less popular than mountain laurel. *Kalmia angustifolia* var. *angustifolia* f. *candida* is a white-flowered form with green stems (unlike the wild type, which has reddish stems). The second variety of *K. angustifolia*, var. *caroliniana*, differs from var. *angustifolia* in having leaves that are densely pubescent beneath, and glabrous calyces. This variety is common in North Carolina, with sporadic occurrences in other southeastern locations.

Kalmia cuneata, white wicky, is one of the rarest shrubs in North America. It is a multistemmed shrub to 5 feet (1.5 m) tall and is the only deciduous member of the genus. The flowers are borne in clusters of three to ten in the upper axils of the previous year's growth. Its creamy white flowers are ½ to ¾ inch (12–19 mm) across and often have a narrow red band within. This species flowers in late spring or early summer, 2 to 3 weeks after *K. latifolia*. It is found in wet areas in eight counties of southeastern North Carolina and adjacent South Carolina.

Kalmia hirsuta, sandhill laurel, is a small shrub to 2 feet (0.6 m) in height with densely pubescent stems and leaves. The leaf margins are strongly revolute. Solitary flowers are borne in the axils of the current year's leaves. The flowers are about ½ inch (12 mm) across and are light pink with red markings around the anther pockets and a red ring near the base of the corolla. This species is found along the coastal plain of the United States from southern South Carolina along the coast of Georgia and northern Florida to extreme southwestern Alabama.

Kalmia ericoides, Cuban laurel, is a 3-foot (0.9-m) shrub with alternate leathery leaves. Most of the plant is pubescent. The flowers are solitary and borne in the axils of the leaves near the ends of the branches, appearing in tight clusters. The corolla is about ½ inch (12 mm) across and light pink with red markings around the anther pockets and a red ring near the base. This species is limited in distribution to the pine barrens of western Cuba, and it appears to be closely related to *K. hirsuta*.

Crosses between species in *Kalmia* are difficult to create, and natural hybrids have never been reported. Only a few controlled interspecific crosses have been successful over the years, and that is unfortunate. Although each species shows a great deal of variability, the variation could be even further increased if the different species were able to readily hybridize with one another. I have done extensive work in crossing the various species in an attempt to produce viable hybrids (Jaynes 1997). A few observations are notable.

Seedlings of crosses between *Kalmia polifolia* and *K. latifolia* were extremely variable, ranging from very weak and miniature to large and vigorous. The hybrids most resembled the female parent (*K. polifolia*). This is to be expected since *K. polifolia* is a natural tetraploid with 48 chromosomes, contributing two sets to the hybrid, while *K. latifolia* contributes only one set. The hybrids are sterile and are probably triploid, with 36 chromosomes. A cross between *K. polifolia* and an induced-tetraploid form of *K. latifolia* might produce more vigorous plants, perhaps more intermediate between the parents, and perhaps fertile. The reciprocal cross, *K. latifolia* × *K. polifolia*, results in no seed set.

Kalmia latifolia × *K. hirsuta* crosses were again highly variable in vigor, habit, leaf shape, and flower color. The hybrids are intermediate between the two species in hardiness, and they are easier to propagate from cuttings than mountain laurel. Some of the hybrids had a compact, multi-branched form, perhaps of horticultural interest. Of the 50 or so hybrids of this cross that flowered for me, only one was fertile. The seedlings from the single fertile plant were grown out and appeared to be the result of a backcross onto mountain laurel. These were then intercrossed to produce some mountain laurel–like plants with smaller leaves and stature. Some second- and third-generation hybrids show resistance to foliar disease and root rot, and some can be grown in full sun in the South (unlike *K. latifolia*), all characteristics that make the plants horticulturally promising.

Crosses between *Kalmia angustifolia* and *K. latifolia* generally produced weak, chlorotic (leaf yellowing) plants that eventually died. Crosses using the white-flowered form of the northern sheep laurel (*K. angustifolia* var. *angustifolia* f. *candida*), however, produced more viable seeds than crosses using the typical form as the seed parent. The resulting hybrids are intermediate between the parents but are more tender and slow to produce flowers. New growth is white to yellow, becoming green as it ages. Flowers are pale pink and sterile. The reciprocal cross failed completely.

The only species cross that is easy to make and generally produces healthy offspring is *Kalmia polifolia* × *K. microphylla*. The hybrids are sterile triploids, some of which are of horticultural interest, and *Kalmia* 'Rocky Top' was selected from this group. The offspring have a more compact habit than the seed parent (*K. polifolia*) and are more tolerant to hot summers and open winters in the northeastern United States; however, the hybrids, as well as the parent species, are often short-lived in this region.

Crosses between *Kalmia hirsuta* and *K. angustifolia* produced weak, chlorotic plants, as did *K. hirsuta* × *K. cuneata* and *K. polifolia* × *K. angustifolia*. The Cuban species, *K. ericoides*, has not been crossed with other species.

Important Traits and Breeding Objectives

Due to the difficulty of crossing different species to create plants of horticultural interest, development of improved laurel cultivars has been confined largely to breeding and selection within species. Of the seven naturally occurring species of *Kalmia*, the mountain laurel (*Kalmia latifolia*) is by far the most important member of the genus in economic terms, as it is sold as an ornamental landscape plant, and the foliage is used for floral displays and Christmas decorations. This species has gained the most attention when it comes to selection and naming of improved plants. Indeed some 80 cultivars have been named.

As with many ornamental plants, perhaps the most important traits for which to breed involve flower characteristics. Flower color (ranging from white and pale pink to deep pink), size, shape, abundance, and pigment pattern are all important in the ornamental value of *Kalmia*. The expanded corolla can be white (*Kalmia latifolia* 'Snowdrift') to light pink (*K. latifolia* 'Pink Frost') to deep reddish pink (*K. latifolia* 'Sarah') or candy stripe (*K. latifolia* 'Peppermint'). Pure white-flowered selections appear to breed true when crossed with other pure white selections. White-flowered cultivars such as *K. latifolia* 'Stillwood' will produce an occasional pink tinge when grown in full sun. Crosses between deep pink- and white-flowered plants will result in seedlings with various amounts of pink. When the white parent is a pure white, the pink is less likely to be expressed in the offspring, as white is usually dominant. When both parents are light to moderate pink, the offspring show a wide range of pink coloring. When crossing the deep pink-colored selections, however, all the seedlings have deep pink coloration.

Bud color in *Kalmia latifolia* ranges from white, in cultivars such as 'Snowdrift', to pink, as in 'Alpine Pink' and 'Pink Surprise', to red, in 'Olympic Fire', 'Sarah', and 'Ostbo Red'. The red bud color is fully expressed only in plants grown in some sunlight. Plants with red buds breed true when intercrossed. Red is recessive relative to white and light pink in flower bud color, but the pigmentation on the inside of the corolla is under separate genetic control and may be white or pink in color, regardless of the color of the bud.

The pigment distribution inside the corolla is highly variable as well. Many cultivars (such as 'Splendens') have spots at the anther pockets. These spots may also form an interrupted band (as in *fuscata* forms of *Kalmia latifolia* and the cultivar 'Freckles'), a narrow continuous band (*fuscata* forms, 'Olympic Wedding', 'Star Cluster'), or a broad, continuous band that almost fills the corolla (*fuscata* forms, 'Bullseye', 'Keepsake' [Plate 13-4], 'Pinwheel'). Presence or absence of a corolla band is controlled by a single dominant gene, with other genes controlling the size and color of the band. Banded plants yield seedlings that are 50% banded when outcrossed to normal plants, and as high as 75% banded when crossed with another banded parent.

Another pigment form is a dark circle at the base of the corolla (as in *Kalmia latifolia* 'Sarah'). Sometimes this circle has five points, which radiate up the creases of the corolla to the margins of the flower. These forms are known as star-ring types. Star-ring plants are rare in the wild, and this pigmentation is controlled by a single dominant gene. Intercrossing star-ring types seems to yield plants similar to the parents in ornamental value, and crosses of star-ring types with plants that have an interrupted band yield plants with interesting flowers. In these offspring, the star-ring is combined with the interrupted band to produce a busy flower that has a star splashed with specks of color near the anther pockets, as in the cultivar 'Peppermint'.

In mountain laurel, the corolla may have five lobes (normal) or up to nine lobes (multilobed). However, no plants have been found yet that reliably and consistently produce multilobed flowers. In the feather-petal types (*Kalmia latifolia* f. *polypetala*), five lobes are cut and range in width from wide to very narrow. This character is controlled by a single recessive gene and can be expressed in many ways, from partially to fully cut. The narrow, straplike petals are most common, but flowers with wide, apple-blossom-like petals are also known. The mountain laurel selection 'Shooting Star' exhibits five deeply cut lobes that are reflexed, and *K. latifolia* 'Bettina' has a reduced corolla. The genes for the feather-petal, 'Shooting Star', and 'Bettina' flower types are all recessive and apparently not linked. All three of these types may yield weak-growing plants.

'Apetala' is a selection with no corolla but functional anthers and pistils. The overall effect of the plant is a sort of fluffy or fuzzy appearance when blooming. This character is also controlled by a single recessive gene. When crossed with normal forms, all the offspring are normal; but when these offspring are backcrossed onto the 'Apetala' parent, 50% of the seedlings have this unusual characteristic.

Variation is also found in the distribution of flowers within the inflorescence. *Kalmia latifolia* 'Heart's Desire' offers tight, ball-shaped inflorescences as something different from the typical loose-flowering form. Cultivars such as 'Silver Dollar' sport flowers larger than typical, and 'Shooting Star' and 'Tightwad' flower later than most mountain laurels. 'Tightwad' has a corolla that refuses to open. This broad range of variation should be looked upon by the plant breeder as an opportunity for improvement of flower forms.

Foliage is also an important ornamental feature, and leaf size, shape, color, and retention should be considered in any breeding program. The *angustata* forms of mountain laurel have willow-like, or strap-shaped, leaves and are rare in the wild. The willow-leaf character is controlled by a single recessive gene. These forms are sometimes sterile, with mis-shapened styles, but this is not always the case, and they can be included in a breeding program, yielding such selections as *Kalmia latifolia* 'Willowcrest'. Other foliage forms of interest to the breeder include ovate leaves or bilobed leaves (with a notch rather than a point at the tip), wavy leaves, or larger-than-typical leaves (as in 'Silver Dollar').

Leaf color can be the typical green or variegated with white, yellow, or yellow-green. Foliage of the cultivar 'Yellow Flush' emerges yellow and after a few weeks turns green. I have made crosses that indicate that green and white or yellow sectoring is maternally inherited. Other types of variegation may be under different genetic control. Variegated mountain laurel offers ornamental potential, but to date few have been worthy of naming.

New shoots (stems) of mountain laurel may be yellow-green or reddish bronze rather than the typical green. Bronzed new growth can be found in 'Bullseye', 'Raspberry Glow', and 'Sarah'. Deep pink-flowered specimens of mountain laurel often have stems and new leaves tinged with red, though this does not always hold true. Red stems usually are found on plants with the darker colored flowers. Plants with pure white flowers lack the reddish pigment and therefore always produce normal green leaves, or foliage that is yellow-green when it first emerges and becomes darker green with maturity.

The overall height, form, vigor, and habit of the plants will also determine their success and usefulness in the landscape. Some forms are compact, distinguished by short internodes and densely clustered leaves. Some of these forms do not bloom profusely and, even when blooming, may have the flowers hidden in the dense foliage. *Kalmia latifolia* f. *obtusata* is similar to the compact type, but the *obtusata* forms have large, thick, and blunt-tipped leaves with thicker stems. Both the compact and the *obtusata* forms are controlled by a single recessive gene. Fortunately, semi-compact types are available, as exemplified by *K. latifolia* 'Carol' and 'Nathan Hale'.

Miniature selections, such as *Kalmia latifolia* f. *myrtifolia*, 'Elf', and

'Minuet', are even smaller. These plants usually have leaves and internodes one-third to one-half that of normal mountain laurel, with flowers somewhat less reduced. These plants may reach 5 feet (1.5 m) tall in 20 years. This characteristic is under the control of a single recessive gene. Seedlings of open-pollinated *myrtifolia* are usually normal in appearance. If these normal seedlings are intercrossed, 25% will be miniature, but a cross between two miniature forms will produce all miniature offspring. Until recently, the miniature forms all had normal flower color (as in 'Elf'), but as a result of combining the miniature character with deep pink and red flower types, new selections are now available. 'Minuet', miniature with banded flowers, was the first to be named; 'Tiddlywinks' and 'Tinkerbell' are rich pink, and 'Little Linda' is red in bud (Plate 13-5).

Some flower and foliage forms are yet to be discovered. Two recent finds include the double-flowered *Kalmia latifolia* 'Madeline', from New Zealand (the opposite side of the world from the native range of the mountain laurel), and 'Creepy', a native North Carolina plant that grows 12 to 18 inches (30–45 cm) high and 16 feet (5 m) across.

Other characters worth considering in the breeding of *Kalmia* include seed capsule appearance and retention, plant hardiness, tolerance to heat and drought, and disease and insect resistance. Since the resulting selection from a breeding program must be further propagated by vegetative means in order to be distributed, ease of propagation (especially via cuttings) is also an important characteristic. Most mountain laurel selections are difficult to root, but 'Carousel', 'Nipmuck', 'Pink Charm', and 'Pink Surprise' are sometimes commercially propagated from cuttings. However, the most common means to commercially produce mountain laurel plants is by micropropagation, or tissue culture.

Hybridization Mechanics

Flowers to be used in hand-pollinated crosses must be selected when the flowers are in bud, before they have opened. In order to avoid contamination of those flowers by pollen from the same flower, emasculation is necessary. This is done by using tweezers to remove the corolla and anthers, leaving only the pistil of the flower (Figure 13-1). With the petals removed as well as the anthers, insects will not be attracted to the flower. Other flower buds should be removed, if they are within a foot of the flower to be pollinated, to further reduce the risk of contamination.

Although *Kalmia* species are primarily pollinated by bumblebees, I found that the powdery pollen can be blown short distances (Jaynes 1997). This provides a possible mechanism for contamination, and caution should be taken to avoid this. One way to avoid potential problems is to use flow-

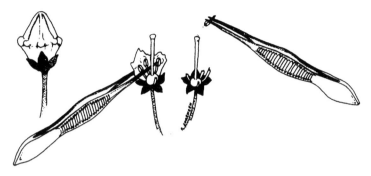

Figure 13-1. Emasculation and pollination process. *Left,* flower bud at proper stage for emasculation. *Center,* removal of the anthers and corolla. *Right,* pollination, usually carried out a day after emasculation. (Illustration by Rita Sorensen-Leonard)

ers near the top of a plant to reduce the chance of pollen falling from above onto the flower to be used in the cross.

Flowers can be pollinated the day after emasculation, unless cool or rainy weather has prevented maturation. In these cases the flower may need an additional day or two to mature. When the stigma is receptive it will appear moist and sticky. Pollinations may be made using the whole anther: if the anther is touched to the stigma, a clump of pollen will adhere to the sticky surface of the stigma. Alternatively, the anther can be tapped above the stigma to loosen a clump of pollen.

When flowering times of two potential parents are different, pollen can be collected and stored for later use. For short-term storage of a week or less, pollen can be kept at room temperature and humidity, out of direct sunlight. For long-term storage, pollen can be placed in a small vial or gelatin capsule, then placed inside a closed larger jar containing silica gel or a similar desiccant. After the pollen has dried (usually 4 to 8 hours), the closed jar should be placed in a freezer at 0 to 20°F (−18 to −7°C), where it can be stored for up to a year. To ship pollen, place the anthers in gelatin capsules, put those into a larger jar with a desiccant, and carefully pack and ship the jar.

Once pollinations are made, seed capsules will begin to ripen if the pollination was successful. As they mature, seed capsules change from green to brown. If collected too soon, the seed may not be ripe; if not collected soon enough, the capsule will dehisce and the seeds will be lost. Once capsules have been harvested, they can be placed in coin envelopes or other similar containers to dry. This usually takes several days. When dry, the seed capsules will open and the tiny *Kalmia* seeds can be shaken loose. If the capsules have been harvested a bit early and the seeds are not readily shaken from the capsule, crush the capsule (on paper) with a wooden block to remove the seeds.

Once seeds have been removed from the capsules, they can be cleaned of dust and debris by gently funneling them down a trough-shaped piece of white paper and letting them fall a short distance onto another piece of paper. If repeated several times, this process eliminates much of the debris, which can support fungal growth during germination.

Kalmia seeds should be stored in a cool, dry location for best results. They may be placed in glassine or coin envelopes and kept in a refrigerator (frost-free) at 40°F (4°C). I found that, of 28 lots of seed stored for more than 10 years, 75% had a germination rate of over 50% (Jaynes 1997). This indicates that *Kalmia* seed may remain viable for years if properly stored. But longevity is variable, and it is best not to take chances with seed from your hand pollinations.

Propagation

Kalmia species vary in their requirements for germination. Fresh *Kalmia latifolia* seed will germinate without further treatment, but cold stratification for 8 weeks, or soaking seed overnight in 200 ppm gibberellin (gibberellic acid, GA$_3$), increases germination by 50%. Seed stored for a year or two will germinate even more readily than fresh seed, since this dry storage overcomes the partial dormancy requirements of fresh seed.

The best temperature for germination and initial growth is between 70 and 75°F (21–24°C). Constant temperatures above 80°F (27°C) reduce survival, and temperatures below 70°F (21°C) slow growth dramatically. Various media are suitable for germination of *Kalmia* seeds, including pure peat or sphagnum moss. Mixes containing more than 15% (by volume) of vermiculite are not recommended. I recommend 3 parts Canadian peat: 1 part perlite (Jaynes 1997). As this medium may deteriorate when stored for more than a couple of months, mix only the amount needed at a given time. This mix should have a pH of about 4.8, and if lower than this it should be raised with a small amount of limestone. I also recommend using clear plastic boxes, 3½ × 7 × 1¾ inches (9 × 18 × 4 cm) high. Half fill these with the soilless mix and gently firm the surface of the mix with a board. Moisten the medium thoroughly before sowing the seed. Once the mix is damp, sow the seeds on the surface of the mix and lightly spritz with water to settle the seed. Do not cover the seeds, as they need light to germinate. Place the sown seed 9 to 12 inches (23–30 cm) below fluorescent lights to begin germination. The seed requires a moist mix and high humidity to germinate, though once the seedlings emerge the surface of the mix should be allowed to dry occasionally to retard algae and moss.

Most *Kalmia* seeds will germinate in 10 to 21 days. Once the seedlings have true leaves, they can be fertilized with an all-purpose water-soluble fertilizer, such as 20-20-20, prepared at the rate of one teaspoon per gallon (about 1 gram per liter) of water. After the first application, this solution may be applied at 2- to 3-week intervals, testing occasionally to prevent salt buildup or pH change.

After germination, seedlings need long days or they may become dormant. Since seed is usually collected in the fall, seedlings are often grown during the winter months, when days are short. In these cases, day length can be extended with the use of artificial light; 75-watt floodlights, turned on from 10 P.M. to 2 A.M., will stimulate the plants into growing as if it were spring. By spring, the seedlings will be large enough to transplant outdoors.

Selected hybrids may be vegetatively propagated by cuttings, grafting, or layering. Propagation is sometimes done by means of tissue culture, but this is generally reserved for commercial operations due to the equipment and expense involved. My earlier book on *Kalmia* gives a thorough discussion of all forms of vegetative propagation (Jaynes 1997).

There is still much to be accomplished in improving and diversifying *Kalmia*. Most of the 80 mountain laurel cultivars have been named within the last 20 years. As with many other plants, important new cultivars are likely to come from the efforts of dedicated amateurs. Public institutions just do not have the funds necessary to do the work. Look at the great success amateurs have had with *Hemerocallis*, *Magnolias*, and *Rhododendrons*. A degree in plant breeding is not required.

Resources

COLLECTIONS

United States

Arnold Arboretum
Harvard University
125 Arborway
Jamaica Plain, MA 02130

Bartlett Arboretum
University of Connecticut at
   Stamford
151 Brookdale Road
Stamford, CT 06903

Callaway Gardens
U.S. Highway 27
P.O. Box 2000
Pine Mountain, GA 31822-2000

Connecticut Arboretum at
   Connecticut College
5625 Connecticut College
270 Mohegan Avenue
New London, CT 06320

Henry Foundation for Botanical
  Research
P.O. Box 7
801 Stony Lane
Gladwyne, PA 19035

Highstead Arboretum
P.O. Box 1097
Redding, CT 06875

Holden Arboretum
9500 Sperry Road
Kirtland, OH 44094

North Carolina Botanical Garden
University of North Carolina
CB Box 3375, Totten Center
Chapel Hill, NC 27599

Planting Fields Arboretum
P.O. Box 58
Oyster Bay, NY 11771

Skylands of Ringwood State Park
New Jersey State Botanical Garden
Ringwood, NJ 07456

Susie Harwood Garden
University of North Carolina at
  Charlotte
Charlotte, NC

U.S. National Arboretum
3501 New York Avenue, N.E.
Washington, DC 20002

Europe

Kalmthout Arboretum
Heuvel 2
2180 Kalmthout
Belgium

Royal Botanic Garden
Inverleith Row
Edinburgh EH3 5LR
Scotland

Royal Horticultural Society's
  Garden, Wisley
Woking, Surrey GU23 6QB
England

Sheffield Park
Uckfield
England

SUPPLIERS

Broken Arrow Nursery
13 Broken Arrow Road
Hamden, CT 06518
U.S.A.
phone: 203-288-1026

Brown's Kalmia and Azalea Nursery
8527 Semiahmoo Drive
Blaine, WA 98230
U.S.A.
phone: 360-371-2489

Cummins Garden
22 Robertsville Road
Marlboro, NJ 07746
U.S.A.
phone: 732-536-2591

Fairweather Gardens
P.O. Box 330
Greenwich, NJ 08323
U.S.A.
phone: 609-451-6261

Forestfarm
990 Tetherow Road
Williams, OR 97544
U.S.A.
phone: 541-846-6963

Glendoick Gardens
Glencarse
Perth PH2 7NS
Scotland
phone: (44) 1738-860205

Greer Gardens
1280 Goodpasture Island Road
Eugene, OR 97401
U.S.A.
phone: 541-686-8266

Heritage Laurels
13313 Fillmore Street
West Olive, MI 49460
U.S.A.
phone: 616-842-4407

Laurel Springs Nursery
401 Regal Street
Hendersonville, NC 28792
U.S.A.
phone: 828-891-1264

Roslyn Nursery
211 Burrs Lane
Dix Hills, NY 11746
U.S.A.
phone: 516-643-9347

Vineland Nurseries
Box 98, Martin Road
Vineland Station, Ontario L0R 2E0
Canada
phone: 905-562-4836

Wayside Gardens
P.O. Box 1
1 Garden Lane
Hodges, SC 29695
U.S.A.
phone: 800-845-1124

Weston Nurseries
P.O. Box 186
E. Main Street, Route 135
Hopkinton, MA 01748
U.S.A.
phone: 508-435-3414

Woodlanders, Inc.
1128 Colleton Avenue
Aiken, SC 29801
U.S.A.
phone: 803-648-7522

INTERNATIONAL REGISTRATION AUTHORITY

Richard A. Jaynes
Broken Arrow Nursery
13 Broken Arrow Road
Hamden, CT 06518
U.S.A.

PLANT SOCIETIES

There is no *Kalmia* society, but many kindred souls may be found in the American Rhododendron Society.

American Rhododendron Society
Deanna Daneri, Executive Director
11 Pinecrest Drive
Fortuna, CA 95540
U.S.A.
phone: 707-725-3043
fax: 707-725-1217

240   Richard A. Jaynes

References and Additional Reading

Dudley, T. R. 1967. Ornamental mountain laurel and a new cultivar: *Kalmia latifolia* 'Bettina'. *American Horticultural Magazine* 46: 245–248.

Ebinger, J. E. 1974. A systematic study of the genus *Kalmia* (Ericaceae). *Rhodora* 76: 315–398.

Fordham, A. J. 1979. *Kalmia latifolia* selections and their propagation. *Journal, American Rhododendron Society* 33: 30–33.

Holmes, M. L. 1956. *Kalmia*, the American laurels. *Baileya* 4: 89–94.

Jaynes, R. A. 1968a. Interspecific crosses in *Kalmia*. *American Journal of Botany* 44: 1120–1125.

———. 1968b. Self incompatibility and inbreeding depression in three laurel (*Kalmia*) species. *Proceedings of the American Society of Horticultural Science* 93: 618–622.

———. 1971a. Laurel selections from seed: True-breeding red-budded mountain laurel. Connecticut Agricultural Experiment Station, Circular 240.

———. 1971b. Seed germination of six *Kalmia* species. *Journal of the American Society of Horticultural Science* 96: 668–672.

———. 1971c. The kalmias and their hybrids. *Quarterly Bulletin of the American Rhododendron Society* 25: 160–164.

———. 1971d. The selection and propagation of improved *Kalmia latifolia* cultivars. *International Plant Propagators' Society, Proceedings* 21: 366–374.

———. 1974. Inheritance of flower and foliage characteristics in mountain laurel (*Kalmia latifolia*). *Journal of the American Society of Horticultural Science* 99: 209–211.

———. 1976. Mountain laurel selections and methods of propagating them. *International Plant Propagators' Society, Proceedings* 26: 233–236.

———. 1981. Inheritance of ornamental traits in mountain laurel, *Kalmia latifolia*. *Journal of Heredity* 72: 245–248.

———. 1982. New mountain laurel selections and their propagation. *International Plant Propagators' Society, Proceedings* 32: 431–434.

———. 1983. Checklist of cultivated laurel, *Kalmia* spp. *Bulletin, American Association of Botanic Gardens and Arboreta* 17: 99–106.

———. 1997. *Kalmia: Mountain Laurel and Related Species*. Portland, Ore.: Timber Press.

Pierce, L. J. 1974. An unusual intergeneric cross. *Quarterly Bulletin of the American Rhododendron Society* 28 (1): 45.

Rehder, A. 1910. Notes on the forms of *Kalmia latifolia*. *Rhodora* 12: 1–3.

Southall, R. M., and J. W. Hardin. 1974. A taxonomic revision of *Kalmia* (Ericaceae). *Journal of the Elisha Mitchell Scientific Society* 90: 1–23.

Plate 10-1. *Hippeastrum brasilianum* (Photo by Alan W. Meerow)

Plate 10-2. *Hippeastrum cybister* (Photo by Alan W. Meerow)

Plate 10-3. *Hippeastrum evansiae* (Photo by Alan W. Meerow)

Plate 10-4. *Hippeastrum papilio* (Photo by Alan W. Meerow)

Plate 10-5. *Hippeastrum petiolatum* (Photo by Alan W. Meerow)

Plate 10-6. *Hippeastrum reticulatum* var. *striatifolium* foliage (Photo by Alan W. Meerow)

Plate 10-7. An unnamed Dutch-type amaryllis hybrid (Photo by Alan W. Meerow)

Plate 11-1. *Penstemon angustifolius* (Photo by Dale T. Lindgren)

Plate 11-2. *Penstemon digitalis* 'Husker Red' spring foliage (Photo by Dale T. Lindgren)

Plate 11-3. *Penstemon pinifolius* 'Mersea Yellow' (Photo by Dale T. Lindgren)

ate 11-4. *Penstemon strictus* (Photo by Dale T. Lindgren)

late 12-1. *Rhododendron fortunei* offers
everal qualities that make it a desirable
lepidote rhododendron for breeding pro-
rams. (Photo by H. Edward Reiley)

Plate 12-2. *Rhododendron* 'Elsie Lee' is an
evergreen azalea with fully double flowers.
(Photo by H. Edward Reiley)

Plate 12-3. *Rhododendron* 'Gibraltar' is a good deciduous azalea. (Photo by H. Edward Reiley)

Plate 12-4. *Rhododendron* 'Hino Crimson' offers the reddest flower color among evergreen azaleas. (Photo by Harold Greer)

Plate 12-5. *Rhododendron* 'Rose Greeley' has excellent fragrance. (Photo by H. Edward Reiley)

Plate 12-6. *Rhododendron strigillosum* is a red-flowered Elepidote rhododendron. (Photo courtesy of the Rhododendron Species Foundation)

Plate 13-1. This collection of field-grown mountain laurel *(Kalmia latifolia)* shows a range of flower color from near red to white. (Photo by Richard A. Jaynes)

Plate 13-2. *Kalmia latifolia* 'Comet' with near-white flowers and a corolla that is almost-petaled. (Photo by Richard A. Jaynes)

Plate 13-3. *Kalmia latifolia* 'Galaxy' combines the 'Shooting Star'-like flower shape with burgundy pigmentation obtained from the form *fuscata*. (Photo by Richard A. Jaynes)

late 13-4. *Kalmia latifolia* 'Keepsake' offers :d buds and burgundy pigmentation on the pen flower. (Photo by Richard A. Jaynes)

Plate 13-5. *Kalmia latifolia* 'Little Linda' was the first miniature or small-leaved cultivar to produce red buds. (Photo by Richard A. Jaynes)

late 14-1. *Camellia* 'April Snow' *(C. japon-ca).* (Photo by William L. Ackerman)

Plate 14-2. *Camellia* 'Dr. Clifford Parks' *(C. reticulata* × *C. japonica).* (Photo by William L. Ackerman)

Plate 14-3. *Camellia* 'E. G. Waterhouse' *(C. saluenensis* × *C. japonica).* (Photo by William L. Ackerman)

Plate 14-4. *Camellia nitidissima.* (Photo by William L. Ackerman)

Plate 14-5. *Camellia* 'Spring Frill' *(C. oleifera* × *C. vernalis).* (Photo by William L. Ackerman)

Plate 14-6. *Camellia* 'Winter's Rose' *(C. oleifera* × *C. hiemalis)*. (Photo by William L. Ackerman)

Plate 15-1. The standard lilac inflorescence shape, as expressed in *Syringa vulgaris* 'Znamya Lenyna', a hybrid introduced from Russia. (Photo by Owen M. Rogers)

Plate 15-2. *Syringa* ×*josiflexa* 'Jesse Hepler', a late-blooming cultivar from the series *Villosae*, showing the looser, more open flower cluster typical of the series. (Photo by Owen M. Rogers)

Plate 15-3. *Syringa reticulata*, showing the nontubular flower form of the subgenus *Ligustrina*. (Photo by Owen M. Rogers)

Plate 15-4. A seedling of *Syringa ×josiflexa* with both radial and staminode doubling. (Photo by Owen M. Rogers)

Plate 15-5. *Syringa ×josiflexa* with both staminode and hose-in-hose doubling. (Photo by Owen M. Rogers)

Plate 15-6. The white-edged purple flowers of *Syringa vulgaris* 'Sensation', with a reversion to the white-flowered 'Hugo de Vries' type. (Photo by Owen M. Rogers)

Plate 16-1. *Magnolia* 'Betty', one of the "Eight Little Girls" released from the breeding program at the U.S. National Arboretum. (Photo by Dorothy J. Callaway)

Plate 16-2. *Magnolia grandiflora* 'Bracken's Brown Beauty' is popular for its neat
pyramidal habit, smaller stature, prolific blooming, and perhaps most importantly, its
cold hardiness. The undersurfaces of the leaves are also a nice rich reddish brown.
(Photo by Dorothy J. Callaway)

Plate 16-3. *Magnolia* 'Butterflies', a cross between *M. acuminata* and *M. denudata*, is among the nicest yellow-flowered precocious magnolias available. (Photo by Dorothy J. Callaway)

Plate 16-4. *Magnolia* 'Joe McDaniel' is an example of the dark flower color found in many Gresham Hybrids. (Photo by Dorothy J. Callaway)

Plate 16-5. *Magnolia kobus* var. *loebneri* 'Leonard Messel' has received a great deal of attention because of its reliable bloom, even after severe winters and/or late freezes. (Photo by Dorothy J. Callaway)

Plate 16-6. *Magnolia liliiflora* is a good parent when breeding for dark flower color, late-blooming flowers, and small size. (Photo by Dorothy J. Callaway)

Plate 16-8. *Magnolia ×soulangiana,* the ever-popular saucer magnolia, resulted from crosses between the reddish purple-flowered *M. liliiflora* and the white-flowered *M. denudata.* (Photo by Dorothy J. Callaway)

ate 16-7. *Magnolia sieboldii* is a member of
e section *Oyama,* which is known for its white
owers with showy, dark maroon stamens.
hoto by Dorothy J. Callaway)

Plate 17-1. *Quercus robur* var. *fastigiata* × *Q. bicolor* (trade name Regal Prince) has the foliage quality of the *Q. bicolor* parent and an erect form derived from the female parent. (Photo by Guy Sternberg)

Plate 17-2. *Quercus ×rosacea (Q. robur × Q. petraea)* is a natural European hybrid that occurs frequently in zones of transition between the deep, rich soils preferred by *Q. robur* and the drier, sandy soils preferred by *Q. petraea*. (Photo by Guy Sternberg)

Plate 17-3. *Quercus ×saulii (Q. montana × Q. alba)* is known for its long-lasting fall color. (Photo by Guy Sternberg)

Plate 17-4. The beautiful leaves of this F₂ *Quercus ×schuettei (Q. macrocarpa × Q. bicolor)* are lustrous and larger than those of either parent, a typical example of the effect of hybrid vigor. (Photo by Guy Sternberg)

14 Breeding Camellias

William L. Ackerman

Camellia belongs to the family Theaceae, tribe Gordonieae, along with eight other genera, namely *Franklinia, Gordonia, Laplacea, Pyrenaria, Schima, Stuartia, Tutcheria,* and *Yunnanea*. Camellias have a long history in the Orient where they have been cultivated for centuries as sources of edible and cosmetic seed oils, for the beverage tea, as symbols in religious ceremonies, as ornamentals, and for making high-quality charcoal.

Important Breeding Materials

Most early *Camellia* cultivars were the result of selections made among open-pollinated seedlings where records may or may not have been kept of the seed parent, and any attempt at identifying the pollen parent was highly speculative. However, the twentieth century has seen extensive intraspecific breeding for ornamental purposes, especially within spring-flowering *Camellia japonica* and *C. reticulata* and fall-flowering *C. sasanqua* and *C. hiemalis* (Feathers and Brown 1978). The vast number of registered cultivars now in existence is strong evidence that camellia growers have been busy. The official cultivar register of the American Camellia Society, *Camellia Nomenclature* (Gonos and Bracci 1996), lists about 5,600 cultivars, while the two-volume *International Camellia Register* (Savige 1993) lists more than 30,000.

It has only been during the past 60 years that systematic hybridization procedures involving detailed records have, to some extent, been followed. Technically, hybridization may occur at three levels, each progressively more difficult to accomplish. These levels are intraspecific, interspecific, and intergeneric hybridization. An intraspecific cross may, for example, occur between two *Camellia japonica* individuals and will yield a *C. japonica* seedling. An interspecific cross combines members of two or more species into one hybrid individual. When hybridization goes a step further and plants from two related genera are successfully crossed, then an intergeneric hybrid has been formed.

Although most hybridization work to date has been done within a very narrow group of species, more than 200 species exist within the genus *Camellia* (Sealy 1958; Chang and Bartholomew 1984). More and more of these species are becoming available each year from the People's Republic of China. Here is the source for progress in the utilization of genetic diversification. Most of the minor species have small flowers of limited commercial value and are difficult to hybridize with commercial cultivars, and it takes many years of crossing and backcrossing to get hybrids that are commercially acceptable. Yet, continued breeding solely with the major horticultural species has reached the stage of diminishing returns within the restricted gene pool. Only by utilizing minor species can we acquire such traits as pleasing floral fragrance; greater tolerance to cold or heat and light intensity; yellow, blue, or purple flower color; new dwarf plant forms; and an extended blooming season (Hanson 1978).

The first documented interspecific hybrids to gain popularity were the Williamsii hybrids (*Camellia* ×*williamsii*), crosses between *C. saluenensis* and *C. japonica* made in the early 1930s by J. C. Williams of Caerhays Castle, England. The Williamsii hybrids were extremely successful in their combination of new flower colors and forms with good plant habit and hardiness. Prominent cultivars include 'Anticipation', 'Brigadoon', 'Citation', 'Donation', 'E. G. Waterhouse' (Plate 14-3), 'J. C. Williams', 'November Pink', and 'St. Ewe'. The success of these hybrids spurred camellia breeders to explore other species combinations and to consider the use of minor species as parents.

The introduction of *Camellia reticulata* cultivars—such as 'Cornelian', 'Crimson Robe', 'Lion Head', 'Professor Tsai', 'Purple Gown', and 'Tali Queen'—from Yunnan, China, into the United States in 1948 and the early 1950s led to its hybridization with *C. japonica*, *C. saluenensis*, and other species. *Camellia reticulata* was a natural for interspecific hybridization. It has large, showy flowers on open, straggly plants. Any hybrid progeny that improved plant characteristics while retaining the commercially desirable flower type would be a distinct improvement. Prominent cultivars resulting from crosses of *C. reticulata* × *C. japonica* include 'Dr. Clifford Parks' (Plate 14-2), 'Forty Niner', 'Howard Asper', and 'Lasca Beauty'. Other cultivars include 'Crimson Crown', 'Diamond Head', 'Harold L. Paige', and 'Royal Robe', from crosses of *C. japonica* × *C. reticulata*, and 'Barbara Clark', 'Dr. Lesley', 'Phyl Doak', and 'Salutation', involving crosses of *C. saluenensis* × *C. reticulata*.

By the early 1960s, camellia breeders advanced to backcross and second-generation hybridizing both with the Williamsii and *Camellia reticulata* hybrid series. It was also at this time that extensive hybridization programs were begun, exploring the species compatibility within the genus. Here, the number of valid interspecific hybrid combinations was expanded from a dozen or so to several hundred species combinations (Ackerman 1971; Parks 1990). Although this work greatly expanded our knowledge of compatibility relationships, only a few of the hybrids attained commercial importance, and then mostly as the genetic foundation for subsequent generations. Among these are 'Baby Bear' (*C. rosaeflora* × *C. tsaii*), 'Carl Tourje' (*C. pitardii* var. *yunnanica* × *C. reticulata*), 'Cornish Snow' (*C. saluenensis* × *C. cuspidata*), 'Sunworshipper' (*C. hongkongensis* × *C. rusticana*), and 'Tiny Princess' (*C. japonica* × *C. fraterna*).

Important Traits and Breeding Objectives

Significant progress comes where there is a clear-cut objective. It is not enough to hybridize haphazardly in hopes of some unforeseen improvement. Thus, you do well to plan ahead, establish an objective, select plant specimens possessing at least one or more of the desired genetic characteristics, and then cross parents that in combination may produce the desired objective. Three objectives that have had varying degrees of success over the past several decades are the search for floral fragrance, greater cold hardiness, and yellow flower color.

Work toward floral fragrance has centered on the hybridization of *Camellia lutchuensis*, and to a lesser extent *C. fraterna* and *C. tsaii*, with large-flowered cultivars of *C. japonica* and *C. rusticana*. Also, efforts have been made to concentrate the faint, elusive fragrance found within some cultivars of *C. japonica*. Cutter (1971, 1973, 1974) was a strong advocate for acquiring highly fragrant cultivars, and it was through his efforts, and those of Finlay (1997), Hallstone (1985), myself (Ackerman 1973), and others, that we have today many promising fragrant-flowered selections, including *Camellia* 'Ack-Scent', 'Alice K. Cutter', 'Cinnamon Cindy', 'Fragrant Pink', 'Scented Gem', and 'Scentuous'.

Of comparable difficulty has been the search for greater cold hardiness. Here, Parks (1968, 1972) concentrated on intraspecific crosses among the most promising *Camellia japonica* cultivars and developed such cultivars as 'April Blush', 'April Dawn', 'April Remembered', 'April Rose', 'April Snow' (Plate 14-1), and 'April Tryst'. In my own work (Ackerman 1989, 1993), I concentrated on crosses involving *C. oleifera* with fall- and spring-flowering cultivars and developed such fall-flowering cultivars as *Camellia* 'Snow Flurry', 'Polar Ice', 'Winter's Beauty', 'Winter's Hope', 'Winter's Interlude', and 'Winter's Rose' (Plate 14-6), as well as the spring-flowering 'Fire

'N Ice', 'Ice Follies', and 'Spring Frill' (Plate 14-5). Both hybridization programs have succeeded in developing more cold-hardy strains. These new
hybrid cultivars are presently extending the cultural range of camellias considerably northward.

The introduction of several small, yellow-flowered species, such as
Camellia nitidissima (Plate 14-4), *C. euphlebia*, and others, from China during the early 1980s has provided plant breeders with a promising new challenge—that is, to transfer the yellow pigmentation into hybrids with commercially acceptable flowers (Xia 1984). Here, not only is there the potential
for yellow-flowered camellias, but also a whole range of exotic colors when
yellow is combined with the existing pinks and reds. What appeared to be
a relatively straightforward task 15 years ago has today proven to be elusive
and, as yet, relatively unrewarding. Briefly, the interspecific crosses have
been difficult, the F_1 hybrids sterile, and the yellow gene(s) apparently
recessive to all color pigment genes (including white) among the standard
cultivars. Plant breeders in China, Japan, Australia, New Zealand, and the
United States have collectively obtained a number of pale creamy colored
hybrids, including the cultivars *Camellia* 'Golden Glow' and 'Honeymoon',
but none comparable to the desired yellow intensity. To date, perhaps the
most significant results have been achieved by Yamaguchi (1990) with the
cultivars 'Shoko', 'Kin-no-gozen', 'Kicho', and 'Kiho'. I have proposed several theoretical solutions (Ackerman 1994), but these will take years to thoroughly evaluate.

Perhaps the ultimate in hybridization is to successfully produce an intergeneric hybrid. In efforts toward obtaining camellia hybrids with greater
cold hardiness, I tried to hybridize *Camellia* with several related genera,
including *Franklinia*, *Gordonia*, *Stuartia*, and *Tutcheria*. This proved to be a
time-consuming, frustrating experience with some academic successes but
with no ultimate practical application (Ackerman and Williams 1982).

Hybridization Mechanics

Camellia, a monoecious genus, has bisexual flowers containing both male
(stamen) and female (pistil) reproductive organs (Figure 14-1). The stamens consist of the anthers (producing pollen grains) borne on a stalk or filament. The pistil consists of an ovary at the base supporting the style, which
is topped with the stigma (Figure 14-2). Pollination takes place through the
activities of a rather wide range of flying insects. Hand pollination consists
of placing mature pollen from the desired male parent onto a receptive
stigma of the desired female parent. Important precautions are necessary to
prevent unwanted pollen from contaminating the cross. This process as-
sures knowing and controlling the parentage.

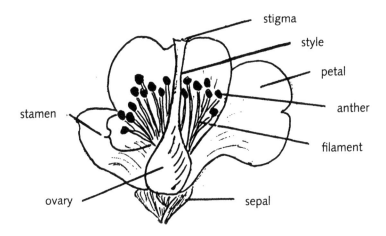

Figure 14-1. Parts of a camellia flower.

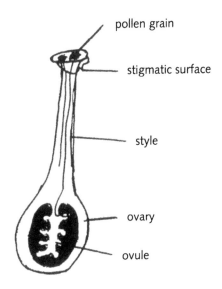

Figure 14-2. Enlarged style and its parts.

Some basic procedures necessary for successful pollinations are as follows:

1. Select flowers in the balloon stage, that is, almost but not quite open (Figure 14-3). If out-of-doors and subject to bee and other activity, the flower must not be open, even slightly. If crosses are being made within a screened greenhouse, these precautions are not as critical.

Figure 14-3. Proper stage for emasculation and pollination.

2. Emasculate the flower. Emasculation involves removing the anthers to prevent self-pollination (Figure 14-4). This is done by cutting a portion of the petals away to expose the reproductive parts, which may be accomplished with a sharp knife, razor blade, or surgical scissors (Figures 14-5). Then, with tweezers, remove the anthers and expose the pistil with its stigma (Figure 14-6).
3. Place the desired pollen on the stigma of the emasculated flower. There are several ways of doing this.
   a. Tweezers can be used to remove one or more stamens, with mature anthers, from the desired male parent, and the pollen rubbed onto the stigma of the desired female parent (Figure 14-7).

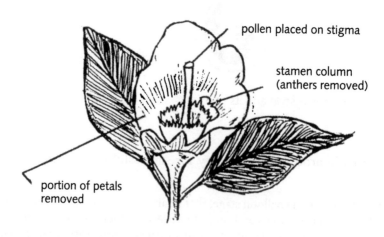

pollen placed on stigma

stamen column
(anthers removed)

portion of petals
removed

Figure 14-4. Flower after emasculation.

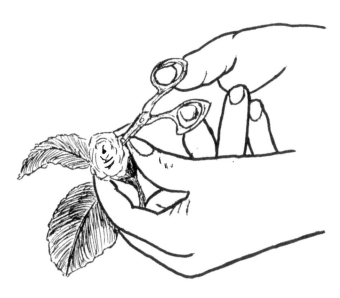

Figure 14-5. Emasculating the flower using surgical scissors.

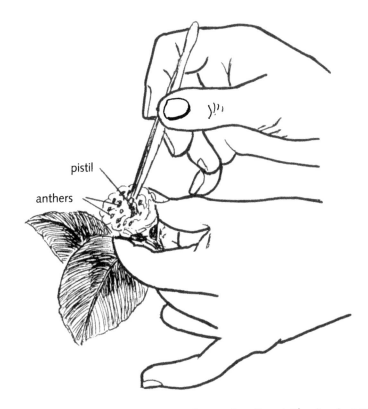

pistil

anthers

Figure 14-6. Removing the anthers and exposing the pistil using tweezers.

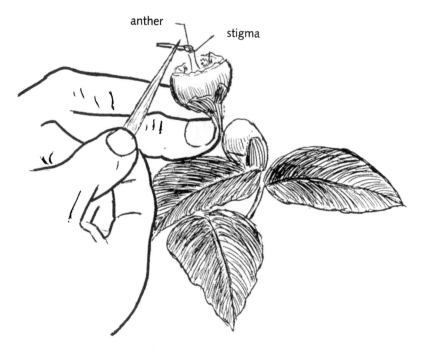

anther

stigma

Figure 14-7. Pollination using a stamen with anther from the pollen parent and applying it to the stigma.

b. A small camel-hair brush, toothpick, wooden matchstick, or your index fingertip (Figure 14-8) may also be used to transfer pollen. The choice of instrument depends largely on whether fresh or stored pollen is used and whether the pollen is plentiful or not. Of those tools listed, the camel-hair brush is perhaps the most wasteful. Whatever instrument is used, it should be sterilized with rubbing alcohol between each successive use of a different pollen.

4. Labels should be applied immediately following the cross. The date and pollen parent are the most critical information. If very large numbers of crosses are made, the pod parent can be added later on those crosses that take; this can be labor-saving with interspecific crosses where expected success rates are low. Use pencil or indelible ink on durable labels that will withstand weather conditions for up to 6 months or more and still be readable. Hang the label as close to the flower as possible, to prevent confusion with other nearby blooms.

5. Whether to cover the pollinated flower is largely dependent on the chances of contamination. Outdoor blooms are, of course, the most susceptible, but even here a properly emasculated flower is of little attraction to bees or other insects. When flowers are to be covered, bags made of nylon netting

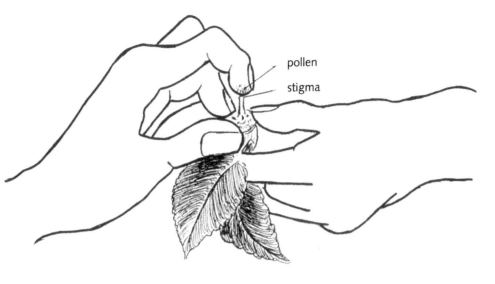

pollen

stigma

Figure 14-8. Pollination using the index finger to apply pollen to the stigma.

are best, as they allow complete air circulation and the least heat buildup, but paper bags are acceptable substitutes. Never use plastic bags.

6. Aftercare. When a seed capsule matures, it splits open and expels anywhere from one to eight seeds. Thus, it is important to cover the capsule with a bag to catch the seed before they spill on the ground. Nylon net or old nylon stockings sewn into small bags do quite well.

Records are extremely important. It is best to keep a special book for recording crosses at the time they are made so you know for how many tags and on which seed parents you will be looking later on. Also, where many parents are used, a record book identifies those crosses that are the most productive in producing offspring. Later on, separate records will be needed at the time of harvesting and planting, and finally one to identify each resulting seedling. Here, one of several coding methods can be quite satisfactory in indicating the individual parentage. The one I like best is to use the last two digits of the year, followed by a dash and then the successive seedling number potted up. Thus, 95-35 would be the thirty-fifth seedling potted in 1995. This information and the parentage are recorded in the record book. In recording each cross, the seed parent is always placed first, followed by an "×" and then the pollen parent.

The parents to be utilized in achieving certain objectives may not flower at the same time and the use of fresh pollen may be impossible, or at least impractical. It is then necessary to collect and store pollen in advance. Anthers should be gathered near the time of pollen dehiscence and filaments should be removed. Spread the anthers out to dry on a sheet of hard-surfaced paper (not porous) for several days at room temperature. The anthers should then be funneled into a small glass vial and stoppered with cotton. The vial, in turn, is stored in a specially prepared screw-top jar: place a 1- to 2-inch (2.5–5 cm) layer of silica gel or anhydrous calcium chloride in the bottom of the jar and cover with a layer of cotton. A number of glass vials of anthers can be stored in one jar. Place the jar in a refrigerator for short-term storage, or in the freezer if storage is longer than several weeks. Remember, moisture is the pollen's worst enemy. If properly air dried and stored, *Camellia* pollen may be held for as long as 6 months or more and still retain substantial viability.

Propagation

GROWING CAMELLIAS FROM SEED

Seed capsules normally split open at maturity to reveal seeds, the outer coat of which is black, hard, and impervious to water. Germination may be hastened by scarifying this hard coat with a file or knife blade. Depending on the number of seeds, they may be sown in pots or deep flats in a light, well-drained medium. It is a good idea to use sterilized media and containers to minimize rot. Likewise, the seeds may be sterilized by soaking them overnight in a 1:10 solution of household bleach. Seeds should be planted so that they are covered with approximately ¼ inch (6 mm) of media. To better stabilize heat and moisture, a glass jar may be inverted over a seed pot, or a glass or plastic covering placed at least several inches above the surface of the seed flat. Camellia seed, upon germination, produce a long tap root of up to 4 inches (10 cm) or more before there is much shoot growth. Many growers break the root tip off when transplanting to encourage lateral root growth.

When involved with interspecific or other wide crosses, a hybridizer is frequently confronted with abortive embryos and/or partially developed seed endosperm. These seeds rarely germinate under the usual procedures. The hybridizer must then resort to aseptic and/or embryo culture methods. Explanation of these techniques is beyond the scope of this chapter and are included in Ackerman (1978) and Irvin (1979).

VEGETATIVE PROPAGATION BY CUTTINGS

Most camellias, with the possible exception of *Camellia reticulata*, root quite readily from cuttings. It is the easiest and surest way of multiplying in quantity replicates of the original parent specimen. Facilities for rooting cuttings can vary greatly, but all follow the same principles: a) provide a light medium for support that will allow good aeration around the cutting base, and b) provide some means of preventing the cutting from drying out during the process of rooting.

In its simplest form, the cutting may be stuck in a media-filled pot and covered with an inverted wide-mouthed jar or plastic cage. The covered pot is then placed in a north-facing window where it will not get direct sunlight. More complex greenhouse facilities may consist of special cutting benches with bottom heat, the use of rooting hormones, and an electronic leaf or timed mechanism operating an intermittent mist system.

The cutting wood should be of the current season's growth almost anytime except when the plant is in a flush of new growth. Depending on the availability of plant material, the cutting can vary from a single leaf and stem down to the next node, to several leaves and a stem length of five or six nodes. Ideally, the cutting should have two to three leaves and a two-node base. In this case, the cut would be made just below the fifth node on the stem, and the lower two leaves removed, leaving the upper three intact. The cut should be tapered and the stem wounded lightly on both sides of the end. If the leaves are quite large, the outer third of each leaf may be trimmed off.

Most garden centers carry rooting hormones (such as indolbutyric acid) that aid and hasten the rooting process. Camellias respond quite well to Hormodin #2 (average cuttings), Hormodin #3 (more dormant cuttings), and Rootone.

Tests have shown that good results may be obtained by using a mixture of 75% coarse sand or perlite and 25% peat as the medium. Garden or potting soil should be avoided, as it is too rich and dense. The mixture should be thoroughly watered before sticking the cuttings, to leach out any impurities.

VEGETATIVE PROPAGATION BY GRAFTING

Grafting is the best method of getting a flowering plant in the shortest time. Hybridizers sometimes use grafting as a technique to get a promising hybrid seedling to flower sooner than would be possible by merely waiting for the seedling to bloom on its own. December through early March is generally considered the best time for grafting, although many grafters claim success during almost any month except during the period of active spring growth.

Vigorous-growing plants should be selected for the rootstock. *Camellia japonica* and *C. sasanqua* cultivars or seedlings are most frequently used, but be wary of using *C. sasanqua* from early to late autumn, since that species has, at least in the Northeast, a tendency to collapse (Baxter 1991).

The most popular kind of grafting for camellias is the cleft graft, although whip grafting, bark grafting (especially in summer), and the cutting graft are also occasionally used. A number of excellent "how-to" books are available. An especially thorough and readable one is by Garner (1988).

Hybridizing Can Be Fun

Hybridizing camellias can provide much pleasure in both anticipation and realization of creating something new. You do not have to be a professional plant breeder! As with most ornamentals, many outstanding camellia cultivars have been developed by backyard hobbyists. Expensive equipment is not a requirement: a few well-selected plants as prospective parents is all that is needed. This can be expanded in complexity and depth as suits the interest and appetite of the gardener.

For those wishing to go beyond the standard cultivars for potential parents, some lesser-known species are readily available. Perhaps the best overall source is Nuccio's Nurseries (see "Suppliers"), which lists some 35 minor species in its catalog. Detailed descriptions of these and many others are given in the back of *Camellia Nomenclature* by Gonos and Bracci (1996). Good luck!

Resources

COLLECTIONS

United States

American Camellia Society
100 Massee Lane
Fort Valley, GA 31030

Atlanta Botanical Garden
P.O. Box 77246
Atlanta, GA 30357

Bayou Bend Garden
P.O. Box 130157
Houston, TX 77219

Bellingrath Gardens
12401 Bellingrath Gardens Road
Theodore, AL 36582

Birmingham Botanical Gardens
2612 Lane Park Road
Birmingham, AL 35223

Brooklyn Botanic Garden
1000 Washington Avenue
Brooklyn, NY 11225

Clemson University Botanical
    Gardens
Clemson University
Clemson, SC 29634

Descanso Gardens
1418 Descanso Drive
La Canada, CA 91011

Huntington Botanical Gardens
1151 Oxford Road
San Marino, CA 91108

Longwood Gardens
P.O. Box 501
409 Conservatory Road
Kennett Square, PA 19348

Norfolk Botanical Garden
Azalea Garden Road
Norfolk, VA 23518

State Botanical Garden of Georgia
2450 S. Milledge Avenue
Athens, GA 30605

Planting Fields Arboretum
P.O. Box 58
Oyster Bay, NY 11771

Australia

E. G. Waterhouse National
   Camellia Garden
Miranda, Sidney area, New South
   Wales

Eryldene (Heritage Trust Garden)
17 McIntosh Street
Gordon, New South Wales 2074

Mount Lofty Annex
Adelaide Botanic Gardens
Mount Lofty Ranges above Adelaide

Royal Melbourne Botanic Gardens
Birdwood Avenue
South Yarra, Melbourne, Victoria

England

Antony Woodland
Antony Road
Torpoint
Cornwall PL11 2QA

Chiswick House
(residence of Duke Devonshire
   until 1892)
London

Marwood Hill Gardens and Nursery
Barnstaple, Devon EX31 4EB

Mount Edgecumbe
Torpoint
Cornwall, near Plymouth

Tregrehan
Cornwall, near St. Austell

France

Parc de Proce
Nantes

Parc Floral de Paris
Château de Vincennes
Paris

Italy

Parks and Gardens
Lucca, near Pisa

Japan

Kamoyama Park
Kamo City, Niigata

Kasayama
Hagi City, Yamaguchi

Komunoyama Park
Ito City, Shizuoka

Municipal Oshima Park
Oshima, Tokyo

Tsubakiyama Forest Park
Miyazaki City, Kyushu

Tsubakiyama Higashi Tazawa
Hiranai-cho, Aomari

New Zealand
The Wellington Botanic Gardens
P.O. Box 2199
Wellington

People's Republic of China
Kunming Institute of Botany Gardens
Kunming, Yunnan Province

SUPPLIERS—UNITED STATES

Retail

Camellia Forest Nursery
125 Carolina Forest Road
Chapel Hill, NC 27516
phone: 919-967-5529

McDonald Garden Centers
1139 Pembrook Avenue
Hampton, VA 23661
phone: 804-722-7463
fax: 804-723-4124

Nuccio's Nurseries
P.O. Box 6160
3555 Chaney Trail
Altadena, CA 91003
phone: 818-794-3383

Roslyn Nursery
211 Burrs Lane
Dix Hills, NY 11746
phone: 516-643-9347
fax: 516-484-1555

Wholesale

Bennett's Creek Nursery
3613 Bridge Road
Suffolk, VA 23435
phone: 804-483-1425 or
    800-343-4611
fax: 804-483-9058

Bond's Nursery Corporation
6420 Del Norte Lane
Dallas, TX 75225
phone: 214-739-8586
fax: 214-739-8238

Hines Nurseries
P.O. Box 1449
Vacaville, CA 95696
phone: 800-777-1097
fax: 707-448-9381

Monrovia Nursery Company
P.O. Box Q
Azusa, CA 91702-1336
phone: 818-334-9321 or
    800-621-6237

Tom Dodd Nurseries
P.O. Drawer 45
Semmes, AL 36575
phone: 205-649-1960 or
    800-226-3633 (DODD)
fax: 205-649-1965

INTERNATIONAL REGISTRATION AUTHORITY

International Camellia Society
Attn: T. J. Savige
Hawksview Road
Wirlinga, New South Wales 2640
Australia

North American Regional
Representative:
American Camellia Society
Attn: Edith Mazzei
1486 Yosemite Circle
Concord, CA 94521
U.S.A.

PLANT SOCIETIES

International Camellia Society
Herbert Short, Membership
41 Galveston Road
East Putney, London SW15 2RZ
England
phone: (44) 181-8706884
fax: (44) 181-8744633

American Camellia Society
Ann Walton, Executive Director
100 Massee Lane
Fort Valley, GA 31030
U.S.A.
phone: 912-967-2358
fax: 912-967-2083

Atlantic Coast Camellia Society
Clara Hahn, Secretary and
   Treasurer
4437 McKee Road
Charlotte, NC 28270
U.S.A.
phone: 704-846-2245

Southern California Camellia
   Society
Bobbie Belcher, Membership
7475 Brydon Road
La Verne, CA 91750-1159
U.S.A.
phone: 909-593-4894

Texas Camellia Society
K. Agee, Membership
Route 13, Box 6820
Nacogdoches, TX 75961
U.S.A.

Australian Camellia Research
   Society
Geoff Sherrington, Membership
4 Jason Court
Nth Balwyn 3104
Australia
phone: (61) 859-8745

Japan Camellia Society
Kaoru Hagiya, President
2-10-52 Nishi-Kobaridai
Niigata-shi 950-21
Japan

References and Additional Reading

Ackerman, W. L. 1971. Genetic and cytological studies with *Camellia* and related genera. *U.S. Agricultural Research Service Technical Bulletin #1427*.
———. 1973. Progeny analysis of scented *Camellia* hybrids. *American Camellia*
   Society Yearbook (1973): 58–68.
———. 1978. Handling *Camellia* seed by aseptic culture. *American Camellia*
   Society Yearbook (1978): 70–74.

————. 1989. History and progress on cold hardiness with *Camellia* in northeastern United States. *International Camellia Society Journal* 21: 81–84.

————. 1993. Camellias for colder climates. *Horticulture* LXXI (5): 28–30.

————. 1994. New thoughts on the hybridization of *Camellia nitidissima*. *International Camellia Society Journal* 26: 115–119.

Ackerman, W. L., and M. Williams. 1982. Intergeneric crosses within Theaceae and the successful hybridization of *Camellia japonica* and *Camellia sasanqua* with *Franklinia alatamaha*. *HortScience* 17 (4): 566–569.

Baxter, L. W., Jr. 1991. The fate of camellias cut back in the autumn. *American Camellia Society Journal* 47 (1): 12–13.

Chang, H. T., and B. Bartholomew. 1984. *Camellias*. Portland, Ore.: Timber Press.

Cutter, R. K. 1971, 1973, and 1974. Interspecific hybridization of camellias with particular reference to fragrance. *American Camellia Society Yearbook* (1971): 86–95, (1973): 68–72, and (1974): 103–107.

Feathers, D. L., and M. H. Brown, eds. 1978. *The Camellia: Its History, Culture, Genetics and a Look into Its Future Development*. Columbia, S.C.: R. L. Bryan.

Finlay, J. 1997. Searching for more fragrance. *International Camellia Society Journal* 29: 64–65.

Garner, R. L. 1988. *The Grafter's Handbook*. London: Cassell Publishers.

Gonos, A. A., and S. Bracci, eds. 1996. *Camellia Nomenclature*. Arcadia, Calif.: Southern California Camellia Society.

Hallstone, K. 1985. Update of camellia flower fragrance in northern California. *American Camellia Society Yearbook* (1985): 90–91.

Hanson, G. P. 1978. The inheritance of floral characters in camellia. *American Camellia Society Yearbook* (1978): 104–114.

Irvin, A. W. 1979. A study of the effects of storage, gibberellic acid, and embryo culture on germination in *Camellia japonica*. *American Camellia Society Yearbook* (1979): 47–57.

Parks, C. R. 1968. Progress towards the development of a more cold resistant camellia. *American Camellia Society Yearbook* (1968): 206–215.

————. 1972. Developing a basis for selecting more winter tolerant camellias. *American Camellia Society Yearbook* (1972): 38–42.

————. 1990. Cross compatibility studies in the genus *Camellia*. *International Camellia Society Journal* 22: 37–54.

Savige, T. J. 1993. *The International Camellia Register*. Singapore: Kyodo Printing.

Sealy, R. J. 1958. *A Revision of the Genus Camellia*. London: The Royal Horticultural Society.

Xia, L. 1984. Seedling breeding with *Camellia chrysantha*. *International Camellia Society Journal* 16: 18–20.

Yamaguchi, T. 1990. New varieties of yellow flowered camellias. *International Camellia Society Journal* 22: 58–59.

15 Breeding Lilacs: Plant of History, Plant for Tomorrow

Owen M. Rogers

The genus *Syringa* contains about 20 species (Pringle 1997), and well over 1500 lilac cultivars are, or have been, in cultivation. *Syringa* has two centers of origin: one in eastern Europe and the other in the Orient. Plants from both sources merged in Persia along the great trade routes, and the common lilac (*Syringa vulgaris*) was introduced into Europe when Count de Busbecq, ambassador of Ferdinand I of Austria, saw the plant in Constantinople and brought it back to Vienna in 1563. From there it went to England and arrived in the United States by the early 1700s. Lilac breeding can be said to have started in the 1800s when Victor Lemoine of Nancy, France, crossed the double *Syringa* 'Azura Plena' with older, single-flowered cultivars and produced the first of a new generation of lilacs with good quality. Because of Lemoine's work, many of the best lilacs in the trade at that time came to be known as "the French Hybrids." Some of those French hybrids, such as 'Mme Lemoine' and 'Président Grévy', are still considered among the best lilacs, but now exceptional forms are produced all over Europe (including eastern Russia), North America, and more recently, the Orient.

Important Breeding Materials

With the genus's diverse background, it should come as no surprise that *Syringa* is taxonomically complex. An up-to-date classification was developed by James Pringle of the Royal Botanical Gardens, Ontario, Canada. His summary includes 2 subgenera, 20 species, and 9 species hybrids that, with two noted exceptions, are known to be in cultivation. Table 15-1 provides information on lilac taxonomy pertinent to this discussion.

In addition to seven color classes recognized by the International Lilac Society, ranging from white to deep purple, one yellow-flowered lilac is

Table 15-1. Lilac Classification

Species known in cultivation, accepted botanical varieties, and validly
named interspecific hybrids of *Syringa*, listed by subgenus and
subspecies (Pringle 1997).

Subgenus *Ligustrina* (Rupr.) K. Koch
  Syringa reticulata (Blume) H. Hare
    subsp. *reticulata*
    subsp. *amurensis* (Rupr.) P. S. Green & M. C. Chang
    subsp. *pekinensis* (Rupr.) P. S. Green & M. C. Chang

Subgenus *Syringa*
  Series *Syringa*
    Syringa vulgaris L.
    Syringa oblata Lindl.
      subsp. *oblata*
      subsp. *dilatata* (Nakai) P. S. Green & M. C. Chang
    Syringa protolaciniata P. S. Green & M. C. Chang
    Syringa afghanica C. K. Schneid.*
    Syringa ×*chinensis* Willdenow (pro sp.) *(S. laciniata* × *S. vulgaris)*
    Syringa ×*hyacinthiflora* Rehder *(S. oblata* × *S. vulgaris)*
    Syringa ×*persica* Linnaeus (pro sp.) *(S. afghanica* × *S. laciniata)*
  Series *Pinnatifoliae* Rehder
    Syringa pinnatifolia Hemsl.
  Series *Pubescentes* (C. K. Schneid.) Lingelsh.
    Syringa pubescens Turcz.
      subsp. *pubescens*
      subsp. *patula* (Palib.) M. C. Chang & X. L. Chen
      subsp. *julianae* (C. K. Schneid.) M. C. Chang & X. L. Chen
      subsp. *microphylla* (Diels) M. C. Chang & X. L. Chen
        var. *microphylla*
        var. *potaninii* (C. K. Schneid.) P. S. Green & M. C. Chang
        var. *flavanthera* (X. L. Chen) M. C. Chang*
    Syringa meyeri C. K. Schneid.
      var. *meyeri*
      var. *spontanea* M. C. Chang*
    Syringa mairei (H. Lév.) Rehder*
    Syringa pinetorum W. W. Sm.*
    Syringa wardii W. W. Sm.*
  Series *Villosae* C. K. Schneid.
    Syringa villosa Vahl
    Syringa emodi Wall. ex Royle
    Syringa wolfii C. K. Schneid.
    Syringa josikaea J. Jacq. ex Rchb.

Species known in cultivation, accepted botanical varieties, and validly named interspecific hybrids of *Syringa*, listed by subgenus and subspecies (Pringle 1997).

Syringa komarowii C. K. Schneid.
  subsp. *komarowii*
  subsp. *reflexa* (C. K. Schneid.) P. S. Green & M. C. Chang
Syringa tomentella Bureau & Franch.
Syringa sweginzowii Koehne & Lingels.
Syringa yunnanensis Franch.
Syringa tibetica P. Y. Bai*
Syringa ×*henryi* C. K. Schneider *(S. josikaea × S. villosa)*
Syringa ×*josiflexa* Preston ex Pringle *(S. josikaea × S. reflexa)*
Syringa ×*nanceiana* McKelvey *(S. xhenryi × S. sweginzowii)*
Syringa ×*prestoniae* McKelvey *(S. reflexa × S. villosa)*
Syringa ×*swegiflexa* Hesse ex Pringle *(S. reflexa × S. sweginzowii)*

*Not known to be in cultivation, or not known to be in cultivation outside China. Plants cultivated under some of these names or nomenclatural synonyms thereof in Europe and North America have been misidentified (see Pringle 1990, 1997).

known (although cream might be a better description): *Syringa vulgaris* 'Primrose', introduced by D. E. Maarse of the Netherlands in 1949. This cultivar is a result of a natural mutation, but the character cannot be used in a breeding program because the mutation for yellow only occurred in the epidermal cells where flower color is determined. Because the mutation did not occur in the tissues that give rise to the pollen and the egg, none of the offspring will have yellow petals. Other natural mutations have occurred in such visible traits as flower color, leaf variegation, or petal shape. Perhaps the most famous one is *S. vulgaris* 'Sensation' (purple florets with a white line around the edge of each petal), also introduced by Maarse, which was a mutation of the white-flowered 'Hugo de Vries' and frequently reverts back to the 'Hugo de Vries' type (Plate 15-6). Most of the other recorded mutations of the common lilac, such as the variegated foliage of 'Aucubaefolia' and 'Dappled Dawn', can be considered as novelties and as such are difficult to find outside of the large collections.

Members of the two lilac subgenera (*Syringa* and *Ligustrina*) will not cross, nor can crosses normally be made between the series within subgenus *Syringa*. The number of possible crosses also varies widely within a series. Some of the known species hybrids, such as *Syringa* ×*persica* and *S.* ×*chinen*-

sis, are sterile and their exact parentage is unknown. Others, such as those species in the series *Villosae,* will cross among themselves but not with anything outside the series. By far the most successful hybrid is *S.* ×*hyacinthiflora* (*S. oblata* × *S. vulgaris*). *Syringa oblata* is an earlier flowering species, blooming about 10 days before *S. vulgaris.* So many successful crosses and backcrosses have been made in this complex that finding a clear dividing line between *S. oblata* and *S. vulgaris* is nearly impossible.

In spite of all these potential problems and barriers to crossing, there is still a wealth of material and variation with which the breeder can work. Flower structure is one such area. The species in series *Syringa* have the standard lilac inflorescence (Plate 15-1), which is called "tight cluster" and is distinct from the looser, more open flower clusters of the species in series *Villosae* (Plate 15-2). Neither flower form bears any similarity to the floret form of the species in the subgenus *Ligustrina,* where the petals of the florets are free and bear little resemblance to the tube flower form of the common lilac (Plate 15-3). In fact, *Syringa reticulata,* the tree lilac, might be considered more closely related to privet (*Ligustrum*) than to the lilac except that it has the capsule seed pods common to all *Syringa* species, as opposed to the drupe-like berry of the privets. Several cultivar selections have been made among tree lilac populations, such as *S. reticulata* 'Ivory Silk', but attempts at crossing have, so far, been unsuccessful.

In addition to the variation in flower and inflorescence form, variation also can be seen in bloom date. Normal bloom time ranges from *Syringa oblata,* which blooms about 10 days earlier than the common lilac (*S. vulgaris*), to the species in the series *Villosae,* which bloom some 10 to 15 days after the common lilac, and ending with the tree lilacs (*S. reticulata*), which bloom a good month after common lilac. Among the blooms that appear over this entire 2-month range, there is also an array of floret size and substance. (Substance refers to larger, firmer petals that are evenly thick along their length and not thinning toward the edge; the total appearance is a thicker, larger mass to the inflorescence.) In a general way, the larger florets with the greatest substance are considered desirable, but that is a personal judgment and a number of breeders would not agree with that observation. Most active lilac breeders tend to concentrate on one of these groups, but no matter which group is chosen, the goal of extending the bloom time is worth considering.

Most lilacs do not have any fall foliage color and remain green right up to leaf fall. In the last 10 years or so, red to crimson fall foliage has been noted in *Syringa oblata* and *S. pubescens* subsp. *patula* (*S. patula*). Perhaps in the future some breeder will be able to develop a group of cultivars that can rival *Euonymus alatus* for the name burning bush. There have also been suggestions that some seed pods show at least an element of fall color. Their color is not nearly as bright as the foliage color, however, and seems to vary from year to year.

With the extreme heterogeneity even among some species, the idea of inbreeding to develop homozygous lines is often suggested. This venture has not been successful, however, because severe inbreeding depression develops, most quickly manifested as flower sterility, which prevents additional progress. On the other hand, if male (or female) sterility could be added to a cultivar ready for release, it would mean no unsightly seed pods, but the basic genetics of sterility have not been elucidated, so breeding for sterility is not often a profitable goal even though the basic material is available.

Important Traits and Breeding Objectives

Every breeder will set different goals, but for the lilac a number of common goals can be gleaned from the new introductions appearing in the marketplace. Certainly superior bloom characteristics would be the most obvious. Large florets, double flowers, and deep colors are all attainable goals. Single flowers are as acceptable if the color is good and the overall flower thryses (the technical term for the lilac inflorescence) presents a good display.

Double flowers are worth striving for regardless of the plant group. There are three forms of flower doubling, and the lilac has them all. The first is radial doubling, in which the number of petals is increased from four to five, six, or more (Plate 15-4). The second form is staminode doubling, where the stamens and sometimes the pistil are turned into petals or petal-like structures (Plates 15-4 and 15-5), and the third type of doubling is hose-in-hose, in which a second, or even a third, complete corolla is located outside the first set of petals (Plate 15-5). From a breeding point of view the staminode doubling is the most difficult to work with. The other two doubling forms involve only the corolla and so the reproductive parts are unchanged and remain fully functional. In staminode doubles the anther, and sometimes the pistil as well, become petals and lose their ability to produce male and female gametes. Frequently a small number of flowers will still produce some pollen and be able to set some seeds, so plants with staminode doubling need not be avoided, but the breeder should be aware of the complication produced by this kind of doubling.

In this day and age it is hard to think of lilacs without fragrance. This has not always been so, and some older lilacs have no, or very little, fragrance. Depending on the series, the flowers can have different fragrances. To me, the odor of *Syringa pubescens* subsp. *patula* smells just like talcum powder, and that fragrance is completely different from the plants in the series *Villosae*. The tree lilac (*S. reticulata*) has yet another odor, so a rich palette of fragrances is available in the genus *Syringa*. The fragrance of the common lilac is complex. It has been described and can be manufactured, but at a prohibitive cost. Therefore, the millions of pounds of lilac fragrance that are produced yearly, mostly for use in laundry soaps, are made from butane. How depressing—but how important the inclusion of a good, true lilac fragrance is as a goal in any breeding program.

The lilac is a temperate zone plant (USDA hardiness zones 3–7). *Syringa vulgaris* requires more hours of chilling than *S. oblata* before the buds will break in the spring. Since *S. oblata* requires less chilling, breeding work aimed at providing suitable plants for the warmer end of the climate range could involve *S. oblata* as a parent. In the 1930s and '40s, Walter B. Clark of southern California used *S. oblata* in his breeding work and introduced a dozen or more cultivars that have been very reliable in the warmer end of the lilac range. A number of enthusiasts have grown lilacs in Florida (zones 9 and 10), and though the plants will survive for several years, they ultimately (at least to date) succumb because the winters that far south do not contain enough hours of chilling to insure good bud break.

Disease and insect resistance should be a goal in most breeding projects, and so it is with the lilacs. Most breeding programs automatically include resistance to disease as a goal. For *Syringa*, such efforts are most often aimed at mildew, a disfiguring, although not fatal, disease. It is most intensive in the southern end of the lilac range, and many forms that show no evidence of the disease in the north are heavily infected in the south. Variation exists in any planting, however, and even in the south some plants are nearly, if not totally, free of the disease. Therefore, by choosing the best parents and practicing strict roguing of any seedlings showing mildew, progress toward mildew-free plants should be possible. Since resistance is easy to find in most lilac species, there is no reason why it could not be automatically included in any breeding program. Resistance to oyster shell scale and the lilac borer have not yet been located. Plant response to oyster shell scale does vary, and those species in the series *Villosae* seem more susceptible. This will lead some breeders to avoid that group and others to concentrate on them because of the value of a truly insect-resistant late-blooming lilac.

The lilac is generally considered to be a large plant (one near my home is over 32 feet [9.6 m] tall), but dwarf forms from 4 to 6 feet (1.2–1.8 m) tall do occur, and others more properly listed as slow growing will remain within bounds for many years—with judicious pruning this period can be extended even longer. Many of the dwarfs are not easily found in the trade, but some such as *Syringa meyeri* 'Palibin' are well known. Within *S. vulgaris*, some relatively dwarf cultivars include the old 'Lucie Baltet' and some of Father John Fiala's introductions, such as 'Little Boy Blue' and 'Miss Muffet'.

Beyond these common goals, every program and every plant breeder will have slightly different objectives. In recent years, growing cultivars suitable for use around one-story houses has become popular. Doubling the number of chromosomes has produced good results in other crops and has been proven to be technically possible in *Syringa*, although tetraploid genetics can be very complicated, especially if there is a lack of basic genetic information, as there is with the lilac. And why not introduce fall foliage color. Some large seedling populations contain plants with varying degrees of purple to reddish color. This short list of possibilities is limited only by the imagination of the plant breeder.

Hybridization Mechanics

Pollen is best collected the day before flower buds open. The anthers in most *Syringa* plants are attached to the corolla tube (Figure 15-1). Therefore, if fat, nearly opened buds are split, then two anthers, which have not shed their pollen, can be collected from each floret. Nip off the top of the bud to reveal the anthers, which can then be squeezed out like toothpaste or removed with sharp tweezers. Other collectors prefer to split the floret top to bottom and scrape the anthers off. Twenty-five to fifty anthers will contain enough pollen for up to 100 pollinations.

For anther storage, I use 00-size gelatin capsules, which are available from nearly any drugstore. Fill the capsules to about one-third full and store them in a small desiccator containing a layer of calcium chloride and capped with a small wad of cotton batting. If a desiccator is used for each pollen, labeling is simplified since a stick-on label on each desiccator is easily seen

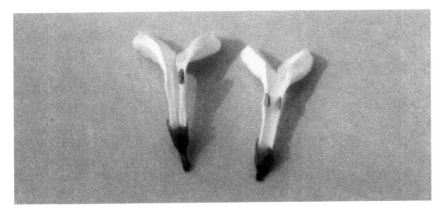

Figure 15-1. Individual *Syringa* flower, showing floral anatomy. (Photo by Owen M. Rogers)

when the breeder is selecting pollen for one day's use. Anthers handled in this manner normally will dry overnight and shed their pollen readily, although some may take as long as 24 hours to dry, especially if the capsules are overfilled. If the pollen is not scheduled to be used the next day, place the desiccators in a refrigerator at 40°F (4°C). This will maintain pollen viability for several months. I have occasionally had success using pollen that is a year old, but if a breeder wanted to do this on a regular basis, much more stringent pollen storage methods, such as a freezer or liquid nitrogen, should be used.

Pollen is normally shed upon anthesis, so open florets cannot be used in controlled crosses and should be removed before the surrounding buds are emasculated. Since anthers are attached to the corolla, removal of the corolla will emasculate the flower and leave the pistil exposed. Any unopened floret (Figure 15-2) that can be emasculated may be used since the stigma of the pistil becomes receptive several days before the floret opens or the pollen is shed normally. Very small buds do not work as well because they cannot be easily emasculated without removing the pistil. As with pollen collection, the technique of emasculation will vary from breeder to breeder. The corolla can be split lengthwise and then removed with tweezers, but

Figure 15-2. A lilac flower at the right stage for emasculation.

this is tedious. I prefer to hold the calyx with the fingers of one hand and tear off the corolla with the other hand using a rolling motion. This allows emasculation of a large number of florets in a matter of minutes, though it does require some practice.

With the flowers emasculated, all you have to do is take the pollen from its capsule and place it on the sigma (Figure 15-3). I use a small watercolor paintbrush with most of the bristles removed. In this way all the stigmas in an inflorescence can be brushed with pollen in a very short time. The brush must be sterilized between pollinations by dipping it in alcohol and allowing it to dry before being reused in another cross. Using several brushes in rotation is convenient. Also, apply a bit of alcohol on any fingers that may have pollen on them. If only a few crosses are to be made, you can use a toothpick or paper matchstick to transfer the pollen, discarding them after each use rather than sterilizing.

After a cross is made, the stigmas need protection from stray pollen. I cover them with a small paper bag closed with a small wire. Other covers may be used, though plastic is not an acceptable cover material because it fosters heat buildup. The bag is only needed until the stigmas begin to brown (5 to 10 days), after which the stigma is no longer receptive, but I

Figure 15-3. A flower after emasculation, ready for pollination.

leave the bag in place so that I can locate the inflorescences that I pollinated. I will admit that by midsummer I often rip open the bottom of the bag to see if fruit has set, but the bag remains to help locate the cross.

Following the cross, record keeping must be accomplished. This may be the last thing done, but it is perhaps the most important step. It is easy to remember crosses made yesterday or even last week, but if any kind of serious plant breeding is planned, record keeping becomes essential. I hang a tag indicating the cross and the date underneath the pollinated inflorescence and also mark the same information on the bag, so if one is lost the other serves as a backup.

Seed should be allowed to ripen on the plant until the seed pod begins to turn brown. Remove the seed head, bag and all, check the tags to be sure they are legible, and group all the bags of one cross into a larger bag. These larger bags can be left in a cool, ventilated area until the seed pods dry. When the pods have dried, collect the seed from individual bags and place them in a seed envelope—with the same attention to labeling as before, of course. Seed is best stored dry for at least a month after collection. A month of stratification at 40°F (4°C) is sometimes suggested to improve germination, or at least the rate of germination, but I have no difficulty with seed sown as soon as the day length begins to lengthen, or about 4 or 5 months after seed collection.

Propagation

Once a superior plant is identified it can be increased by vegetative propagation. Historically, lilacs were increased by budding or grafting. Some nurseries still use these techniques, but with the advent of rooting hormones and micropropagation, so-called own-rooted plants are possible and are recommended, since any suckers produced from own-rooted plants will be the same as the original shoots, not the understock.

Final Note

Lilac breeding is both easy (you don't even have to bend down) and rewarding. The Count de Busbecq really did start something when he introduced the lilac to Europe—so many opportunities are still waiting to be explored within the lilacs that there will be work for both the professional and the amateur plant breeder for many years to come. There is really nothing like the "high" felt when you go out some bright spring morning, see a bush blooming for the first time, and realize that you are the first person on the face of the earth who has seen that flower.

Resources

COLLECTIONS

Since so many lilac cultivars have been named, no one nursery can carry more than a small number of them. Anyone desiring to assess or just view a significant number of plants should consider visiting one of the following large lilac collections that exist around the world. This list could be expanded considerably by including private collections, which often contain several hundred different forms, and by including new collections just being started in such places as Italy and Poland. Up-to-date information on these and other collections can be obtained from the International Lilac Society.

Arnold Arboretum
Harvard University
125 Arborway
Jamaica Plain, MA 02130
U.S.A.

Highland Botanical Park
180 Reservoir Avenue
Rochester, NY 14620
U.S.A.

Niagara Parks
P.O. Box 150
Niagara Falls, ON L2E 6T2
Canada

Royal Botanical Gardens
P.O. Box 399
Hamilton, Ontario L8N 3H8
Canada

Central Botanic Garden
Moscow, Russia

National Trust Garden
Norman's Farm
Stowmarket, Suffolk
England IP14 4SF

SUPPLIERS—NORTH AMERICA

Country Lace Lilacs
10202 N.E. 279th Street
Battle Ground, WA 98604
phone: 206-687-1874
Lilacs are produced on their own roots and are shipped bare root. The selection changes annually. Owner is interested in plant exchanges.

Fox Hill Nursery
347 Lunt Road
Freeport, ME 04032
phone: 207-729-1511
Lilacs are produced on their own roots and shipped bare root, container, and balled and burlapped (B & B). Many uncommon selections are available.

Grape Hill Gardens
1232 Devereaux Road
Clyde, NY 14433
A large and comprehensive collection containing rare lilacs not available elsewhere.

Heard Gardens Ltd.
5355 Merle Hay Road
Johnston, IA 50131
phone: 515-276-4533
Lilacs are produced on their own roots and are shipped bare root. Approximately 40 selections are available.

The Lilac Farm
P.O. Box 272-C
Cambridge Springs, PA 16403
phone: 814-398-2528 or 800-542-4158
Lilacs are produced from rooted cuttings and are shipped via UPS in a moistened wrap. A broad selection is available.

Margaretten Park
38570 N. Bouquet Canyon Road
Leona, CA 93550
A large collection of southern acclimated lilacs that includes many introductions from Joel Margaretten.

Pepiniere Select Plus Nursery
R.R. #1
Brinston, Ontario K0E 1C0
Canada
phone: 613-652-1775
Lilacs are produced on their own roots or are micropropagated and are shipped bare root. Up to 800 lilac taxa will be available. Distribution center located in United States for quicker service.

Wedge Nursery
R.R. #2, Box 114
Albert Lea, MN 56007
phone: 507-373-5225
Lilacs are produced on their own roots and are shipped bare root and in containers. Approximately 140 selections are available.

INTERNATIONAL REGISTRATION AUTHORITY

Royal Botanical Gardens
Attn: Freek Vrugtman
P.O. Box 399
Hamilton, Ontario L8N 3H8
Canada
fax: 905-577-0375

PLANT SOCIETIES
International Lilac Society
David Gressley, Secretary
c/o The Holden Arboretum
9500 Sperry Road
Kirtland, OH 44094-5172
U.S.A.

References and Additional Reading

Dvorak, J., Jr. 1956. A special scientific publication of the International Lilac Society, Inc. Ed. John L. Fiala.—A complete description of all the cultivars grown at the Morton Arboretum with detailed drawings of the florets of those cultivars. (Available through the International Lilac Society, Owen M. Rogers, Plant Biology Department, University of New Hampshire, Durham, NH 03824 U.S.A.)

Fiala, J. L. 1988. *Lilacs: The Genus Syringa*. Portland, Ore.: Timber Press.— The most recent and complete lilac reference. Includes sections on hybridization and chromosome doubling. Contains more than 400 color plates.

McKelvey, S. 1928. *The Lilac: A Monograph*. New York: Macmillan.—A very detailed reference of all the lilacs known up to 1928.

Pringle, J. 1990. An updated summary of currently accepted botanical nomenclature at the specific and varietal levels in *Syringa. Lilac* 19 (4): 75–80.

————. 1997. An updated summary of classification in *Syringa* at the ranks of species, subspecies, and variety. *Lilac* 26 (1): 19–26.

16 Breeding Magnolias

Dorothy J. Callaway

More than 100 magnolia hybrids are in cultivation today, and the number continues to increase. The majority of those hybrids were not produced by professional plant breeders but by amateurs or gardeners who might not consider themselves plant breeders at all. Breeding magnolias can be a rewarding hobby, and it is not difficult. All that is required are, of course, magnolia flowers, a few simple tools, and a little practice.

Key Groups for Breeding

The genus *Magnolia* comprises about 80 species native to the Americas and southeastern Asia. Of the species, only about 30 are cultivated. The genus is broken down into 2 subgenera and 11 sections. It is easy to think of magnolias in two separate groups, and the taxonomic subgenera fall along these same lines: magnolias that bloom in the summer (subgenus *Magnolia*), and magnolias that bloom before the leaves are produced in the spring (subgenus *Yulania*). The latter species are sometimes called "precocious." The two species in section *Tulipastrum* (subgenus *Yulania*) straddle the fence a bit, blooming just as the leaves emerge in spring. Table 16-1 includes a listing of all the cultivated species, along with the corresponding taxonomic subgenera and sections. Some of the most important species, in terms of breeding and hybrids in cultivation, are discussed further in the chapter.

Chromosome number is an essential biological consideration for breeding magnolias. The $2n$ number of chromosomes in magnolias is most often 38 (diploid), 76 (tetraploid), or 114 (hexaploid). In magnolias, species within a section are closely related and, in most cases, have the same number of chromosomes. Obtaining hybrids from parents with the same chromosome number is usually easier than hybridizing plants with different chromo-

Table 16-1. Cultivated Species of *Magnolia*

Species arranged by subgenus and section, with chromosome numbers indicated for each section.

Subgenus *MAGNOLIA*
Section *Magnolia* ($2n = 38$)
  Magnolia virginiana
    var. *australis*
  Section *Rhytidospermum* ($2n = 38$)
  Magnolia fraseri
    var. *pyramidata*
  Magnolia hypoleuca
  Magnolia macrophylla
    var. *ashei*
  Magnolia officinalis
  Magnolia rostrata
  Magnolia tripetala
Section *Oyama* ($2n = 38$)
  Magnolia globosa
  Magnolia sieboldii
  Magnolia sinensis
  Magnolia wilsonii
Section *Theorhodon* (various
    chromosome numbers)
  Magnolia grandiflora ($2n = 114$)

Subgenus *YULANIA*
Section *Yulania* ($2n = 114$)
  Magnolia campbellii
    var. *alba*
    var. *mollicomata*
  Magnolia dawsoniana
  Magnolia denudata
  Magnolia sargentiana
    var. *robusta*
  Magnolia sprengeri
    var. *elongata*
  Magnolia zenii
Section *Buergeria* ($2n = 38$)
  Magnolia biondii
  Magnolia cylindrica
  Magnolia kobus
    var. *loebneri*
    var. *stellata*
  Magnolia salicifolia
Section *Tulipastrum* ($2n = 76$)
  Magnolia acuminata
    var. *subcordata*
  Magnolia liliiflora

some numbers. Therefore crosses within a section are usually more successful than crosses between sections. Intersectional crosses often, but not always, result in hybrids that are partially sterile.

It has often been shown that plants with a higher ploidy level (tetraploid as compared to diploid) have correspondingly larger flowers and leaves. Despite this observation, *Magnolia macrophylla*, only a diploid, has the largest flowers and leaves of the genus. This indicates that flower size is also genetic in origin. Kehr (1991) describes a polyploid form of *M. kobus* that has flowers of typical size, but with thicker and wider tepals, further supporting a genetic basis for flower size.

Experienced magnolia breeders (see Kehr 1998) have noted that seemingly sterile hybrids, such as triploids, sometimes function with relative fertility when used as a pollen parent. Similarly, pentaploid ($5n$) hybrids may be at least partially fertile. Some hybrids of the *Magnolia ×soulangiana* complex were inter-hybridized to develop subsequent *M. ×soulangiana* derivatives. These latter hybrids have segregated into a huge range of chromosome numbers from $3n$ to $8n$. The selection pressure appears to have been in the direction of higher ploidy level due to larger flowers and other desirable traits exhibited in those plants with higher chromosome numbers.

Increasing the chromosome number, or ploidy, of some magnolias would be beneficial in breeding magnolias that might not otherwise be crossed because of their different chromosome numbers. Increasing a plant's chromosome number can be done by treating the plant with colchicine. Magnolia breeder August Kehr has perfected the method of treating magnolias with colchicine, and those interested are referred to his writings (Kehr 1985, 1996).

Important Breeding Materials

Most of the breeding work done with magnolias has involved the deciduous, spring-blooming species. Section *Yulania* species are popular for their large flowers on leafless branches in the spring, and these characteristics are often selected for in breeding programs. The oldest and most common magnolia hybrid known today is *Magnolia ×soulangiana* (Plate 16-8), a cross between the white-flowered *M. denudata* (of section *Yulania*) and the deep purple-flowered *M. liliiflora* (of section *Tulipastrum*). The resulting hybrids are various shades of pink and purple, from almost white to dark purple. They are intermediate between the two parents in size, bloom time, and usually flower color. Some of the hybrids have, themselves, been used as parents in further hybridization work.

Magnolia campbellii, another species in section *Yulania*, is prized for its "cup-and-saucer" flowers; the inner whorl of petals stands upright like hands folded in prayer, while the outer petals lie flat. There are drawbacks to the cultivation of *M. campbellii*, however, such as the long time from seed to bloom (up to 25 years!). If this species were crossed with one that blooms when young, perhaps the resulting hybrid would have a reasonably short time from seed to bloom and still yield the attractive cup-and-saucer flower form. This was one objective of the late D. Todd Gresham, whose Gresham hybrids come in a broad range of flower colors and are widely popular today. Gresham crossed *M. ×veitchii* (a cross between *M. campbellii* and *M. denudata*) with *M. liliiflora* and *M. ×soulangiana* 'Lennei Alba' to create a series of hybrids ranging in flower color from white to deep reddish purple. He hoped that the cup-and-saucer shape of the flowers might be inherited from the *campbellii* grandparent. Although some Gresham hybrids show a trace of the cup-and-saucer shape, they do not approach the grandeur of *M.*

campbellii in that regard. There are, however, plenty of qualities in the Gresham hybrids that make them good choices for the garden. Gresham's crosses produced a wide variety in flower color, flower shape, and bloom season. Most of these hybrids bloom at a relatively early age (sometimes just a year or two from a rooted cutting) and are vigorous and fast-growing. Gresham himself named only about a dozen of these plants before his death in 1969, but the original seedlings from his crosses still exist and continue to be evaluated and used as parents for further breeding. Gresham hybrids are too numerous to list all, but some of the more popular ones include 'Full Eclipse', 'Joe McDaniel' (Plate 16-4), 'Jon Jon', 'Royal Crown', 'Sweet Sixteen', 'Tina Durio', and 'Todd Gresham'.

Magnolia liliiflora is an important parent when trying to create hybrids with dark-colored flowers, since it has the darkest reddish purple color of any species (Plate 16-6). As a member of section *Tulipastrum*, it blooms just as the leaves emerge and is also a good parent when trying to create late-blooming hybrids. In addition, *M. liliiflora* is the species with the smallest mature size (under 15 feet, or 1.5 m), and more breeding work could be done for smaller hybrids.

Magnolia acuminata, the cucumbertree, has recently become among the most important in breeding programs due to its yellow flower color (rare among magnolias) and its great cold hardiness. Crosses with spring bloomers in sections *Yulania* and *Buergeria* have yielded tough plants that produce yellow flowers before the leaves in spring, but later than most spring bloomers. This gives the hybrids an edge when dealing with late freezes that often harm flower buds of typical spring bloomers. There are two varieties of *M. acuminata:* the typical (northern) variety, which has yellowish green flowers, and var. *subcordata*, the southern version, with flowers of a more pronounced yellow. The catch is that when using the southern variety as a parent to enhance yellow flower color in the hybrids, the breeder risks losing the hardiness. When using the northern type to impart hardiness as well as yellow flower color, the flower color may not be as intense as with var. *subcordata*. In both varieties, the yellow carotenoid pigment is maternally inherited, so the yellow coloration is only passed to the next generation if *M. acuminata* is used as the female parent. However, using this species as the pollen parent in crosses with pink or purple forms could produce desirable late-blooming pink or purple hybrids.

Magnolia acuminata has been crossed with *M. liliiflora*, its sister in section *Tulipastrum*, to produce the hybrid known as *M. ×brooklynensis*. The flowers of these offspring have a combination of yellow, green, pink, and purple coloring within the same flower. They are typically grown by collectors and do not often appear in the general nursery trade, but one of the cultivars, *M. ×brooklynensis* 'Woodsman', is a popular parent in some breeding programs. Backcrossing *M.* ×*brooklynensis* selections with *M. acuminata* produces yellow bloomers such as *Magnolia* 'Yellow Bird'. Crossing these hybrids with a pink- or purple-flowered plant could potentially produce a late-blooming pink or purple form.

Magnolias in section *Buergeria* are early bloomers and have flowers that appear star-like, especially in *Magnolia kobus* var. *stellata* and *M. kobus* var. *loebneri*. Typical *M. kobus* and *M. salicifolia* have flowers with wider and fewer petals, but the overall starry look is there. These species, too, are among the toughest and most cold-hardy magnolias. Many crosses have been made between the species or varieties in this group, and they exhibit a range of flower characteristics from relatively few petals to more than 35, flower colors from white to rosy pink, and habits from small rounded shrubs (various forms of *M. kobus* var. *stellata*) to medium upright trees (*M. kobus* var. *loebneri* 'Merrill') to very large trees (typical *M. kobus* or *M. salicifolia*). Among the most cold-hardy is *M. kobus* var. *loebneri* 'Leonard Messel' (Plate 16-5), with pink flowers that emerge from frost-resistant buds. Again, this is a plus when those spring frosts come around. Crosses between species in this section and species in section *Yulania* or *Tulipastrum* are fairly common and can yield interesting hybrids. Notable examples are the "Eight Little Girls" (*M. liliiflora* × *M. kobus* var. *stellata*), *Magnolia* 'Marillyn' (*M. kobus* × *M. liliiflora* 'Nigra'), and *Magnolia* 'Gold Star' (*M. acuminata* var. *subcordata* 'Miss Honeybee' × *M. kobus* var. *stellata*).

The southern magnolia, *Magnolia grandiflora* (of section *Theorhodon*), is the primary evergreen magnolia found in cultivation. The leaves are very glossy green, thick, and leathery, and the large white flowers are intensely fragrant. Although breeders have attempted to create yellow- or pink-flowered evergreen magnolias by crossing with *M. acuminata* or a pink-flowered species, these have proven futile. Species in section *Rhytidospermum* are known as the bigleaf species and have large (sometimes to 3 feet [0.9 m]) leaves arranged in false whorls at the ends of the branches. These species seem to cross easily within the section and produce interesting hybrids with combinations of characteristics from the parents. Species of this section have also been successfully crossed with *M. virginiana* (of section *Magnolia*) and *M. sieboldii* (of section *Oyama*).

Magnolias in section *Oyama* are small, summer-blooming shrubs with white flowers and deep reddish maroon stamens. These plants are suitable for smaller gardens, and the stamen color is an interesting characteristic. The species of section *Oyama* are not very heat tolerant, and the cross of *Magnolia globosa* × *M. virginiana* has produced a hybrid known as *Magnolia* 'Porcelain Dove', which bears maroon-colored stamens on fragrant white flowers yet is more heat tolerant than the *Oyama* magnolias due to the influence of *M. virginiana*. *Magnolia virginiana* is a fragrant species with nice glossy green leaves that are silvery beneath. It is suspected that natural hybrids between that species and *M. grandiflora* are abundant and appear to most often resemble the latter species.

Important Traits and Breeding Objectives

The specific goals of different breeding programs may vary, but a few general objectives might be considered by any beginning magnolia breeder. Obvious objectives include larger flowers, increased flower fragrance, flower durability, and desirable flower color or shape. Larger-flowered hybrids could result from crosses using large-flowered parents. Many of the Gresham hybrids produce very large flowers, as do *Magnolia campbellii*, *M. sargentiana* var. *robusta*, and *M. grandiflora*. Fragrant hybrids could result from the use of fragrant parents like *M. grandiflora*, *M. virginiana*, and members of section *Buergeria*, as well as hybrids such as 'Porcelain Dove' and 'Heaven Scent'.

Yellow-flowered magnolia hybrids are quite popular now, and the yellow-flowered *Magnolia acuminata* is involved in these crosses. Many of the yellows such as 'Butterflies' [PP#7456] (Plate 16-3), 'Elizabeth', 'Ivory Chalice', 'Yellow Fever', and 'Yellow Garland' are crosses between *M. acuminata* and the white-flowered, precocious *M. denudata*. The white or pale pink forms of *M.* ×*soulangiana* are also good parents in crosses with *M. acuminata*, as in *Magnolia* 'Yellow Lantern'. In all these hybrids, *M. acuminata* has imparted hardiness and later flowering as well as yellow flower color, and this combination of traits is hard to beat. The hybrid called 'Gold Star' is a cross between *M. acuminata* and *M. kobus* var. *stellata*, and it is rising in popularity due to its hardiness and nice foliage as well as the pale yellow, star-like flowers.

Hybrids with apricot- or peach-colored flowers, like *Magnolia* 'Peachy' and 'Coral Lake', are beginning to appear in the trade. 'Peachy' is a cross between *M. acuminata* and *M. sprengeri* 'Diva'. 'Coral Lake' is of unknown parentage, but it is likely a cross between *M. acuminata* and a pink- or rose-flowered plant. Near-red flowers would be desirable in magnolias, and some of the deep reddish purple species (especially *M. liliiflora*) and cultivars (*M. campbellii* var. *mollicomata* 'Lanarth', *M.* ×*soulangiana* 'Lennei', *Magnolia* 'Vulcan', and others) would be good places to start.

Many a magnolia breeder has dreamed of creating a pink- or yellow-flowered evergreen magnolia, and crosses of *Magnolia grandiflora* with yellow or pink parents have been tried, but to date all such crosses have produced offspring that are nearly indistinguishable from *M. grandiflora*. These crosses could theoretically be more successful with induction of polyploidy in the plant to be crossed with the hexaploid *M. grandiflora*.

One of the most commonly pursued commodities in the magnolia trade is a precocious magnolia that is hardy and is a reliable bloomer, in spite of spring frosts. Late-blooming species make good parents when breeding with this concept in mind. These later blooming plants are more likely to escape frost damage. *Magnolia acuminata*, *M. liliiflora*, and *M.* ×*brooklynensis* hybrids are good choices for delaying bloom in their offspring, as are some of the later flowering Gresham hybrids. The more cold-tolerant selections of *M. kobus* var. *stellata* and var. *loebneri* are excellent choices in breeding for hardy flower buds. Perhaps most notable in this group for its bud hardiness and reliability is *M. kobus* var. *loebneri* 'Leonard Messel', a pink-flowered cultivar that has received praises from northern and midwestern gardeners for its performance. *Magnolia* 'Daybreak', a cross by August E. Kehr using *M.* ×*brooklynensis* 'Woodsman' and the Gresham hybrid 'Tina Durio' as parents, is reported to be quite bud hardy. Hybrids like these will have a long-lasting place in gardens of colder climates. Another attraction for colder climates would be a cold-hardy evergreen magnolia. Hardy selections of *M. grandiflora*, like 'Bracken's Brown Beauty' [Plant Patent #5520] (Plate 16-2), 'Edith Bogue', 'Simpson', 'Victoria', and others, are excellent starting points for a breeding program with this goal in mind.

At the other extreme, there is a market in the warmer zones for plants similar to the *Oyama* magnolias but more heat tolerant. These magnolias—*Magnolia globosa*, *M. sieboldii* (Plate 16-7), *M. sinensis*, and *M. wilsonii*—are exceptional because of the maroon stamens held in a ring in the center of white flowers. These are small shrubs at maturity, are summer blooming, and can be quite cold hardy (*M. sieboldii* does well in zone 4). But these species do not do well in the heat of southern summers. *Magnolia* 'Porcelain Dove' (*M. globosa* × *M. virginiana*) is more heat tolerant than the magnolias of section *Oyama*, but the stamens are not as deep red as in those species. Further crosses along this line could produce nice hybrids for southern gardens. And what about an evergreen, large-flowered *Oyama* magnolia? Theoretically, an induced polyploid form of a species of section *Oyama* could be crossed with *M. grandiflora* for just such a beauty.

The habit or form of a plant may be as important as flower attributes. Dwarf, small-statured, or slow-growing plants are popular with people who maintain smaller gardens. Most magnolias become large trees, and many home gardeners do not have sufficient space for such. *Magnolia liliiflora* is the species with the smallest ultimate height and would be useful in crosses to create smaller hybrids. Some of the most popular magnolia hybrids are crosses between *M. liliiflora* and *M. kobus* var. *stellata*. The resulting hybrids, known as the "Eight Little Girls," are 'Ann', 'Betty' (Plate 16-1), 'Jane', 'Judy', 'Pinkie', 'Randy', 'Ricki', and 'Susan'. A main attraction of these plants is their small stature. They are shrubs up to about 12 feet (3.6 m) tall at maturity with pinkish purple flowers. The "girls" vary slightly in hardiness, bloom time, and flower color.

Some selections of *Magnolia kobus* var. *stellata* and var. *loebneri* would also be useful in creating hybrids of small stature. Smaller cultivars of *M. grandiflora*, such as 'Little Gem' and 'Bracken's Brown Beauty' [PP#5520], have become very popular as gardeners shy away from the typical forms of *M. grandiflora* that become towering monsters over time. Trees with a particular habit, such as pyramidal or rounded, may be desirable, and selection for these traits is especially evident within *M. grandiflora*. The cultivar 'Hasse', a very narrow, columnar form, is increasing in popularity, and both 'Little Gem' and 'Bracken's Brown Beauty' exhibit a neat, dense, pyramidal habit even without the help of pruners. Within the precocious species, *M. kobus* var. *loebneri* 'Merrill' is sometimes chosen for its upright form, as opposed to the more typical rounded form of other cultivars in that group. Variability of leaf characteristics, especially within *M. grandiflora*, can be exploited by breeding for leaf shape, size, glossiness, or evergreenness. Deciduous hybrids such as *Magnolia* 'Wada's Memory' and 'Gold Star' have nice reddish bronze new growth in the spring, and this could be selected for as well.

Sometimes selections are made for more practical reasons such as ease of propagation. This is an important characteristic because no matter how beautiful and desirable a hybrid is, if it cannot be propagated it will not gain popularity in the trade.

Hybridization Mechanics

The first step in breeding magnolias is to collect pollen from flowers of the plant to be used as the male parent. General guidelines for pollen collection and storage are given here, but the reader who is looking for more information will find it in the articles listed at the end of this chapter. The best of these is Savage (1978), and the author is greatly appreciative of Savage's willingness to share this information.

A difficult aspect of collecting pollen is knowing exactly when the flower is at the right maturity. Ideally, flowers should be harvested about one day before they open, and with a little practice this becomes fairly easy to estimate. Remember that an individual magnolia flower will have mature, receptive stigmas before the stamens are mature and that the weather will affect the speed of maturation of the flower. The warmer the weather, the faster the flower matures. The beginning magnolia breeder may want to collect flowers every day until becoming proficient at determining the right stage of maturity. Flowers ready for pollen collection should have stamens that are pulling away from the gynoecium (female flower parts) rather than pressing against it.

Pollen collection is best done in the middle of the day when the dew has dried. Pollen may be collected in two ways: by harvesting only the stamens, or by harvesting the entire flower. Most breeders prefer to harvest the entire flower, which is easier for handling and record keeping. Therefore the collection of flowers rather than stamens is outlined here; however, if individual stamens are to be collected, the same procedure can be followed with only slight, but obvious, modifications.

Begin by cutting the flowers from the plant and removing all tepals. Cut the gynoecium straight across, above the tips of the anthers, and place the gynandrophore cut side down on white paper in a draft-free area until the pollen is shed. Glass or waxed paper can be substituted for the white paper, but these make it more difficult to see the pollen. Record keeping is important at all stages of plant breeding, and the paper or glass should serve as a place to record the name of the plant from which each flower came, as well as the date pollen was collected and any other pertinent information.

Pollen is usually shed the day following the cutting of the flower. Pollen will have fallen in a circle or halo around the gynoecium. Remove the gynandrophore from the paper once the pollen has been released. Carefully fold the pollen-covered paper to create a channel or funnel to aid in pouring the pollen into a small, white, 2 × 3 inch (5 × 8 cm) envelope (or a gelatin capsule) labeled with the plant name and date of pollen collection. Then seal the envelope flap and seams with tape to keep pollen from leaking out. The envelopes should be placed in a tightly sealed jar about half full of a desiccant. If the pollen becomes damp, it is susceptible to spoilage by molds and mildew that render the pollen inviable. The jar containing the desiccant and envelopes of pollen can usually be stored in the refrigerator for short periods of time (a few months) or in the freezer at about 0°F (−18°C) for a year or two without much loss of viability. Again, this depends on how well the humidity is controlled.

Having successfully collected pollen, the next task of the magnolia hybridizer is to select receptive stigmas on which to dust the pollen. Select several buds on the intended female parent plant, choosing buds that are low enough to reach and are about two days away from opening. The bud should have shed all but a single perule (bud scale). Clip the tip off of the bud, leaving a hole about ¼ inch (0.5 cm) in diameter. As much of the tepals should be left as possible since these will help protect the flower after pollination.

Once the tip of the flower bud has been removed, the gynoecium should be visible. The stigmas should be reflexed (curled back) and should appear wet and sticky. Open the envelope containing the pollen and dip a pipe cleaner into it. A small artist's watercolor paintbrush can be substi-

tuted for the pipe cleaner, but be sure to clean the bristles in alcohol between pollinations to avoid unwanted pollen contamination. Pipe cleaners
are disposable and new ones should be used for each pollination, or they
should be cleaned between pollinations. Quickly remove the pollen-coated
pipe cleaner from the envelope and insert it into the opening in the flower
bud. Cover the stigmas with pollen, being careful not to damage the gynoecium. After pollination, tie the flower's tepals shut at the tip of the bud
with small twine or a rubber band. This will protect the gynoecium and
keep out unwanted pollen. Label the cross carefully with a tag and marker
that will withstand weather. In a few days, the twine or rubber band must be
removed. Failure to do so can result in the development of fungi that rot the
flower under warm, moist conditions. At the same time, cover the flower
with a mesh bag to keep the fruit from being eaten by animals as they
develop. Pieces of nylon stocking work well for this. Keep the fruit covered
for protection until the seeds are harvested.

Evaluation of hybrids is an important part of any breeding program.
This usually means simply growing the hybrids from seed to maturity to see
what their characteristics are and whether or not they are superior to what
is currently in the trade. It is also a good time to test their true hybridity and
determine whether or not they are fertile. If the hybrids are from species
that require many years to bloom, this maturation time may be shortened by
chip-budding or side-grafting the hybrid onto limbs of a mature magnolia.

Throughout the hybridization process, good record keeping is essential.
At the very least, the parentage, direction of the cross, and other pertinent
information about the parents should be recorded and made part of the label
for the resulting progeny. The rule for recording a cross is to always list the
seed (female) parent first, followed by the pollen (male) parent. Other useful information includes notes on date of cross, number of crosses and the
percent that were successful, seed set of the cross, percent germination of
seeds, percentage of seedlings that were hybrids, and descriptions of the
hybrids and how they may differ from one another. Though this information may not seem very important, especially if it is negative, it does
provide a record of hybridization work upon which other breeders can build.

Propagation

The magnolia fruit is an aggregate of follicles called a follicetum. When
the seeds are ready to be collected, the fruit will split to reveal red- or
orange-coated seeds. The fruit are great treats for wildlife, so use a mesh bag
or nylon stockings to protect your crosses until you harvest the seeds. The
fruit can be picked before they are completely ripe and placed in a warm, dry
spot for several days until they open.

The colorful outer coat of the seeds should be removed before the seeds are planted. This can be done by soaking the seeds in water for up to 3 days, then squeezing the seeds or rubbing them across a screen to remove the coat. The seeds should then be washed in mild soapy water to remove the oily film, and then rinsed with clear water.

Magnolia seeds need a cold treatment before they will germinate. This treatment can be achieved by planting seeds outdoors in fall (but again, protection from animals is necessary), but the most common method involves storing the seeds in the refrigerator until spring. Cleaned seeds should be wrapped in damp (but not soaking wet) sphagnum moss, placed in plastic bags, and kept in a household refrigerator at 33–40°F (0.5–4°C). Seeds that become dried out will lose viability, as will seeds that stay soggy or become infected with fungal growth. A bit of fungicide or a rinse in a 1:10 chlorine bleach: water solution before packaging should help deter fungal growth. Seeds should be ready to plant in 3 to 4 months but may be stored under refrigerated conditions for longer periods if necessary. Sow seeds in a standard soilless potting medium and protect from birds and rodents. Optimum temperature for germination is about 70°F (21°C). Germination may occur anywhere from several weeks to a few months after sowing, depending on the species and the conditions.

After hybrid progeny are evaluated, hybrids selected for naming and introduction should be propagated by vegetative means. Magnolias are commonly propagated by cuttings or grafting (chip-budding or side-grafting). These methods are discussed further in Callaway (1994).

Would-be plant breeders can get started on their way to creating hybrid magnolias with just a little practice using the information given here. Anyone interested in further reading should consult the references at the end of this chapter. There are so many possibilities within the genus *Magnolia*, and there is always room for experimentation. By beginning with just a few simple crosses, magnolia enthusiasts can become magnolia breeders, presenting a whole new reason to enjoy growing the plants.

Resources

COLLECTIONS

The following are public gardens that offer nice collections of magnolias. Many private gardeners also have wonderful magnolia collections, and many of the nurseries listed under "Suppliers" have display gardens. Anyone interested in learning more should contact the Magnolia Society.

North America

Arnold Arboretum
Harvard University
125 Arborway
Jamaica Plain, MA 02130

Barnes Foundation Arboretum
300 N. Latch's Lane
Merion Station, PA 19066

Brooklyn Botanic Garden
1000 Washington Avenue
Brooklyn, NY 11225

Henry Foundation for Botanical
    Research
P.O. Box 7
801 Stony Lane
Gladwyne, PA 19035

Morris Arboretum of the University
    of Pennsylvania
9414 Meadowbrook Avenue
Philadelphia, PA 19118

Royal Botanical Gardens
P.O. Box 399
Hamilton, Ontario L8N 3H8

Strybing Arboretum and Botanical
    Gardens
Golden Gate Park
9th Avenue at Lincoln Way
San Francisco, CA 94122

U.S. National Arboretum
3501 New York Avenue, N.E.
Washington, DC 20002

Washington Park Arboretum
University of Washington
Box 358010
Seattle, WA 98195

Europe

Caerhays Castle
St. Austell, Cornwall
England

Chyverton
Truro, Cornwall
England

Herkenrode
Wespelaar
Belgium

Kalmthout Arboretum
Heuvel 2
2180 Kalmthout
Belgium

Les Parcs de France
Ingrannes
France

Norrauramov
Bjuv
Sweden

Pépinières de Kérisnel
Société d'Initiatives et de
    Coopération Agricoles
29250 St.-Pol-de-Léon
France

Royal Botanic Garden
Inverleith Row
Edinburgh EH3 5LR
Scotland

Royal Horticultural Society's
    Garden, Wisley
Woking, Surrey GU23 6QB
England

Trewithen Nurseries
Grampound Road
Truro, Cornwall TR2
England

Vico Morcote
Lugano
Switzerland

Asia and the Pacific

Blumhardt, Oswald
No. 9 R.D. 1386-SH14
Whangarei
New Zealand

Chollipo Arboretum
Chungchongnam-do 352-33
South Korea

Kunming Botanical Garden
Kunming, Yunnan
China

SUPPLIERS

The following is a partial list of mail-order suppliers of magnolias. These were chosen because they specialize in, or offer a wide selection of, magnolias. A more complete list, including wholesale nurseries, can be obtained from the Magnolia Society.

United States

Fairweather Gardens
P.O. Box 330
Greenwich, NJ 08323
phone: 856-451-6261
fax: 856-451-0303

Louisiana Nursery
5853 Highway 182
Opelousas, LA 70570
phone: 318-948-3696
fax: 318-942-6404

Gossler Farms Nursery
1200 Weaver Road
Springfield, OR 97478-9691
phone: 541-746-3922
fax: 541-744-7924

Roslyn Nursery
211 Burrs Lane
Dix Hills, NY 11746
phone: 631-643-9347
fax: 631-427-0894

Greer Gardens
1280 Goodpasture Island Road
Eugene, OR 97401-1794
phone: 541-686-8266 or
    800-548-0111
fax: 541-686-0910

Wavecrest Nurseries
2509 Lakeshore Drive
Fennville, MI 49408
phone: 616-543-4175
fax: 616-543-4100

Europe

Bulkyard Plants
P.O. Box 56
2770 AB Boskoop
The Netherlands
phone: (31) 172-213095 or 212005
fax: (31) 172-216173 or 213402

Burncoose and South Down
   Nurseries
Gwennap
Redruth, Cornwall TR16 6BJ
England
phone: (44) 1209-861112
fax: (44) 1209-860011

C.E.C.E.
Avenue Leopold III n. 12
7130 Bray (Binche)
Belgium
phone: (32) 64-338215
fax: (32) 64-369462

Eisenhut, Otto
6575 San Nazzaro/Ticino
Switzerland
phone: (41) 91-795-18-67
fax: (41) 91-795-30-29

Esveld, Firma C.
Rijneveld 72
2771 XS Boskoop
The Netherlands
phone: (31) 1722-13289 or 14616

Mallet Court Nursery
Curry Mallet
Taunton, Somerset TA3 6SY
England
phone: (44) 1823-480748
fax: (44) 1823-481009

Pépinières de Kérisnel
Société d'Initiatives et de
   Coopération Agricoles
29250 St.-Pol-de-Léon
France
phone: (33) 98-690710
fax: (33) 98-290102

Plantekassen
Jægersborg Alle 172
2820 Gentofte
Denmark
phone: (45) 39658213

Zetas Nursery
Gä Södertäljevägen 194
141 70 Huddinge
Sweden
phone: (46) 8-6460391
fax: (46) 8-6466400

Zwijnenburg, Pieter, Jr.
Halve Raak 18
2771 AD Boskoop
The Netherlands
phone: (31) 1722-1632
fax: (31) 1722-18474

New Zealand

Blumhardt, Oswald
No. 9 R.D. 1386-SH14
Whangarei

Jury Nurseries
P.O. Box 65
Urenui, North Taranaki

INTERNATIONAL REGISTRATION AUTHORITY
The Magnolia Society, Inc.
Attn: Dorothy J. Callaway
6616 81st Street
Cabin John, MD 20818
U.S.A.
phone and fax: 301-320-4296

PLANT SOCIETIES
The Magnolia Society, Inc.
Roberta D. Hagen, Secretary
6616 81st Street
Cabin John, MD 20818
U.S.A.
phone and fax: 301-320-4296

References and Additional Reading

Callaway, D. J. 1994. *The World of Magnolias*. Portland, Ore.: Timber Press.

Gardiner, J. M. 1989. *Magnolias*. Chester, Conn.: Globe Pequot Press.

Hopkins, H. 1990. A look backward at backcrossing. *Journal of the Magnolia Society* 25 (2): 1–5.

Jonsson, L. 1987. How easy is pollen collecting? *Journal of the Magnolia Society* 22 (2): 1–3.

Kehr, A. E. 1985. Inducing polyploidy in magnolias. *Journal of the Magnolia Society* 20 (2): 6–9.

————. 1991. Magnolia improvement by polyploidy. *Journal of the Magnolia Society* 26 (2): 1–3.

————. 1996. Woody plant polyploidy. *American Nurseryman* 183 (3): 38–47.

————. 1998. New genetic traits in magnolias. *Journal of the Magnolia Society* 33 (1): 1–6.

Ledvina, D. 1984. Creating hybrids. *Journal of the Magnolia Society* 20 (2): 25–26.

McDaniel, J. C. 1974. Get in on the ground floor of magnolia hybridizing. *Journal of the Magnolia Society* 10 (2): 13–14.

————. 1975. Hybridizing section Rhytidospermum. *Journal of the Magnolia Society* 11 (1): 9–11.

Santamour, F. S. 1965a. Biochemical studies in *Magnolia* I. Floral anthocyanins. *Bulletin of the Morris Arboretum* 16 (3): 43–48.

————. 1965b. Biochemical studies in *Magnolia* II. Leucoanthocyanins in leaves. *Bulletin of the Morris Arboretum* 16 (4): 63–64.

————. 1966. Biochemical studies in *Magnolia* IV. Flavonols and flavones. *Bulletin of the Morris Arboretum* 17 (4): 65–58.

————. 1969. Cytology of *Magnolia* hybrids I. *Bulletin of the Morris Arboretum* 20 (4): 63–65.

———. 1970a. Cytology of *Magnolia* hybrids II. *M.* ×*soulangiana* hybrids. *Bulletin of the Morris Arboretum* 21 (3): 58–61.

———. 1970b. Cytology of *Magnolia* hybrids III. Intra-sectional hybrids. *Bulletin of the Morris Arboretum* 21 (4): 80–81.

———. 1970c. Implications of cytology and biochemistry for magnolia hybridization. *Journal of the Magnolia Society* 7 (2): 8–10.

Savage, P. J. 1978. Gathering gold dust. *Journal of the Magnolia Society* 14 (1): 11–18.

Treseder, N. G. 1978. *Magnolias*. London: Faber and Faber.

17 Breeding Oaks: A New Frontier

Guy Sternberg

The oaks (*Quercus*)—trees of the Druids—are the predominate genus of broad-leaved trees in the Northern Hemisphere. This fascinating and variable group probably is represented by more species, covering a greater basal area over a more diverse ecological range, than any other kind of tree. From centers of differentiation in India and Mexico, some 500 oak species have evolved to cover much of the planet north of the equator. The oaks' combined value for timber, wildlife, and ornamental purposes may be without parallel in the natural world.

Oaks are notorious for their sexual infidelity. Natural oak hybrids can be found in almost any habitat where two or more interfertile species occur within sight of one another (Palmer 1948; Sternberg 1990). One oak taxon, historically recognized by many authorities as a true species (*Quercus undulata*), has been found to be a hybrid grex involving perhaps seven parent species (Tucker 1961). Some of our most beautiful and vigorous oak trees are hybrids, and the genus obviously has unimaginable potential for genetic tinkering. Yet, surprisingly few people have attempted to experiment with oaks through controlled breeding.

The primary reason for this becomes apparent when one considers that, after successful pollination (and selection of superior progeny), vegetative propagation of the selected clonal material is necessary. Without this vegetative propagation, the fruits of the breeder's work survive only in the ortet (the original F_1 progeny) and can never be shared with the horticultural world. The new plant must be reproduced in identical genetic (or at least phenotypic) form to be useful in the nursery trade, or even to be eligible for a plant patent.

But attempts at asexual oak propagation by grafting or budding can be frustrated by delayed graft incompatibilities that prevent lignification of the graft union, resulting in graft failure several years after a seemingly successful graft. This failure is superficially analogous to human blood typing, or to tissue rejection in a human organ transplant, and it has discouraged the development of more than one outstanding oak cultivar. The cause has been traced to incompatibility problems with the peroxidase enzyme, which promotes the necessary lignification of the graft union only if peroxidase isozymes of the scion and understock match (Santamour 1988, 1992).

Some promising cultivars of pin oak (*Quercus palustris*), for example, disappeared from the nursery trade about a decade after they were introduced, because the trees began to fail at the graft line. Electrophoretic analysis of cambial enzyme profiles of some of these failing grafted plants confirms the presence of incompatible enzyme bands. Close familial relationships between stock and scion are not particularly helpful either, just as blood types cannot be predicted from parent to offspring in humans. If the electrophoretic bands do not match, the graft will fail, even if a seedling is being grafted onto its own parent.

Cutting propagation of this genus has been even trickier than grafting, and few nurseries have attempted this procedure. Successful tissue culture of oaks is even more elusive. The propagation situation with oaks has been so problematic that, at some major nurseries in the United States, 90% of the plants, of all types, are propagated vegetatively, but 90% of the remaining (seed-grown) plants are oaks.

All this is changing rapidly. The compatibility of an oak graft now can be predicted in advance through electrophoretic enzyme allele separation analysis. Putative natural hybrids also can be identified through electrophoresis, using primers in a microbiological technique known as PCR (polymerase chain reaction) to replicate genetic material for RFLPS (restriction fragment length polymorphism studies) and analysis of IPMP (isozyme protein migration patterns) (Arnheim et al. 1990; Hamrick 1991; Martinez 1991; Riggs 1991).

The graft incompatibility problem generally is serious only in certain subgeneric groups of oaks. Several researchers are perfecting techniques for rooting hardened softwood cuttings, and the same species that seem to pose the most problems with grafting seem to display the most promise for cutting propagation. Tissue culture techniques for oaks are advancing as well, with the commercial production of rooted explants likely in the near future. We thus should expect to see the propagation roadblocks for oaks fall in rapid order.

Taxonomy and Breeding Materials

As research opens the door for the development of oak cultivars, tree breeders are turning to the oaks with renewed excitement. Oaks can be crossed to combine features such as evergreen or deciduous foliage, myriad growth forms, red or gold fall colors, and adaptability to nearly any soil and climate, and to produce heterosis, or hybrid vigor (Sternberg 1990). The only significant limitation, once we master the basic horticultural techniques involved, is our inability to produce successful hybrids between generic and subgeneric groups (Tucker 1990). Some knowledge of subgeneric classification thus is a prerequisite for oak breeding.

The oak genus, *Quercus*, is closely related to the tan oaks, genus *Lithocarpus*. Both bear acorns, but the two genera will not interbreed. Oaks and tan oaks are classified in the same family with beeches (*Fagus*) and chestnuts (*Castanea* and *Castanopsis*) too, as well as with the lesser-known tropical genera *Trigonobalanus*, *Colombobalanus*, and *Formanodendron*, but each genus forms a distinct and exclusive breeding group.

Among oak authorities, there is disagreement regarding intrageneric taxonomic classification within the true oak genus *Quercus*. Oaks rebel with delight against the neat little boundaries devised by systematists to categorize them. A few authorities, frustrated by this, even suggest classifying all oaks under one of two super-species; others find reason to split each of the commonly recognized species into several more. The phylogenetic approach currently accepted by most authorities (Nixon 1993) recognizes two distinct groups at the subgenus level (see chart): the ring-cupped oaks (subgenus *Cyclobalanopsis*) of Asia, and the scale-cupped oaks (subgenus *Quercus*), which are distributed throughout the range of the genus.

Subgenus *Quercus* usually is divided further into three sections, although some of these sections arguably could be raised to the subgeneric level. Section *Lobatae* (or subgenus *Erythrobalanus*) comprises the red oaks of the Western Hemisphere, ranging from Canada south as far as Colombia. Section *Protobalanus* is a small group from western North America, commonly known as the golden (or intermediate) oaks. Section *Quercus* (frequently labeled *Lepidobalanus* or *Leucobalanus* in older literature) is the largest and most diverse group, with distribution in Europe, Asia, Africa, and throughout most of the genus range in the Western Hemisphere. This group, known as the white oaks, sometimes is subdivided further into subsections, loosely defined as the white oak group *sensu stricto*, the Turkish oaks, and the holly oaks.

Virtually none of the species in any of the sectional or subgeneric groups will cross with any species from a different group (Tucker 1990). Within groups, though, and even across the supposed subsectional lines

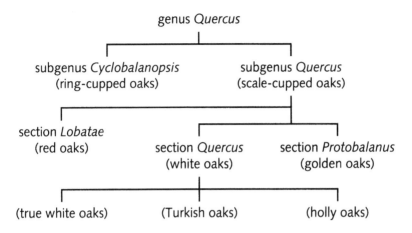

that separate the Turkish oaks and the holly oaks, almost anything goes. Nearly every oak species studied has been found to cross with at least one other oak species, producing viable progeny. Much of the natural variation in the beautiful white oak (*Quercus alba*), for example, has been traced to natural introgression. This is the residual genetic effect of past hybridization with 11 other oaks from the same taxonomic section (Hardin 1975). The variable bur oak (*Q. macrocarpa*) also displays considerable heterozygosity from the influence of past hybridization.

History

Although not yet popular with North American breeders, oaks have been studied extensively elsewhere in pollination experiments. Most notable among these studies might be the work of Piatnitsky in the 1930s in the Ukraine, which involved 200,000 pollinations representing 47 different interspecific crosses (Radu 1995). Most American breeding projects have focused more narrowly upon two, or a few, interfertile species, or upon intraspecific improvement breeding.

The most well known oak breeder in North America was the late Walter Cottam, who developed the many beautiful hybrid oaks now growing at the arboretum of the University of Utah in Salt Lake City (Cottam et al. 1982). These plantings were replicated at the Shields Grove collection in Davis, California, under the care of John Tucker of the University of California. Tucker ranks with Cornelius Muller (formerly of the U.S. Department of Agriculture), Frank Santamour (of the U.S. National Arboretum), Kevin Nixon (of Cornell University in New York), and Richard Jensen (of Notre Dame University in Indiana) among the foremost modern authorities on hybrid oak studies in North America.

Earlier names associated with hybridization in oaks include Aimee Camus of France, who compiled the monographic atlas *Les Chênes* in the 1930s, and William Trelease of the United States, who contributed the most comprehensive treatment of American oaks ever accomplished, in the 1920s. The Michaux father-and-son team of France (1780s–1820s), Charles Sprague Sargent of the Arnold Arboretum (1890s–1920s), and Professor Joe McDaniel of the University of Illinois (1960s–1970s) also were preeminent among those who have made significant contributions toward our understanding of hybridization in the oaks.

François André (the younger) Michaux was the first to describe a hybrid oak in North America. It was a cross of willow oak (*Quercus phellos*) with red oak (*Q. rubra*), a cross widely recognized now as one of our most commonly encountered and easily identified oak hybrids.

Some impressive oak hybrids develop under natural conditions at the interface of two distinct habitats, each with its own characteristic oak species. One example is prevalent in uniform hybrid populations, or swarms, near Lubbock, Texas. There *Quercus havardii*, a dwarf white oak species of sandy soils, meets *Q. mohriana*, a related white oak that grows on adjacent limestone areas. Such hybrids may combine survival attributes from each parent, enabling them to occupy a transitional habitat preferred by neither (Muller 1952; Sternberg 1990). Similar examples can be found among the red oaks as well, such as those in the Apostle Islands region of western Lake Superior involving *Q. rubra* and *Q. ellipsoidalis* (Isebrands 1994).

In a grove of sibling individuals, a lone hybrid often will become the most outstanding specimen due to hybrid vigor. The United States national champion specimen of the hybrid oak cross *Quercus muhlenbergii* × *Q. macrocarpa* in Sangamon County, Illinois, for example, stands out among ancient specimens of the parent species *Q. muhlenbergii* growing in the same grove because it has become nearly twice as large (Sternberg 1990).

Miguel Marquez of El Paso, Texas, developed the Marquez Special Edition oak hybrids now becoming available from nurseries in the United States. He has been a pioneer in hybridization within the white oak group, including the crossing of tender evergreen species with hardy deciduous species. Some of the results of this breeding work can be seen growing as far north as the Oikos Tree Crops collection in Kalamazoo, Michigan.

Important Traits and Breeding Objectives

Historically, hybrid cultivar development in oaks has depended almost exclusively on selection from natural crosses. These open-pollinated hybrids exhibit variable characteristics, with the best individuals combining the most desirable features of each parent. Controlled crosses have significant practical advantages, however. The provenance of each line thus can be traced, if parents from known sources are used; this facilitates descriptions for plant patent application and can help predict the adaptability of the hybrid progeny to specific climate zones. Controlled crosses also build upon the preselection of parent individuals exhibiting the most pronounced display of desired features, thus bypassing the randomness inherent in selection from available natural hybrids.

When selecting oaks for breeding, certain traits may stand out as having both the need and the potential for improvement. The common European or English oak, *Quercus robur*, is very easy to graft and transplant, and fastigiate individuals frequently will contribute their unique upright habit of growth in varying degrees to hybrid offspring. All these traits can be useful in a hybrid progeny. This species nonetheless has certain deficiencies when grown in much of North America, such as susceptibility to winter injury and mildew damage, drab summer foliage, and a notorious lack of fall color. The other parent of an English oak hybrid, therefore, should be selected to contribute superior performance in these areas, as desired.

Magnificent hybrids of English oak with hardy and colorful North American oak species are being developed at North Dakota State University, Schmidt Nursery in Oregon, Oikos Nursery in Michigan, Cully Nursery in Illinois, and Starhill Forest, also in Illinois. Some of these hybrids display good fall color, others have lustrous bicolored leaves during the growing season, and all show excellent hardiness and disease resistance, which are traits inherited from their American parents. Yet each has some degree of fastigiate or narrow-pyramidal form, all are easy to propagate, and most seem to develop a fibrous, easily transplanted root system—characteristics of the English parent. All should share traits common to both parents, such as strength and longevity, and several exhibit the hybrid vigor that will make them popular with nurseries and landscapers (Plate 17-1).

Those who work with the genus assert that there is no such thing as a bad oak, but that each species has special strengths to offer in a hybridization program. Horticultural adaptability (for transplanting and vegetative propagation) is a definite strength of the English oak for use in hybridization programs involving the white oak taxonomic section *Quercus*. *Quercus robur* is one of the most popular oaks of all, and it has furnished more named cultivars than any other oak species. Another European species, cork oak (*Q. suber*), and an Asian species, Chinese cork oak (*Q. variabilis*), each could contribute stunning corky bark to a hybrid progeny, and they might be crossed with other species for fall color or increased cold hardiness.

Among the American oaks, white oak (*Quercus alba*), chestnut oak (*Q. montana*), and swamp chestnut oak (*Q. michauxii*) could be used within the same white oak taxonomic group to impart brilliant fall color. Bur oak (*Q.*

macrocarpa) can offer its large acorn size, hardiness, and adaptability to difficult growing conditions, as well as its own textured, corky bark. The tropical species *Q. insignis* has even larger, brightly colored acorns, nearly the size of tangerines, which would be stunning on a hybrid tree that could survive in temperate climates.

Chinkapin oak (*Quercus muhlenbergii*) could contribute its adaptability to alkaline soils; dwarf chinkapin oak (*Q. prinoides*) might yield progeny of reduced stature, suitable for smaller landscapes. Swamp white oak (*Q. bicolor*) and overcup oak (*Q. lyrata*) could offer root systems adapted to poorly drained soil, and valley oak (*Q. lobata*) might add small leaf size and a weeping form. Post oak (*Q. stellata*) could confer drought resistance, and the multiple-stemmed Rocky Mountain oak (*Q. gambelii*) might contribute a freely sprouting, lignotuberous growth habit for barrier plantings. Any of these species might be crossed with the hardiest evergreen white oaks, such as Texas live oak (*Q. fusiformis*) or scrub live oak (*Q. turbinella*), especially if the evergreen parent is chosen from the coldest part of its natural range, to give the breeder a cold-hardy, semievergreen oak.

Most of the species in the white oak taxonomic section are long lived, strong wooded, and relatively resistant to oak wilt (*Ceratocystis fagacearum*), the primary disease affecting oaks in North America. One cross in this section, a special selection of *Quercus ×saulii* (*Q. montana × Q. alba*) developed by Starhill Forest Arboretum in Illinois, has some of the most brilliant and long-lasting fall color of any tree (Plate 17-3); it also has a symmetrical pyramidal form, lustrous summer leaves with bright undersides that flash in the wind, and excellent vigor. Such a plant should be expected to thrive on harsh rocky or dry sites and could have a potential life span of several centuries, since both parent species exhibit such characteristics. In this example, the ornamental characteristics of both species coincided, and the selected hybrid individual inherited them in combination, outperforming either parent and all its siblings (Sternberg 1992).

Within the red oak taxonomic section *Lobatae*, breeding efforts might concentrate on producing individuals with strong, wide branching angles, good wound closure, ease of propagation and transplanting, or extremely rapid growth. The red oaks in general are faster growing than the white oaks, and almost any red oak has outstanding fall color, so these features should be accentuated by choosing superior individuals as parents. Red oaks generally are more brittle and prone to decay than the white oaks, though, and much more susceptible to oak wilt. Unfortunately, the strength, disease resistance, and longevity of the white oaks cannot be bred into the red oaks, since the two groups are not interfertile. Much can be done, however, to make the most of the virtues already present within the red oak group.

Golden oaks (section *Protobalanus*) cannot be crossed with white oaks or red oaks, but they will cross among themselves. This is a small group, with limited winter hardiness, so any interspecific breeding program involving the golden oaks probably should be tailored to the local market and areas with a similar climate. The real potential for breeding in this group might be the opportunity to enhance the ornamental characteristics of its variable flagship species, canyon live oak (*Quercus chrysolepis*), by intraspecific crossing to develop selections with features such as large, brightly colored acorns, predictable growth habit, or increased cold hardiness.

Other primary characteristics to consider when breeding oaks include a particular branching habit, ornamental leaf shape, or fruiting characteristic (size, taste, color), and the tendency to be evergreen, deciduous, or marcescent (with foliage that browns but clings into the dormant season) also should be considered. Traits affecting cultural adaptability to nursery production must be factored in as well, including straight and uniform growth, resistance to nursery diseases, hardening off for winter storage, and development of visual appeal at a young age.

In addition, controlled crossing allows for the potential combination of characteristics from two promising species that could not be grown near enough to each other to cross naturally. The large, spectacularly ruffled evergreen foliage of *Quercus resinosa*, a species that grows on tropical American volcanoes, might combine magnificently with the equally large deciduous foliage of *Q. dentata*, a winter-hardy Asian species, yielding many magnificent progeny. The hardiness of such a cross would need to be tested, but several beautiful hybrid oaks developed in Europe have used species like English oak (*Q. robur*) or Turkish oak (*Q. cerris*) to enhance the winter hardiness of evergreen species such as holly oak (*Q. ilex*).

State and industry foresters also select for vigorous trees with straight boles that self-prune, shedding lower branches to produce clear lumber. Seed orchards of such selected individuals are established to furnish superior open-pollinated seed for reforestation. Careful attention to the adaptive provenance of the trees in each seed orchard ensures the best combination of vigor and hardiness for any particular planting region. Due to the economies of scale (and perhaps to the recognized need for genetic diversity in any forest), once the orchard trees have been produced by breeding or selection, open pollination among these superior parents normally is used to produce progeny for general reforestation.

Hybridization Mechanics

Oaks depend on random pollen dissemination by wind (they are anemophilous), and so they must produce copious amounts of pollen to ensure that some of it gets to the right place. Pendent staminate catkins are conspicuous in spring, ripening just as the leaves begin to expand, so pollen collection is a relatively simple task where the source tree has limbs low enough to reach. Pollen from the donor tree should be harvested by picking catkins before the male flowers begin to shed. The catkins are picked with tweezers into paper collecting bags and stored in a dry place until the pollen is released. Pollen can be shaken onto filter paper once the catkins ripen, and the free pollen then should be stored in sterile plastic or glass containers in the refrigerator until the designated pistillate flowers are receptive.

The pistillate flowers that develop in the leaf axils are tiny and inconspicuous. In order to attempt a controlled cross, the female flowers must be located and covered before the pollen ripens, to avoid pollen contamination. Some breeders use plastic bags to isolate the female flowers, but plastic can trap heat and kill the shoot in warm or sunny climates unless it is shaded. Paper bags minimize this problem, but they are more easily damaged by wind and rain. The bag should be placed over the twig after all emerging staminate catkins have been removed. Seal the bag with a cotton gasket wrapped around the twig inside the neck of the bag and cinch it securely with string or wire ties.

Oak pollen can be stored for longer periods, such as until the next flowering season, in the following manner:

1. Sift the pollen through a sieve to remove debris and break up any clumps.
2. Place the sifted pollen in an open plastic container, such as a film can without the lid.
3. Carefully place the open container of pollen upright into a larger container with a drying agent such as calcium chloride crystals, taking care not to allow the desiccant to come into direct contact with the pollen.
4. Seal the outer container, allow the pollen to dry overnight, and place the sealed container in a freezer.

To reactivate the pollen following storage, bring the container up to room temperature, open it, and replace the desiccant with water. Then reseal the container, and allow the pollen to rehydrate overnight at room temperature (Marquez 1995).

The common tool for dispensing pollen, available in any kitchen, is a basting syringe with an opening about ⅛ inch (3 mm) in diameter. The pollen may be sprayed through a small puncture into the bag covering the pistillate flowers, and the puncture then must be sealed with tape to prevent the entry of unwanted airborne pollen; this step may be repeated after a few days to ensure that the female flower receives pollen at the correct time (Marquez 1991).

Each pollination bag should be labeled with a color or numerical code that refers to a log book. The log should record the identity of the parent trees and the dates of pollen collection, bagging, and pollination. The bag should be removed when the risk of exposure to airborne pollen has expired, but the label must remain fastened securely to the twig until harvest. If the pollination is successful, the acorns will mature normally; unsuccessful pollinations will abort.

The mature fruit should be harvested when slightly green, as soon as they can be pulled from the acorn cap without tearing the hilum (the zone of attachment to the cap). This will minimize exposure of the fruit to insects and seed predators, and prevents the nightmare of finding your precious ripe acorns already fallen, lying on the ground, indistinguishable from thousands of open-pollinated acorns. If early harvest is not desired, re-bag the fruit in late summer to protect them, and wait for them to abscise in the bags.

Most red oaks, except coast live oak (*Quercus agrifolia*), emory oak (*Q. emoryi*), occasionally silverleaf oak (*Q. hypoleucoides*), and possibly some Mexican or tropical American species not commonly encountered, require two growing seasons for their acorns to mature. Golden oaks also take 2 years; all will display only "nubbins" or "acornetts" during the first year after pollination. Wait until the second year to harvest them, when they have reached full size and have ripened. White oak types, at least the ones found in North America and most of those from Europe, ripen their fruit the first year.

Propagation

Acorns picked while still green should be after-ripened for a few days if needed, or until they turn their characteristic ripe color and the cap loosens. Keep them in a cool, shady place with high humidity. Some species (particularly the red oaks) may be stratified over winter, but it is best to plant all acorns directly outdoors in the fall if possible. Plant them shallowly, on their sides, and mulch the seedbed to control excessive fluctuations in temperature.

All oak acorns are sought by rodents and birds for food, even after they have germinated. Wire-mesh guards can provide secure protection if properly installed. A sheet of hardware cloth with a mesh size smaller than the acorn diameter (and smaller than the head size of your local rodent species) can be placed directly on the seedbed or flat and secured along its edges. The seedlings will grow up through the wire mesh, which must be left in place throughout the first growing season to prevent hungry seed predators from tearing up seedlings to feast on the remnants of the cotyledons.

Field-grown seedlings should be transplanted or undercut in the early spring following their first growing season, unless they were seeded directly into their permanent locations. Most oaks develop deep tap roots in their early years, and a vigorous 2-year-old seedling can be difficult to dig from a seedbed. Protect outplanted seedlings from browsing herbivores with commercial tree shelters or fencing until they reach a non-vulnerable size, if necessary. The type of protection required, and the duration of the protection period, will vary with the abundance and species of browsing mammals present.

Some of the hybrid characteristics of your cross will become apparent during the first year. Fall color, leaf shape, and hybrid vigor manifest early, furnishing some degree of optimism that your seedling tree truly is a hybrid and not a victim of the ubiquitous stray pollen that loves to creep into any controlled cross that isn't perfectly and promptly sealed. Other characteristics, like bark and growth form, develop gradually over time. It is crucial that, during all this time, the tags, log books, maps, and other records of a hybridization program are carefully maintained; loss of such records can be disastrous, especially if multiple crosses are involved and the seedling progeny cannot be distinguished in the field.

Plant breeding and hybrid selection with the oaks provides a fascinating opportunity to work with what is one of the most genetically diverse and productive of all tree families, breaking new ground with every step. It is an opportunity that, once discovered, is difficult to ignore.

Resources

COLLECTIONS

North America

Arnold Arboretum
Harvard University
125 Arborway
Jamaica Plain, MA 02130

Holden Arboretum
9500 Sperry Road
Kirtland, OH 44094-5172

Mexican National Oak Collection
Louise Wardle Camacho Botanic
   Garden
11 Oriente 2407
Puebla, Puebla State
Mexico

Morton Arboretum
Route 53
Lisle, IL 60532

North American Plant Preservation
   Council Collection
Starhill Forest
Route 1, Box 272
Petersburg, IL 62675

Red Butte Gardens
University of Utah Arboretum
18A De Trobriand Street
Salt Lake City, UT 84113

Shields Grove
Davis Arboretum
University of California
Davis, CA 95616

Europe

Arboretum National des Barres
45290 Nogent-sur-Vernisson
France

Arboretum Simeria
Street Biscaria 1
2625 Simeria, Jud Hunedoara
Romania

Arboretum Trompenburg
Groene Wetering 46
3062 PC Rotterdam
The Netherlands

Arboretum Waasland
Kriekelaarstraat 29
B-9100 Nieuwkerken
Belgium

Sir Harold Hillier Arboretum
Jermyns Lane
Ampfield, Near Romsey
Hampshire S051 0QA
England

Royal Botanic Gardens, Kew
Richmond, Surrey TW9 3AB
England

Westonbirt Arboretum
Tetbury, Gloucestershire GL8 8QS
England

New Zealand

Hackfalls Arboretum
P.O. Box 3
Tiniroto via Gisborne

SUPPLIERS

United States

Forestfarm
990 Tetherow Road
Williams, OR 97544

Forrest Keeling Nursery
Highway 79S Box 135
Elsberry, MO 63343

King Nursery
6849 Route 34
Oswego, IL 60543

Oikos Tree Crops
P.O. Box 19425
Kalamazoo, MI 49019

Possibility Place
7548 W. Manhattan-Monee Road
Monee, IL 60449

Trees That Please
9 Gilcrease Lane
Los Lunas, NM 87031

Woodlanders
1128 Colleton Avenue
Aiken, SC 29801

Europe

Boomkwekerij
M. M. Bomer
Vagevuurstraat 6
4882 NK-Zundert
The Netherlands

Spécialiste Français du Chêne
Pépinières
D. Bastard
49600 St.-Philbert-en-Mauges
France

Mallet Court Nursery
Curry Mallet
Taunton, Somerset TA3 6SY
England

INTERNATIONAL REGISTRATION AUTHORITY

American Association of Botanical Gardens and Arboreta
Attn: Steven Clemants
Brooklyn Botanic Garden
1000 Washington Avenue
Brooklyn, NY 11225
U.S.A.

PLANT SOCIETIES

International Oak Society
c/o Richard Jensen
Dept. of Biology
St. Mary's College
Notre Dame, IN 46556
U.S.A.

References and Additional Reading

Arnheim, N., T. White, and W. E. Rainey. 1990. Application of PCR: Organismal and population biology. *BioScience* 40 (3).

Cottam, W. P., J. M. Tucker, and F. S. Santamour. 1982. *Oak Hybridization at the University of Utah.* State Arboretum of Utah publication no. 1.

Hamrick, J. 1991. Department of Botany, University of Georgia. Personal communication.

Hardin, J. W. 1975. Hybridization and introgression in *Quercus alba.* Paper no. 4477, Journal Series of the North Carolina Agricultural Experiment Station, Raleigh, North Carolina.

Isebrands, J. G. 1994. U.S. Forest Service, Rhinelander, Wisconsin. Personal communication.

Marquez, M. 1991–1995. El Paso, Texas. Personal communications.

Martinez, C. L. 1991. STA Laboratories, Longmont, Colorado. Personal communication.

Muller, C. H. 1952. Ecological control of hybridization in *Quercus:* A factor in the mechanism of evolution. *Evolution: International Journal of Organic Evolution* 6 (2).

Nixon, K. C. 1993. Infrageneric classification of *Quercus* (Fagaceae) and typification of sectional names. *Annales des Science Forestières* 50 (Suppl. 1): 25s–34s.

Palmer, E. J. 1948. Hybrid oaks of North America. *Journal of the Arnold Arboretum* XXIX (1).

Radu, S. 1995. Oaks of Europe and Asia: Occurrence, ecology and amenity values. Arboretum Simeria, Romania. *Journal of the International Oak Society* 6.

Riggs, L. 1991. Genetic Resource Consultants, Berkeley, California. Personal communication.

Santamour, F. S., Jr. 1988. Cambial peroxidase enzymes related to graft incompatibility in red oak. *Journal of Environmental Horticulture* (September).

———. 1992. United States National Arboretum, Washington, D.C. Personal communication.

Sternberg, G. 1990. Sturdy as an oak: Natural and selected oak hybrids. *American Nurseryman* (15 July).

———. 1992. American oaks in the landscape. *Journal of the International Oak Society* (March).

Tucker, J. 1961. Studies in the *Quercus undulata* complex. *American Journal of Botany* 48 (March).

———. 1990. Hybridization in California oaks. *Fremontia* 18 (3).

Appendix: Sources of Plant Breeding Supplies

Many of the breeding supplies mentioned in this book are readily available locally. Pipe cleaners and artist's brushes for use in hand pollinating can usually be found in craft stores or the craft department of discount stores, as can desiccants such as silica gel. Gelatin capsules, often used to store pollen, may be found at pharmacies. Jeweler's tags found at office supply stores or discount stores can be used for labeling crosses. Many nursery suppliers and chemical suppliers have rooting hormones, gibberellic acid, colchicine, and other such compounds. The following are some mail-order sources for many of these items.

Aldrich Chemical Co.
940 E. Saint Paul Avenue
Milwaukee, WI 53233
U.S.A.
phone: 414-273-3850
Chemical supplier

A. M. Leonard
241 Fox Drive
P.O. Box 816
Piqua, OH 45356
U.S.A.
phone: 800-543-8955
fax: 800-433-0633
Horticultural supplier aimed at home gardeners

Hummert International
4500 Earth City Expressway
Earth City, MO 63045
U.S.A.
phone: 314-506-4500 or 800-325-3055
fax: 314-506-4510
Large horticultural supplier

MacKenzie Nursery Supply, Inc.
P.O. Box 322
3891 Shepard Road
Perry, OH 44081
U.S.A.
phone: 216-259-3517 or 800-777-5030
fax: 216-259-3004
Horticultural supplier

Nasco Science
901 Janesville Avenue
Fort Atkinson, WI 53538-0901
U.S.A.
phone: 414-563-2446 or 800-558-9595
fax: 414-563-8296
Scientific and chemical supplier

Research Organics, Inc.
4353 E. 49th Street
Cleveland, OH 44125-1083
U.S.A.
phone: 800-321-0570
Chemical supplier

Sigma Chemical Company
P.O. Box 14508
St. Louis, MO 63178
U.S.A.
phone: 314-771-5750 or 800-325-3010
Laboratory and chemical supplier

Glossary

This glossary includes many of the terms used in this book. For further reading, please see the references given at the end of the glossary.

allele: one of the alternative forms of a specific gene that occurs at the same locus on homologous chromosomes. For example, red and white may be alleles of a gene for color.

anther: the part of the stamen that bears pollen.

anthocyanin: a red, purple, or blue pigment found in various plants; especially common in flower petals.

bilateral symmetry: composed of two corresponding halves, each a mirror image of the other; usually used to describe flowers.

calyx: a collective term for all the sepals in a flower.

chimera: a portion of a plant composed of two or more genetically distinct tissues growing adjacent to each other, originating via spontaneous or induced mutation.

corona: a crown- or trumpet-shaped outgrowth of petals, especially prominent in daffodils.

cultivar: from "cultivated variety"; a variety that has arisen in cultivation.

dehisce: referring to fruit, to split open when ripe, usually along distinct lines or sutures, to release seeds.

dominant allele: the allele that is expressed in a gene by masking the affect of the alternate allele. For example, if red and white are alleles for flower color and if red is dominant, then all plants carrying both alleles would have red flowers, the white allele being masked.

electrophoresis: a system for separating different enzymes based on the differential movement of charged molecules in solution through a porous medium (such as filter paper or a gel) in an electric field.

emasculation: removal of the anthers from a flower or bud.

epiphytic: growing on another plant for support only (is not parasitic).

follicetum: a fruiting structure made up of an aggregate of follicles.

floret: one of many small individual flowers that make up a larger inflorescence.

genotype: the genetic makeup of a plant (as opposed to its outward appearance, or phenotype).

germplasm: all the hereditary material in a species.

gynandrophore: the central axis of the flower, including the male and female floral structures.

gynoecium: a collective term for the female parts of the flower.

heterozygous: having both dominant and recessive alleles on a gene for a particular characteristic.

homozygous: having identical alleles for genes on each of the matching chromosomes in a pair.

inflorescence: a cluster of flowers, as in the head of a sunflower or a spike of grass; made up of florets.

interspecific: between species.

intraspecific: within a species.

isozymes: different forms of the same enzyme.

lithophytic: growing on rocks for support.

monoecious: having separate male and female flowers on the same plant.

ortet: a plant from which material was taken for vegetative propagation; the original single ancestor of a clone.

ovary: the basal portion of the pistil that becomes the fruit when fertilized.

perianth: the combination of the calyx and corolla or tepals in a flower.

phenotype: the physical appearance of a plant.

pistil: the female part of the flower.

ploidy: referring to the number of chromosomes.

radial symmetry: used to describe flowers that can be bisected into identical halves along more than one axis, forming mirror images.

recessive: a genetic characteristic that is not expressed in the presence of a comparable but dominant allele in a heterozygous situation.

revolute: having margins rolled downward, toward the lower side.

rhizomatous: having underground, horizontal stems.

rosettes: a crowded, circular cluster of leaves that radiate from a crown close to the ground.

scape: a leafless flower stalk arising from the ground.

scarification: the scratching or scoring of a thick seed coat to allow absorption of water; sometimes necessary for seeds to germinate.

somatic: referring to the vegetative phase of plants; the usually diploid cells that make up the nonreproductive, vegetative tissue.

spadix: a spike of flowers enclosed in a spathe or sheath-like bract.

spathe: a sheath-like bract enclosing a spike of flowers (the spadix).

sport: a plant or portion of a plant that arises from mutation; phenotypically it exceeds the normal range of variation for that particular species.

staminode: a sterile stamen that does not produce pollen.

stigma: the portion of a carpel upon which the pollen germinates.

style: a slender, stalk-like extension of the pistil that extends from the ovary to the stigma; the tissue through which the pollen tube grows.

tepals: parts of the perianth that are not differentiated into distinct petals and sepals.

tetraploid: an organism with twice the diploid number of chromosomes; written as $4n$.

twin scaling: a method of propagating bulbous plants.

variegated: describing leaves that lack chlorophyll in certain areas, thus appearing yellowish or white.

vernalization: a regimen of exposure to low temperatures required by some plants for the induction of early flowering and/or breaking of bud dormancy.

Other Useful References

Capon, B. 1990. *Botany for Gardeners: An Introduction and Guide.* Portland, Ore.: Timber Press.

King, R. C., and W. D. Stansfield. 1985. *A Dictionary of Genetics.* 3rd ed. New York: Oxford University Press.

Little, R. J., and E. E. Jones. 1980. *A Dictionary of Botany.* New York: Van Nostrand Reinhold.

Notes on Contributors

WILLIAM L. ACKERMAN, PH.D., received a B.S. in horticulture and an M.S. in plant genetics from Rutgers University and a Ph.D. in botany (plant genetics) from the University of Maryland. He served with the U.S. Department of Agriculture at the Plant Introduction Station, Chico, California, as a pomologist and later as research horticulturist in charge of the Plant Introduction Station in Glenn Dale, Maryland, involved in the research and evaluation of tree fruit crops and ornamentals. From 1974 until retirement in 1984, Ackerman served as senior research horticulturist at the U.S. National Arboretum where he was leader of the Woody and Herbaceous Plant Breeding and Cytogenetics Program. He is still active as a research collaborator at the National Arboretum. Ackerman has authored 176 articles and released 105 new cultivars into the nursery trade, including 52 camellias. In 1999 he received the American Horticultural Society's Luther Burbank award for "extraordinary achievements in the field of plant breeding."

M. BRETT CALLAWAY, PH.D., is a corn breeder/geneticist and currently works as research coordinator for South America for Pioneer Hi-Bred International, Inc. He received B.S. and M.S. degrees in horticulture at the University of Georgia and a Ph.D. in plant breeding and biometrics at Cornell University. Callaway was co-editor of *Crop Improvement for Sustainable Agriculture*, published by the University of Nebraska Press in 1993, and author of numerous articles in popular and technical publications. He has a continuing interest in the pawpaw (*Asimina triloba*) and in efforts to promote commercialization of this native fruit tree.

DOROTHY J. CALLAWAY received a B.S. in horticulture at the University of Georgia and an M.S. in botany (plant taxonomy) at the L. H. Bailey Hortorium at Cornell University. She received her hands-on experience with magnolias as co-owner of Sweetbay Farm, a mail-order magnolia nursery. Callaway is author of *The World of Magnolias*, published in 1994 by Timber Press, and numerous articles on magnolias and pawpaws (*Asimina*). She currently serves as international registrar for Magnoliaceae and as editor and a member of the board of trustees for the Magnolia Society. After living in Brazil for a year, the Callaways now live and garden in Baxter, Iowa.

ELISE HAVENS and her husband, RICHARD, own Grant Mitsch Novelty Daffodils in Hubbard, Oregon. The business was established by Havens' parents, Grant and Amy Mitsch. Mr. Mitsch maintained an extensive and innovative hybridizing program that is being continued by the Havenses. Resulting hybrids are offered through their nursery. Havens also has a background in mathematics and computers, with a B.S. in math and experience in system maintenance and design.

RICHARD J. HENNY, PH.D., a professor of horticulture with the University of Florida since 1976, specializes in breeding ornamental aroids including *Anthurium*, *Aglaonema*, *Spathiphyllum*, and *Dieffenbachia*. The focus of his work includes the study of factors controlling flowering, pollination, and seed set and the genetics of various important ornamental traits. He has published numerous scientific and popular articles pertaining to breeding systems of ornamental aroids. He has also named and released 12 commercial cultivars.

RICHARD A. JAYNES, PH.D., worked at the Connecticut Agricultural Experiment Station for 25 years as plant breeder and horticulturist. In 1984 he resigned to establish Broken Arrow Nursery in Hamden, Connecticut, and continue his work breeding and selecting laurels. He has received several awards for his work with chestnut trees and laurels, including the Jackson Dawson Medal for horticultural achievement presented by the Massachusetts Horticultural Society. Jaynes is author of numerous publications, most notably *Kalmia: Mountain Laurel and Related Species*, published by Timber Press in 1997.

DALE T. LINDGREN, PH.D., is professor of horticulture at the University of Nebraska West Central Research and Extension Center in North Platte. He holds a B.S. in horticulture and agronomy from the University of Nebraska and an M.S. and a Ph.D. from the University of Wisconsin in plant breeding and genetics. Lindgren is continuing the West Central Research and Extension Center program of developing ornamental plants adapted to soil and climatic conditions of the Great Plains, with emphasis on native plants. Lindgren's plant breeding activities have received state and national recognition, including having *Penstemon digitalis* 'Husker Red' selected as the 1996 Perennial Plant of the Year by the Perennial Plant Association. He has released 18 cultivars of horticultural plants.

CURRIER MCEWEN, M.D., professor emeritus and former dean of the New York University School of Medicine, became interested in Japanese and Siberian irises almost accidentally more than 40 years ago. In addition to many medical articles and books, his publications include *The Japanese Iris* (1990), *The Siberian Iris* (1996), and more than 100 horticultural articles. His gardens on the coast of Maine, where every year he grows thousands of hybrids, have been the subject of numerous features. The first hybridizer to induce tetraploidy in Japanese and Siberian irises, Dr. McEwen has bred, registered, and introduced 98 Siberian irises, 34 Japanese irises, and 43 daylilies. He has received many awards and medals, including the Hybridizer's Medal of the American Iris Society, the comparable Foster Memorial Plaque of the British Iris Society, and the American Horticultural Society's Luther Burbank Award, created to recognize extraordinary achievement in the field of plant breeding.

ALAN W. MEEROW, PH.D., received his B.S. degree in botany and environmental horticulture at the University of California at Davis, and his M.S. and Ph.D. at the University of Florida. His Master's thesis and Ph.D. dissertation involved taxonomic study of the genus *Eucharis* in the family· Amaryllidaceae. Meerow, formerly a professor at the University of Florida, currently serves as a research geneticist in tropical ornamentals at the USDA's Subtropical Horticulture Research Station in Miami, Florida, and is a research associate of Fairchild Tropical Garden in Miami. He has received numerous awards and grants, and has published more than 150 technical, trade, and popular publications.

TED L. PETIT, PH.D., is the owner of Le Petit Jardin, a mail-order nursery specializing in daylilies. He has been hybridizing daylilies for more than a decade and has introduced more than 100 daylily cultivars. He received his Ph.D. in psychology and neuroscience from the University of Florida and is currently a professor at the University of Toronto. In addition to many scientific articles and books on brain research, Petit has written a number of articles on daylilies for the American Hemerocallis Society's *The Daylily Journal*. Every year in his gardens in north Florida he grows tens of thousands of daylily hybrids. He is co-author of *The Color Encyclopedia of Daylilies*, published by Timber Press in 2000.

H. EDWARD REILEY is a retired educator who has grown rhododendrons and azaleas for many years. He has experience in growing these plants in the nursery and the landscape, and is also an experienced propagator of rhododendrons and azaleas. A resident of Maryland, he is a charter member of the Mason-Dixon chapter of the American Rhododendron Society. Reiley is author of *Success with Rhododendrons and Azaleas*, published by Timber Press in 1995.

OWEN M. ROGERS, PH.D., has degrees in floriculture, horticulture, and plant breeding. He is a retired professor of horticulture and former chair of the Plant Science Department at the University of New Hampshire, where for 36 years he conducted research on genetics of ornamental plants, with emphasis on late-blooming lilac species. In retirement he is on the board of directors of the International Lilac Society and serves on the Governor's Lilac and Wildflower Commission as well as the board of the Wentworth-Coolidge historic site (site of the oldest lilacs in New Hampshire). He is also active in the establishment of a lilac arboretum at the Veterans Hospital in Manchester, New Hampshire. Rogers serves as a lecturer for two landscape symposia and has authored numerous articles on lilacs.

PETER SHALIT, M.D., PH.D., has been growing gesneriads indoors under lights for 35 years. He is a lifetime member of the American Gloxinia and Gesneriad Society and a founding member of the Gesneriad Hybridizers Association. He has a B.S. in botany from Cornell University and a Ph.D. in genetics and M.D. degrees from the University of Washington. Breeding gesneriads has been one of his favorite hobbies for many years, and his first named hybrid, *Sinningia* 'Bewitched', was released in 1995. By profession he is an internal medicine physician. He lives in Seattle, Washington, in a house filled with plants and cats.

JEFFREY L. SMITH, PH.D., has been a member of the African Violet Society of America for more than 20 years. During that time, he has written numerous articles for *African Violet Magazine* and currently writes a genetics advice column, "In Search of New Violets." Smith's research in African violet genetics has produced several commercial plants, including the Genetic series and the Tomorrow's series. He is currently writing a book on African violets for Timber Press and is working on the taxonomy of the genus *Saintpaulia*.

GUY STERNBERG is a registered landscape architect, certified professional arborist, and horticultural photographer with a degree in horticulture from Purdue University. Sternberg maintains Starhill Forest, a private research arboretum, and is developing oak selections for the nursery trade. He has grown oak species and hybrids for more than 30 years and has assembled the official North American oak living collection recognized by the North American Plant Preservation Council. He has served on the staff of the Illinois Department of Natural Resources for nearly three decades and holds an adjunct research associate appointment with the Illinois State Museum Botany Department. Sternberg also has served as a charter member, statewide director, and chapter president of the Illinois Native Plant Society, and as a founding member and first president of the International Oak Society. He has published several articles, papers, and books on oaks and native trees. He is co-author (with Jim Wilson) of *Landscaping with Native Trees* and will serve as lead author and photographer for the planned genus monograph on oaks for Timber Press.

JAMES W. WILKINS JR., M.D., is a dermatologist in Jackson, Michigan. He was introduced to hostas and their hybridizing by Ralph H. (Herb) Benedict. Dr. Wilkins is an avid gardener and has been growing and hybridizing hostas for 15 years. He is active in the Michigan Hosta Society, on the board of the Great Lakes Region of the American Hosta Society, and president of the American Hosta Society. He often lectures on shade gardening, and his former garden was featured on PBS's *The Victory Garden*. He and his wife, Sandy, are creating a new garden in rural Jackson.

Index of Plant Names